The 'New Inflation' and Monetary Policy

The 'New Inflation' and Monetary Policy

Proceedings of a Conference organised by the Banca Commerciale Italiana and the Department of Economics of Università Bocconi in Milan, 1974

Edited by
Mario Monti

First published 1976 *by*
THE MACMILLAN PRESS LTD
London and Basingstoke
Associated companies in New York
Dublin Melbourne Johannesburg and Madras

SBN 333 18845 4

Printed in Great Britain by
WESTERN PRINTING SERVICES LTD
Bristol

Contents

Foreword *Gaetano Stammati* vii
Notes on the Contributors ix
Editor's Introduction *Mario Monti* xiv

PART ONE

1 Real and Monetary Factors in Economic Fluctuations
Sir John Hicks 3
Discussion of Chapter 1 *Giuseppe Di Nardi* 14

2 Inflation, Money and the Role of Fiscal Arrangements: An Analytic Framework for the Inflation Problem
Karl Brunner 25
Discussion of Chapter 2 *Mario Monti* 82

3 Some Economic Implications of the Indexing of Financial Assets, with Special Reference to Mortgages
Franco Modigliani 90
Discussion of Chapter 3 *Siro Lombardini* 117

4 The 'New Inflation' and Flexible Exchange Rates
Robert A. Mundell 142
Discussion of Chapter 4 *Luigi Spaventa* 160

PART TWO

5 Address *Emilio Colombo* 167

6 Address *Guido Carli* 173

PART THREE

7 Report on the European Economic Community *Ugo Mosca* 185

8 Report on the United States (1) *James L. Pierce* 197

9 Report on the United States (2) *Albert E. Burger* 205

10 Report on Japan *Chiaki Nishiyama* 225

11 Report on Brazil *Américo Oswaldo Campiglia* 246

12 Report on the United Kingdom (1) *Paul Bareau* 256

13 Report on the United Kingdom (2) *Brian Quinn* 262

14 Report on Italy *Antonio Fazio* 265

15 Report on France *Pierre Berger* 277

16 Report on the Federal Republic of Germany *Kurt Andreas* 289

Concluding Remarks *Innocenzo Gasparini* 297

Index of Names 303

Index of Subjects 305

Foreword

The publication of the conference proceedings collected in this volume comes at a time when the world-wide malady which has generally come to be called 'inflation' is still in full force. This process, which was once seen as producing an 'euphoric' state of the economy, is today accompanied by recessionary phenomena. The coexistence of inflation with recession has brought with it new names for the phenomenon such as 'stagflation', 'slumpflation' and most recently 'unempflation'. For present purposes we have called the phenomenon, as it appears in the title of this conference, the 'new inflation' in order to indicate the variety of aspects or phenomena associated with the recent explosion of prices as well as the variety of causes, often interrelated, that help to bring such a process into being.

The persistence, or better the slowness in the slackening of the inflationary phenomenon, despite the rigid monetary and fiscal policies adopted in all countries, has led the experts to predict that price increases will continue for some months at rates much higher than we have normally been accustomed to during the last quarter century. This confirms the 'new' character of the present inflation and obliges us to learn to live with it, or at the very least to admit its very different nature. This special nature justifies, indeed makes necessary, its being brought to the attention not only of experts, but of the public at large.

The recognition of the role modern economic theory assigns to the banking system in feeding and supporting inflationary pressures through the supply of money has encouraged the Banca Commerciale Italiana in conjunction with the Department of Economics of the Università Bocconi to propose this conference.

While it is true that modern theory often explains banking behaviour as a function of exogenous variables controlled by the monetary authorities, there remains the possibility, even under this favourable hypothesis, that the control of these exogenous variables is simply a reaction to the existence of monetary disequilibrium caused, or permitted, by the behaviour of the banking system. Thus there is a distinct possibility of the co-responsibility of the monetary authorities and the banking system.

Modern theory also emphasises the central role played by the banks' investment decisions. Here is a more direct link, through the supply of money, between the action of the banking system and inflation.

In organising this conference with the aim of finding a valid explanation of the new inflation, the management of the Banca Commerciale Italiana has been motivated by what, with Benedetto Croce, one might call an 'ethical impulse for knowledge'. In fact the great Neapolitan philosopher emphasised that knowledge is always 'an act of comprehension and intelligence that results from an exigence of everyday life which cannot be overcome by direct action without first posing and resolving a theoretical problem, which dispels the illusions, the doubts and the obscurity surrounding reality, and which is the act of thought'.

Besides this initial motivation there is another, expressed by the desire, which a bank such as ours naturally has, to fulfil a social responsibility in various ways in the cultural field, whether or not they regard the economy. This represents a long and enduring tradition, in England as in Italy. The great bankers and the great families of bankers have traditionally found it natural to intersperse the more or less arid work in their banks with the desire to study, to write and also to surround themselves with the beautiful things continually created by groups of artists nearby.

The Banca Commerciale Italiana has been inspired by this tradition throughout its eighty years of existence as the publications which bear its name and the projects that it has supported bear witness.

We are particularly proud to have been able to bring together for this conference such a large number of distinguished economists from all countries for discussions at a high technical level. In addition, the presence of high government officials at the conference demonstrates to the experts the desire for a guide to action of those responsible for economic policy, as well as emphasising the prominent links between inflation and important aspects of social and political reality.

GAETANO STAMMATI

Notes on the Contributors

Kurt Andreas is a director of the Deutsche Bundesbank and head of its Credit Department. He was previously at the Research Department of the Deutsche Bundesbank.

Paul Bareau is economic consultant to Barclays Bank and to the International Publishing Corporation. He was previously Economic Editor of the *News Chronicle*, an adviser to the U.K. Treasury, editor of the *Statist* and for a time Lecturer in Comparative Banking at the London School of Economics. Among his publications are *The City of London* and *The Future of the Sterling Area.*

Pierre Berger is Directeur Général des Etudes at the Banque de France. He is also Director of the Centre d'Etudes Supérieures de Banque. Among his contributions to monetary economics are *La monnaie et ses mécanismes* and *Le marché monétaire.*

Karl Brunner is Professor of Economics at both the Graduate School of Management of the University of Rochester and the University of Bern. He was educated at the University of Zurich and was later Professor of Economics at the University of California at Los Angeles and at the Ohio State University. Among Professor Brunner's recent publications have been *Targets and Indicators of Monetary Policy* (1969) and *Survey of Selected Issues in Monetary Theory* (1971). He is the founder of the *Journal of Money, Credit and Banking* and of the *Journal of Monetary Economics.*

Albert E. Burger is Assistant Vice President of the Federal Reserve Bank of St. Louis. A graduate of Oklahoma State University and of Purdue University, he is the author of *The Money Supply Process* (1971) and of several articles on monetary policy and international economics.

Américo Oswaldo Campiglia is Managing Director of Itau-Investment and Financing Co. and Vice President of Banco Frances e Brasileiro S.A. He is also President of Comit of Brasil-Consulting S.A., of Tecoplan S.A. and of ACREFI-Investment and Financing Enterprises Association. A former Professor of Finance and Costs at the University of Sâo Paulo, he has published several studies of industrial economics and finance, including *Control Systems in Industrial Production* (1967) and *Inflation and Development: the Brasilian Experience* (1975).

Guido Carli was Governor of the Banca d'Italia at the time of this Conference. He resigned in August 1975 after fifteen years in office and is now President of Ente per gli studi monetari, bancari e finanziari

Luigi Einaudi. He was previously Manager of the Ufficio Italiano dei Cambi, President of Mediocredito Centrale, Minister of Foreign Trade and General Manager of the Banca d'Italia. He has also been Executive Director of the International Monetary Fund, Director of the Bank for International Settlements and member of several other international financial committees. He is the author of many essays on monetary policy and the international financial system, among which are *Verso il multilateralismo degli scambi e la convertibilità delle monete* and *Evoluzione della legislazione italiana sul controllo degli scambi e dei cambi.*

Emilio Colombo, Italian Minister of the Treasury, has been a Member of Parliament since 1948 and Prime Minister in 1970–72. Before becoming Treasury Minister for the first time in 1963, he had been a member of the Constituent Assembly in 1946–48 and Under Secretary of Agriculture and of Public Works, as well as Minister of Agriculture, of Foreign Trade, and of Industry and Commerce. He has also been Minister of Finance and Minister in charge of the Italian Representation to the United Nations. As Prime Minister and Treasury Minister, he has represented Italy at most international financial meetings and EEC ministerial councils. He is the author of several articles on monetary and financial problems.

Giuseppe Di Nardi is Professor of Economics at the Università di Roma. He was formerly Professor of Economics at the Università di Bari and the Università di Napoli. Among his many publications are *Le banche di emissione nel secolo XIX* (1953), *Lezioni di economia dello sviluppo* (1963), *Economia della produzione* (1970) and *Il controllo sociale dell'economia* (1972).

Antonio Fazio is head of the Research Department of the Banca d'Italia. He was previously responsible for the Econometric Unit and for the Money Market Unit of the Research Department. Among other publications, he is the author of *Monetary Base and the Control of Credit in Italy* (1969) and co-author of *M2BI: A Revised Version of the Model of the Financial Sector of the Italian Economy* (1974) and of *Demand and Supply of Bank Credit in Italy* (1974).

Innocenzo Gasparini is Professor of Economics and Dean of the Faculty of Economics at Università Bocconi, Milano. He is also Rector of Università Bocconi and President of the Società Italiana degli Economisti. Professor Gasparini was educated at Università Bocconi, Oxford University, Stanford University and the University of Chicago and was later Professor of Economics at the Universities of Sassari, Padova and Venezia. Among his publications are *Sviluppo economico e ruolo dell'agricoltura* (1953), *Alcuni problemi di equilibrio monetario* (1954), *L'offerta di fonti di energia nello sviluppo economico* (1960) and *Programmazione economica nazionale e regionale e politica a medio e lungo termine* (1972).

Sir John Hicks, who was awarded the Nobel Memorial Prize for

Economics in 1972, is Professor Emeritus at All Souls College, Oxford. A graduate of Oxford University, he was Professor of Political Economy at the University of Oxford from 1952 to 1965, having previously been a lecturer at the London School of Economics and Professor of Economics at the University of Manchester. Among his fundamental contributions to economic theory are *Value and Capital* (1939), *Capital and Growth* (1965), *Critical Essays in Monetary Theory* (1967), *Capital and Time* (1973) and *The Crisis in Keynesian Economics* (1974).

Siro Lombardini is Professor of Economic Policy at the Università di Torino. He was educated at the Università Cattolica, Milano, at the London School of Economics and at the University of Chicago. Professor Lombardini has been a member of several governmental consultative committees and Chairman of the Price Control Commission. He is a member of the Technical-Scientific Committee on Economic Planning. He is the author, among other publications, of *Il monopolio nella teoria economica* (1953), *L'analisi della domanda nella teoria economica* (1957), and *Modern Monopolies in Economic Development* (1971).

Franco Modigliani is Professor of Economics and Institute Professor at Massachusetts Institute of Technology, Cambridge, Mass. He was previously Professor of Economics at the University of Illinois, at the Carnegie Institute of Technology and at Northwestern University. Professor Modigliani is also Academic Consultant to the Board of Governors of the Federal Reserve System and Econometric Consultant to the Banca d'Italia. He was President of the Econometric Society in 1962 and has been elected President of the American Economic Association for 1976. He is co-author of *National Incomes and International Trade* (1953) and *The Role of Anticipations and Plans in Economic Behavior* (1961) and author of many important articles on economic theory and on financial and monetary economics.

Mario Monti is Professor of Economics at the Università di Torino and Professor of Monetary Theory and Policy at Università Bocconi, Milano. He was educated at Università Bocconi and Yale University. Among his publications in monetary economics are *A Theoretical Model of Bank Behavior and Its Implications for Monetary Policy* (1971) and *Per un'analisi mensile della politica monetaria e finanziaria italiana* (1974).

Ugo Mosca is Director General for Economic and Financial Affairs at the Commission of the European Communities since 1967. A graduate of the Universities of Milano and Firenze, he entered the Italian Diplomatic Service in 1939 and held various economic posts at the Ministry of Foreign Affairs before becoming Deputy Permanent Representative of Italy to the EEC in 1961. Dr Mosca is a member of several economic committees of the Communities and the author of articles on international financial problems.

Robert A. Mundell is Professor of Economics at Columbia University (at the University of Waterloo, Ontario, at the time of this Conference) and Professor of International Economics at the Graduate Institute of International Studies in Geneva. Educated at the University of British Columbia, Massachusetts Institute of Technology and the London School of Economics, he has also been Professor of Economics at the University of Chicago. Professor Mundell has been a consultant to the World Bank, the Board of Governors of the Federal Reserve System, the US Treasury and the European Communities. His recent publications include *International Economics* (1968), *Monetary Problems of the International Economy* (co-editor, 1969) and *Monetary Theory: Inflation, Interest and Growth in the World Economy* (1971).

Chiaki Nishiyama is Professor of Economics, Director of the Institute of Industrial Relations and Chairman of the Center for Modern Economics at Rikkyo University, Tokyo. He is also adviser to the Wage Committee of the Japan Federation of Economic Organizations and has been a member of various committees of the Japanese Government. Among Professor Nishiyama's contributions to economic theory and monetary economics are *Free Economy: Its Politics and Principles* (1974) and *A Monetary History and Analysis of the Japanese Economy, 1868–1970* (co-author, 1974).

James L. Pierce is consultant to the Committee on Banking, Currency and Housing, US House of Representatives. At the time of this Conference he was Associate Director, Division of Research and Statistics, Board of Governors of the Federal Reserve System and a member of the Graduate Faculty of the University of Maryland. Dr Pierce, who had previously been Assistant Professor of Economics at Yale University and Staff Member of the Cowles Foundation, is the author of various essays in monetary economics, including *Interest Rates and Their Prospects in the Recovery* (1975) and *Bank Management and Portfolio Behavior* (co-author, 1975).

Brian Quinn is Assistant to the Chief Cashier at the Bank of England. He was an economist at the Bank at the time of this Conference. He had previously been an economist at the International Monetary Fund and resident representative of the IMF in Freetown, Sierra Leone. Dr Quinn has published articles on international financial problems and is co-author of the IMF's *Surveys of African Economies*.

Luigi Spaventa is Professor of Economics at the Università di Roma. He was educated at the Università di Roma and at Cambridge University, and was later Professor of Economics at the Università di Palermo and at the Università di Perugia. Professor Spaventa, for several years an adviser to the Italian Government, has published many essays on capital theory and on economic policy problems, among which are *Realism without Parables in Capital Theory* (1968), *Rate of Profit, Rate of Growth, and Capital Intensity in a Simple Production Model* (1970), *Il controllo dell'economia nel breve periodo* (co-author, 1970), *Some Internal and External Effects of the Rise in the Price of Oil* (co-author, 1974).

Gaetano Stammati has been Chairman of Banca Commerciale Italiana from 1972 to February 1976, when he became the Italian Minister of Finance. He is also Professor of Economic Policy at the Università di Roma. He graduated from the Università di Napoli and was later Chief of Cabinet of the Minister of Foreign Trade and of the Minister of Finance, Director General of Taxation at the Ministry of Finance, Director General at the Ministry of State Participations, Chief of Cabinet and Director General at the Ministry of the Treasury, and Auditor-General. Professor Stammati has also been a member of several committees on reform of the international monetary system and of the European Communities. Among his publications are *Capitalismo e Socialismo di fronte al problema del prezzo*, *Il problema economico della ricostruzione*, *Imposta generale sulla entrata*, *La finanza pubblica* and *Il sistema monetario internazionale*.

Editor's Introduction

This collection of essays on *The 'New Inflation' and Monetary Policy* brings together the papers presented to the Conference organised by the Banca Commerciale Italiana and the Department of Economics of Università Bocconi, which was held in Milan in June 1974.

Professor Gaetano Stammati explains in his foreword the aims of the Conference and Professor Innocenzo Gasparini sums up in his concluding remarks the varied positions that have emerged. The purpose of this introduction is to outline the subject of the book and illustrate its contents.

The general issue underlying all contributions is the interaction between monetary policy and the recent – and current – inflation experienced by most countries of the world. It involves both a discussion of the role of monetary policy in generating and feeding inflation, and an inquiry into the structural changes imposed by inflation in the analytic frameworks and implementation procedures of monetary policy.

The magnitude and peculiarity of inflationary trends in the early 1970s – particularly in 1973 and 1974 – has led many to use the term 'new inflation'. Others object that there is really nothing new in this inflationary episode. Whatever its merits as an accurate definition of the current inflation, this provocative reference to a 'new inflation' has proved a useful heuristic device. The reader will note that several contributors offer a penetrating analysis particularly where they propose to show, or to deny, the 'new' features of inflation.

This was essentially our motivation in formulating the subject of the Conference – and in confirming it as the title of this volume.

The rate of inflation in most industrial countries will probably be somewhat lower when the book is published than it was at the time of the Conference. Since the exceptionally high level of that rate was itself a prominent indicator of a new situation, resort to the term 'new inflation' may seem less warranted, or at least less timely, to the reader.

Upon further reflection, however, it may be concluded that the current inflation is showing a new character in its decelerating phase, at least as it did until it was accelerating. Most forecasts, for example, warn that even a recession of relatively great severity is going to reduce inflation in most countries much less and much more slowly than in the past. There must be something new also in the public opinion's response to inflation, if one looks at the general satisfaction in realising that the rate of inflation is gradually lowering to levels which would have seemed incredibly high only two or three years ago.

The contributors have been asked to explore the relationships between the features of the current inflation – whether a new or an old phenomenon in their view – and monetary policy. The latter has been considered not only as an instrument of *stabilisation* policy, but also as a set of institutional arrangements aimed at obtaining an efficient monetary and financial *structure*. This is an important aspect, because inflationary conditions, besides prompting specific compensating actions by the monetary authorities, alter the working of the system through which means of payment are provided and funds are allocated through the economy.

Domestic monetary policies, in the wide sense mentioned above, are the direct object of most papers collected here. But all of them emphasise the links between monetary policy and other economic policies, fiscal policy in particular, as well as its relationships with the real aspects of the economy and the international monetary system.

In the first section of the book, four distinguished academic economists present original theoretical essays on certain broad aspects of the current inflation which appear of crucial importance in assessing how new this phenomenon is and what special problems it implies for monetary policy.

Professor Sir John Hicks reconsiders the role of real and monetary factors in economic fluctuations. His analysis helps us to place our current inflationary experience in a historical perspective and guides the reader in identifying both the experiences on which the various theories of business cycles have been based in the past and thus the elements they can still provide for an explanation of current problems.

One of the new conditions characterising most countries in recent years is certainly the unprecedented size of the government budget relative to the economic system. Professor Karl Brunner presents a detailed analytic framework in which the role of the budget process in generating inflation and in conditioning monetary policy is explored. His analysis partly resolves the conflict between Keynesian economics and traditional monetarism and specifies a set of structural arrangements which should guide the government sector's fiscal and monetary operations if a non-inflationary environment is to be created.

Another apparently new aspect of inflation can be seen in the increasing attention given to the problem of how 'to live with' inflation, and to indexing in particular. Professor Franco Modigliani considers the role of indexing financial assets and examines its effects not only on the distribution of income and wealth but also in maintaining well-functioning capital markets, with ample opportunities for financial intermediation, portfolio diversification and resulting efficient allocation of resources. A special case is made for the indexation of mortgages.

It has also been discussed in recent years whether the transition to an international monetary system with a relatively high degree of exchange-rate flexibility is to some extent responsible for the 'new inflation'. Professor Robert A. Mundell's paper deals with this question and places recent national and international monetary policies in a theoretical framework enriched with some historical flashbacks.

These papers of course generated a great deal of lively discussion at the Conference. Comments by the principal debaters – Professors Giuseppe Di Nardi, Mario Monti, Siro Lombardini and Luigi Spaventa respectively – have been included in this book and helped in stimulating the discussion from the floor. Lack of space unfortunately prevents us from including the comments from the floor. In some cases, however, authors have revised their papers for publication in the light of the general discussion.

While of considerable interest in themselves, the four theoretical papers had another significant purpose, that of providing both a systematic framework and a set of specific stimuli for submitting and discussing a series of papers reporting on the inflationary experiences of several countries.

Italian Treasury Minister Emilio Colombo and Governor Guido Carli of the Banca d'Italia delivered addresses to the Conference. Their papers provide the reader with interesting insights into the formulation of monetary policy in a country experiencing unusual inflationary pressures and into the participation of that country in official discussions on the international monetary system in recent years.

In the final section of the book, prominent economists and central bank officials report on the actual record of inflation and monetary policy in selected countries. Each gives a description of policies pursued and of the process which led to their adoption and discusses how the special features of the 'new inflation' have been influencing the analytic framework, the selection of objectives and the implementation of monetary policy, as well as its relationships with other instruments of economic policy.

A comparison of inflationary trends and monetary policies in major industrial regions is offered by the reports on the European Economic Community (Dr Ugo Mosca), the United States (Dr James L. Pierce and Dr Albert E. Burger) and Japan (Professor Chiaki Nishiyama). A paper on Brazil (Professor Américo O. Campiglia) has been added for the peculiar experience of that country, especially as regards indexation.

The analysis then focuses on the four main countries within the EEC, the United Kingdom (Mr Paul Bareau and Mr Brian Quinn), Italy (Dr Antonio Fazio), France (M. Pierre Berger) and the Federal Republic of Germany (Dr Kurt Andreas).

Material supplied from so many and diverse sources cannot be wholly homogeneous, whatever effort is made by the programme committee of a Conference and individual authors. In the case of the present subject, this may well turn out to be an advantage, to the extent that it enables the reader to identify differences in the approach and in the underlying theoretical views of the monetary authorities of the various countries.

A few issues may be mentioned here among the many on which authors of country reports make their contrasting opinions clear, often stimulated by basic questions asked in the theoretical papers referred to above. How does the issue of money illusion bear upon appropriate monetary analysis and policy and, in connection with this, are monetary indicators – interest rates and rates of change in monetary aggregates, in particular – to be observed in nominal or in real terms? Is the present rate of inflation perceived as a substantially exogenous factor in the case of relatively small, open economies; and to what extent is it reasonable to attribute it to the supply behaviour of non-industrial countries and oil-exporting countries in particular? How does the 'new inflation' affect the relative performance of monetary and fiscal policies? Should new structural arrangements – such as the indexing of financial assets, or the payment of interest on demand deposits in countries where it is presently prohibited – be taken into serious consideration as devices for improving the performance of the monetary system under strong inflationary conditions?

The reader will not find conclusive answers to most of these and similar problems in the book. It is hoped, however, that some clarification of the issues has been achieved, in their theoretical foundations as well as in their practical implications. If the next world boom – as most observers believe – brings with it a new outbreak of the uncomfortable features known as the 'new inflation', this clearer view might prove particularly useful.

The editor acknowledges his debt to all the distinguished contributors to this book and to Professor Innocenzo Gasparini, Professor Gaetano Stammati and Dr Sergio Siglienti, with whom he had the pleasure to serve in the programme committee of the Conference.

March 1975 MARIO MONTI

Part One

1 Real and Monetary Factors in Economic Fluctuations

Sir John Hicks

Nearly twenty-five years ago I published a book called *A Contribution to the Theory of the Trade Cycle*. Though it is just called 'Trade Cycle' on the back, the full title was very seriously meant. I was not writing a textbook, or treatise, on economic fluctuations; I was simply exploring a particular model which, at the time of writing, appeared to have some relevance. Now, when I look back at what I wrote, I am even more inclined to insist upon the limitation of what I was doing than I was then.

The immediate stimulus to the writing of my book was Harrod's *Economic Dynamics*. But even before I read Harrod, I had been lecturing on the cycle. In my lectures I had taken a more historical approach, and I am now rather sorry that more of that did not survive into the book. Some of it I would now like to bring back. I can only sketch the history; nevertheless I would like to begin from the historical end.

One of the advantages of beginning in that way is that it forces one at once to face the question: what is it that we are talking about? I believe that there are two things which are easily confused, but which it is quite essential to distinguish. There are on the one hand the cycles that are made by statisticians; there are on the other the cycles that are clearly marked in public sentiment, the cycles which the historian, even if he is not particularly numerically inclined, cannot possibly overlook. Statisticians, analysing time-series, can always discover cycles; for any time-series can always be analysed, by well-established methods, into trend and fluctuations about trend. The fluctuations, indeed, may be irregular; but it does not need much tolerance (and a good deal of tolerance is usually exhibited) to reduce them to a cyclical, or quasi-cyclical, pattern. Even the most irregular fluctuations can be exhibited as a superimposition of one sort of cycle upon another – 'cycle on epicycle, orb on orb' – the Ptolemaic parallel is very apparent. It seems to me that it is very doubtful if we need a theory of cycles *in that sense*. I think that they are better left to *ad hoc* analysis by the microeconomist.

The cycles I want to talk about are the other kind, which I shall allow myself to call the true economic cycles. We can talk much more sense about them when we have made the distinction. For we shall not want to take it for granted that true economic cycles have always been with us, or must always be with us. They may or they may not. And they may easily change their character, quite fundamentally, over time.

The true economic cycle is fairly long; so, if we are to have a good number of them to discuss, we must go quite a long way back. Not indeed to the eighteenth-century pre-history, which has been explored by T. S. Ashton – to whom, in my thinking about cycles, I owe a considerable debt. It is enough to go back to that remarkable series of very well-marked cycles, in the middle of the nineteenth century. There were (at least) four of them, running (from high point to high point) 1825–37, 1837–47, 1847–57, 1857–67. The ten-year cycle which Jevons associated with sunspots! I shall venture to call it the *classical* cycle (for one may feel confident that in this application *classical* will be neither confusing nor misleading). There is no doubt about the reality of the classical cycle; it vastly impressed contemporaries, and it has affected thinking about cycles ever since.

The classical cycle, of course, was primarily a British phenomenon; but it was not confined to Britain. It is readily recognisable in France (you cannot tell the story of the Second Empire without it) and it had its repercussions in the United States. It was indeed a Frenchman, writing in the eighteen-sixties, who gave the first comprehensive analysis of it; so Schumpeter (who, in my view, is much too deeply involved with the cycles of the statisticians) would like us to call all ten-year (or more or less ten-year) fluctuations Juglars! On my reading of the history Clement Juglar has his historical place.

The classical cycle was very regular; but in the years which followed, the regularity was not maintained. Those who look for cycles can find them, between 1870 and 1914; but they are less well marked than they were in the classical epoch (as we had better call it). There was just one outstanding exception; the trade crisis of 1907, which centred on the United States, seemed to repeat the earlier pattern. And so it was that in the years just before 1914 economists again became cycle-conscious (Aftalion, Pigou, Robertson).

In the inter-war 'epoch' there were three peaks, in 1920, 1929 and 1937. Thus, though the cycle appeared to be a little shorter, the classical pattern appeared to have returned. But then, after 1950, the fluctuations became irregular, as they were before 1914. So we may sum up (of course very roughly, but sufficiently for my purpose) by saying that there have been two epochs, 1820–70 and 1920–40, with very well-marked cycles; and two, 1870–1914 and since 1950, in which regular cycles are distinctly harder to trace. For theoretical purposes, at least, that is the kind of picture we should have in our minds.

It is not surprising, in the light of this experience, that the classical pattern should have had a great influence on subsequent thinking; when economists, such as Hawtrey or Lavington, write on *the* cycle, it is the classical pattern which (one feels) they have mainly in mind. So let us look at it more closely, keeping in mind (now) its historical reference.

The course was roughly as follows. Out of its (say) ten years, two or three were years of depression, four or five years of recovery and normal operation. There followed a year or two of boom or 'overheating', leading to a crisis. After the crisis there was another depression and the next cycle began.

There was a certain symmetry between boom, on the one hand, and slump (or depression) on the other. It is probable that the symmetry extended to output and employment, the modern indicators, but these were less stressed in 'classical' times than they are nowadays. There was little information, in the classical epoch, about output in general; and not much about employment. It was obvious that there was unemployment in the slump; what happened in the boom was rather obscure. What struck observers was the movement of prices and of interest rates (especially short rates). A boom, it was recognised, was a time of high prices and high rates of interest; in a depression prices were low and rates of interest low. (It should be emphasised that the prices in question were wholesale prices – what we now call commodity prices; there was less information about retail prices and it would seem probable that the swing in retail prices, if it existed, was much less.) What is important is that in the classical epoch not output and employment but prices and interest rates were regarded as the key variables.

Now these of course were monetary phenomena, essentially monetary phenomena. When Hawtrey said that 'the trade cycle is a purely monetary phenomenon' it was the classical cycle of which he was surely thinking; and for the classical cycle what he said still seems to me to be broadly correct. There is indeed a contemporary analysis, in John Stuart Mill's *Principles*, which comes to much the same thing. Why do prices rise in the boom? It could hardly be that output is low, so spending on output must be increased. This could only happen if the supply of money is increased, or if it is circulating more rapidly, or (most probably) both at once. Mill already showed how this would happen. The boom starts by businessmen becoming more 'optimistic' and as a consequence of their optimism keeping less money idle. So the velocity of circulation rises and prices rise. The rise in prices engenders expectations of further rises; this further increases 'optimism' and further increases the velocity of circulation. But the businessmen do not have the money to do all they want to do; so they borrow from the banks, who share their optimism, and are therefore very ready to give them the credit which they require. Thus there is an increase in bank credit, which we would nowadays reckon to be an increase in the supply of money.

At last the point comes (so the story goes) when the banks (and perhaps some other businesses also) feel themselves to be overexpanded; credit is restricted and there is a crisis. Credit is shaken, confidence is shaken. The weaker concerns go bankrupt, being unable to meet their obligations. Prices fall because of forced sales, and there is an outbreak of unemployment. Not until the 'mess' has been cleared up can there be a recovery.

That, in very broad outline, is the monetary theory of the cycle – the theory which J. S. Mill, already, had got from Henry Thornton. A cycle which was a 'purely monetary phenomenon' would have, I think, to be something like that. And though there were doubtless many cross-currents (such as have been elucidated by Robin Matthews and John Hughes in their books on two of those cycles) I would myself be prepared to admit that the classical cycles were mainly like that. I believe, accordingly, that one ought to begin with the monetary theory (which is capable, of course, of vastly more elaboration that I have given to it), though, as we shall see, much more than the monetary theory, in the end, is required.

The problem of the cycle, on the monetary theory, is one of 'Banking Policy and the Price Level' (as Robertson, as late as 1926, so far as the title, but not the substance, of his book was concerned, was still to regard it). The slump is a consequence of the boom; so, to cure slumps, booms must first be cured. The objective is stabilisation. Now when one looks, on this line of thought, at what I called my second epoch, it is not surprising that there was, at least to begin with, greater stability. Booms were interrupted before they had gone too far. The chief reason for this was not better banking policy (though there probably was in some ways rather better banking policy) but that London remained the financial centre of the world, at a time when British economic growth was (relatively) slowing up. Thus a strain communicated itself to London at an early stage of expansion, so that the international banking system was less inclined to permit 'overheating' than it had been in the first (classical) epoch. The reappearance of the classical cycle, with its accompanying crisis, at the end of the second epoch, fits in. For the economic centre was then beginning to shift to the more dynamic, and more unstable, American economy.

That much can still be done with the monetary theory; but for the second epoch as a whole it is less than fully satisfactory. It was already found, by contemporaries, to be unsatisfactory. For it was hard to see that all of the 'abortive booms' could be interpreted as booms of the old sort, cut short by an earlier application of monetary restriction. The monetary restriction, sometimes at least, was by no means evident. So we got the beginnings of the accelerator theory, which seemed to show the possibility of a boom petering out by itself.

Before enlarging upon that, I turn to my third epoch, 1920–40, which of course is crucial. There were crises in 1920 and 1929, and a high point, hardly a crisis, in 1937. They fit, superficially, into the classical pattern; but the resemblance is in fact no more than superficial.

I shall dwell for a moment on 1920. The immediate post-war situation, in nearly all countries, was highly inflationary; there were some, such as Germany, where nothing was done to check the inflation, so that Germany proceeded to monetary disaster. In the United States, and in Britain, a check was imposed; and the result, in both countries, was severe depression – the slump of 1921.

But let us look at what happened a little more closely. The crucial date, for monetary policy, was January 1920. It was in that month that the American banks imposed a severe restriction of credit, raising their discount rates to 6 or 7 per cent (a very high rate in those days). The corresponding action in Britain was three months later (April). The turn in prices, in both countries, followed in May. But though the fall began in May, it was initially quite slow, not enough to check the boom in other respects. The real slump occurred in the autumn. It was between October 1920 and the summer of 1921 that there was the great fall in wholesale prices (nearly 50 per cent) accompanied by massive unemployment.

Thus there was a rather long lag between the monetary restriction (beginning in January 1920) and the slump (nearly a year later). This has been interpreted in two ways. Those who hold to a monetary explanation have pointed to the length of time for which the monetary restriction was maintained. It was not until the spring of 1921 that the American banks began to relax; while the bank rate of the Bank of England was held at 7 per cent for a whole year (April to April). It has often been thought, by later commentators, that this was doing more than was necessary. One can nevertheless understand how it was thought at the time that a prolonged experience of dear money was needed in order to convince the public that inflation was over. The remarkable discovery has lately been made that Keynes himself (who was later to become so ardent an expansionist) was advising the maintenance of high bank rate for 'at least a year' in February 1920.

The other alternative is to look for a non-monetary explanation. This is possible; it has been done (in particular by Pigou). I myself find it hard to believe that the chief responsibility (for good or evil) is not to be laid upon monetary policy; it is nevertheless very possible that some part of the explanation is to be found elsewhere.

It is insisted, on this alternative view, that the high prices of 1919 were largely due to real shortages. It inevitably took time, after the damage done by the War, for the productive system of the world to return to some sort of order. It was always likely that as production recovered, prices would come down – or, if they did not actually fall, that the rise in prices would be moderated. The change from the hectic and disorderly production of 1919, making do as best it could with short supplies, to the quite different organisation involved in more normal operation, was bound to be a shock. It was likely to lead to unemployment, since old processes would be terminated before new could be started. Such considerations can hardly go the whole way to explain what happened; but they may point to a contributing factor.

Pigou was writing long after the event; later experience may have played some part in the formation of the view he came to take on 1920. I turn to that – in particular to what is clearly the centre-piece of the whole story, the Great Depression of 1929–33.

The first thing to be said about that is that it was a *double* slump. It began with the Wall Street crash of 1929, a repetition, at least at first sight, of that of 1907, leading to a depression just as that had done. But the recovery from the depression, which on previous experience might have been expected to follow within a year or two, did not take place. Instead there was a second slump, superimposed upon the first. Now there is no doubt at all that this second slump was monetary in character; it is to be explained by the fragility of the international monetary system, reconstructed no more than very imperfectly after the First World War. First of all came the European monetary collapse, beginning with the Kreditanstalt crash in July 1931; there followed, as a consequence of that, the 1933 crisis in America. Not until that had been worked off could recovery begin.

The monetary character of the second slump was easy to recognise; it was easy to see where the blame must lie. So the monetary system of the world, as it had grown up over the centuries, was called in question. It was generally resolved that nothing like it was ever to occur again. The crash was attributed (at least in part justly) to monetary restriction; so monetary restriction, at least of that sort, should henceforward be removed. In the 'classical' trade boom, as I explained, banks at the end ran out of cash; as long as the (ultimate) monetary reserve consisted of precious metals, that in the end was bound to happen. In the new monetary system, as established after the Second World War, it was not to happen. The government (or banking system) of a particular country might run out of international reserves; but it did not have to restrict credit, and force a depression, if it found itself in that position. It could just depreciate its exchange, reducing the value of its own money in terms of international money. And international money itself was not strictly tied to gold; the international money was in fact not gold but the American dollar. As long as the Americans supplied the dollars that were required (and it seemed for long that they had no objection) there was no monetary constraint on expansion, so there was no need for a boom to come to an end in the 'classical' manner.

If this were in fact the whole story, the trade cycle would be finished. Our historical approach would be doubly justified, for the Cycle would have passed into history, and in history we could leave it. It would indeed have left other problems behind it – problems of inflation – but with them I am not directly concerned. I have nevertheless left open the possibility, of which Pigou and Robertson (and other early accelerationists) were well aware, that there is something else. It is time to give it more serious consideration.

I shall take the acceleration theory in its modern form, which is deeply influenced by Keynes (1936). It is not in Keynes, but it has (I think one may say) in one form or another become a part of Keynesian teaching. In its Keynesian form it was first put forward by Samuelson (1938), but it owes much to others, especially, perhaps, to Harrod and Kaldor. My own *Contribution* (1950) is an elaborate (I now think too elaborate) version. I was careful, in my book, to leave a place for monetary influences; but the greater part of the book is concerned with the accelerator model.

The accelerator model not only neglects money; it pays little attention even to prices. It proceeds almost entirely in real terms. And it assumes that its real magnitudes can be aggregated, so that it can proceed, in the conventional macroeconomic manner, in terms of output and employment, saving and investment.

In its simplest form, the accelerator model is very violent; too violent, indeed, to make sense. If saving is geared to output, but investment (net investment) to rate of change of output, saving equals investment gives $sY = cgY$; so $s = cg$ (the Harrod equation) is a condition of equilibrium. But it is an equilibrium that is inherently unstable. Any 'chance' increase in output, raising the rate of growth of output, will induce more investment (the accelerator), but that will have a multiplier effect which will raise output further. Output, however, cannot, at any time, be indefinitely extensible. Thus if the initial equilibrium position was one of less than (Keynesian) full employment, any (expansionary) disturbance would drive the economy up to its full employment 'ceiling'; but on the ceiling output would have to increase less rapidly than on the way to the ceiling. This would put the accelerator into reverse; and there is nothing in the simple model which would stop the downward fluctuation, short of complete collapse.

Not even in 1932 (after monetary disaster, of which the accelerator theory takes no account) was there complete collapse; somehow, to some extent, a bottom, or 'floor' was found. Thus if the accelerator model was to fit the facts (any facts) it required to be modified, or 'cooled'. In my own version I introduced two 'coolants'; others however have been suggested, and I would not now give particular preference to those which I included in my book.

The first of my 'coolants' was the introduction of lags. It is instantaneous adjustment which is so explosive; but it is hard to believe that effects on consumption and investment do not take time to operate. I was able to show that lagged repercussions would not merely lengthen the time that would be taken by the whole process, but would probably dampen the fluctuation considerably. With quite plausible lags, we can readily explain how a boom might peter out without ever reaching a ceiling; and a slump might pass into recovery without ever reaching a floor. This might not happen, but it could happen. The range of phenomena which the model could deal with would thus be considerably widened.

My other 'coolant' was autonomous investment. Harrod himself had been reluctant to suppose that all investment activity is closely geared to current output; he allowed for the probable existence of a 'long-range investment' which is relatively independent. I preferred a different description, which was just meant to mark off a part of investment not geared to current output, whether long range or not. Again with an eye to historical application, I was anxious that the model should not pretend to explain too much. It was easy to show that if one admitted autonomous investment that provided a floor.

My autonomous investment has been much criticised, but I think that on the whole I would stand by it. I would grant that many things which one might put into the 'autonomous' pigeon-hole would provide no more than a temporary floor; if output continued for very long at the low (slump) level, the support which they gave would fade out. But a temporary floor, if it held for some time, would provide a breathing-space; and in a breathing-space new investment could more confidently be undertaken. In spite of the 'pessimism', properly associated with such a situation, *some* people might surely come round, in the breathing-space, to the view that the depression would not go on for ever.

Two other 'coolants' which I did not use in my book, must now be mentioned. One is 'non-linearity' – the rejection of the Harrodian proportionality between output (or income) and consumption (and therefore saving), which I formally maintained. If, at a low level of output, saving (net saving) disappears, there can clearly be equilibrium with no net investment, so that mere maintenance of capital (gross investment = depreciation) is sufficient to establish a floor. The introduction of such non-linearity is usually associated with distributional considerations, but it need not be so associated. With Friedman's consumption function, consumption depending on *permanent income*, the saving ratio (saving/current income) will be high when income is rising, or abnormally high, low when income is falling, or abnormally low. But much the same effect can be represented by lags.

Finally, and perhaps more importantly, there is a qualification which needs to be introduced into the accelerator itself. Why should investment be geared to rate of change of current output, even with a lag? Only if a rise in output requires an increase in capacity. I was careful, at least at one point in my book, to emphasise the elasticity of capacity; one should think of increased output being produced, in the first place, from existing capacity; only when there was reason to expect that the increased output would go on being required would capacity be increased. But this must mean that on the floor, where there surely is excess capacity, a rise in final demand will not induce a significant amount of investment; only when output has expanded towards a normal level will the accelerator get to work. It also means that at the 'collision' with the ceiling, arrears of investment, to meet the requirements of that level of output, will still remain to be made up; so it appears to be possible for the economy to remain on its ceiling for longer – indeed far longer – than I supposed. So even a boom which is due to 'explosive' investment – so that it does not peter out – may be less explosive than it appears in my model.

It must however be admitted that when the model is modified in these latter ways, it changes its character. It ceases to be a mathematical model, such as might conceivably be used as an econometric hypothesis. Mathematics (or some of it) has provided some illuminating exercises; but it cannot be applied as it stands. The view which I now take about it is the same as that which was taken, in the end, by Dennis Robertson who, when he looked back at his own early work, concluded:

> As to stylised models of the cycle, of the kind now so fashionable, they doubtless have their uses, provided their limitations are clearly understood. We must wait with respectful patience while the econometricians decide whether their elaborate methods are really capable of covering such models with flesh and blood. But I confess that to me at least the forces at work seem so complex, the question whether even the few selected parameters can be relied upon to stay put through the cycle or between cycles so doubtful, that I wonder whether more truth will not in the end be wrung from interpretative studies of the crude data.
>
> (That is from the introduction which he wrote in 1948 to the reprint of his 'Study of Industrial Fluctuation', originally published in 1915.)

In this paper, as in my book, I have found myself obliged to treat the monetary theory and the 'real' or accelerator theory rather separately. They are certainly very different in character; but can we build a bridge?

Let us go back, in the first place, to the classical cycle. I have granted that in the classical cycle the boom was brought to an end by a monetary constraint; but may not the accelerator mechanism also have been operating? As we have been reinterpreting it, it seems to fit in. One would expect, in the light of what has been said, that in the early stages of recovery there would be no great strain on capacity, so no strong accelerator; but that after a while there would be much more induced investment – so that recovery would pass into boom, which is what seems to have happened. And only at that stage would there be a monetary strain. What would have happened, in those days, if there had been no monetary constraint – if the supply of money had been extensible, as it has been, on the whole, since 1950? That, I think, is the critical question: a question to which, I fear, econometrics will be unable to answer. We can only speculate. There would clearly have been more inflation than there was; but would the booms, unchecked monetarily, nevertheless have come to an end from real causes? My own feeling (one can not be positive) is that they probably would. For I see no reason why the basic accelerator model should not apply.

One must hold fast to autonomous investment. But there are (at least) two kinds of autonomous investment which need to be distinguished. One is that which springs from invention – the typical industrial need for embodiment of invention in new kinds of fixed capital. At the classical stage, at least, such investment must surely be regarded as autonomous. The other is public investment, the amount of which must surely be regarded as variable, at least to some extent, as a matter of policy. Autonomous investment, of either type, must itself be subject to fluctuation, as I said.

In the classical epoch (surely) the main kind of autonomous investment was the first. And it must, at that stage at least, have tended to fluctuate. Thus, although a strong burst of autonomous investment might have kept the economy on its ceiling for a time, even when induced investment was fading, such a condition could hardly in those conditions have lasted indefinitely. Even in the absence of monetary restraint, there must in the end have been a downturn. It is true that a slump, occurring in that way, would probably have been less violent than classical slumps were in practice (the accelerator model, when suitably 'cooled' does not exhibit more than a gradual decline), still some decline from the level of activity reached in the boom would have been likely to occur.

But then, how in these terms do we explain the prolonged boom (for that surely is what in these terms it has been) of the last twenty years? Absence of monetary restraint would not now seem to be a sufficient explanation. Nor, I think, can it be explained by the widespread adoption of more or less Keynesian policies. Public investment has proved too inflexible to be a very efficient regulator; and tax policy, at least as so far operated, too weak. The principal explanation, I now feel, is the change in character of invention, and thus of investment that depends on invention. In the classical epoch research into new techniques was not organised; now it is. There has therefore been a stronger flow of this kind of investment activity; it has been limited by real scarcities, but by little else. Thus the economy has been kept, for a long time, pressing upon its ceiling; as in the classical epoch it would not have been kept.

Can we rely upon such a condition continuing? It may do so, but I rather doubt it. One may point on the one hand to the abortive investments, and investment projects, the sputniks, Concordes and Chunnels, which look so like the absurdities whose exposure accompanied the breaking of classical booms. One may also point to the real constraints which have appeared, in these last two years, not from full employment of labour, but from scarcity of primary products. Such bottlenecks can be broken, but it takes time to break them. In the interim there may well be a pause.

I am not suggesting that if such things occur (and they may not) they would very usefully be analysed in the terms I have been using. I have tried to suggest that cycle theories should be looked at against the experience on which they have been based, or which has suggested them. The problems which we have now to face are very different from those which faced our predecessors in the classical epoch, or those of the semi-classical epoch between the Wars. For their proper consideration we doubtless need new theories. But from the older theories something can still be learned.

Discussion of Chapter 1

Giuseppe Di Nardi

INTRODUCTION

I have followed Professor Hicks's very stimulating and perceptive work for many years, indeed I could say decades. His presentation here today, as so many of his previous writings, gives cause for reflection. While it is sometimes possible to disagree with some of Professor Hicks's opinions, this is not so with his rigorous and unexceptionable logic. Today, as in the past, I find many points on which I agree with Professor Hicks. This has not, however, prevented me from formulating some additional observations, which may lead to rather different conclusions.

To give some order to my talk I shall concentrate attention on three basic points. First, I shall briefly consider the method required for the study of the dynamic reality of the economy as expressed in the business cycle. Then I shall discuss the central theme that Professor Hicks's paper has opened for discussion. This concerns whether the causes of cycles, and determinants of their turning points, are to be found in the variability of the money supply or are due to some other cause such as scarcity in the real sector. Finally I shall try to use my comments on the first two points as a basis for formulating some conclusions about the problem we have before us today, that is, the nature of the inflationary process spreading over the western world.

1. THE METHOD OF APPROACH

I agree with the use of history as an aid in analysing the problem of the explanation of cycles. Professor Hicks has admitted that he would have liked to have made more use of history in the developments of the arguments that appeared in his book, *A Contribution to the Theory of the Trade Cycle*. My agreement, however, is in the sense of using history in the *verification* of a theory. In order to understand history a *guide* is necessary. Theory is this guide. In fact, this is just how Professor Hicks uses history in his paper. He uses a specific set of principles to classify a number of economic cycles, regrouping them according to their outstanding characteristics, and finally he outlines their differing conceptual characteristics. These, in fact, represent the different 'theories' of economic cycles.

Many different cycle theories appear to have explanatory power. Confronting the theories with the historical facts provides a method of verification. What criteria might be chosen to distinguish among the theories?

Professor Hicks himself points out that his *Contribution* is the analysis of a *particular pattern of cycles*; therefore it is not and cannot be *the* theory of cycles.

The various theories appear as subjective interpretations of a very complex and changing reality.

The detailed study of historical movement to identify 'the cycles that are clearly marked in public sentiment', as Professor Hicks suggests in his presentation, seems to be the most appropriate method to use in the presence of such a large variety of theoretical models.

I agree with this method because it seems to me the most suited to the empirical character of economics. My agreement on this point is not only one of intellectual judgement but also one of practical experience. In fact, the 'cycles that are made by statisticians' that Professor Hicks refers to are not similar in all countries and in all epochs. For example, it has never been possible to identify or measure cycles in the Italian economy even in the classic period of the nineteenth century which was characterised by free trade and a cohesive international monetary system. Thus I prefer to study fluctuations through the historical analysis of their manifestations, and consequently to use the comparative method utilising historical observation to establish *analogies* among cyclical sequences of the industrial economies of the world, in order to obtain, inductively, regularities that can be used as the basis for the formulation of general theories of the cycle.

I arrived at this conclusion at the end of the thirties when, trying to verify the internal coherence of the general equilibrium model, I came to the conclusion that each attempt to substitute a process analysis, in itself temporal, for the simple identification of the necessary conditions of the *final state of equilibrium*, broke the equilibrium scheme and opened the way to fluctuating movement in the economy.[1]

In those years people debated whether it was possible to dynamise the static general equilibrium model or whether dynamic theory could not be better identified in the theory of cycles given that the equilibrium appeared as the exception and the cycle as the rule of real economic movements.

However, I must point out that when scholars used to identify the dynamic theory of the economic system in the theory of cycle, they usually had in mind the cycles that Sir John says 'are made by statisticians', rather than the very different cycles 'that are clearly

[1] G. Di Nardi, 'Interdipendenza e indeterminazione dinamica nella teoria economica', *Giornale degli Economisti*, 1 (1942) par. 2; translated in French in *Economies et Sociétés*, ISEA, Paris, n°· 9, Nov 1967.

marked in public sentiment' and which the historian cannot ignore.

We are interested precisely in these types of cycles. We want to know if they are really inevitable or if they can change over time; if they have their origin in a variable money supply or in the scarcity of real goods that monetary manoeuvres cannot eliminate.

2. REAL AND MONETARY FACTORS

From the analysis of the facts of a long period of about 150 years in the history of capitalism, Professor Hicks draws a distinction between two epochs. The first shows well-marked cycles during the periods 1820–70 and 1920–40. The second one, also divided in two periods from 1870 to 1914 and from 1950 to the present, does not show such regular cycles as during the first epoch.

During the first epoch, 1820–70, Professor Hicks finds four rather regular cycles of about ten years, regular enough to identify as the '*Classical Cycle*'. Analysis of the events of the period reveals the clear *monetary origin* of these cycles.

This also seems to Professor Hicks to be the case for the period between the two World Wars where there were three turning points, 1920 – 1929 – 1937. In this period, the cycles appear shorter, but rather similar to the 'classical' type.

The way that Professor Hicks succeeds in identifying the monetary origin of these cycles is very interesting to me. He points out that while the phase of prosperity is in full swing, *banks start to experience a shortage of liquidity*. They thus become more hesitant to grant loans. At the same time, firms become less optimistic because they feel compelled to liquidate inventories quickly as a result of credit restrictions. Prices fall and the depression, which shows itself in terms of unemployment, gets under way.

Professor Hicks rightly says, 'the problem of the cycle, in the monetary theory, is one of 'Banking Policy and the Price Level'.

I would give an inexact impression of Professor Hicks's views if I were to say that he proposes a monetary explanation of economic fluctuations. Indeed he points out that 'much more than the monetary theory' is required for a complete explanation of cycles.

In fact, later in his paper, when he explains the cycles of the second epoch, he puts the emphasis on real factors, that is on the explanation of the cycles in terms of *real shortages*. In this he starts from the observation that the *accelerator theory*, which tends to ignore prices and only emphasises real quantities (production and investment), already demonstrates how an expansionary phase of the cycle may run out of steam without any reference to credit restriction.

It is not necessary for me to go through all the steps of the analysis developed by Professor Hicks in his paper to point out the importance of the accelerator in the explanation of cyclical fluctuations, neither is it necessary to recall the improvements he proposes to the simplified accelerator theory which he considers as 'too violent'.

My greatest interest, in fact, is in the concluding parts of this analysis. Professor Hicks says both in his paper as well as in his 1950 book that the monetary and real aspects of the theory of cycles have been treated separately, but he asks himself whether it is possible to construct a link between the two causes.

Professor Hicks locates the crucial point of this attempt in the following problem: what would happen if a boom, determined by induced investment according to the accelerator theory, were not followed by monetary restriction? He acknowledges that there certainly would be more inflation than associated with a boom controlled by restrictive monetary policy. He also responds positively to the question of whether or not such a boom could be brought to an end by real causes, even in the absence of monetary restriction.

From my point of view, the link between the two explanations of cycles is here, and I think that it represents *more than a link*—a *complete and sufficient explanation*. By this I mean that in the determination and in the development of the cycle, monetary policy has only the potentiality to *dampen* fluctuations which are essentially determined by real factors. I have arrived at this particular conclusion by reflection on the evidence that Professor Hicks has presented, both in his résumé of the historical facts that he uses to sustain his explanation of the monetary origins of the Classical Cycle, and in his modification of the accelerator analysis through the integration of the effects of lags and autonomous investment, or 'coolants', as he calls them.

I want to indicate briefly how I have arrived at this opinion. First, I asked myself why, in the Classical Cycle, the shift from boom to depression is generated by a reaction by the banking system to the first symptoms of a shortage of liquidity. My response was that in the epoch to which Professor Hicks's monetary cycles refer, banking policy was very sensitive to the rules of bank-note convertibility. Even in periods when convertibility was suspended – usually because of difficulties due to the budget and to the balance of international payments – banking policy showed some indulgence towards the Exchequer but not towards the private sector. I want to emphasise that even in periods of suspension of convertibility the central banks felt obliged to be strict in controlling credit in order not to compromise the future return to note convertibility.

Italian banks of the last century often infringed the orthodox rules of banking behaviour, both in an effort to support the public finances of a newly formed state and to satisfy private sector pressure, with the objective of aiding the economic development of the country. These banks were subject to the severe judgement of the international financial community, which resulted in the sale of Italian securities on the Paris and Zurich markets and caused an outflow of foreign capital from our country.[2]

The orthodox methods of credit control depended on the nature of the monetary system. The nature of the monetary system depended in turn on a particular conception of money. I want to stress that the convertible money of the period remained essentially a commodity money and on that account susceptible to conditions of real scarcity. If the signal for credit restriction was sent out from the central banks, this came about because a position of real scarcity was revealed by the movement of metal reserves, a position of real scarcity that would have cooled the boom and provoked a recession anyhow.

It is evident that this is not a stylised explanation of the cycle. It is an explanation that relies on the observation of events and also on a theory to identify the functions of money and relate the movements of the real sector of the economy with the variables of the monetary system.

This discussion obviously revives ancient controversies. The discussions that raged throughout the eighteenth and in the beginning of the nineteenth century turned on the distinction between money, the effective means of payments, and credit, that could only transfer current payment commitments, in terms of the transfer of real resources, into the future.

It is not convenient to reintroduce here a doctrinal debate that appears to have been forgotten with the passage of time. I only refer to it to demonstrate my agreement with Professor Hicks, for I too believe that old theories are still valid and may still be instructive.

The old theory of effective money and the system of convertibility that is founded on it, say that the tightness of credit that interrupts the boom is the consequence of the conditions of effective scarcity of real resources. Consequently the cycle, even when it appears superficially to be due to a change in expectations by the banks caused by a lack of liquidity, shows itself on closer observation to be the result of pressure on the supply of real resources. Credit can only offset this to the extent that it is possible to mobilise the liquid resources desired by the banks and obtain foreign loans. When the banks resort to credit restriction it implies that such possibilities are already nearly exhausted.

I arrive at this explanation in the same manner as Professor Hicks in his analysis of the Classical Cycle. But I believe that there is, in addition, a confirmation of this explanation in Professor Hicks's interpretation of the great slump of 1929–33. He says that this was a double depression and that the second one was certainly of a monetary character. The consequence of that crisis was that, 'the monetary system of the world,

[2] See my *Le Banche di emissione in Italia nel sec. XIX* (Turin: UTET, 1953).

as it had grown up over the centuries, was called in question'. The responsibility for the crisis fell, therefore, on the state of the international monetary system. After the Second World War, it was decided that a new monetary system should be adopted. The most important characteristic of the new system was to be the elimination of credit restrictions, and thus the elimination of the cause of the severity of economic fluctuations. To this end the function of international means of payment was taken from gold and linked to the US dollar, a currency not immediately convertible into gold.

I find no difficulty in accepting Professor Hicks's judgement on the new monetary system when he says: 'As long as the Americans supplied the dollars that were required (and it seemed for long that they had no objection), there was no monetary constraint on expansion, so there was no need for a boom to come to an end in the "classical" manner.'

In truth, it seemed like that for a long time. At any rate it allows us to understand the long boom from 1950 to 1970. But what has happened in recent years, in particular in Italy, leads, I think, to additional support for the view that I have expressed above – namely that monetary factors can permit a temporary masking of the scarcity that develops in an economy in the last stages of expansion, but that it cannot prevent it. Thus the depression comes about because of real factors, even in the absence of credit restrictions.

It seems to me that this was visible enough by the end of the long boom of 1950–70. Its exceptional duration was made possible not only by a continuous wave of technical progress aided by systematic research, as Professor Hicks has explained, but also by the absence of credit restriction. The boom finished none the less with a dramatic manifestation of the tendency towards scarcity of real resources which appeared clearly during the last months of 1973.

These observations should confirm that, in addition to the implications of the accelerator which show how a cycle can originate independently of money and prices, there are other reasons that place doubt on the belief that cycles would not arrive in the absence of restrictive monetary policy.

My opinion is that the elimination of credit restrictions can put off the moment of the depression but it cannot eliminate it and that, therefore, cyclical fluctuations are always due to the emergence of scarcity in the real sector of the economy. Even the 'Classical Cycle' fits this interpretation for the monetary crisis which precedes the depression is the first manifestation of a deeper disequilibrium taking place in the real structure of the economic system.

3. INFLATION

In his paper Professor Hicks proposes a rethinking of research he carried out some twenty-five years ago, research that enriched our scientific literature with an explanation of economic cycles in terms of a model based on the interaction of the multiplier and accelerator, with the introduction of an *n*-period lag distribution of induced investment to avoid the explosive results of instantaneous adjustment, and with the consideration of investment autonomous from current production to allow a floor to the cycle.

Professor Hicks's cycle is produced in the real sector of the economy without reference to monetary factors.

In his paper Professor Hicks proposes a review of this model of the cycle in the light of historical experience. At the end of his review he has found a strong justification for his model, even if he has had to admit that it may not be suitable as a guide for econometric research.

Professor Hicks's major interest is the historical verification of his theoretical model, which is already considered as one of the major efforts of contemporary thought in this field of economics. However, I believe that our task, and mine in particular in the present circumstances, is different and consists essentially in drawing from the theory of cycles some reflections on the phenomena of the new inflation which is the object of this conference.

The link between the two themes is very close. In this regard I recall that Hawtrey used to say that the economic cycle is nothing more than a replica of true monetary inflation or deflation on a smaller scale.[3] Professor Hicks as well, at the end of his paper, draws attention in passing to the pressure that can be produced in the expansionary phase of a cycle not hindered by monetary restriction, as was the case in effect from 1950.

This is the point where the hints thrown out by Professor Hicks suggest a link between the theory of cycles and the theory of inflation.

It is superfluous to say that there are no contradictions between the explanation of the cycle that ignores monetary factors and the identification of inflation with the expansionary phase and depression with the recessionary phase of the cycle. This identification is one of outward appearance. This can also be understood as a recognition of the co-responsibility of monetary policy in the development of economic cycles. But this is a line of analysis quite different from that which directly attributes the capacity to avoid a depression, once the boom has broken, to the supply of money.

It seems to me that the path to be followed in the analysis of the actual state of affairs is to be found right at the end of Professor Hicks's paper when he asks how 'the prolonged boom of the last twenty years' can be best explained. I can accept his interpretation of the preponderant role played by autonomous investment generated by organised research, but it seems to me that his thesis cannot explain the whole experience.

[3] See G. Haberler, *Prosperity and Depression* (New York: Atheneum, 1963), p. 16.

It does not seem to me general enough. For example, it seems insufficient for the explanation of the Italian experience.

Since I am more directly interested in the Italian experience I am led to attribute a greater weight to other categories of autonomous investment, for example public investment supported by a basically expansive monetary policy, even if marked by regret for short periods. My explanation is mainly of a Keynesian type and draws more directly on Domar's model than on the Hicksian interpretation of cycles.

The Domar model, as is well known, consists of the conditions of equilibrium between the rate of increase of aggregate demand and the rate of increase of the system's productive capacity. Both rates are determined by net investment. On one side net investment determines the rate of increase of money income via the multiplier and on the other it acts on productive capacity by means of the average social productivity of investment goods which increases the stock of capital. Knowing that equilibrium requires the equality of the two rates of increase, it is easy to show that such a system runs on a razor's edge. Thus it can easily generate inflation if aggregate demand grows at a rate higher than productive capacity, or fall into recession if the growth of productive capacity is not promptly and fully utilised to satisfy aggregate demand.

This description of the mode of operation of the system is certainly very condensed by comparison with the precision of the conclusions discussed in the formal model, but this description is sufficient as an intuitive explanation of the possibility of a prolonged inflation and how this can degenerate into recession and unemployment.

Let us first note that some portion of total investment is taken up by public investment, a portion that tends to rise with the rise in the production of output and also because public spending is largely used to bring the economy to full employment.

Let us also note that even private investment does not always generate an immediate increase in productive capacity. It should be obvious that productive capacity does not become available and operative in synchronisation with the rise in money income generated by the expenditure necessary to produce it. The time-lag between these two magnitudes depends not only on the 'construction period' of capital goods, which could be considered as a cause of inflation if stocks of goods or unused capacity were not available to meet a rise in aggregate demand. More important to my mind is the lengthening of the time-lag that results when the proportion of autonomous investment in total investment rises, and the further lengthening if the proportion of expenditure for public works and general construction projects in autonomous investment rises. The major part of such investment consists technically of various forms of social overhead capital, whose utilisation is often retarded by the lack of or retard in complementary investment. In such a case the productive capacity cannot be immediately utilised. The increased availability of money income does not correspond to an equivalent increase in the supply of commercial goods and services. In such circumstances the equilibrium between demand and supply can only be established through rising prices.

From these observations I maintain that it is not possible to deduce that the long boom of 1950–70 was solely sustained by continuous technical progress, as Professor Hicks tries to explain. The application of Keynesian policies, either to combat recession at its first signs or to satisfy the always largely unfulfilled demand for public goods, was also of importance. These policies have generated, first, the creeping inflation of the 1960s and then, through the accumulation over the years of means of payment not balanced by real goods, the inflation that we are currently suffering. Keynes, however, had already pointed out in chapter 21 of the *General Theory* that given the importance of money as a link between the present and the future, there could be a rise in prices even before the system had reached full employment.[4] This reference is not made without purpose. It links up with the observations made above concerning the relation between effective money and real scarcity.

One can also assume the opposite case, although not realistically in current conditions. Aggregate investment could generate an excess of productive capacity in relation to the rate of growth of the aggregate demand, because of a high proportion of induced to total investment. In this case there would be excess capacity and prices would tend to decrease. This case is not common, at least it never occurred in the long ascending phase of the present cycle. These assumptions do not seem very realistic even if theoretically plausible because of the incomes' inflation which adds to and reinforces the support of aggregate demand.

The goal of men of science, today as always, is to discover instruments of action to control the movement of the economy in the aim of progress and stability.

The first problem is how to slow down the cyclical expansion as it nears its ceiling.

The other problem is how to slow down the recession when the action of the accelerator works in a recessionary way, that is, in conditions of excess capacity.

The classic instruments of intervention are monetary and fiscal policy, the latter taken in the larger sense of public expenditure policy. It is possible to slow an expansionary phase by using both instruments in a convergent manner. By this I mean that monetary policy is to be used in a *selective manner* in order to obtain a restriction of credit while at the same time allowing finance for private investment capable of creating new productive capacity utilisable in a short time. In this way

[4] J. M. Keynes, *General Theory* (London: Macmillan, 1936), 4, 5, pp. 298–304

the production of real goods is promoted and the excess of purchasing power is neutralised.

The use of the other instrument, fiscal policy, must be regulated to reduce the public investments that do not contribute to new capacity formation in the short term. This involves the postponement of programmes of social investment until the next recession.

In the opposite case, where one wants to slow a recession because the available productive capacity is excessive in relation to aggregate demand, monetary policy acts in an expansionary manner by increasing the finance available to the public sector of the economy to carry out social investment programmes which contribute to supporting aggregate demand in the short term but not to the creation of new productive capacity.

At the same time public expenditure policy is integrated with monetary policy to favour the rapid execution of public works programmes.

The conditions required for the efficient operation of stabilising actions is an appropriate and efficient institutional organisation capable of planning public expenditure in a manner much less rigid than is traditional.

In putting forward this stabilisation policy scheme, the scope of which is to slow down the inflation that seems to be in the nature of Keynesian policies for the support of aggregate demand, I hasten to add that I am conscious of the practical difficulties and the institutional obstacles which make its actual application nearly impossible.

I believe many of us have already noticed that in many countries, and especially in Italy, public expenditure contributes more to the aggravation of cycles than to their correction.

The scheme of stabilisation policy that I have proposed here, I had already put forward some years ago[5] and discussed on many occasions. And yet, to this date, nothing has been done in Italy to organise public administration in such a way that it would allow the regulation of public spending for anti-cyclical purposes.

Everyone agrees in condemning credit restriction. But no one has ever shown the will to act decisively, and in advance, to arrange alternative instruments, which may act as a complement to the control of the supply of money. The necessity of such action has been expressed many times in the literature,[6] but it appears that governments and the bureaucracies do not intend to relinquish their power to determine public expenditure according to discretionary and related opportunistic motives.

The fact is that inflation continues unabated and now threatens to

[5] G. Di Nardi, 'Le politiche di impiego dei mezzi per lo sviluppo economico', *Rivista di Politica Economica* (1956).

[6] Among the most recent see John Cornwall, 'The Ceiling and the Domar Effect as Stabilizers', *Kyklos*, 1 (1974).

topple the productive structure and civil order. I personally do not believe that inflation is a calamity to which we must develop our ability to adapt. I believe, on the contrary, that inflation concerns a malfunction of the economic system, a malfunction that governments can control if they are predisposed to create the organisation necessary to do it. It seems to me that automatic stabilising instruments will work if men firmly intend that they should and are willing to organise them so that they can function efficiently and properly.

2 Inflation, Money and the Role of Fiscal Arrangements: an Analytic Framework for the Inflation Problem*

Karl Brunner

I INTRODUCTION

A persistent and world-wide inflation has attracted public attention. The space allotted in newspapers and the efforts invested in political rhetoric or the rapid succession of policy programmes reflects the general concern. The public discussion also produced a remarkable array of ideas and beliefs bearing on the inflation problem. This array can be usefully classified into three major groups according to the following two criteria: (i) the dependence or independence of price movements with respect to current and past evolutions of market conditions, and (ii) the occurrence or non-occurrence of a dominant impulse pattern driving the inflationary process.

'Institutionalist' theories of inflation claim that prices move autonomously and independently from evolving market condition. Price movements emerge in this view as a response to specific 'sociological and sociopsychological' forces or institutional arrangements. The variety of 'institutionalist' theories can be ordered according to the social patterns selected by diverse explanations. These patterns produce the dominant impulse conditioning the general motion of the price-level.[1]

* This paper is based on discussions and joint work developed over many years with Allan H. Meltzer. This collaboration over many years has substantially influenced this paper. It forms part of a project supported by a grant from the National Science Foundation. This support is gratefully acknowledged.

[1] Most cost push ideas belong to this class of inflation theories. Some uses of the cost-push terminology however involve ideas consistent with the price-theoretical explanations. Institutionalist explanations subsume of course Galbraithian ideas, the monopoly theory of inflation sanctioned by the *New York Times*, etc.

Price theoretical explanations assert on the other hand that prices respond systematically to changing market conditions. They join institutionalist explanations however in the recognition of dominant impulse forces accountable for the broad movements in the price level. The precise nature of impulses emphasised by price-theoretical explanations differs of course radically from the patterns considered by institutionalist ideas. Moreover, different versions of price-theoretical explanations locate the inflationary impulse force either with fiscal, monetary or 'Wicksellian' processes.[2]

The remaining inflation theories form a group of essentially 'eclectic-agnostic' explanations. They share in general with the price-theoretical explanations the rejection of the 'institutionalist' emphasis on 'autonomous' price movements proceeding independently of market conditions. But they also reject the idea of a systematic and dominant impulse force. The driving force emerges from a sequence of random events usually appearing in the 'real sector' of the economy.[3]

This paper does not attend to the collection of 'institutionalist' or 'eclectic-agnostic' ideas. They fail to explain observed inflation experiences for a variety of reasons. It is also contended that the Wicksellian version of price-theoretical explanations encounters serious difficulties when confronted with observations. The Wicksellian conjecture may contribute to the description of transient spurts in prices, but it fails to advance our understanding of persistent increases in prices maintained over a longer period, involving moreover episodes of sustained accelerations (or decelerations) in price movements.[4] These persistent patterns form the observable phenomenon requiring our analytical attention.

The literature on growth theory joins monetary theory in the consensus that our phenomenon is 'essentially a monetary problem'. This

[2] The reader may find a more detailed description of the range of inflation theories in my papers 'Monetary Management, Domestic Inflation and Imported Inflation', published in *National Monetary Policies and the International Financial System* (Chicago and London, 1974) edited by Robert Z. Aliber; and 'Is Inflation Really Intractable?' published in *Währungsstabilität in einer integrierten Welt. Beiträge zur Geldtheorie und Geldpolitik* (Frankfurt and Berlin, 1974).

[3] The reader should note Peter Fortune's interesting piece, 'An Evaluation of Anti-Inflation Policies in the United States', New England Economic Review, Jan/Feb 1974, Federal Reserve Bank of Boston. Fortune never refers to the large monetary acceleration observed in 1972 when discussing the accelerating price movements in 1973. He emphasises only real factors (failing wheat crops, oil embargo, devaluation, etc.).

[4] The reader will find a more detailed discussion in the papers mentioned in footnote 2. It should also be noted that Western European political development tended to lower quite generally the private sector's anticipated real net yield on real capital. This has been reflected in a falling proportion of investment to gross national product in several European countries. It is thus most improbable that the recent inflation experiences can be interpreted as a Wicksellian process.

means, that inflations emerge and disappear, accelerate or decay according to the evolution of monetary growth. This literature recognises the monetary impulse as the dominant force generating our inflation experiences. Some portions of macro-theory still seem to contest this view however. Major importance is attributed to fiscal policies, i.e. to the government sector's expenditure and taxing policies. These views have been forcefully articulated by various members of the Council of Economic Advisers serving under Presidents Kennedy and Johnson. Monetarists argued on the other hand that fiscal policies exert only a transient effect on both nominal and real values.

The analytic framework offered in this paper partly resolves this conflict. Traditional monetarists and Keynesians may not be appeased by the partial resolution involving a reinterpretation of the economic impact resulting from fiscal policies. This reinterpretation is based on price-theoretical considerations modifying traditional fiscalist and monetarist propositions. In particular, it will be shown that fiscal policies exert both a short-run and a long-run effect. They also affect in the long-run both nominal and real values. We shall also note that the long-run nominal effects are essentially due to the fact that fiscal policies and fiscal arrangements are the long-run determinants of financial stock variables. Lastly, fiscal policies partly determine in the long run the private sector's level of 'normal output'. The subsequent analysis of the inflation problem thus assigns a central role to the evolution of the budget process. But such attribution is not based on traditional Keynesian multiplier reasoning. Moreover, the proposition that inflation is 'essentially a monetary phenomenon' remains valid. But its very validity leads us to examine the processes conditioning the evolution of monetary growth. The resulting analysis of the interaction between the monetary system, asset markets and the budget process, combined with a price-theoretically guided incorporation of fiscal policy, substantially modifies antecedent pieces of monetarist theorising.[5]

[5] It should be emphasised that these ideas gradually emerged in our discussions over the past six years. We presented our first piece bearing on these issues in June 1970 at the First Konstanz Conference on Monetary Theory and Monetary Policy. It was included in the subsequent *Proceedings* published by Kredit and Kapital, 1972. A second piece 'Money, Debt and Economic Activity' was published in the *Journal of Political Economy* (1972). A third paper was presented at the National Bureau Conference on Inflation in November 1971 and subsequently published in the supplementary issue of February 1973 of the *Journal of Money, Credit and Banking*. Two other papers have been presented at conferences. One was presented at a Conference on Inflation in April 1973 at Tulane University and another, bearing particularly on international aspects, at a conference in Paris in March 1974. The first was thoroughly redrafted and will be included with other papers from the Conference on 'Monetarism' held at Brown University on 2 November 1974 in a volume to be published in 1976 by North Holland Publishing Co. The second paper will be included in a volume edited by Emile Classen and Pascal Salin and also published in 1976 by North Holland Publishing Co.

II THE ANALYTIC FRAMEWORK

II.1 A GENERAL DESCRIPTION

It seems useful to begin with a stylised summary of the economic process depicted in the subsequent analysis. The interaction between four distinct processes determines the evolution of prices and output. The short-run process describes the responses of prices, output, interest rate, market value of real capital, money stock and total bank credit, produced by the simultaneous adjustment of asset and output markets relative to inherited stocks or financial and real assets. The short-run equilibrium will be represented subsequently in terms of a demand and supply configuration in the output market. The movements of the intersection between output demand and producers supply traces the path of the short-run system. This path describes an adjustment to the intermediate-run financial stock-flow equilibrium position, an adjustment determined by the operation of the government sector's budget constraint.

The short-run equilibrium supplemented with the budget process conditions the rate of change of financial stocks (monetary base and government securities). Changes in these stocks gradually modify the short-run system in accordance with the government sector's fiscal arrangements. The adjustments imposed via the asset markets on the short-run equilibrium position converge, with tax revenues sufficiently responsive to current conditions, to a state of financial stock-flow equilibrium. A persistent inflation requires under the circumstances intermittent changes in fiscal policies. The nature of the fiscal arrangements and the pattern of fiscal policies thus occurs with a central importance in our subsequent analysis of inflation as a process generating a persistent rise in prices maintained over substantial periods. This formulation eliminates temporary movements or once-for-all adjustments in the price-level. Such phenomena do not constitute the inflation problem under consideration in this paper.

The interaction between short- and intermediate-run processes does not exhaust the evolution of prices and output over time. Two longer-run processes gradually modify the intermediate run financial stock flow equilibrium position. These longer-run processes adjust output to a 'normal output' via gradual changes in efficiency wages. This involves also a corresponding convergence of the employment stock to the private sector's 'normal employment level'. The wage and employment stock adjustment determines thus a motion of the intermediate-run system to a point consistent with the economy's normal output. Lastly, accumulation of real stocks and investment in human capital modify normal output over time. This magnitude is further conditioned by fiscal policies of the government sector. Changes in tax rates affect the long-run stock of real capital or the stock of capital invested in human skills. Moreover, absorption of labour and output by the government sector also affects normal output. Fiscal arrangements and fiscal policies thus determine the longer-run inflationary drift imposed on an economy via two distinct but interrelated channels. They position the intermediate-run system relative to normal output, and they condition the level of normal output. It will be argued in the last sections of the paper that Western countries increasingly follow a pattern of economic policies, particularly fiscal policies, which accelerate the inflationary impact of the budget process and retard the growth of normal output. An entrenched and apparently intractable inflation problem thus emerges.

II.2 PRESENTATION OF THE MODEL

(a) *The Output Market*

The short-run equilibrium system combines three markets: an output market and two asset markets. The system expresses the interaction between the three markets. The output market is introduced first. Equation (1a) describes the equilibrium condition

$$\text{(1a)} \quad y = d[i - \pi, p, ap, P, W_n, W_h, e] + g$$
$$d_1, d_2, < 0 < d_3, d_4, d_5, d_6, d_7$$

on the output market, with y denoting the private sector's output, d the private sector's real demand (absorption) and g the government sector's absorption of output. The private sector's demand depends on the real rate on financial assets $(i - \pi)$ defined as the nominal rate i minus the credit market's anticipated rate of inflation π, the current price-level of output p, the anticipated price-level ap, the asset price-level (market value of real capital) P, non-human wealth W_n, human wealth W_h and the anticipated net yield e on real capital. The two wealth magnitudes are defined by equations (1b) and (1c). Equation (1b) introduces the private sector's total wealth as the sum of the market value of existing real capital (PK), the market value of outstanding government securities (vS), and lastly the

$$\text{(1b)} \quad W_n = PK + v(i, \tau_n) . S + (1 + \omega)B; \; v_1, v_2 < 0$$

$$\text{(1c)} \quad W_h = W(ay, aw, lg, q, \tau_h)$$
$$W_1, W_2, W_3, W_4 > 0 > W_5$$

monetary system's net contribution to the public's wealth $(1 + \omega)B$. The element ω expresses the monetary system's net worth multiplier. This magnitude is necessarily positive due to the occurrence of real resources required to operate the banking system and not included in K. Furthermore, ω may also absorb the Pesek-Saving effect produced by a non-competitive banking system. The letter v in the second term refers to the market value of securities per unit. It depends on the (index of) market rates i and the tax parameter τ_n summarising the relevant information about the tax schedule applicable to income from non-human wealth. The elasticity of v with respect to i [expressed by the formula $\varepsilon(v,i)$] is confined to the negative unit interval. It reflects the maturity structure of outstanding securities. With S consisting completely of consols $\varepsilon(v,i) = -1$. The value of $\varepsilon(v,i)$ moves closer to zero with shorter maturities.

Human wealth depends on anticipated output ay, the anticipated wage rate aw, the government sector's absorption of labour lg, the stock of human capital q inherited from the past and the tax parameters summarising the appropriate information concerning the tax schedule applicable to income from labour. This formulation expresses an underlying postulate bearing on the regularity of income distribution between ownership of real capital and labour. This postulate also conditions the formulation of the anticipated net yield e on real capital

(1d) $$e = n/K$$

$$\text{with } n = n(ay,\tau_n,u);\; n_1 > 0 > n_2, n_3$$

The magnitude n expresses the net real income derived from ownership of real capital. It depends on the anticipated real income ay in a manner governed by the patterns of income distribution, the tax schedule applicable to income from ownership of non-human wealth, and an uncertainty term u summarising the market's evaluation of the content of property rights. This term reflects in particular the private sector's anticipations bearing on the evolution of new institutions modifying property rights or entitlements. Moreover, the emergence of persistent inflation in societies governed by somewhat unstable political processes generates pervasive uncertainties concerning the future course of government policy. Such uncertainty lowers n and e. The degree of such uncertainty could be related to the frequency of changes in policies. It could also be associated with the range and frequency of changes in discretionary arrangements or interpretations of existing laws or rulings. The growing obscurity and complexity of legal or regulatory arrangements reflected in the relative demand for legal and accounting services in the private sector also appears to influence the level of uncertainty. An examination of bureaucratic behaviour might suggest that the level of pervasive uncertainty grows in the longer run with lg, the absorption of labour services and the relative increase of output absorption by the government sector.[6]

[6] This assertion implies that $\gamma = g.y^{-1}$ and $lg.L^{-1}$ (L = labour force) should be included among the determinants of e. The suggestion is made in order to draw attention to some unfinished business in macro theory. The government sector could be considered as a production process absorbing output g from the private sector and labour services lg as inputs. But what is the output and how does it feed back to the

The description of the output market is completed with the presentation of the producers' supply behaviour. Equation (1e) introduces supply behaviour in form of a price-setting function.

(1e) $p = p[cu(y,K,q),fw]$ $p_1,p_2>0$ and $cu_1>0>c_2,c_3$

The price-level of output depends on the rate of capacity utilisation *cu* and the efficiency wage *fw*. The efficiency wage is defined as the ratio of the private sector's wage bill to normal output *ny*, i.e. we write

$$fw = \frac{w.\overline{lp}}{ny}$$

where $\overline{lp}$ is the 'normal' amount of labour absorbed by the private sector, *ny* the associated normal output and *w* the money wage. The utilisation rate *cu* depends positively on output and negatively on two capital stocks. The first expresses the real resources available for productive activities accumulated over the past. The second involves the inherited capital of human skills and relevant productive information also acquired by past investment.

The reader should note in this context that the occurrence of an aggregate output variable associated with a correspondingly aggregated price-level neither implies nor presupposes that our analysis is confined to a single commodity world (i.e. a 'one potato world'). Such misinterpretations of the specification should be carefully avoided. The formulation involves an empirical constraint imposed on the subsequent analysis. It is implicitly asserted that variations in relative prices among components of output are not significant with respect to the problems pursued in this paper. In particular, it is argued that relative price changes between output components are of second or third order of importance for the analysis of some aggregative processes (e.g. the inflation problem) compared to the variations in the asset price *P* relative to the output price-level *p*, or compared to relative variations in interest rates. The specification thus reflects a judgement (hypothesis) concerning the relevant order of magnitudes or aspects bearing on our problem.

(b) *A Rationale for the Non-Keynesian Asset Markets*

The explicit emphasis on the relative changes of *P* and *p* deserve some attention. We may discern two distinct procedures in aggregative analysis. One strand imposes the equality $P = p$ for all relevant horizons. The other strand abolishes the interaction of the two price-levels and

---

behaviour of the private sector? The government produces goods competing with or complementing consumables offered by the private sector, or modifying the anticipated yield on real capital. This array of problems requires an approach using a variety of analytical developments emerging in recent years.

removes any relative variations between P and p by eliminating P from the analysis. The first procedure may be represented by Witte or Foley-Sidrauski.[7] It postulates a stock-flow interaction with a current price determined by the stock relationship. The flow analysis describes the response of producers' supply behaviour bearing on new production to this price. This means that P is determined on the asset markets by the portfolio adjustments of investors. This price is moreover equated to p, the price regulating new production, and the latter magnitude emerges from the interaction of $p = P$ with a rising supply curve describing the producers' behaviour.

The second procedure occurs implicitly in many textbook versions of Keynesian analysis, or appears imbedded in econometric models cast in a Keynesian mould. According to this analysis real capital inherited from the past is frozen into the portfolios of individual agents' wealth positions. It exists and decays beyond any portfolio adjustments proceeding on the market. No asset price P can emerge under the circumstances and relative variations of P and p cannot guide investment or consumption. The output price is the only relevant price recognised by this analysis.[8]

The two procedures may be usefully distinguished according to their implicit position concerning two types of transaction costs. The 'Keynesian strand' assumes that the first type of transaction costs, i.e. costs pertaining to the turnover of existing assets, prohibit portfolio adjustments involving real assets. The Foley-Sidrauski-Witte procedure assumes that these costs are sufficiently low for direct or indirect transactions. The second type of transaction costs bear on the costs of information concerning newly produced assets and the costs of integrating the new acquisitions into an established operation. The second type of transaction costs slips (over the shorter run) a wedge between P and p. They also permit a range of relative variations of these two prices. These variations form an important channel for the transmission of monetary and fiscal impulses. Our analysis assigns in this manner substantial significance to the operation of the second type of transaction costs. The occurrence of the first type of transaction costs is not denied. It is claimed however that a useful approximation for aggregative analysis can be made by combining relatively moderate transaction (turnover)

[7] The reader should note the paper by James Witte, 'The Micro-Foundations of the Social Investment Function', *Journal of Political Economy* (Oct 1963); and the work jointly performed by Duncan Foley and Miguel Sidrauski, 'Portfolio Choice, Investment, and Growth', *The American Economic Review* (Mar 1970).

[8] A qualification should be attached to this description. One could still recognise the occurrence of a shadow price attached to the resources. This shadow price reflects in the usual way the implicit value of the resource constraint. It could be used according to the Foley-Sidrauski-Witte procedure to determine new production activity. The fact remains that no such shadow price appeared in the analysis.

costs over some segments of real assets with a shadow price interpretation over the remaining segment.[9]

The relative turnover costs of inherited real assets bear on an important issue for aggregative analysis. The nature of the transmission mechanism forms one of the major substantive issues in contemporary macro theory. Alternative views are essentially conditioned by the underlying hypotheses governing the substitution relations centered on money. Keynesian analysis constrains these substitutions to a narrow subset of all available assets. Money substitutes only with 'bonds'. This is consistent with a uniformly forbidding level of transaction costs over the whole spectrum of real assets. It follows therefore that Keynesian analysis recognised only two asset markets, a credit market (or financial assets market) and the money market. Walras law is applied to eliminate the credit market and there remains the money market proximately determining the rate of interest. Monetarist analysis on the other hand asserts the substitutability of money in all directions over most of the available assets, including in particular real assets. It is not denied that various asset types suffer very different transaction costs. These costs delay the adjustments and absorb minor shifts and shocks imposed on the economy. They modify or obstruct the transmission of comparatively minor monetary or fiscal impulses. It is nevertheless claimed that persistent or large impulses eventually prevail. They will induce portfolio adjustments reaching substantially beyond financial assets. This pattern justifies for purposes of a useful analysis about the gross contours of an economy an approximation involving a general range of substitutions.

(c) *The Asset Markets*

The recognition of a general range implies an admission of three asset markets into the analysis. The money market and credit market is necessarily supplemented with a real asset market. The latter is eliminated from explicit consideration by virtue of the Walras law and the analysis actually proceeds with the interaction between two asset markets. This involves also a change in the interpretation of the money market. The proximate determination of interest rate is now assigned to the credit market. The money market on the other hand determines proximately the asset price of real capital P. Equations (2) and (3) introduce the two asset markets.

[9] It was noted before that the asset price P can be given both a market and a shadow price interpretation. In either case it affects in combination with p aggregate demand, capital accumulation and the long-run level of normal output. It has been argued on occasion that classical and Keynesian analysis differ according to the assumption made with respect to the transaction (turnover) costs of real capital. With low turnover costs a classical analysis emerges, whereas forbidding transaction costs establish a Keynesian pattern. This characterisation misses however some crucial elements incorporated in this paper's analysis.

(2) $a(i,p,P,W_n,W_h,e,\ldots).\ UB = \sigma(i-\pi,p,ap,P,W_n,W_h,e,S)$

$a_1,a_3,a_4,a_5,>0>a_6,a_2;\ \sigma_1,\sigma_4<0<\sigma_2,\sigma_3,\sigma_7,\sigma_8$

(3) $m(i,p,P,W_n,W_h,e,\ldots).\ UB = \lambda(i,ap,e,p,P,W_n,W_h)$

$m_1,m_2,m_6,>0>m_3,m_4,m_5;\ \lambda_1,\lambda_2,\lambda_3<0<\lambda_4,\lambda_5,\lambda_6,\lambda_7.$

The credit market expressed by equation (2) juxtaposes the banks' absorption of earning assets and the public's asset supply. The banks' absorption is introduced as a product of asset multiplier and the ('unborrowed') monetary base *UB* adjusted in the usual way for changes in reserve requirements. The asset multiplier may be usefully understood to form a semi-reduced form derived from underlying relations describing the public's and the banks' relevant allocation patterns.[10] The banks divide assets between earning assets and base money, they partition base money between borrowed and unborrowed amounts and set the relative conditions on liabilities. The public divides money balances between currency and demand deposits and total deposits between time and demand deposits. These allocation patterns depend on relative prices, interest rates and wealth. It follows that the asset multiplier depends via the allocation patterns on the same range of variables. The public's asset supply σ to banks can be thought of as the sum of the public's desired loan liability position plus the excess supply of outstanding government securities not absorbed by private portfolios at given market conditions.[11]

The money market equation describes the interaction between money stock and money demand. The money stock is introduced as a product of monetary multiplier *m* and monetary base. The monetary multiplier depends also on the allocation patterns underlying the asset multiplier. The dependence however exhibits substantially different properties. Still, the monetary multiplier depends necessarily on the same range of variables with a sensitivity conditioned by the monetary regime.[12] Money demand also depends on this range of variables. It depends thus in particular, as does the public's asset supply, on the anticipated net real yield on real capital *e*. This magnitude affects money demand negatively and asset supply positively. This circumstance expresses the nature of the substitution relations asserted in monetarist analysis.

The opposite response of σ and λ to variations in the anticipated net yield *e* is not the only difference between the two behaviour functions. An increase in the anticipated price level *ap* raises the asset supply, but

[10] The reader is referred to my paper 'A Diagrammatic Exposition of the Money Supply Process', *Schweizerische Zeitschrift für Volkswirtschaft und Statistik* (1974).

[11] This may be stated as follows: $\sigma = L^d + S - \delta$ where L^d = desired loan liability position, S = stock of government securities outstanding, δ = public's desired security portfolio.

[12] This point has been elaborated in my paper on 'A Diagrammatic Exposition of the Money Supply Process', noted under footnote 10.

lowers money demand. Moreover, σ depends on the real rate $(i - \pi)$ on financial assets, whereas λ depends on the nominal rate i. An increase in the anticipated rate of inflation π occurring at a constant real rate $(i - \pi)$ lowers money demand with no effect on asset supply. It should also be noted that money demand is substantially more sensitive to variations in wealth positions than the public's asset supply.[13] Lastly, the public's asset supply includes explicitly the stock of government securities S outstanding with a derivative equal to unity. This variable occurs only implicitly in money demand as a component of non-human wealth. The construction of the public's asset supply as the sum of desired loan liabilities plus the excess supply of securities not absorbed in private portfolios determines this pattern. These differences reveal that σ and λ describe distinct behaviour patterns and the two functions are not mirror images. The essential difference between the two behaviour functions follows from the broadened spectrum of substitution relations.

(d) *The Budget Process*

The equations introduced thus far describe the short-run system. They describe the interaction between asset markets and output markets in response to change in fiscal policies or the financial stock variables UB and S. The next equation plays a central role for both intermediate-run and longer-run analysis. Equation (4) presents the government sector's budget.

$$(4) \qquad pg + w.lg + I(i).S - t(p,ry;\tau_h,\tau_n) = U\mathring{B} + \mathring{S}$$

$$I_1,t_1,t_2,t_3,t_4,t_5 > 0 \text{ and } ry = y + \frac{w.lg}{p} + \frac{I.S}{p}$$

Total government expenditures are a sum of three components, pg measures the nominal expenditures on output acquired from private producers and $w.lg$ indicates the value of labour services used in the government sector with w describing the average wage offered. The last term, $I(i).S$, includes the government sector's payment of interest on the outstanding debt. The expression $I(i)$ states the average interest payment per security. Its dependence on i reflects the maturity structure. The elasticity $\varepsilon(I,i)$ is unity whenever the stock of securities has a maturity less than the time period built into the analysis. On the other hand, with S composed solely of consols, $\varepsilon(I,i)$ approaches in the shorter-run almost zero. For steady state analysis however it would be generally appropriate to equate $\varepsilon(I,i)$ with unity.

Tax accruals t are subtracted on the left of equation (4) from total government expenditures. Tax revenues depend positively on output

[13] This follows from the fact that $\delta\sigma/\delta W = \delta L^d/\delta W - \delta\sigma/\delta W$. The two terms defining $\delta\sigma/\delta W$ exhibit opposite signs.

price p and received real income ry and the tax parameters. Received real income is the sum of output, the government sector's real wage bill and the real value of total interest payments received from the government sector. The properties of the tax revenue function assume a major importance in our subsequent analysis of the inflation problem. The right side of equation (4) states that the deficit is either financed by borrowing through sales of securities, $\mathring{S}$, or through creation of base money $U\mathring{B}$. It is actually immaterial whether the government obtains a variety of direct or indirect advances from the central bank or whether the central bank only purchases securities on the open market. The institutional obfuscation of the relevant operation does not detract from the fact that deficits are either financed by selling securities outside the government sector or by creating base money.

(e) *Equations Bearing on Longer-Run Aspects*

The system of four equations describes completely the response of the short-run process and the adjustment to a position of financial stock-flow equilibrium. This process will be explored in some detail with the aid of diagrams in the next section. We still need to introduce two equations bearing on the longer-run processes.

$$(5)\quad \frac{\mathring{w}}{w} = \int_0^t \beta[t-\tau,\tau].h[\tau,I(t)].[y(\tau) - ny(\tau)]d\tau + \frac{a\mathring{p}}{ap}$$

$$(6)\quad ny = f[\overline{lp}.\overline{lu}.q,K]; f_1,f_2 > 0$$

$$\overline{lp} = \overline{par}.POP.(1-\bar{u}) - lg$$

Equation (5) describes the wage adjustment process which moves the intermediate-run position gradually into coincidence with normal output. This wage adjustment governs implicitly the adjustment of the employment stock to a 'normal employment level' associated with normal output. Equation (6) determines the level of normal output. The wage adjustment equation will not be explicitly incorporated into the analysis of adjustment processes. This portion of our work will be developed at another occasion. It guides however our interpretation of longer-run processes and expresses our conjecture about an 'inherently stable' and shock absorbing private sector. It is sufficient at this stage to clarify in a somewhat intuitive manner the crucial mechanism linking intermediate-run and longer-run positions of the economic system. The rationale underlying equation (5) views wage adjustment as a process producing and disseminating information over the economic system. One set of signals bears on the rate of inflation anticipated by suppliers on the labour market and demanders on the output market. The reader should note that $a\mathring{p}/ap$ coincides with π in the steady state, but not, in general, over the adjustment processes. These expectations refer to differently mixed groups of economic agents with differently distributed information costs. The behaviour of the two anticipation rates is thus expected to be different over at least an intermediate run. Another set of signals pertains to the state of output and labour markets. An output below normal output produces signals gradually retarding, and outputs above normal yield signals gradually accelerating wage movements. The information disseminated by market processes does not link current wage changes with current market positions. This information is distributed over time. Moreover, its import is subsequently reassessed according to the information level realised at a later stage. These two aspects of the information process are expressed by the term β and h multiplying the deviations of output from normal output under the integral. The β function describes the probabilities according to which pieces of information about market conditions are distributed over time. It describes simultaneously a forward and backward distribution and satisfies the conditions (5a).

$$\text{(5a)} \quad \int_{-\infty}^{t} \beta(t - \tau,\tau)d\tau = \int_{t}^{\infty} \beta(t,\tau)d\tau = 1$$

The expression $\beta(t,\tau)$ describes the probability that a signal produced by a given output deviation in t is absorbed by agents in $(t + \tau)$. The operation of the market system shapes the nature of this distribution, whether it is stretched out over time or rather compressed. Furthermore, the magnitude of the information impulse conveyed by this probability process is modified by information I available at point t. This modification of the magnitude is expressed by the h-function. Its operation is best understood with an example. Suppose some negative output deviations emerged in the recent past but suppliers of labour assess the signals from current information to mean a short and shallow deviation barely affecting the dominant mass of workers. This information lowers the value of h and lowers the effect of negative output deviations on wage adjustments. We also note that the same set of signals simultaneously affects $a\mathring{p}/ap$. Both effects moderate the response of wages to an emerging contraction of output. It is furthermore conjectured that institutional arrangements affect the speed of adjustments of the employment stock through modifications of the h functions. Powerful labour unions introduce possibly an asymmetry into h, small values being associated with negative and large with positive output deviations. This may result from the circumstance that a majority of union members with seniority entitlements is not much affected by a retardation of activity. The survival probability of a union hierarchy is not raised by speedy response to negative deviations. It is probably raised on the other hand by a speedy response to positive deviations. Some aspects of pervasive allusions to a 'wage push' can thus be effectively incorporated into our analysis. The major contention implicit in traditional ideas of a 'wage push' remains however unacceptable, viz. that wages (or prices) do *not* respond to evolving market conditions and are essentially controlled by specific institutional patterns. We should however consider the possibility that institutional arrangements *do* condition the wage adjustment process in important respects. These considerations do not imply the absence or removal of any mechanisms pushing intermediate-run positions towards normal output. They imply that variations in institutional arrangements affect the relevant horizon of the process. This means also that the social cost of an anti-inflationary policy may depend significantly on prevailing institutional patterns and past policies.

The same institutional arrangements stretching the wage adjustment over time may also lower the level of normal output. This level is explained in equation (6). It depends on the stock of real capital K and the amount of labour lp absorbed by the private sector. The latter magnitude is weighted with the normal utilisation rate $\overline{lu}$ of labour and an index of the accumulated capital of human skills and technological knowledge q. This capital is formed by suitable investments similarly to the stock of real capital. The labour amount lp is defined as the difference between the employed normal labour force $\overline{par}.POP(l - \bar{u})$ and the labour lg absorbed by the government sector. The normal employed labour force is explained in terms of the total population POP, the normal participation rate $\overline{par}$ and the normal unemployment rate $\bar{u}$. The normal state magnitudes occurring in the description of normal output are indicated with a bar. Equation (6) thus suggests that fiscal policies raising lg, or increasing $(i - \pi)$ via larger g, lower lp or K and compress normal output. Taxes, subsidy and benefit policies which lower incentives to acquire skill and knowledge capital, or raise the normal unemployment rate, also lower or retard the normal output level. This linkage between fiscal policy and normal output involves a long-run 'crowding out' effect substantially more important than the much discussed short-run 'crowding out' effects.

III THE IMPLICATIONS OF THE MODEL

The analysis proceeds in a series of steps gradually developing the building blocks required for our inflation problem. The lowest building blocks are the responses of the asset markets. These responses are shortly discussed in section 1. We proceed next in section 2 to an analysis of the short-run system and examine its responses by means of a diagrammatic presentation. Section 3 inserts the budget process into the diagram and discusses the intermediate-run financial stock-flow adjustment. Section 4 investigates analytically the dynamic implications of fiscal arrangements and budget process. The last section attends to an analysis of the longer-run state. It pursues particularly the role of fiscal policies and fiscal arrangements in longer-run inflationary experiences.

III.1 THE RESPONSE OF THE ASSET MARKETS

The subsequent short-run analysis assumes that anticipated output ay and anticipated price-level ap depend partly on current output and price-level. Anticipated output ay depends also on the capital stock K. This section examines responses of interest rate i and asset price P generated by the interaction between asset markets. The feedbacks via the output market are not incorporated into this asset market analysis. The patterns required for the analysis in the following sections are listed in Table I.

TABLE I The Response Patterns of the Asset Markets

The elasticity of y with respect to x is denoted by $\varepsilon(y,x)$

1. the response to UB

$$\varepsilon(i,UB|AM) \sim -\frac{\varepsilon(MM,P) - \varepsilon(CM,P)}{\Delta} < 0$$

$$\varepsilon(P,UB|AM) \sim -\frac{\varepsilon(CM,i) - \varepsilon(MM,i)}{\Delta} > 0$$

where $\Delta = \varepsilon(CM,i).\varepsilon(MM,P) - \varepsilon(MM,i).\varepsilon(CM,P) < 0$

and
$$\varepsilon(CM,i) = \varepsilon(a,i) - \varepsilon(\sigma,i-\pi)\frac{i}{i-\pi} > 0$$
$$\varepsilon(MM,i) = \varepsilon(m,i) - \varepsilon(\lambda,i) > 0$$
$$\varepsilon(CM,P = \varepsilon(a,P) - \varepsilon(\sigma,P) > 0$$
$$\varepsilon(MM,P) = \varepsilon(m,P) - \varepsilon(\lambda,P) < 0$$

The fundamental order postulates are

$$\varepsilon(CM,i) > \varepsilon(MM,i) > 0 \text{ and } |\varepsilon(MM,P)| > \varepsilon(CM,P) > 0$$

The elasticities of a, m, σ and λ with respect to i and P include the effect of variations in i and P via non-human wealth W_n. Inspection of the four expressions above shows that they can be understood as interest rate or asset price elasticities of the excess supply of bank credit on the credit market (for CM) and of the excess supply of money on the money market (for MM). It should also be noted that the responses of i and P are approximations. The real balance effect is omitted in order to simplify the expressions. This effect involves an expression proportional to $(1 + \omega)UB.W_n^{-1}$ and remains at a negligible order.

2. The response to S

$$\varepsilon(i,S|AM) \sim \frac{\varepsilon(MM,P)}{\Delta} \cdot \frac{S}{aB} > 0$$

$$\varepsilon(P,S|AM) \sim -\frac{\varepsilon(MM,i)}{\Delta}\frac{S}{aB} > 0$$

In order to simplify, the real security effect via W_n has been omitted. It is proportional to $vS.W_n^{-1}$ and is of small order.

3. The response to y

$$\varepsilon(i,y|AM) = -\frac{\varepsilon(CM,y).\varepsilon(MM,P) - \varepsilon(MM,y).\varepsilon(CM,P)}{\Delta} > 0$$

$$\varepsilon(P,y|AM) = -\frac{\varepsilon(MM,y).\varepsilon(CM,i) - \varepsilon(CM,y).\varepsilon(MM,i)}{\Delta} \gtrless 0$$

where $\varepsilon(CM,y) = \varepsilon(a,y) - \varepsilon(\sigma,p).\varepsilon(p,y) - \varepsilon(\sigma,e).\varepsilon(e,ay).\varepsilon(ay,y) < 0$

$$\varepsilon(MM,y) = \varepsilon(m,y) - \varepsilon(\lambda,p).\varepsilon(p,y) - [\varepsilon(\lambda,W_h).\varepsilon(W_h,ay) + \varepsilon(\lambda,e).\varepsilon(e,ay)].\varepsilon(ay,y) < 0$$

The term involving $\varepsilon(\sigma,W_h)$ is deleted in $\varepsilon(CM,y)$. It is of comparatively small importance. It is however included in $\varepsilon(MM,y)$. This term emerges because of a partial dependence of *ay* on *y* expressible by an elasticity $0 < \varepsilon(ay,y) < 1$. The sign of $\varepsilon(CM,y)$ *is* unambiguously negative. The sign of $e(MM,y)$ depends on the bracketed term containing the two components with opposite sign. In order to simplify the account the term is approximated by zero (Note: the discussion of the budget process will use expressions for $\varepsilon(CM,y)$ and $\varepsilon(MM,y)$ with *p* held constant.) These modified terms are

$$\varepsilon(CM,y) = \varepsilon(a,y) - \varepsilon(\sigma,e).\varepsilon(e,ay).\varepsilon(ay,y) < 0$$
$$\varepsilon(MM,y) = \varepsilon(m,y) \sim 0$$

The responses of *i* and *P* under these conditions are

$$\varepsilon(i,y|AM) > 0 \text{ and } \varepsilon(P,y|AM) > 0.$$

4. The response to *p*

$$\varepsilon(i,p|AM) = \frac{\varepsilon(\sigma,p).\varepsilon(MM,P) - \varepsilon(\lambda,p).\varepsilon(CM,P)}{\Delta} > 0$$

$$\varepsilon(P,p|AM) = \frac{\varepsilon(\lambda,p).\varepsilon(CM,i) - \varepsilon(\sigma,p).\varepsilon(MM,i)}{\Delta} < 0$$

provided $\varepsilon(\lambda,p) \leqslant \varepsilon(\sigma,p)$

5. The response to π

$$\varepsilon(i,\pi|AM) = -\frac{\varepsilon(MM,P)}{\Delta}.\varepsilon(\sigma,i-\pi)\frac{\pi}{i-\pi} > 0$$

$$\varepsilon(P,\pi|AM) = +\frac{\varepsilon(MM,i)}{\Delta}.\varepsilon(\sigma,i-\pi)\frac{\pi}{i-\pi} > 0$$

6. The response to *ap*

$$\varepsilon(i,ap|AM) = \frac{\varepsilon(\sigma,ap).\varepsilon(MM,P) - \varepsilon(\lambda,ap).\varepsilon(CM,P)}{\Delta} > 0$$

$$\varepsilon(P,ap|AM) = \frac{\varepsilon(\lambda,ap).\varepsilon(CM,i) - \varepsilon(\sigma,ap).\varepsilon(MM,i)}{\Delta} > 0$$

provided $|\varepsilon(\lambda,ap)| \leqslant \varepsilon(\sigma,ap)$

7. The response to an increase in *K* (holding *p* constant)

$$\varepsilon(i,K|AM) = \frac{\varepsilon(\sigma,e).\varepsilon(e,K).\varepsilon(MM,P) - [\varepsilon(\lambda,W_n).\frac{PK}{W_n} + \varepsilon(\lambda,e).\varepsilon(e,K)].\varepsilon(CM,P)}{\Delta} > 0$$

$$\varepsilon(P,K|AM) = \frac{[\varepsilon(\lambda,W_n)\frac{PK}{W_n} + \varepsilon(\lambda,e).\varepsilon(e,K)].\varepsilon(CM,i) - \varepsilon(\sigma,e).\varepsilon(e,K).\varepsilon(CM,i)}{\Delta} < 0$$

Note that $\varepsilon(e,K) = \varepsilon(n,ay).\varepsilon(ay,K) - 1 > -1$ and less than 0.
It is assumed that *ay* is partly adjusted to changes in available real resources.

The responses to changes in the base and the outstanding stock of government securities reveal some important properties of the generalised substitution relations centred around money. The interest rate moves proportional to the reciprocal of an average interest elasticity over the asset markets with weights determined by the asset price elasticities of the excess supply of bank credit on the credit market, $\varepsilon(CM,P)$, and of the excess supply of the money market, $\varepsilon(MM,P)$. The sign of the elasticity of i with respect to UB implied by the asset markets (AM) equations, i.e. $\varepsilon(i,UB|AM)$, is uniquely determined by the signs of underlying elasticities. The reader should note that the conditioning label AM is inserted into the elasticity expression, $\varepsilon(i,UB|AM)$, to emphasise that the response of i to UB is determined just by the interaction of asset markets. The response of P on the other hand depends on a fundamental order constraint. It is postulated that the interest elasticity [$\varepsilon(CM,i)$] of the excess supply of bank credit exceeds the interest elasticity [$\varepsilon(MM,i)$] of the excess supply of money. This postulate involves *no* assumption about the absolute magnitude of $\varepsilon(MM,i)$. The transmission of monetary impulses occurs independently of such an assumption. With $\varepsilon(CM,i) > \varepsilon(MM,i) > 0$ an increase in the base simultaneously lowers i and raises P.

The role of the order constraint can be clarified with an examination of its denial. With $\varepsilon(CM,i) = \varepsilon(MM,i)$ the asset price level P does not respond to the base and we obtain

$$(7) \quad \begin{aligned} \varepsilon(i,UB|AM) &= -\frac{1}{\varepsilon(MM,i)} \\ \varepsilon(P,UB|AM) &= \end{aligned}$$

The analysis produces under the conditions stated a Keynesian pattern. The only transmission channel conveying monetary impulses operates via interest rates. Moreover, the response of interest rates depends on interest elasticities of the money market according to standard Keynesian money market theory. With $\varepsilon(CM,i)$ moderately less than $\varepsilon(MM,i)$ monetary impulses exert negligible influences on the economy and for large values of $\varepsilon(MM,i)$ relative to $\varepsilon(CM,i)$, even perverse effects.

An increase in the stock of government securities raises both interest rates i and asset price P. It conveys thus partially offsetting signals to the output market. This pattern affects the intermediate-run financial stock-flow adjustment to be examined in a subsequent section. The responses associated with S depend on the relative substitutability between money and financial assets on the one side and between financial assets and real capital on the other side. A dominant substitution relation between financial assets and money produces the pattern observed. Under the circumstances an increase in financial assets lowers their money price and raises the price of real capital. The real rates of return on financial and real assets diverge in the short-run in response to changes in S relative to the money stock and K. Adjustments in K and the price-levels p and P impose in the long run a convergence of the real rates.

Two aspects of inflation are included among the patterns examined in Table I. An increase in the credit market's anticipated rate of inflation raises both i and P. Moreover, the response increases with the prevailing level of inflationary anticipations. An increase of the purchaser's anticipated price-level ap raises the asset price level P. The effect on i depends on the relative sensitivity of money demand λ and the public's asset supply σ to variations in ap. With $\varepsilon(\sigma,ap) \sim |\varepsilon(\lambda,ap)|$ an increase of ap raises the interest rate i by a modest proportion. The net impulse conveyed to the output market remains consequently expansive. An increase in the current price-level imposes on the other hand adjustments on the asset markets transmitting deflationary impulses to the output market. The interest rate i rises and the asset price P falls. Lastly, an increase in human wealth works dominantly through an increase in money demand to raise i and lower P.

An economy's growth patterns operate on the asset markets via longer-run adjustments of the capital stocks K, q and also the employment stock lp. They modify asset market conditions via the producer's price setting responses and changes in human wealth. The previous results determine the short-run impact of a persistent growth in q and lp. These channels operate via the price setting function on p. An increase in q raises normal output ny, and lowers (without wage adjustment) the efficiency wage and p. The results are partly modified by an expanding money demand resulting from the effect generated by q via human wealth. Changes in the capital stock K affect capacity utilisation, the efficiency wage, non-human wealth and the anticipated yield e on real capital. We require for the purposes of our subsequent arguments particularly the effects conveyed by the e and W_n channels. The result is shown in Table I, point 7. An increase of K affects i quite negligibly with probably a small rise in the context of pure asset market adjustments. The asset price P on the other hand is definitely lowered. An inspection of the formula shows that the response of P to K is actually proportional to the negative value of the elasticity $\varepsilon(P,UB|AM)$, with a positive proportionality factor. Values in excess of unity for this factor seem probable. With $\varepsilon(P,UB|AM)$ somewhat below unity, the product defining the response of P to K centres around unity.

III.2 A DIAGRAMMATIC DESCRIPTION OF THE SHORT-RUN SYSTEM

Important aspects of the intermediate-run and longer-run adjustment process can be usefully clarified by means of a pseudo-Marshallian diagram. Figure 1 juxtaposes a demand and supply curve in a price-output plane. The vertical line measures output-price p and the horizontal line the private sector's output y. The supply curve s represents the price setting function introduced in equation (1d). The slope of the curve expresses the elasticity $\varepsilon(p,y|s)$ of this function. The position of the curve is lowered with increases in real capital K and human skill capital q. It rises with increasing efficiency wages fw. The demand curve is somewhat less Marshallian in nature and involves actually an equilibrium condition spanning several markets. It is thus a pseudo-demand curve, representing the locus of all p, y-values satisfying the output *and* the asset markets. The properties of this $(d + g)$ curve are obtained by replacing the arguments i and P in the d function with their respective

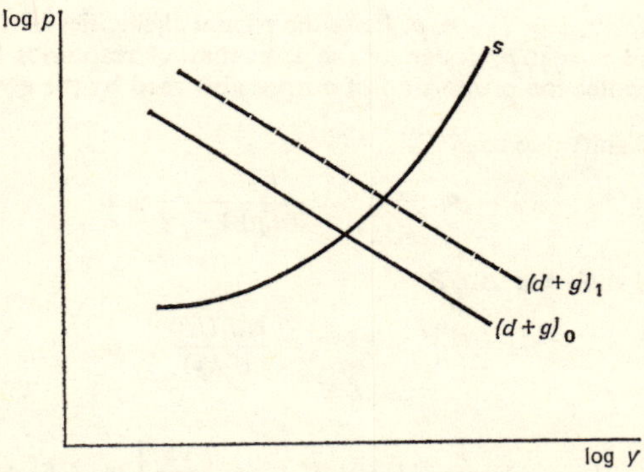

Figure 1. A shift in the $(d + g)$ line from $(d + g)_0$ to $(d + g)_1$ as a result of an increase in g, UB or S. Price rises and output expands depending on the slopes of the two lines.

solutions obtained from the asset markets. Suitable differentiation produces the slope of the curve listed in Table II.1. The slope is unambiguously negative. We may also conjecture that it is less than unity in absolute value. This conjecture is influenced by an implication of the homogeneity condition imposed on the d-function. Homogeneity implies that

$$(8) \qquad -\varepsilon(d,p) = \varepsilon(d,ap) + \varepsilon(d,P) + \varepsilon(d,W_n) + \varepsilon(d,W_h) > 0$$

where $\varepsilon(d,P)$ describes the partial elasticity of d with respect to P not incorporating the effect of P via non-human wealth W_n. The implication suggests that $\varepsilon(d,p) < -1$.

TABLE II Properties of the Pseudo-Demand Curve

1. The slope of the curve $d + g$ is expressed by

$$\varepsilon(p,y|d+g) = \frac{1-(1-\gamma)\cdot\bar{\varepsilon}(d,y)}{\varepsilon(d,p)\cdot(1-\gamma)} < 0$$

where

$$\bar{\varepsilon}(d,y) = \left[\varepsilon(d,i-\pi)\frac{i}{i-\pi} + \varepsilon(d,W_n).\varepsilon(v,i)\frac{vS}{W_n}\right].\varepsilon(i,y|AM) + \left[\varepsilon(d,P) + \varepsilon(d,W_n)\frac{PK}{W_n}\right].\varepsilon(P,y|AM) + \varepsilon(d,e).\varepsilon(e,y) > 0$$

$$\bar{\varepsilon}(d,p) = \varepsilon(d,p) + \left[\varepsilon(d,i-\pi)\frac{i}{i-\pi} + \varepsilon(d,W_n).\varepsilon(v,i)\frac{vS}{W_n}\right].\varepsilon(i,p|AM) + \left[\varepsilon(d,P) + \varepsilon(d,W_n)\frac{PK}{W_n}\right].\varepsilon(P,p|AM) < 0$$

Note: the $\varepsilon(d,x)$, $x = i - \pi, p, P$ are the partial elasticities of d. The $\varepsilon(v,z|AM)$ $v = i, P$ and $z = y, p$, designate the asset market responses listed in Table I Lastly, γ denotes the proportion of output absorbed by the government sector.

2. The vertical shift due to g

$$\varepsilon(p,g|d+g) = -\frac{1}{\bar{\varepsilon}(d,p)}\frac{\gamma}{1-\gamma} > 0$$

3. The vertical shift due to UB

$$\varepsilon(p,UB|d+g) = -\frac{\bar{\varepsilon}(d,UB)}{\bar{\varepsilon}(d,p)} > 0$$

where

$$\bar{\varepsilon}(d,UB) = \left[\varepsilon(d,i-\pi)\frac{i}{i-\pi} + \varepsilon(d,W_n).\varepsilon(v,i)\frac{vS}{W_n}\right].\varepsilon(i,UB|AM) + \left[\varepsilon(d,P) + \varepsilon(d,W_n)\frac{PK}{W_n}\right].\varepsilon(P,UB|AM) + \varepsilon(d,W_n)\frac{(1+\omega)UB}{W_n} > 0$$

4. The vertical shift due to S

$$\varepsilon(p,S|d+g) = -\frac{\bar{\varepsilon}(d,S)}{\bar{\varepsilon}(d,p)} > 0$$

$$\bar{\varepsilon}(d,S) = \left[\varepsilon(d,i-\pi)\frac{i}{i-\pi} + \varepsilon(d,W_n).\varepsilon(v,i)\frac{vS}{W_n}\right].\varepsilon(i,S|AM) + \left[\varepsilon(d,P) + \varepsilon(d,W_n)\frac{PK}{W_n}\right].\varepsilon(P,S|AM) + \varepsilon(d,W_n)\frac{vS}{W_n} > 0$$

5. The vertical shift due to K

$$\varepsilon(p,K|d+g) = -\frac{\bar{\varepsilon}(d,K)}{\bar{\varepsilon}(d,p)} < 0$$

with

$$\bar{\varepsilon}(d,K) = \varepsilon(d,W_n)\frac{PK}{W_n} + \left[\varepsilon(d,i-\pi)\frac{i}{i-\pi} + \varepsilon(d,W_n).\varepsilon(v,i)\frac{vS}{W_n}\right].\varepsilon(i,K|AM) + \left[\varepsilon(d,P) + \varepsilon(d,W_n)\frac{PK}{W_n}\right].\varepsilon(P,K|AM) + \varepsilon(d,W_h).\varepsilon(W_h,ay).\varepsilon(ay,K + \varepsilon(d,e).\varepsilon(e,K)$$

The position of the $(d + g)$ line depends on the financial stock variables *UB* and *S*, the fiscal policy variables g, τ_h, τ_n, the stock of real capital and anticipations. Changes in these variables modify the position of the $(d + g)$ line. Some of these modifications form an essential strand of the intermediate-run financial stock-flow adjustment process. The relevant shifts in $(d + g)$ for our purposes are due to changes in *g*, *UB* and *S*. Points 2, 3 and 4 in Table II describe the modifications applied to $(d + g)$ as a result of such changes.

The response in the position of $(d + g)$ is presented in form of vertical shift elasticities. We note that all shift elasticities are positive. Increases in financial stocks and government expenditures *g* raise the $(d + g)$ curve. But we also note that the vertical shifts listed differ substantially. The shift elasticity of *g* is proportional to $\gamma(1 - \gamma)^{-1}$, a magnitude probably centred below one-half over a group of major countries. The proportionality factor is the reciprocal of the total price-elasticity of demand $\bar{\varepsilon}(d,p)$. This magnitude may be centred around -2. We obtain thus a shift elasticity with a general order of at most one-fifth. An increase in *g* by 10 per cent thus raises $(d + g)$ probably by less than 2 per cent. Suppose furthermore that the slopes of $(d + g)$ and *s* are approximately equal around the equilibrium point. The short-run elasticity $\varepsilon(p,g/OAM)$ of *p* with respect to *g*, taking account of the full interaction between output and asset markets, settles under the circumstances at around 1/10. The same assumptions also imply that a 10 per cent increase in *g* raises *y* by approximately 1 per cent.

The results depend of course on the assumptions made concerning the relative magnitude of the various elasticities. Table III introduces some variation in the assumptions pertaining to the slope of the *s* curve and the total price elasticity $\bar{\varepsilon}(d,p)$ of the *d* function. Inspection of the table shows that a flatter supply curve naturally raises the response of output. A lower price elasticity of *d* on the other hand does not lower the response of the price level. Neither does it raise the response of output. Even a much lower price-elasticity $\varepsilon(d,p)$ and a flat supply curve yields an elasticity $\varepsilon(y,g/OAM)$ of *y* with respect to *g* still not exceeding one-fifth. But this result was produced by an assumption concerning the total price elasticity $\bar{\varepsilon}(d,p)$ implying that the wealth and asset price elasticities of the *d* function are of an order approximately one-fifth. This implication seems quite unreasonable and difficult to accept. It is thus concluded that government expenditures certainly exert a shorter-run effect on *p* and *y*. The elasticity of *p* with respect to *g* remains however moderate over activity ranges not exceeding normal utilisation rates. Moreover, the elasticity of output with respect to *g* should not be expected to exceed one-fifth and remains probably below this benchmark.

Both shift elasticities for *UB* and *S* are positive. The numerator of the *UB* shift is unambiguously positive, whereas the numerator of the *S* shift is a sum of two components with opposite sign. This circumstance follows from the implication of the asset market interaction noted in Table I. Changes in *S* induce offsetting impulses via *i* and *P*. It is postulated however that the effect conveyed via the *P* channel prevails over the effect conveyed via the *i* channel. It will be established in the subsequent section that a positive *S* shift forms a necessary condition of a dynamically stable stock-flow adjustment process. It follows however that the *S* shift is a small fraction of the *UB* shift. Prices and output increase in response to an expansion of both financial stocks, but the increase due to a change in *UB* is a multiple of the effect exerted by *S*. The *UB* shift exceeds probably also the *g* shift. We obtain for $\gamma = 0{\cdot}25$ a *g*-shift of 0·16 in Table III. The *UB* shift is conjectured to be approximately 0·4 to 0·5. Even a massive $\gamma = 0{\cdot}4$ still yields a *g* shift (0·33) below the conjectured *UB* shift.

The responses of the short-run system occur in context of an economy with changing resources expressed by changes in *K*, *q* or *lp*. A clarification of the major mechanism adjusting an economy to the cumulative impact of growth (positive or negative) requires a paragraph exploring their implications for the short-run equilibrium system. An increase in *K* lowers the supply curve and produces probably a small downward shift for the 'demand' curve. The intersection moves consequently along the demand curve. Output expands and with constant financial stocks prices fall. An increase in 'human capital' *q* produces a similar pattern. The effect of growth pattern on the short-run equilibrium remains however quite modest. Their important operation over time cannot be explained in terms of a short-run equilibrium system. They gradually modify the position of normal output *ny* via the long-run production function. This also modifies the gap between actual and normal output $(y - ny)$ and operates on the wage adjustment processes. A rapid increase in *ny* relative to the short-run system gradually lowers efficiency wages (not necessarily money wages) and moves the intersection point of the short-run equilibrium system to the right in Figure 1. The role of the wage adjustment process will be further explored in the section bearing on long-run aspects.

The interaction between output and asset markets determines price-level *p*, output *y*, interest rate *i*, asset price *P*, money stock and the volume of bank credit. The system of three markets can be solved for these variables in terms of the financial stocks and the fiscal policy variables. We obtain thus the solution functions for *p* and *y*

$$(9) \qquad p = p[UB, S, g, \tau_h, \tau_n;\ K, \pi, ap]$$
$$y = y[UB, S, g, \tau_h, \tau_n;\ K, \pi, ap]$$

The properties of these solution functions with respect to the selected arguments are expressed by suitable elasticities. It appears useful to

TABLE III Short-Run Response of Price and Output to a 10% Increase in Government Expenditures g Under Different Assumptions

maintained assumption $\gamma = 0{\cdot}25$
$(1-\gamma).\bar{\varepsilon}(d,y) = 0{\cdot}4$

	$(d+g)$ slope $= -0{\cdot}87$	$(d+g)$ slope $= -0{\cdot}87$	$(d+g)$ slope $= -1{\cdot}75$	$(d+g)$ slope $= -1{\cdot}75$
	$\bar{\varepsilon}(d,p) = -2$	$\bar{\varepsilon}(d,p) = -2$	$\bar{\varepsilon}(d,p) = -1$	$\bar{\varepsilon}(d,p) = -1$
	$s -$ slope $= (d+g)$ slope	$s -$ slope $= 0$	$s -$ slope $= (d+g)$ slope	$s -$ slope $= 0$
shift-elasticity	0·16	0·16	0·33	0·33
$\hat{p}.100$	0·80%	0	1·60%	2%
$\hat{y}.100$	approx. 1%	approx. 2%	approx. 1%	approx. 2%

introduce the elasticities with respect to UB, S, and g in terms of the geometric concepts applied in our previous discussion. We write thus

$$(10) \quad \varepsilon(p,g/OAM) = -\frac{\varepsilon(p,g/d+g). \quad \varepsilon(p,y/s)}{\varepsilon(p,y/d+g) - \varepsilon(p,y/s)} > 0$$

$$\varepsilon(y,g/OAM) = -\frac{\varepsilon(p,g/d+g)}{\varepsilon(p,y/d+g) - \varepsilon(p,y/s)} > 0$$

The other elasticities are easily obtained by replacing g in the expression above with the variable selected. The expressions above imply that the ratios between the different short-run responses of p and y are equal to the corresponding ratios of the respective shift elasticities for the $(d + g)$ line. The ordering of these shift elasticities between UB, S and g thus carries over to the response of the major economic variables.

III.3 THE INTERMEDIATE-RUN ADJUSTMENT AND THE STOCK-FLOW EQUILIBRIUM POSITION

The financial stock-flow adjustment process emerges from the interaction between the short-run position of the economy and the budget process. The budget equation associates to every position of the economy, represented by the triple (p,y,i) a magnitude of the deficit (or surplus). These imbalances in the budget produce changes in financial stocks modifying the position of $(d + g)$. A short-run equilibrium producing deficits or surpluses can thus not persist. The financial impulses unleashed by budget imbalances impose continuous adjustment on the asset markets feeding back to the output market.

The interaction between the short-run equilibrium position and the budget process is explored somewhat further in Figure 2. A third line was added in this diagram. The *bbe* curve represents an equation obtained by replacing first the interest rate variable i in the component of total government expenditures describing interest payments with its solution from the asset markets. The expression for total government expenditures obtained in this manner is set equal to tax revenues. The resulting equation implicitly defines a relation between p and y. The *bbe* line represents consequently the locus of all $p - y$ combinations satisfying for any given values of the remaining variables the asset market equations and the requirements of a balanced budget. All points on the *bbe* line generate by construction a balanced budget. The space above or to the right of the line describes all states producing a budget surplus, and all points to the left or below the line describe states producing a budget deficit. The position of the line depends on fiscal policies, expressed by expenditures g, $w.lg$, or tax rates τ_h, τ_n, and the inherited financial stocks. Changes in these magnitudes shift the *bbe* line. Similarly, the slope of the *bbe* line is determined by the fiscal arrangements characterising the budget process. Three conditions describe for our

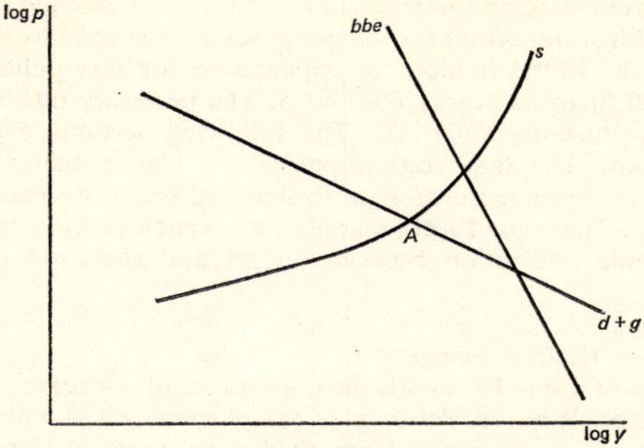

(a)

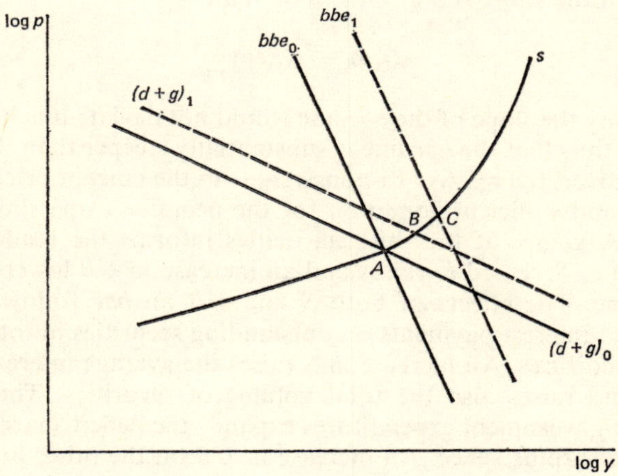

(b)

Figure 2.

purposes the nature of fiscal arrangements. One condition pertains to expenditure policies and differentiates between programmes approximately formulated in real or nominal terms. The other two conditions apply to the tax revenue function. The responsiveness of tax revenues to current conditions affects the results and so does the lagging of revenues relative to their determining factors. The line drawn in the diagram assumes a non-lagged and responsive tax revenue function with an expenditure policy addressing real expenditures.

The subsequent analysis requires an explicit description of the properties defining the *bbe* line. Alternative fiscal arrangements can be effectively characterised in terms of comparative slopes and shifts of the *bbe* line. Most important for our purposes are the responses of the *bbe* line (i.e. the shifts) induced by expenditure (or tax) policies and by changes in financial stocks *UB* and *S*. The necessary information has been assembled in Table IV. The following sections explore their implications. The first section presents a diagrammatic discussion based on tax revenue functions with standard responsiveness to current conditions. The second section applies an explicit analytic treatment to the dynamic interaction between budget and short-run equilibrium position.

(a) *The Tax Revenue Function*

Inspection of Table IV reveals the importance of adequately responsive tax revenues. With an elasticity of tax revenues $\varepsilon(t,p)$ with respect to current prices p sufficiently large all denominators of slope and shift expressions are negative. The positive terms in the denominators are probably in the short-run at most 0·5. With

$$\varepsilon(t,y) = \varepsilon(t,ry)\frac{y}{ry}$$

around unity the slope of the *bbe* line would not deviate much from -2. One notes thus that the *bbe* line is substantially steeper than the $(d + g)$ line. Moreover, the relative responsiveness to the current price-level is a necessary and sufficient condition for the negative slope shown in the diagram. A glance at the shift elasticities informs the reader that an increase in g, S, w and lg raises and an increase in *UB* lowers (slightly) the *bbe* line. The effects of both *S* and *UB* on *bbe* follow from the inclusion of interest payments on outstanding securities in total government expenditures. An increase in *S* raises the average interest paid per security and raises also the total volume of securities. The resulting increase in government expenditures expands the deficit space and compresses the surplus space. An increase in *UB* on the other hand lowers interest rates, lowers consequently interest payments and total government expenditures by a smallish amount. An inspection of the *S* and *UB* shifts immediately shows that the *S* shift exceeds the *UB* shift by a multiple.

Consider now the relative position of the lines in Figure 2*a*. The budget process determines under the circumstances a deficit. The intersection between $(d + g)$ and s lies below and to the left of the *bbe* line. The horizontal distance of the state point from the *bbe* line offers an index for the magnitude of this deficit. There emerges under the circumstances a continuous increase in the base *UB* or the stock of securities *S*. Suppose for the moment that the deficit is financed with base money. The base expands and the position of the $(d + g)$ line slides upwards according to the positive shift elasticity listed in Table II. The *bbe* line

TABLE IV The Properties of the *bbe* Line

1. The slope

$\varepsilon(p,y|bbe) =$

$$\frac{\varepsilon(t,ry)\dfrac{y}{ry}\left[1 + \varepsilon(I,i).\varepsilon(i,y|AM)\dfrac{IS}{py}\right] - \varepsilon(I,i).\varepsilon(i,y|AM)\dfrac{IS}{t}}{\dfrac{pg}{t} - \varepsilon(t,p) + \varepsilon(I,i).\varepsilon(i,p|AM).E_1 + E_2 + \varepsilon(t,ry)\dfrac{y}{ry}.\dfrac{w.1g + IS}{t}.\dfrac{t}{py}}$$

Where $E_1 = 1 - \varepsilon(t,ry)\dfrac{y}{ry}.\dfrac{t}{py} > 0$

$$E_2 = \varepsilon(w,p).\frac{w.lg}{t}\left[l - \varepsilon(t,ry)\frac{y}{ry}.\frac{t}{pt}\right] > 0$$

With $\varepsilon(t,ry)\dfrac{y}{ry} \sim 1$ the numerator is approximately unity. The denominator depends substantially on E_2. For the shorter run $\varepsilon(w,p) = 0$ and consequently $E_2 = 0$. Moreover, $E_1 < 1$, $\varepsilon(I,i) < 1/2$ and $\varepsilon(i,p|AM)$ is comparatively small. The third term of the denominator is thus quite small. The last term of the denominator is about one-half of the proportion of (net) taxes to the nominal value of output py. This is again a smallish fraction. It follows thus that with $pg.t^{-1} < 1/2$ and $\varepsilon(t,p) \geqslant 1$ the denominator is negative with numerical value at least 1/2. The slope is under the circumstances around -2 and substantially larger numerically than the slope of the $(d + g)$ line.

Suppose now that $t.(py)^{-1} \sim 1/4$ and $w.lg.t^{-1} \sim 2/5$. We obtain thus for the extreme value of $\varepsilon(w,p) = 1$ beyond the shorter run a value of $E_2 = 0{\cdot}3$. The denominator is substantially raised algebraically by $\varepsilon(w,p) > 0$ but remains negative even with $\varepsilon(w,p) = 1$, provided $\varepsilon(t,p) \geqslant 1$. The slope falls however from -2 to -5. The longer-run *bbe* line is thus much steeper.

2. The vertical shift due to a change in g

$$\varepsilon(p,g|bbe) = -\frac{1}{\Delta}.\frac{pg}{t} > 0$$

where Δ is the denominator of the slope expression

3. The horizontal shift due to a change in g

$$\varepsilon(y,g|bbe) = -\frac{1}{\varepsilon(I,i).\varepsilon(i,y|AM)\left[1-\varepsilon(t,ry)\dfrac{y}{ry}.\dfrac{t}{py}\right]-\varepsilon(t,ry)\dfrac{y}{ry}}.\frac{pg}{t} \quad 0$$

This shift elasticity is approximately equal to the proportion $pg.t^{-1}$.

4. The vertical shift due to lg

$$\varepsilon(p,lg|bbe) = -\frac{\dfrac{w.lg}{t}\left[1-\varepsilon(t,ry)\dfrac{y}{ry}.\dfrac{t}{py}\right] + \varepsilon(I,i).\varepsilon(i,lg|AM)\dfrac{IS}{t}}{\Delta} > 0$$

5. The vertical shift due to UB

$$\varepsilon(p,UB|bbe = -\frac{\varepsilon(I,i).\varepsilon(i,UB|AM)\dfrac{IS}{t}\left[[1 - \varepsilon(t,ry)\dfrac{y}{ry}.\dfrac{t}{py}\right]}{\Delta} < 0$$

6. The vertical shift due to S

$$\varepsilon(p,S|bbe) = -\frac{[1+\varepsilon(I,i).\varepsilon(i,S|AM)]\left[1-\varepsilon(t,ry)\frac{y}{ry}\cdot\frac{t}{py}\right]}{\Delta}\cdot\frac{IS}{t} > 0$$

Note that $\varepsilon(p,S|bbe) > |\varepsilon(p,UB|bbe)|$

7. We require for the discussion in the text a shift elasticity with respect to w. Adjustments in w are impounded into shifts and not into the slope. This procedure seems to offer some advantages for some problems.

$$\varepsilon(p,w|bbe) = -\frac{\frac{w.lg}{t}\left[1-\varepsilon(t,ry)\frac{y}{ry}\cdot\frac{t}{py}\right]+\varepsilon(I,i).\varepsilon(i,w|AM)\frac{IS}{t}}{\Delta^*} > 0$$

$$\Delta^* = \Delta - E_2.$$

8. For low responsiveness of tax revenues to current prices, i.e. $\varepsilon(t,p)$ sufficiently below unity, the slope of *bbe* turns positive.

9. In case of a nominal expenditure policy, i.e. pg is predetermined in lieu of g, slope and shift expressions have a denominator Δ^{**}

$$\Delta^{**} = \Delta - \frac{pg}{t}$$

This denominator is algebraically smaller and numerically larger. The slope will not deviate much from -1 under the circumstances.

---

on the other hand moves negligibly downwards to meet the rising $(d + g)$ line. The process eventually terminates when all three lines intersect at the same point. This intersection defines a position of financial stock-flow equilibrium. At the prevailing state the budget is balanced and imposes no further adjustments on the asset markets with feedbacks to the output market.

Suppose however that the deficit is financed with issues of new securities. The stock S increases and the $(d + g)$ line rises according to the positive shift elasticity for S listed in Table II. But the motion of the $(d + g)$ line is much slower in this case. This follows from a shift elasticity for S substantially smaller than the shift elasticity of UB. The rate of output expansion and the rate of price increases resulting from movements of $(d + g)$ along s towards the joint intersection with *bbe* is thus substantially smaller for deficits financed with securities.

But this is not the complete story, even within the partial domain of financial stock flow equilibrium disregarding longer-run aspects. An expanding stock of S also raises the *bbe* line (note the shift-elasticity in Table IV). The *bbe* line thus moves ahead of the $(d + g)$ lines. Convergence to a stock-flow equilibrium requires under the circumstances some constraints on the relative motions of the two lines. These constraints cannot be clarified within the diagram and need some analytic attention. It is clear however that a positive shift elasticity of $(d + g)$

with respect to S is a necessary but not a sufficient condition for a stable stock-flow adjustment process. We also note that for any deficit financed with new securities the eventual position of *bbe* will be above the final position realised when the deficit is financed with base money. The final stock-flow equilibrium associated with the initial position in Figure 2*a* depends therefore on the mode of financing the deficit. An increasing reliance on securities moves the final equilibrium upwards along the *s* curve. It follows that the total increase in prices measured from initial position to final equilibrium position is larger for any given deficit financed with securities. The rate at which the system moves however from initial to final position is much larger for deficits financed with base money.

An important implication occurs in Figure 2*b*. The discussion begins with a position of stock-flow equilibrium characterised by the intersection of the three lines $(d + g)_0$, s and bbe_0 in point A. Suppose now that government expenditures are raised. This shifts both *bbe* and the $(d + g)$ line into new positions $(d + g)_1$ and bbe_1 above their respective previous positions. It is important to note that the vertical and horizontal shift of the *bbe* line substantially exceeds the corresponding shift of the $(d + g)$ line. This pattern yields important implications bearing on the role of fiscal policies. The movement of the short-run system from point A to point B in Figure 2*b* describes the pure fiscal effect uncontaminated with feedbacks from asset market adjustments to changing financial stocks. But the pure fiscal effect of a fiscal policy action does not exhaust the total effect of the increase in government expenditures. The total effect is expressed by the change in position from A to C. We note that the fiscal effect of fiscal policy explains only a part of the total effect. The portion B to C of the total effect expresses the financial effect of the fiscal policy.

The relative order of fiscal and monetary effect can be estimated with the aid of the formula describing the response of prices p in terms of slopes and shift. We repeat the formula obtained for the short-run equilibrium and add the corresponding statement for the stock-flow equilibrium (i.e. the intersection between *bbe* and *s*)

$$(11) \quad \varepsilon(p,g/OAM) = \frac{\varepsilon(p,g/d + g). \quad \varepsilon(p,y/s)}{\varepsilon(p,y/d + g) - \varepsilon(p,y/s)}$$

$$\varepsilon(p,g/bbe - s) = \frac{\varepsilon(p,g/bbe). \quad \varepsilon(p,y/s)}{\varepsilon(p,y/bbe) - \varepsilon(p,y/s)}$$

where the OAM conditioning in the first expression describes the interaction of all markets revealed by $(d + g)$ and s, and the conditioning $bbe - s$ describes the price response determined by the intersection between *bbe* and *s*. Some assumptions are introduced to fix the components of the expressions in the formula above. It is specifically assumed that tax revenues are proportional with respect to prices and output, nominal government expenditures on output are about 40 per cent of tax revenues, and the elasticity of interest payments with respect to p and y roughly 0·25. The slope of the *bbe* line is under the circumstances approximately minus 2 compared to a slope about $-0{\cdot}80$ for the $(d + g)$ line. The shift elasticity for *bbe* with respect to g is moreover about 1·1, compared to at most 0·2 for $(d + g)$. Lastly, it is postulated that $\varepsilon(p,y/d + g) \sim \varepsilon(p,y/s)$, the symmetry assumption previously used. All this implies that the total response of p to g represented by the intersection between *bbe* and s is approximately 3 times the pure fiscal effect on p. It should also be noted that the excess of the total effect over the pure fiscal effect depends substantially on the slope of the supply curve relative to the slope of the demand curve. It is easily demonstrable that, under the order conditions specified, the (relative) excess of the total effect remains above 2, even for a relatively small slope of the supply curve.[14]

A nominal expenditure policy modifies somewhat the patterns discussed in the previous paragraphs. Inspection of Table IV reveals that the slope of the *bbe* line falls algebraically (rises numerically) by moving to a nominal expenditure policy. Under the assumptions made above concerning interest payments and responsiveness of tax revenues the slope rises to about minus one, just exceeding moderately the slope of $(d + g)$ in numerical value. The shift elasticity of *bbe* with respect to g is also lowered from about 1·1 to approximately 0·5. These changes suggest a moderation of the relative excess of the total effect of fiscal policy, and they lower consequently the monetary effect relative to the pure fiscal effect. The total effect seems actually lowered to about 2·2 times the pure fiscal effect. A nominal expenditure policy thus constrains the monetary effect of a fiscal policy by a substantial margin. This consequence will be further substantiated in the section exploring explicitly the dynamic analysis.

(b) *The Stability of the Stock-Flow Adjustment*

The intermediate run stock-flow adjustment process can be reduced to

[14] The formulae used to compare the total effect assumes implicitly that the position of the *bbe* line, once fixed at *bbe*, by an increase in g, remains subsequently in this position. This imposes a constraint on the financing of the deficit defined by the following condition

$$\varepsilon(p,UB|bbe)\frac{dUB}{UB} + \varepsilon(p,S|bbe)\frac{dS}{S} = 0$$

$$\text{i.e. } \frac{dUB}{dS} = -\frac{\varepsilon(p,S|bbe)}{\varepsilon(p,UB|bbe)} \cdot \frac{UB_1}{S_1} > 0$$

The *bbe* line will not be affected by the increase in financial stocks and stay at bbe_1 whenever the ratio of new base money to new securities is proportional to the inherited ratio of base to outstanding securities with a proportionality factor determined by the two vertical shift elasticities.

a single differential equation. An examination of this differential equation determines the dynamic properties of the system's motion. This analysis is prepared by solving simultaneously the output and asset markets for output y, interest rate i, price level p and asset price-level P in terms of the financial stocks UB, S, the fiscal variables g, τ_h, and τ_n, the anticipation variables π and ap and the money wage w. The properties of these solutions have been explored in the discussion of the short-run equilibrium system represented by the intersection of the $(d + g)$ and the s curve. The solution functions obtained are used to replace p, i and y occurring in the budget deficit in terms of the variables relatively predetermined with respect to the short-run equilibrium system. We derive in particular equation (12)

$$(12) \quad U\mathring{B} + \mathring{S} = f[UB,S;\, g,w.lg,\tau_h,\tau_n;\, \pi,ap]$$

Introduction of a financial parameter allows us to reduce the equation containing two stock variables to a single stock equation. The parameter μ describes the proportion of the deficit (surplus) financed with the aid of new base money.

$$(13) \quad UB = UB_0 + \mu D$$

$$S = S_0 + (1 - \mu)D$$

Equation (13) defines the relation between the financial stocks and μ, with B_0 and S_0 the initial magnitudes modified by open market purchases and D the cumulated sum (the integral) of the budget deficit. The differential equation is accordingly converted to the following expression:

$$(14) \quad \mathring{D} = F[D;\, g,w.lg,\tau_h,\tau_n;\pi,ap,\mu]$$

The process described by this equation is stable for any negative derivative of F with respect to D. This derivative can be constituted in a stepwise fashion. We note first, that F_D is a linear combination of derivatives of the deficit function f with respect to UB and S. Specifically

$$(15) \quad F_D = f_{UB}\mu + f_S(1 - \mu)$$

The next step presents the derivatives of f_{UB} and f_S in terms of properties of the price-setting function, the tax-revenue function and also the short-run equilibrium system. We write thus

$$(16) \quad f_{UB} = \frac{t}{UB}\Big[\varepsilon(y,UB\,|\,OAM).\Big[\varepsilon(p,y\,|\,s).E - \varepsilon(t,ry)\frac{y}{ry}\Big] + \varepsilon(I,i).\varepsilon(i,UB\,|\,OAM)\Big[1 - \varepsilon(t,ry)\frac{t}{p.ry}\Big]\frac{IS}{t}\Big] < 0$$

$$fs = \frac{t}{S}\Big[\varepsilon(y,S|OAM).\Big[\varepsilon(p,y|s).E - \varepsilon(t,ry)\frac{y}{ry}\Big] + \Big[1 + \varepsilon(I,i).\varepsilon(i,S|OAM)\Big]\Big[1 - \varepsilon(t,ry)\frac{t}{p.ry}\Big]\frac{IS}{t}\Big]$$

where

$$(17) \quad E = \frac{pg}{t} - \varepsilon(t,p) + \varepsilon(t,ry)\frac{I.S}{p.ry} < 0$$

The derivative of the deficit function with respect to *UB* is a weighted sum of two components with weights $t.UB^{-1}$ and $IS.UB^{-1}$. The first component multiplies the elasticity $\varepsilon(y,UB|OAM)$ of output with respect to *UB*, representing the flow equilibrium system, with a bracketed term containing *E* depending on the fiscal arrangements bearing on expenditure policies and the responsiveness of tax revenues. This bracketed term is negative for all arrangements involving a sufficient degree of responsiveness in tax revenues. The second component is a product of $\varepsilon(I,i)$ and $\varepsilon(i,UB|OAM)$, the response of *i* to *UB* including feedbacks via the output market. The first elasticity is small in the short-run (i.e. nearer to zero than to unity) and converges to unity with the extension of the analytic horizon. The second elasticity is possibly positive but remains quite small. The second component of f_{UB} may consequently have a positive sign. Its magnitude is confined however to a negligible level. Lastly, the weight attached to the second component is a small fraction of the weight attached to the first component. The first weight $t.UB^{-1}$, expressing the ratio of tax revenues to the base, is a multiple of unity, whereas the second weight is the ratio of interest payments *IS* to the base. The ratio is a fraction of unity. We conclude thus with some assurance that f_{UB} is negative.

The derivative f_S of the deficit function with respect to *S* is again a weighted sum of two components with weights $t.S^{-1}$ and $IS.S^{-1}$. The first component is the product of $\varepsilon(y,S|OAM)$, the response of *y* to *S* determined by the short-run equilibrium system, with the identical expression *E* occurring in the first component of f_{UB}. A positive value of the elasticity, i.e. $\varepsilon(y,S|OAM) > 0$, postulated for the short-run equilibrium system, assigns a negative value to the first component of f_S. The second component is unambiguously positive however. It actually exceeds unity. This fact reflects the 'double' effect of an increase of *S* on interest payments via higher interest rates and a larger outstanding stock of securities *S*. An inspection of the weights assigned to the two components indicates that they are 3 to 4 times smaller (in the USA) than the corresponding weights composing the linear combination defining f_{UB}. But the *ratios* of the weights occurring in the two derivatives of the *F* function are identical. It follows that the negative component is weighted about ten times more (i.e. in the proportion *t* to *IS*) than the positive component with a value somewhat above unity. We note under the circumstances that for tax revenues sufficiently large relative to interest payments the derivative f_S will be negative. The derivative will turn positive whenever interest payments appear with sufficient weight in total government expenditures.

The patterns surrounding the two derivatives of the deficit function imply that the linear combination (15) defining the derivative F_D is negative for *all* admissible values of μ. The stabilising feedback from the budget to the money supply process is strengthened by nominal expenditure policies. Such policies lower the price sensitivity of expenditures relative to the price sensitivity of tax revenues and increase numerically the negative component in the derivatives f_{UB} and f_S. Smaller responsiveness of t combined with real expenditure policies lowers on the other hand the stabilising feedback to the asset markets via the budget.

Throughout the discussion thus far we neglected wage adjustments. Money wages were held constant and the s line remained consequently in a given position. It seems appropriate to relax this assumption in order to examine the role of the government sector's wage bill in the financial stock-flow process. It is postulated for this purpose that money wages w depend partly on the price-level and respond over the intermediate run to changes in the price-level. We postulate in particular that $\varepsilon(w,p) \leqslant 1$. The first step involves a description of the responses of the flow equilibrium position (p,y) to changes in $x = UB$, S and g, incorporating modifications of the s-curve due to adjustments in w induced by changes in p. The derived expressions $\varepsilon(p,x \mid OAM,s)$ can be derived from the geometric description in terms of slopes and shifts of $(d + g)$ and s.

The general pattern of such descriptions has already been used in previous sections. We require at this stage a specification of the shift elasticity for s. The expression $\varepsilon(p,w/s).\varepsilon(w,p).\varepsilon(p,x/OAM,s)$ describes the required feedback response in the position of s. The geometric representation of the response patterns thus yields

$$\varepsilon(p,x/OAM,s) = \frac{-\varepsilon(p,x/d+g).\varepsilon(p,y/s) + \varepsilon(p,y/d+g).\varepsilon(p,w/s).\varepsilon(w,p).\varepsilon(p,x/OAM,s)}{\varepsilon(p,y/d+g) - \varepsilon(p,y/s)}$$

$$\varepsilon(y,x/OAM,s) = \frac{-\varepsilon(p,x/d+g) + \varepsilon(p,w/s).\varepsilon(w,p).\varepsilon(p,x/OAM,s)}{\varepsilon(p,y/d+g) - \varepsilon(p,y/s)}$$

$$x = UB,S,g$$

An appropriate rearrangement determines

$$\varepsilon(p,x/OAM,s) = \frac{-\varepsilon(p,x/d+g).\varepsilon(p,y/s)}{\varepsilon(p,y/d+g)[1 - \varepsilon(p,w/s).\varepsilon(w,p)] - \varepsilon(p,y/s)} > 0$$

$$\varepsilon(y,x/OAM,s) = -\frac{\varepsilon(p,x/d+g)}{\varepsilon(p,y/d+g)-\varepsilon(p,y/s)}\left[1+\frac{\varepsilon(p,w/s).\varepsilon(w,p).\varepsilon(p,y/s)}{\Delta}\right]$$

with $\Delta = \varepsilon(p,y/d+g)[1-\varepsilon(p,w/s).\varepsilon(w,p)] - \varepsilon(p,y/s) < 0$

We note the simple result implied by the condition $\varepsilon(p,w/s).\varepsilon(w,p) \sim 1$. We obtain under these conditions

$$\varepsilon(y,x/OAM,s) \sim 0 \text{ and } \varepsilon(p,x/OAM,s) \sim \varepsilon(p,x/d+g)$$

The range of relevant parameter values for the product $\varepsilon(p,w/s).\varepsilon(w,p)$ characterising wage adjustments are probably confined to the closed unit interval. Our previous results obtained with a fixed *s* line correspond to $\varepsilon(p,w/s).\varepsilon(w,p) = 0$. This state characterises short-run processes and produces a dominant pattern of output responses. The polar extreme in the range implies that the price-level absorbs via the wage adjustments all impulses and output remains unaffected. We conjecture that the relevant parameter values produce over the intermediate run a value for $\varepsilon(p,w/s).\varepsilon(w,p)$ in the open unit interval still producing a noticeable output response. The results clearly establish that wage adjustment reinforces the price response and dampens the output response.

The modification introduced with wage adjustments changes little in the dynamics of the intermediate run financial stock-flow process. The deficit function is again transformed with the aid of the solutions from the flow equilibrium system into a differential equation determining the motion of *D*. The endogenous variables, *p*, *i* and *y* occurring in the deficit function are replaced by appropriate solutions as before. The major difference occurs in the present case in the properties of the *p* and *y* function. With $\varepsilon(p,w/s).\varepsilon(w,p) = 0$ the *p* function was simply given by the price setting function, whereas it appears now as a solution function with *UB*, *S* and *g* as argument and properties established in the previous paragraphs. The derivative of the deficit function with respect to *D* is again a linear combination of derivatives with respect to *B* and *S* with weights μ and $(1-\mu)$.

(16a)

$$f_{UB} = \frac{t}{UB}\left[\varepsilon(y,UB|OAM)\left[\varepsilon(p,y|s).E^* - \varepsilon(t,ry)\frac{y}{ry}\right] + \varepsilon(I,i).\varepsilon(i,UB|OAM)\left[1-\varepsilon(t,ry)\frac{t}{p.ry}\right]\frac{IS}{t}\right]$$

$$f_S = \frac{t}{S}\left[\varepsilon(y,S|OAM)\left[\varepsilon(p,y|s).E^* - \varepsilon(t,ry)\frac{y}{ry}\right] + [1+\varepsilon(I,i).\varepsilon(i,S|OAM)]\left[1-\varepsilon(t,ry)\frac{t}{p.ry}\right]\frac{IS}{t}\right]$$

where

$$(17a)\quad E^* = E + \varepsilon(w,p)\frac{w.lg}{t} + \frac{w.lg}{t}.\varepsilon(t,ry)\frac{t}{p.ry}[1 - \varepsilon(w,p)]$$

where E has been defined under equation (17). Note that with $\varepsilon(w,p) > 0$ the term $E^* > E$. The responsiveness of wages thus raises algebraically the first component of the two derivatives. Both changes narrow somewhat the constraints imposed on a stable process. All situations involving a substantial magnitude of relative interest payments require probably a minimal value for μ to prevent the destabilising influence from a numerically small but positive derivative f_S. Instability reflects under the circumstances an inadequate financing procedure of the government.

(c) *The Response of the Financial Stock Equilibrium*
Suppose now that the stock-flow process is determined by a fiscal arrangement assuring stability. The process converges under the circumstances to the stock-flow equilibrium position defined by the balanced budget equation

$$(18)\quad F[D;\mu,B_0,S_0,g,lg,\tau_h,\tau_n;\ \pi,ap,K] = 0$$

This equation determines the equilibrium value D^e of the financial stock as an implicit function of fiscal policy, monetary policy expressed by the financial parameter μ and the magnitudes B_0 and S_0 and the anticipation variables. The short-run system composed of output and asset markets responds to this equilibrium stock D^e and its composition determined by μ. This may be formally expressed by replacing first UB and S in the short-run equilibrium system with the expressions in terms of D and μ introduced in equation (13). In a second step D is replaced with the implicit function derived from the balanced budget equation. This procedure reveals that the behaviour of the price-level beyond the shorter horizons depends crucially on the behaviour of financial stocks. But the latter behaviour is centrally determined by fiscal policies. Fiscal policy emerges thus as a longer-run determinant of financial stocks and consequently the longer-run behaviour of price-movements.

The patterns involved depend on the properties of the implicit function derivable from the deficit function F. We may consider the budget equation as a proximate determinant of the equilibrium stock D depending on μ, UB_0, S_0, g, and τ. For any admissible monetary policy (μ, UB_0, S_0) and fiscal policy (g,lg,τ_h,τ_n) the equation determines simultaneously the stock D and its composition UB and S. The response of these equilibria stocks with respect to g is given by

$$(19)\quad \varepsilon(D,g) = -\frac{\varepsilon(y,g\,|\,OAM,s).E+\dfrac{pg}{t}+\varepsilon(I,i).\varepsilon(i,g\,|\,OAM,s)\dfrac{IS}{t}}{E_1.\dfrac{\mu D}{UB}+E_2.\dfrac{(1-\mu)D}{S}} > 0$$

where E = the expression defined under equation (17).

$$\text{and} \quad E_1 = \varepsilon(y,UB|OAM).E + \varepsilon(I,i).\varepsilon(i,UB|OAM)\frac{IS}{t} < 0$$

$$E_2 = \varepsilon(y,S|OAM).E + [1 + \varepsilon(I,i).\varepsilon(i,S|OAM)]\frac{IS}{S} < 0$$

The positive sign of expression (19) is assured by the inequalities $|E| < 1$ and $\varepsilon(y,g|OAM) < pg.t^{-1}$. The formula incorporates an adjustment of money wages to price changes. We note that this lowers numerically the expression E above. The same procedure determines also the following patterns $\varepsilon(D,\mu) < 0$; $\varepsilon(D,UB_0) < 0$; $\varepsilon(D,S_0) < 0$. The denominators of all expressions are identical. It follows that the numerical magnitude of all response elasticities of D falls whenever μ increases.

(d) *Fiscal Effect, Financial Effect and Inflation*

The equilibrium financial stocks determined by the budget equation can be used to describe the total price movements associated with given fiscal actions. Suppose government expenditures g are raised from g_0 to g_1. The resulting increase in prices from the initial position to time t can be expressed for the two modes of financing a deficit by equation (20):

$$(20) \quad (a) \quad \log\frac{P_t}{P_0} = \varepsilon(p,g|OAM).\log\frac{g_1}{g_0} + \varepsilon(p,UB|OAM)\log\frac{UB_t}{UB_0}$$

$$(b) \quad \log\frac{P_t}{P_0} = \varepsilon(p,g|OAM)\log\frac{g_1}{g_0} + \varepsilon(p,S|OAM)\log\frac{S_t}{S_0}$$

where $UB_t \leqslant \delta^1[S; g_1,\tau_h,\tau_n, \ldots]$

$S_t \leqslant \delta^2[UB; g_1,\tau_h,\tau_n, \ldots]$

The functions δ^1 and δ^1 are the equilibrium functions derived from the deficit function with properties discussed in previous paragraphs. The total effect of government expenditure on the price-level thus appears as a sum of two components. The first component measures the 'direct' fiscal effect discussed in the context of the short-run equilibrium of the system. The second component describes the monetary or the debt effect of the fiscal action. The comparative order of magnitudes of $\varepsilon(p,g|OAM)$, $\varepsilon(p,UB|OAM)$ and $\varepsilon(p,S|OAM)$ determine the interpretation of price movements induced by expanding outlays g. With $\varepsilon(p,g|OAM)$ larger than $\varepsilon(p,S|OAM)$, but also much smaller than $\varepsilon(p,UB|OAM)$, the second component emerges already with some weight at an early stage for a UB-financed deficit. It remains on the other hand at a negligible level of importance over a substantial time in case of an S-financed deficit. We also note that the occurrence of persistent price movements does not depend on continuous increases in expenditures by the government sector. Intermittent increases are sufficient to maintain a persistent increase in the second component. The resulting price increase will be large with fiscal arrangements producing a low responsiveness of tax revenues and a policy concentrating on real expenditures.

One may wonder at this point whether a deficit financed with issues of securities can effectively explain our inflation problem. It is clearly established that an S-financed deficit does produce a larger total change in the price-level. This does not imply however that a financial policy of intermittently maintained deficits financed with new securities can effectively explain observed rates of inflation, and particularly the inflationary accelerations observed over the past ten years. Some further reflections bearing on the orders of magnitude implicit in the analysis should caution us in this respect. It was already noted in earlier paragraphs that even with symmetrically sloping $(d + g)$ and s curves the fiscal effect associated with a 10 per cent increase in g raises p over a shorter-run adjustment by around 1 per cent. Suppose furthermore, that the deficit created determines a 20 per cent rate of increase in S and combine this with $\varepsilon(p,S|OAM) \leqslant 1/10$. It follows that the second component contributes at most 2 per cent to a prevailing rate of inflation. Increasing government expenditures financed with new securities thus induce a moderate initial bulge in price movements lowered subsequently to a modest level of inflation. This pattern holds even for large deficits, substantial increases in real expenditures and huge relative increases in S.

This result of the intermediate run analysis is reinforced by placing the problem into the context of a growing economy. It was shown that an expanding labour absorption lp and growing capital stocks K and q gradually shift the supply curve to the right with comparatively little modification of the demand curve. The short-run equilibrium moves therefore closer to the budget line for any initial position exhibiting a deficit with a non-lagged tax revenue function. The relative increase in the stock of securities associated with the deficits gently moves the demand curve $d + g$ to the right at a rate substantially less (in rough contours) than the movement of the supply curve. Economic growth moves the short-run equilibrium towards the *bbe* line and accelerates thus the closing of the deficit. The very modest rate of inflation produced by an expanding stock of securities is probably more than offset under the circumstances by economic growth. It appears thus unlikely that the observed levels and accelerations of inflation allow a useful reduction to deficits financed with issues of securities. The elasticity $\varepsilon(p,UB|OAM)$ exceeds $\varepsilon(p,S|OAM)$ by a large factor. The magnitude of observed inflation thus clearly suggests that our attention be addressed to deficits financed with new base money. Inflation still emerges in this manner as an essentially monetary phenomenon. But it also appears that this monetary phenomenon is partly determined by the fiscal policies pursued and the fiscal arrangements established. These policies and arrangements condition the money supply process and contribute to determine the longer run monetary growth.

(e) *A Final Comment on Fiscal and Monetary Policy*
The previous sections elaborated the central role of fiscal policy for all explanations of monetary trends. It follows that questions bearing on persistent and sustained accelerations (or decelerations) of inflation direct our attention to fiscal arrangements and policies. But our analysis also revealed that these policies and arrangements are not quite sufficient to explain our phenomenon. Its emergence and magnitude is substantially affected by the stance of monetary policy expressed by (μ, UB_0, S_0). The last paragraph in the previous sections argued that with $\mu = 0$ even large increases in g generating large deficits cannot adequately explain the observed rate of inflation. The analysis of fiscal policy and fiscal arrangement must be supplemented therefore by an examination of μ.

The substantial cost of developing a functioning market for securities, or the cost of access to such a market existing in various countries also affects the prevailing value of μ. Lastly, the level of μ reveals the governments' traditional propensity for inflationary finance. The public's difficulty to perceive and appreciate the nature of inflationary finance encourages the governments' disposition. These considerations also assign a low probability to inflationary developments evolving independently of fiscal policies and fiscal arrangements, simply driven by pure open market operations raising UB_0 and lowering S_0. A central bank could modify these 'initial' magnitudes autonomously relative to current budget processes. Open market operations raise the $(d + g)$ line, and persistent operations eventually move the short-run equilibrium intersection into the surplus space. A persistent inflation at a constant rate requires however intermittent acceleration of open market purchases. The resulting pattern of rising UB, falling S and a permanent budget surplus does not apply to any inflation experienced in the recent past. Any relevant explanation must fully recognise the role of fiscal policy in the determination of monetary growth.

IV ASPECTS OF LONGER-RUN PROCESSES

IV.1 THE STABILISING ROLE OF WAGE ADJUSTMENTS

The wage adjustment process determines the link between the intermediate run and the longer-run adjustment of the economy. Its operation can be recognised in general terms by means of Figure 3. Figure 3*a* juxtaposes an intermediate-run financial stock-flow equilibrium with

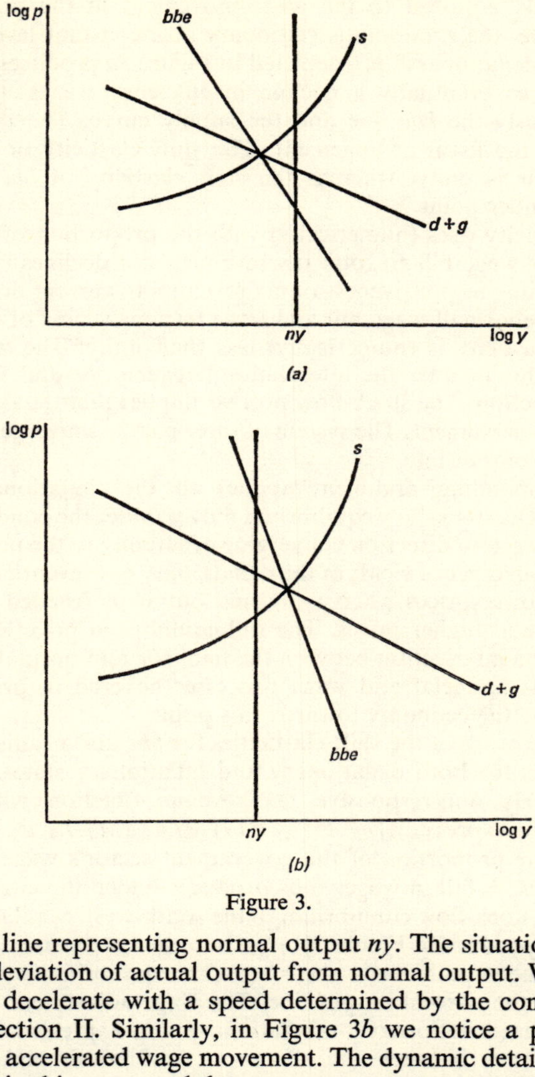

Figure 3.

the vertical line representing normal output *ny*. The situation describes a negative deviation of actual output from normal output. Wage movements thus decelerate with a speed determined by the conditions discussed in section II. Similarly, in Figure 3*b* we notice a positive gap inducing an accelerated wage movement. The dynamic detail is however disregarded in this paper and the argument concentrates on the fact that a negative deviation decelerates wages, a sustained gap lowers the relative change, and a negative gap persisting over a longer horizon actually lowers wages. The patterns determined by this wage adjustment are substantially conditioned by the government sector's wage policies and the prevalence of economic growth raising particularly *y* and *K*.

Suppose for the moment that wage rates in the government sector are competitively adjusted to the wage movement in the private sector. Furthermore, the economy is stationary at a constant level of normal output. A 'deflationary' gap depicted in Figure 3*a* produces under these circumstances eventually a decline in efficiency wages which lowers simultaneously the *bbe* line and the supply curve. The relative shifts depend on the fiscal arrangement. The shift elasticity of supply with respect to w is unity, whereas the shift elasticity of *bbe* is listed in Table IV under point 7.

The elasticity rises (numerically) with the proportion of the government sector wage bill to total tax revenues and declines (numerically) with increasing responsiveness of tax revenues to current price p. With a comparatively small wage bill and large responsiveness of tax revenues the shift elasticity is (numerically) less than unity. The wage process pushes in this manner the intersection between *bbe* and s in a south-eastern direction. The stock-flow process implies that the demand curve follows this movement. The system of three curves converge thus toward the normal output line.

A corresponding argument applies to the 'inflationary gap' in Figure 3*b*. The stock-flow equilibrium moves under the conditions stated in a north-western direction converging eventually to the normal output line. The convergence yields in the deflationary case eventually a normal output at lower prices whereas normal output is reached in the inflationary case at higher prices. The full equilibrium price level is determined by the intersection between the final *bbe* and normal output line. The various financial and wage processes covered in previous paragraphs drive the economy towards this point.

A reverse order of the shift elasticities for *bbe* and s radically changes the patterns for both deflationary and inflationary states. Consider a comparatively non-responsive tax revenue function with an $\varepsilon(t,p)$ exceeding the expression $[pg\,.\,t^{-1} + \varepsilon(I,i)\,.\,\varepsilon(i,p \mid AM)\,.\,IS\,.\,t^{-1}]$ by a margin less than the proportion of the government sector's wage bill to total tax revenues. A fall in wages thus produces under the circumstances a path of the stock-flow equilibrium to the south-west. Similarly, the same conditions produce in Figure 3*b* a path to the north-east. In both cases the adjustment path leads the short-run equilibrium system further away from the normal output line. The wage adjustment process thus increases the deflationary or inflationary gap expressed by the horizontal distance between the short-run equilibrium and the normal output line. The conditions responsible for this disequilibrating pattern include a competitively adjusted wage level in the government sector (independent of productivity considerations), a comparatively low responsiveness of tax revenues supplemented with a relatively high wage bill of the government sector. Removal of some conditions prevent the disequilibrating pattern. A small response of government wage level to market determined wages or an independent wage policy of the government sector lowers the relative shift elasticity of the *bbe* line to negligible proportions and thus assures convergence to normal output. The corresponding result applies to the inflationary gap in Figure 3*b*

The instability produced by the relative shift elasticities should not be understood as an inherent property of the wage adjustment process. The instability is determined by a destabilising feedback from wave movements to the money stock. The shift of the *bbe* line pushes the prevalent state into the surplus space and the monetary base declines at an excessive rate relative to the fall in wages. The instability results thus basically from a perverse money supply mechanism determined by the budget process. A suitable modification of the budget process could rearrange the money supply mechanism and assure unobstructed operation of an equilibrating wage adjustment. With the perverse feedback in the money supply mechanism removed the stock-flow system converges to a point on the normal output line. A balanced budget rule would achieve this result. This rule implies that the *bbe* line follows the intersection between $(d + g)$ and s towards the *ny* line. Another rule stipulates that fiscal policy be adjusted to achieve a balanced budget at normal output with inherited price level p. A short-run equilibrium to the left of *ny* necessarily expands the financial stocks under the circumstances. The $(d + g)$ line increases while s sinks away under the pressures of wage adjustment. The path moves in this case on a shorter trajectory towards the *ny* line. A similar argument applies also to the inflationary gap.

Let us remove now the constraint of a stationary economy. Economic growth, reflected by rising q and K, raises the level of normal output. The normal output line moves gradually to the right at a speed determined by the expansion rate in K and q. The *bbe* line still falls when money wages eventually decline. The downward shift in supply is reinforced by the effect of increasing K and q. The total vertical shift is defined by the formula

$$\varepsilon(p,fw|s)\frac{dw}{w} - \varepsilon(p,fw|s).\varepsilon(ny,q)\frac{dq}{q} + [\varepsilon(p,K|s) - \varepsilon(p,fw|s).(ny,K)]\frac{dK}{K}$$

$$< \varepsilon(p,fw|s)\frac{dw}{w} \qquad < \frac{dq}{q}, \frac{dK}{K}$$

This expression is approximately equal to

$$\frac{dw}{w} - \varepsilon(ny,q).\frac{dq}{q} + [\varepsilon(p,K|s) - \varepsilon(ny,K)].\frac{dK}{K} < \frac{dw}{w}$$

Economic growth thus offsets to some extent the instability determined by the conditions introducing a perverse money supply mechanism. We also note that the supply curve moves already to the right when rising money wages have sufficiently retarded to be overcome by the influence of q and K on efficiency wages. Falling efficiency wages dislodge the supply curve and the stock-flow system moves towards the *ny* line. The performance of the system is still improved however with any removal of the perverse money supply feedback examined above.

The effect of economic growth remains somewhat ambiguous in the inflationary case of Figure 3*b*. The normal output line moves to the right, but growth enlarges in this case the excess shift of the *bbe* line and the stock-flow system moves to the north-east away from the *ny* line.

The remarks above concerning removal of perverse feedbacks in the money supply process can of course be extended. A suitable choice of fiscal policies assures in the deflationary case a positive monetary growth alleviating the burden of the wage adjustment process. An increase in government expenditures slides the *bbe* line in Figure 3*a* along the supply curve and raises the $(d + g)$ line. The state point moves closer to the normal output line and the deficit reinforces the operation of the wage process and also minimises reliance on this process. This fiscal policy of course raises the final price level determined by the *bbe* and *ny* lines. The corresponding policy with some appropriate reductions in expenditures and the resulting surplus would reinforce the operation of the wage adjustments in the inflationary case. The ultimate price-level is relatively lowered by this policy. These fiscal policy changes should be viewed as a longer-run control device generating stabilising money supply responses.

The possibility of fiscal policies alleviating the burden imposed on the wage adjustment process associated with the implicit money supply behaviour may appear very alluring. The possibility exists, and its very existence produces an essentially asymmetric realisation. The incentive structure confronting policy makers and legislators assigns small rewards to reductions of expenditures (or increases in tax rates) in periods corresponding to Figure 3*b*. The rewards attached to expanding expenditures appear on the other hand very substantial in periods corresponding to Figure 3*a*. The probabilities affecting fiscal policy actions are thus heavily loaded in favour of accelerating fiscal policies in deflationary episodes supplemented with fiscal expansions over inflationary periods. This pattern induces a drift of *bbe* to the right at a rate exceeding the growth rate of the normal output line. This pattern implies a long-run drift in the price-level determined by the intersection between *bbe* and *ny*. Prices accelerate, intermittently driven by a rising *bbe* line sliding upwards along the normal output line.

The discussion in earlier paragraphs suggests the existence of a trade-off between stabilising fiscal policies and stabilising fiscal arrangements. A tax revenue at least proportional to the price-level *p*, supplemented with nominal expenditure policy and an independent or substantially lagged government wage policy assures an excess shift of the supply curve relative to the *bbe* curve under the pressures of wage adjustments. Suitable fiscal arrangements substitute in this manner for discretionary policy actions with long-run inflationary propensities. A long-run concern for a non-inflationary environment establishes a preference for the reliance on suitably adjusted fiscal arrangements. These arrangements should of course include a rule confining monetary growth within a specified control band. This rule of monetary control implicitly constrains the budget and the financial parameter.

IV.2 SOME LONG-RUN PATTERNS AFFECTING THE POSITION OF THE NORMAL OUTPUT LINE

The previous sections of the paper explored the role of fiscal policies bearing on the behaviour of the intermediate-run system and the long-run movement of the *bbe* line. The long-run effect of fiscal policy on normal output still requires some attention. An examination of the long-run conditions yields information bearing on the system's stock of real capital or capital intensity.

A few adjustments in the formulation simplify somewhat the necessary long-run analysis. Extensive use of homogeneity properties suggests that W_h be made homogeneous of degree one with respect to p (via *aw* and *ap*). It is also postulated that W_h is linear homogeneous with respect to y and *lg*. Lastly, UB_0 and S_0 are set equal to zero, so that $B = \mu D$ and $S = (1 - \mu)D$. Human capital q is disregarded here and its explicit incorporation developed at another occasion. Lastly, in order to simplify the argument the long run considers a stationary state. The relevant propositions are not affected by this simplification.[15]

The analysis begins with the *OAM* system consisting of output and asset markets. The first long-run condition involves replacement of *ap* with $p(1 + \pi)$ in all market equations. Moreover, the two crucial conditions defining the long-run state are used to remove P and i from the *OAM* system. Equation (22) introduces the two long-run conditions

$$(21)\quad p = \mathrm{P}$$

$$i = F_K + \pi$$

We also note that $e = F_K$ and this relation is used to replace e. The modification of F_K by the impact of the tax parameter is neglected here. The two conditions (21) state the equality of the two price-levels supplemented with the equality between nominal interest rate and the sum of the marginal product of real capital and the anticipated inflation rate. Lastly, all occurrences of y, whether in the output market equation or

[15] It should also be noted that a consistent long-run analysis requires that the production function and the price-setting function (and also the money-wage function) cannot be introduced independently. Their respective properties must satisfy some consistent conditions. We need not delve into these problems at this stage however. The procedure implicitly removes an independent price-setting function.

as arguments of W_h, are replaced by the production function. The replacement of P, i and e yields an *OAM* system jointly determining p, K and μ as a function of the fiscal variables fi, (g, lg, τ_n, τ_h), anticipated inflation rate π, and the level of financial stocks D. The long-run *OAM* system thus determines the price-level, the stock of real capital and the distribution of the financial stocks between government securities and base money (or total money stock). It is thus not possible in the long run to set arbitrarily monetary and fiscal policies. One of the policy parameters must be adjusted to the others by the system's interaction. Monetary policy μ was selected for this purpose in order to concentrate on the long-run effect of fiscal policy.

These long-run effects on K and the financial stocks are developed in a stepwise fashion yielding the necessary building blocks. The argument begins with the two asset market equations, *i.e.* the *AM* system. Each equation defines implicitly a relation between μ and K. These are depicted in Figure 4. The horizontal axis measures log K and the

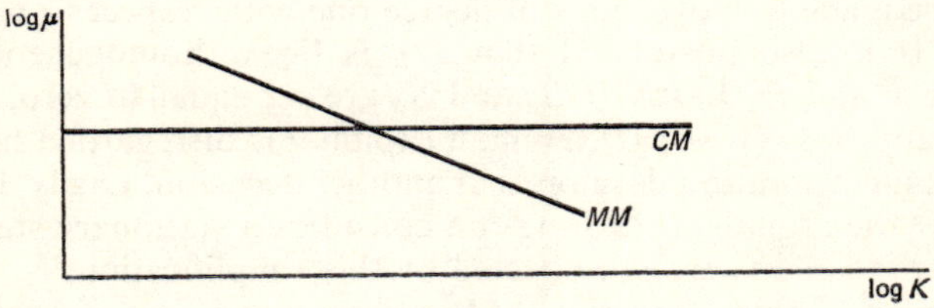

Figure 4.

vertical axis log μ. The *CM* line describes the relation determined by the credit market equation and the *MM* line reflects the money market equation. The properties of these lines, derived from the asset market equations, are described in Table V. Vanishing wealth elasticities of σ and offsetting effects (on σ) of the real rate $(i - \pi)$ on financial assets and of the anticipated net yield e on real capital suggest an approximation of the *CM* line with a horizontal. The slope of the *MM* line on the other hand is definitely negative and is approximately equal to minus the total elasticity $\bar{\varepsilon}(\lambda, K)$ of money demand with respect to the stock of real capital. This elasticity is determined by the wealth elasticities and the capital yield elasticity $\varepsilon(\lambda, e)$. The larger (numerically) these elasticities the steeper is the *MM* line. It seems probable that the slope centres in the neighbourhood of unity.

The position of both lines depends on the price-level and the fiscal variables. Inspection of the asset market equation immediately shows however that *CM* and *MM* are not affected by variations in g directly. A change in g does not modify their position. Table V indicates however that variations in p, π, and lg shift the two curves and change the

TABLE V The Properties of the Long-Run *LM* and *MM* Lines

In order to simplify the results the elasticities of the asset and monetary multiplier with respect to K and μ were approximated with zero.

1. the slope of the lines
   a) the CM line

$$\varepsilon(\mu, K/CM) = -\frac{\varepsilon(\sigma,K)}{1-\varepsilon(\sigma,\mu)} \sim 0$$

where

$$\varepsilon(\sigma,K) = [\varepsilon(\sigma,i-\pi) + \varepsilon(\sigma,e)].\varepsilon(F_K,K) + \varepsilon(\sigma,W_n)\frac{PK}{W_n} + \varepsilon(\sigma,W_h).\varepsilon(W_h,K) \sim 0$$

and

$$-\varepsilon(\sigma,\mu) = \frac{S}{aB}\cdot\frac{\mu}{1-\mu}$$

   b) the *MM* line

$$\varepsilon(\mu, K/MM) = -\frac{\bar{\varepsilon}(\lambda,K)}{1-\varepsilon(\lambda,\mu)} \sim -\varepsilon(\lambda,K) < 0$$

where

$$\bar{\varepsilon}(\lambda,K) = \varepsilon(\lambda,W_n)\frac{PK}{W_n} + \varepsilon(\lambda,W_h).\varepsilon(W_h,K) + \left[\varepsilon(\lambda,e) + \varepsilon(\lambda,i)\frac{F_K}{i}\right]\varepsilon(F_K,K) > 0$$

$$\varepsilon(\lambda,\mu) = \varepsilon(\lambda,W_n)\frac{D}{W_n}\text{ ; of small order}$$

2. The vertical shift elasticities of *CM* and *MM*
   a) *wrt* price-level p

$$\varepsilon(\mu,p/CM) = \frac{\bar{\varepsilon}(\sigma,p)}{1+\frac{S}{aB}\frac{\mu}{1-\mu}} \sim -\frac{1-\frac{S}{aB}}{1+\frac{S}{aB}\frac{\mu}{1-\mu}} = -\frac{(1-\mu)[aB-S]}{(1-\mu)aB+\mu S} < 0$$

$$\varepsilon(\mu,p/MM) = -\frac{\bar{\varepsilon}(\lambda,p)}{1-\varepsilon(\lambda,\mu)} \sim -1$$

The homogeneity conditions determine that

$$\bar{\varepsilon}(\sigma,p) = \varepsilon(\sigma,p) + \varepsilon(\sigma,ap) + \varepsilon(\sigma,P) + \varepsilon(\sigma,W_n)\frac{PK}{W_n} + \varepsilon(W_h,p) \sim 1 - \varepsilon(\sigma,S) = 1 - \frac{S}{aB}$$

$$\bar{\varepsilon}(\lambda,p) = \varepsilon(\lambda,p) + \varepsilon(\lambda,ap) + \varepsilon(\lambda,P) + \varepsilon(\lambda,W_n)\frac{PK}{W_n} + \varepsilon(\lambda,W_h).\varepsilon(W_h,p) \sim 1$$

The latter magnitude is approximately unity. It is slightly below unity by the amount

$$\varepsilon(\lambda,W_n)\frac{S+(1+\omega)B}{W_n}$$

The difference is of small order and is neglected.

b) *wrt* π

$$\varepsilon(\mu,\pi/CM) = -\frac{-\bar{\varepsilon}(\sigma,\pi)}{1+\frac{S}{aB}\cdot\frac{\mu}{1-\mu}} < 0$$

$$\bar{\varepsilon}(\sigma,\pi) = -\ \varepsilon(\sigma,i-\pi)\frac{\pi}{i-\pi} + \varepsilon(\sigma,ap)\frac{\pi}{1-\pi} > 0$$

$$\varepsilon(\mu,\pi/MM) = -\ \frac{\bar{\varepsilon}(\lambda,\pi)}{1-\varepsilon(\lambda,\mu)} \sim -\ \bar{\varepsilon}(\lambda,\pi) \sim 0$$

$$\bar{\varepsilon}(\lambda,\pi) = \varepsilon(\lambda,ap)\frac{\pi}{1+\pi} + \varepsilon(\lambda,W_h).\varepsilon(W_h,ap)\frac{\pi}{1+\pi} + \varepsilon(\lambda,i)\frac{\pi}{i}$$

c) *wrt* lg

$$\varepsilon(\mu,lg/CM) = -\ \frac{\bar{\varepsilon}(\sigma,lg)}{1+\dfrac{S}{aB}\cdot\dfrac{\mu}{1-\mu}} > 0$$

$$\bar{\varepsilon}(\sigma,lg) \sim -\varepsilon(\sigma,e).\varepsilon(F_K,lp)\frac{lg}{lp} < 0$$

$$\varepsilon(\mu,lg/MM) = -\ \frac{\bar{\varepsilon}(\lambda,lg)}{1-\varepsilon(\lambda,\mu)} \sim -\ \bar{\varepsilon}(\lambda,lg) < 0$$

$$\bar{\varepsilon}(\lambda,g) = \varepsilon(\lambda,W_h).\varepsilon(W_h,lg) - \varepsilon(\lambda,e).\varepsilon(F_K,lp)\frac{lg}{lp} > 0$$

---

intersection determining the asset market solution for K and μ. The shift elasticities with respect to the price-level p assume (approximately) a very simple form. Both shifts are negative. An increase in p thus pushes both lines downward. It follows immediately that μ declines in response to an increase in p. More information is required to determine the response of K. The relative order of the two shifts is important for a definite result. The table establishes that the MM shift is approximately unity numerically. Moreover, the CM shift is (numerically) less than unity by its very form.

The CM shift is thus definitely smaller than the MM shift and the intersection moves therefore to the south-west. An increase in p lowers consequently both K and μ. The fall in K is accompanied under the circumstances with a shift in financial stocks from base money (or money generally) to securities. Variations in p induce in this manner a substitution relation between real and (non-money) financial assets on the asset market.

Variation in the anticipated rate of inflation π yields a different pattern. An increase in π lowers the CM line with little effect on the MM line. This is due to the fact that π operates on λ via ap and W_h and the two arguments affect λ with opposite signs. It follows that an increase in π pushes the intersection point between the two lines along the CM line, and the intersection moves in a south-eastern direction. An increase in π therefore lowers μ and raises K. Rising inflationary anticipations thus reallocate assets away from money towards all other assets.

We consider lastly the impact of changes in the government's absorption of labour lg. Increasing labour absorption raises the CM line and lowers the MM line. The intersection point thus moves to the north-west. An increase of lg raises μ and lowers K. The lower K is accompanied in this case with a shift from securities to money. Real assets and financial assets operate under the circumstances as complements in response to changes in lg.

The results of the asset market interaction may be assembled for subsequent reference as follows

$$\begin{aligned} &\varepsilon\,(K,p/AM < 0 > \varepsilon(\mu,p/AM) \\ (22)\quad &\varepsilon(K,\pi/AM) > 0 > \varepsilon(\mu,\pi/AM) \\ &\varepsilon(K,lg/AM) < 0 < \varepsilon(\mu,lg/AM) \\ &\varepsilon(K,g/AM) = 0 = \varepsilon(\mu,g/AM) \end{aligned}$$

The asset market responses provide the building blocks required for an adequate description of the responses of p, K and μ determined by the interaction over the whole OAM system. We obtain first the response of the price-level p to π and fi. The solutions obtained from the AM system are used for this purpose to replace all occurrences of K and μ in the output market equation. Moreover, the output variable y on the left of the output market equation is replaced by the production function. The output market equation, thus modified, immediately determines the OAM response of p with respect to π and fi. These responses are derived by suitable differentiation and are assembled in Table VI.

TABLE VI The Response of p over the OAM·system *wrt* π and fiscal variables

1. $\varepsilon(p,g/OAM) = \dfrac{\gamma}{\text{den}(OAM)} > 0$

where the denominator .den(OAM) expressing the interaction over the OAM system is defined as follows:

$$\text{den}\,(OAM) = \varepsilon(F,K).\varepsilon(K,p/AM) - (1-\gamma)\varepsilon(d,p/OAM)$$

and where

$$\varepsilon(d,p/OAM) = \bar{\varepsilon}(d,p) + \bar{\varepsilon}(d,K).\varepsilon(K,p/AM) + \varepsilon(d,\mu).\varepsilon(\mu,p/AM)$$

$$\bar{\varepsilon}(d,p) = \varepsilon(d,p) + \varepsilon(d,ap) + \varepsilon(d,P) + \varepsilon(d,W_n)\frac{PK}{W_n} + \varepsilon(d,W_h).\varepsilon(W_h,p)$$

The homogeneity properties imply

$$\bar{\varepsilon}(d,p) = -\,\varepsilon(d,W_n)\frac{S+(1+\omega)UB}{W_n} = -\,\varepsilon(d,W_n)\frac{(1+\omega.\mu)D}{W_n} < 0$$

$$\begin{aligned} \bar{\varepsilon}(d,K) = &\Big[\overset{-}{\varepsilon(d,i}-\pi) + \overset{+}{\varepsilon(d,e)}\Big].\varepsilon(F_K,K) + \varepsilon(d,W_n)\frac{PK}{W_n} \\ &+ \varepsilon(d,W_h).\varepsilon(W_h,ny).\varepsilon(F,K) \\ &\sim \varepsilon(d,W_n)\frac{PK}{W_n} + \varepsilon(d,W_h)\frac{p.ny}{p.ny+w.lg}.\varepsilon(F,K) \end{aligned}$$

and

$$\varepsilon(d,\mu) = \varepsilon(d,W_n)\frac{\omega.\mu D}{W_n}$$

With the aid of these components of den(OAM) the denominator can be converted into the following expression:

$$\text{den}(OAM) = \varepsilon(K,p/AM)\Big[\varepsilon(F,K)\Big(1 - (1-\gamma).\varepsilon(d,W_h)\frac{p.ny}{p.ny + w.lg}\Big) - (1-\gamma).\varepsilon(d,W_n)\frac{PK}{W_n}\Big] + \varepsilon(d,W_n)\frac{D}{W_n}\Big[1 + \omega.\mu[1 - \varepsilon(\mu,p\,|\,AM)]\Big]$$

2.

$$\varepsilon(p,lg/OAM) = \frac{(1-\gamma).\varepsilon(d,lg/OAM) + \varepsilon(F,lp)\frac{lg}{lp}}{\text{den }(OAM)} \gtrless 0$$

where

$$\varepsilon(d,lg/OAM) = \varepsilon(d,W_h).\varepsilon(W_h,lg) + \bar{\varepsilon}(d,K).\varepsilon(K,lg\,|\,AM + \varepsilon(d,\mu)\varepsilon(\mu,lg\,|\,AM)$$

Approximating $\varepsilon(d,W_h)$ and $\bar{\varepsilon}(d,K)$ with unity we obtain

$$\varepsilon(d,lg/OAM) \sim \frac{w.lp}{p.ny + w.lg}\frac{lg}{lp} + \varepsilon(K,lg/AM) + R$$

where 0 is a positive term. The second term, i.e. $\varepsilon(K,lg/AM)$ is negative and numerically substantially below unity. It is also noteworthy that an increasing proportion of labour absorption lg/lp by the government sector raises the elasticity $\varepsilon(p,lg/OAM)$ algebraically and eventually assures the positive sign. It is assumed that the offsetting components of $\varepsilon(d,lg/OAM)$ hold this elasticity at a small level relative to $\varepsilon(F,lp)\frac{lg}{lp}$.

3.

$$\varepsilon(p,\pi/OAM) = (1-\gamma)\frac{\varepsilon(d,ap)\frac{\pi}{1+\pi} + \varepsilon(d,K).\varepsilon(K,\pi\,|\,AM) + \varepsilon(d,\mu).\varepsilon(\mu,\pi\,|\,AM)}{den\ (OAM)} > 0$$

All component expressions have already been defined.

The elasticity of the price-level p with respect to government absorption g of output is positive. An expanding absorption raises the price-level independent of the mode of financing the deficit. The price response measured by the elasticity simply reflects the role of prices in adjusting competing claims made by the private and the government sector on the private sector's output. The elasticity $\varepsilon(p,g/OAM)$ is proportional to the government's absorption ratio γ and it increases with this ratio. The proportionality factor is the reciprocal of an expression, denoted with den(OAM) summarising the total net effect of price changes on the excess supply of the output market, taking full account of the interaction with the asset markets. A necessary and sufficient condition for a positive price response to g is a positive net effect of price variations on the excess supply of output, and a sufficient condition for that to occur is the following inequality

$$(23) \qquad \varepsilon(F,K) < \frac{(1-\gamma).\varepsilon(d,W_n)\dfrac{PK}{W_n}}{1-(1-\gamma).\varepsilon(d,W_h)\dfrac{p.ny}{p.ny+w.lg}}$$

This condition is immediately derived from the last line under point 1 in Table VI. Sufficiently large wealth elasticities of aggregate demand assure thus a positive response of p to g. The standard estimates of $\varepsilon(F,K)$, much nearer to zero than to unity, and the implication of the permanent income hypothesis yielding for $\varepsilon(d,W_h)$ a value equal to the proportion of consumption to private aggregate demand, jointly determine that the inequality is satisfied. Positive responses of p are also obtained with respect to government absorption lg of labour and the anticipated rate of inflation π. Moreover, the response of p to lg increases with a rising relative labour absorption lg/lp. An expansion of a *large* bureaucracy raises the price-level substantially more. An inspection of the various building blocks constituting $\varepsilon(p,\pi/OAM)$ also determines that the response of p with respect to π rises with the established inflationary anticipations. Larger anticipations raise the response of the price-level.

With the price responses at our disposal the responses of K and μ determined by the full interaction of the OAM system can be easily described.

The results can now be immediately stated as follows:

$$\begin{aligned}
&\varepsilon(K,g/OAM) = \overset{-}{\varepsilon(K,p/AM)}.\overset{+}{\varepsilon(p,g/OAM)} < 0\\
&\varepsilon(K,lg/OAM) = \overset{-}{\varepsilon(K,lg/AM)} + \overset{-}{\varepsilon(K,p/AM)}.\overset{+}{\varepsilon(p,lg/OAM)} < 0\\
(24) \quad &\varepsilon(K,\pi/OAM) = \overset{+}{\varepsilon(K,\pi/AM)} + \overset{-}{\varepsilon(K,p/AM)}.\overset{+}{\varepsilon(p,\pi/OAM)} \sim 0\\
&\varepsilon(\mu,g/OAM) = \overset{-}{\varepsilon(\mu,p/AM)}.\overset{+}{\varepsilon(p,g/OAM)} < 0\\
&\varepsilon(\mu,lg/OAM) = \overset{+}{\varepsilon(\mu,lg/AM)} + \varepsilon(\mu,p/AM).\overset{+}{\varepsilon(p,lg/OAM)} \sim 0\\
&\varepsilon(\mu,\pi/OAM) = \overset{-}{\varepsilon(\mu,\pi/AM)} + \overset{-}{\varepsilon(\mu,p/AM)}.\overset{+}{\varepsilon\,(p,lg/OAM)} < 0
\end{aligned}$$

An increase in government's output absorption g lowers K and μ. The decline in capital intensity is thus accompanied by a shift in financial assets from money to securities. An increasing labour absorption *lg* also lowers *K* but exerts only a relatively minor effect on μ. Lastly, rising inflationary anticipations shift the composition of financial assets towards securities, and exert a minor effect on *K*. The capital stock suffers two offsetting influences, a positive portfolio effect produced by the interaction of asset markets, and a negative feedback effect via the price responses on the output market. Inflation *per se* yields therefore no significant effect on the economy's capital intensity, whereas expansionary fiscal actions, expressed by increasing *g* or *lg*, lower the economy's capital intensity. It follows that increasing *g* or *lg* lower the economy's normal output. Both *g* and *lg* lower *ny* via lower *K*, and *lg* lowers in addition also the long-run value of the private sector's labour absorption *lp*. Expansionary fiscal policy simultaneously shifts the *bbe* line and the normal output line. The *bbe* line is pushed up and the normal output is shifted to the left. The *bbe* shift dominates the analysis of inflation and price-level effects and the shift in normal output affects the long-run welfare effects of fiscal policy.

IV.3 FISCAL POLICY, PRICE-LEVEL AND INFLATION

The analysis developed thus far used the *level* of financial stocks *D* as a predetermined variable. The effect of *D* on *p*, *K* and μ can be read off by inspection. One obtains from the homogeneity conditions immediately

$$\varepsilon\,(p,D/OAM) = 1;\ \varepsilon(K,D/OAM) = 0 = \varepsilon(\mu,D/OAM).$$

The fixation of *D* is a useful device to obtain important blocks. Moreover, the level of *D* is quite irrelevant for the welfare implications of fiscal policy expressed by the position of the normal output line. A complete analysis of the real effects of fiscal policy usefully bypasses the determination of *D*. An analysis of price-level and inflation rate on the other hand requires careful attention to the budget-process conditioning the behaviour of *D* in the longer run. An examination of *D* thus requires some analysis of the expression defining the deficit. We repeat initially the description of the deficit def

$$(25)\quad \text{def} = p(g + rw.lg) + I(1 - \mu)D - t(p,ry;\ldots)$$

where *rw* is the real wage expressible as a function of *K* and *lp* with the usual properties. The deficit is obviously a function of *p*, *K* (via *rw*, *I* and *ry*) and μ. The expression is thus converted into

$$(26)\quad \mathring{D} = \text{def}[p(D,\pi,fi),K(\pi,fi),\mu(\pi,fi);fi]$$

or shorter

$$(26a)\quad \mathring{D} = \text{def}[D;\pi,fi]$$

The homogeneity properties of the *OAM* system determine a comparatively simple derivative of def with respect to D. We obtain

$$(27)\quad \text{def}_D = \frac{t}{D}\left[\frac{p.\text{reg}}{t} + \frac{I(1-\mu)D}{t} - \varepsilon(t,p)\right]$$
$$= \frac{t}{D}\left[1 + \frac{\text{def}}{t} - \varepsilon(t,p)\right]$$

where reg $= g + rw.lg$ indicating total real expenditures of the government sector net of interest payments. It is immediately obvious that a sufficiently large relative deficit def$.t^{-1}$ assures a positive derivative def_D. A large deficit thus initiates an accelerated increase of financial stocks and possibly also an accelerated increase in the price-level proportional to the expansion in D. Under the conditions laid down relative price changes $\hat{p}$ are equal to relative changes $\hat{D}$ in D. It is noteworthy, however, that with $\varepsilon(t,p) > 1$ this instability does not persist. It only occurs over an initial phase of the process with a magnitude and length determined by the level of the deficit and the degree of progressivity of tax revenues, i.e. by the magnitude of $\varepsilon(t,p) - 1 > 0$. A progressive tax arrangement implies that the process unleashed by an initial deficit raises t by more than def. The deficit declines continuously relative to t under the circumstances and with $\varepsilon(t,p,) > 1$ the derivative def_D eventually becomes negative. The evolution can be described with the aid of Figure 5. The vertical measures $\mathring{D}$ and the horizontal D. The

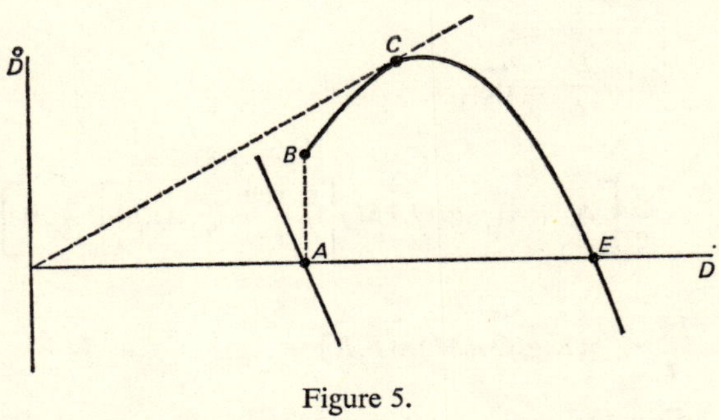

Figure 5.

position A describes an inherited stock equilibrium with a stable neighbourhood expressed by a negatively sloping line. This slope determines a vanishing $\mathring{D}$ as D increases (i.e. as $\mathring{D} > 0$). Suppose now that the equilibrium is disrupted by an increase in g raising the deficit to the vertical distance A–B. It is assumed that the relative deficit (i.e. def$/t$) is large compared to $\varepsilon(t,p)$, so that an unstable process is initiated. This instability is depicted by a rising curve from B to C reflecting a positive derivative def_D. But the slope of this curve continuously declines as D (or p) increases. The relative change $\hat{D}$ reaches a maximum at C and so does the inflation rate. The slope declines further beyond this point and eventually the line descends to intersect the horizontal at a new equilibrium point at E. A large deficit thus imposes some momentum over an initial phase, but eventually inflation must recede whenever fiscal variables are held constant. The initial phase of instability may convey a sense that inflation proceeds on its own momentum, independent of fiscal policies. But this phase cannot last with a non-homogeneous deficit function. A constant fiscal policy is sufficient under the circumstances to terminate eventually inflation. Persistent inflation requires an activist fiscal policy, and such a policy will produce repeated waves of inflationary acceleration whenever executed in large magnitudes.[16]

Let us examine however the equilibrium responses of D to variations in fiscal policy. These equilibrium responses provide useful information about the longer-run direction of financial stocks and the price-level. The response of D to changes in g and lg obtained in previous sections require some modification at this stage. The elasticity of D with respect to g under long-run conditions appears as follows

$$(28) \quad \varepsilon(D,g/OAM\text{-}bbe) = -\frac{\overline{\text{def}_g}}{\overline{\text{def}_D}}$$

and

$$\text{def}_g \frac{g}{t} = \overline{\text{def}}$$

$$\text{def}_D \frac{D}{t} = \overline{\text{def}_D}$$

where

$$(28a) \quad \text{def}_g = \frac{t}{g}\left[\text{A} + \varepsilon(p,g/OAM)\left[\frac{p.\text{reg}}{t} - \varepsilon(t,p)\right] + 0\right] > 0$$

and

$$(28b) \quad A = \frac{pg}{t} + \varepsilon(K,g/OAM),\varepsilon(F,K) \times$$

$$\times \left[\frac{rw.lg}{t} - \varepsilon(t,ry)\frac{ny + rw.lg}{ry}\right] + \frac{(1-\mu).I.D}{t} \times$$

$$\times \left[\varepsilon(I,F_K).\varepsilon(F_K,K).\varepsilon(K,g/OAM) - \frac{\mu}{1-\mu}.\varepsilon(\mu,g/OAM)\right] > 0$$

[16] A more developed dynamic analysis would incorporate assumptions about π. This analysis can be found in a paper 'Fiscal Policy, the Price-Level and Inflation' presented at a conference in Helsinki in August 1975. The paper demonstrates that stability still holds with adaptively formed expectations. Similar conditions apply to existence and stability of solutions under rational expectations.

The A term is unambiguously positive. The second term is negative, but it is also a small fraction. The last term 0 is proportional to the fraction of interest payments measured with respect to the nominal value of received income and remains thus at a negligible level. The negative second term expresses the effect of g on the budget exerted via the price-level p. It follows therefore that a progressive tax schedule introduces a negative feedback attenuating the response of D to g. The attenuation increases with the progressivity of the tax schedule. Weak progressivity lowers the numerical value of $\varepsilon(t,p)$ close to unity and the difference $[p.\text{reg}.t^{-1} - \varepsilon(t,p)]$ falls to a small order (because $p.g.\text{reg} + IS = t$). The A term on the other hand expresses three channels conveying the effect of g on the deficit. The first component $p.g.t^{-1}$ describes the direct effect, the second component and part of the last component describe the effect exerted via K, and the remaining part of the last component describes the effect transmitted via μ. An inspection of the formula reveals that the effects via K and μ raise the total non-price effect substantially above the 'direct effect' and thus raise the long-run response of D.

The elasticity of D with respect to lg has a form quite similar to $\varepsilon(D,g/OAM\text{–}bbe)$. The difference appears in the A term, the direct effect is measured by the expression

$$(29) \quad \frac{w.lg}{t} + \varepsilon(t,ry)\frac{ny}{ry}\varepsilon(F,lp)\frac{lg}{lp}$$

Approximately equal proportions of pg and $w.lg$ to tax revenues t imply that the direct effect of lg in def_{lg} exceeds the direct effect of g in def_g. It follows under the circumstances that the numerator of $\varepsilon(D,lg/OAM\text{–}bbe)$ exceeds the numerator of $\varepsilon(D,g/OAM\text{–}bbe)$. This excess increases moreover with the relative absorption lg/lp of labour lg by the government sector. Larger relative labour absorption by the government thus raises the responsiveness of D to further increases in lg and reinforces the reaction of the price-level. Intermittent expansions of the ratio lg/lp form in this manner an important element of a persistent and erratic inflation.

The argument developed thus far was based on a non-homogeneous (in p) deficit function. It is sufficient for this case to emerge that $\varepsilon(t,p) > 1$, or that expenditures be fixed in nominal terms. But suppose that the actual degree of progressivity is weak and further weakened by delays in tax payments induced by inflationary experiences. It seems appropriate under the circumstances to examine the state of affairs with a tax revenue function homogeneous of degree one with respect to p. The deficit function is also linear-homogeneous in this case. The deficit equation can be written in the following form as a result.

$$(30) \quad \mathring{D} = \text{def}\,[D,\pi; fi] = \overline{\text{def}}\,[\pi; fi].D$$

The deficit function is again obtained after replacing all endogenous variables occurring in the budget expression with the aid of their respective *OAM* solutions. The second equation on the right of (30) yields

(31) $$\frac{\mathring{D}}{D} = \overline{\text{def}}\,[\pi; fi]$$

in the absence of growth the relative change $\hat{D}$ is equal to the rate of inflation $\hat{p}$. If we combine this equation with the assumption that expectations are formed adaptively, we obtain

(32) $$\dot{\pi} = h[\overline{\text{def}}\,(\pi; fi) - \pi]$$

The stability conditions require that

$$\text{def}_{\pi} < 1$$

Necessary and sufficient conditions for this inequality were discussed in another paper.[17] If stability is not assured, inflation accelerates continuously even at a constant and unchanging fiscal policy. But inflation persists at a *steady* rate in this case even in long-run equilibrium. This equilibrium is characterised by the condition

$$\pi = \overline{\text{def}}\,(\pi; fi)$$

This equation could also be derived under the assumption of rational expectations expressed by

$$\pi = \hat{p}$$

The stability conditions of adaptive expectations occur as the existence condition for the solution under rational expectations. Figure 6 may help us to perceive the problem.

The horizontal measures π and the vertical the deficit per unit of cumulated deficit, i.e. $\overline{\text{def}} = \text{def}/D$. The π line is a 45 degree line bisecting the positive quadrant. The def line represents the association of $\overline{\text{def}}$

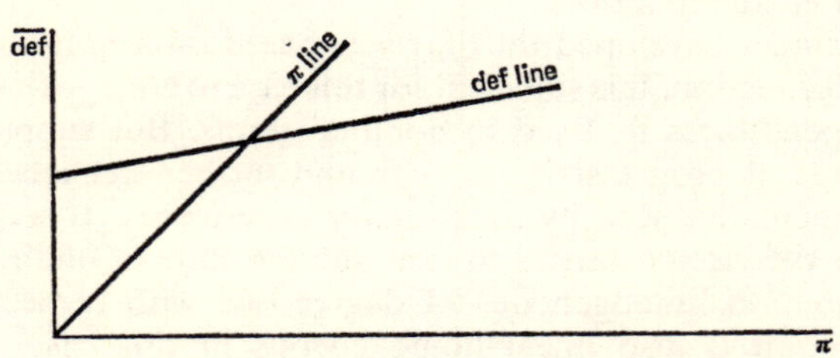

Figure 6.

[17] The reader is again referred to the paper noted under footnote 16.

with π, given the fiscal variables *fi*. The intersection determines a permanent rate of inflation associated with a fiscal policy indexed by the intercept of the $\overline{\text{def}}$ line on the vertical axis. Obviously, permanent inflation increases with the algebraic value of the slope of the $\overline{\text{def}}$ line and the level of expansionary fiscal policies. Steady inflation persists even with an unchanging fiscal policy. This implication contrasts sharply with the non-homogeneous case. Inflation can only be lowered and eventually terminated by suitable reductions of the deficit. Such reductions lower the intercept of the def line. Moreover, the previous analysis demonstrated that every reduction of π brought about by a fall in *g* or *lg* raises *K* and the private sector's normal output. This gain in output measures implicitly the social cost of steady inflation. This social cost does not include yet the traditional 'Chicago measure' of the cost of inflation. An explicit inclusion of this measure requires adding real balances as an argument in the production function. It is sufficient however at this stage to note that the traditional Chicago measure underestimates the full social cost of steady and fully anticipated inflation. The full cost includes the output loss imposed permanently by the fiscal policies responsible for the long-run inflationary patterns.

CONCLUSION

The inflation problem approached in this paper subsumes a persistent rate of increase in the general price-level maintained over a lengthy interval of time. The analysis is not immediately or *per se* interested in temporary price movements or once-and-for-all price adjustments. It includes however appropriate attention to waves of accelerations and decelerations typically characterising inflationary experiences.

The paper presented an analytic framework jointly developed with Allan H. Meltzer over the past six years explaining the evolution of an economy in terms of a superposition of three distinct processes. A short-run flow equilibrium describes the shorter-run responses of output and asset markets to inherited stocks of financial and real assets and prevailing anticipations. The interaction between the government sector's budget process and the short-run flow equilibrium determines changes in financial stocks with the resulting adjustments of output and asset markets. This interaction describes an intermediate-run process adjusting the stocks of financial assets to an equilibrium level fixed by underlying fiscal policy patterns. The change in financial stocks imposes an adjustment on asset markets modifying continuously the short-run flow equilibrium system. An intermediate-run financial stock-flow equilibrium is established whenever the short-run flow equilibrium system produces in the context of a given fiscal policy a balanced budget. Lastly, capital accumulation (not explicitly incorporated in this paper) and wage adjustments move the intermediate-run system towards a longer-run position. This position is determined by the interaction of fiscal policies and inherited resources.

The analysis fully accepts the proposition that 'inflation is essentially a monetary phenomenon'. It also recognises however that changes in fiscal policy exert some direct influence on price movements associated with the reallocation of resources between private and government sector implicitly imposed on the economy by variations in fiscal policy. The relevant orders of magnitude associated with the 'direct' fiscal effect of fiscal policy remains comparatively small. The fiscal effect of fiscal policy cannot explain under the circumstances the inflationary experiences observed in recent years. The fiscal effect contributes at most to relatively minor and intermittent spurts in the price-level. But the fiscal effect of fiscal policy does not exhaust the total effect of fiscal policy. The financial effect supplements and probably exceeds the fiscal effect. The financial effect is produced via adjustments in financial stocks determined by the government's budget process.

The analytic framework thus directs examinations of the inflation problem beyond the immediately observable monetary growth to the underlying budget process. This process conditions the longer-run growth patterns of the money stock. The inflation problem can be usefully approached under the circumstances by an examination of the interaction between budget process expressed by a long-run balanced budget position (*bbe* line) and the private sector's normal output. Policies pushing the long-run *bbe* line upwards as a result of persistent expansion of real expenditures by the government sector impose adjustments on the short- and intermediate-run system generating an accelerated monetary growth and a maintained inflation. The inflation problem is thus reduced to a set of institutions and aspects of political processes controlling the longer-run evolution of the budget process. And it appears that over the past ten years a new phenomenon, a 'new inflation' indeed emerged in some sense. It is however not new in the sense frequently alluded to in 'institutionalist' explanations denying dependence of price-wage movements on evolving market conditions. The central association and causal relation between monetary growth and price movements remains indisputably at work. The new element in the inflation problem must be recognised in the role of the budget process and the effect of political processes on persistent and even expanding deficits. The effect on the financial stocks (reflected by the long-run position of the balanced budget line) is moreover reinforced by the conseqences on normal output. Increasing absorption of output, and labour by the government sector lowers the private sector's capital intensity and available labour supply. Fiscal policy thus lowers in the long run the private sector's normal output. The social cost of erratic inflation conditioned by the prevailing financial evolutions produced by government policies is amplified by the long-run effects of the underlying fiscal patterns on the level of normal output. The Keynesian heritage of activist fiscal policies has been gradually changed over the post-war period. There emerged an uncontrollable monster, exemplified most dramatically by Italian and English experiences, which threatens the economic welfare of the citizens and eventually endangers the institutions of an open society.

Discussion of Chapter 2

Mario Monti

This remarkable paper is the most articulate statement that Professor Brunner has offered so far on his (and Allan H. Meltzer's) particular brand of monetarism, which I shall call 'fiscal monetarism'.

I will first briefly describe the message of the paper as I understand it, for the benefit of those readers who may have not found its analytic framework too appealing. I will then turn to a few comments on certain aspects of the framework itself.

'FISCAL MONETARISM' AND MONETARISM

Karl Brunner's is of course a monetarist analysis of the inflation problem. *Macroeconomic variables*, and the output price level in particular, are largely determined by the behaviour of *monetary aggregates*, especially total bank credit. These in turn are influenced by *base money* (or the monetary base) through a process that has been clarified in recent years by Brunner and Meltzer among others.

In this paper Brunner goes one step and a half further. He explains in detail how base money, usually treated as an exogenous instrument, is in fact determined to a great extent by the *budget process*. And he also hints at some features of the *institutional and political process* lying behind the formulation of the budget.

The budget deficit is either financed through creation of base money or through sales of government securities outside the government sector (inclusive of the central bank). Because of its effects on these financial stocks, fiscal policy is reinstated as the main channel of public influence on the economic system.

Fiscal policy, of course, already had this role in the economics of Keynes, and even more so in Keynesian economics, but had lost it in monetarist theory. As Brunner and Meltzer noted in commenting on Milton Friedman's 'Theoretical Framework for Monetary Analysis', 'one of the more striking features of Friedman's analysis is that in fifty-five pages of text, much of it devoted to short-run or short-term adjustments, the fiscal role of government is mentioned only once and only to be dismissed. Changes in government expenditure and taxes, apparently, have so little effect that they can be ignored entirely.'[1]

[1] K. Brunner and A. H. Meltzer, 'Friedman's Monetary Theory', *Journal of Political Economy* (Sept–Oct 1972), p. 842.

However, the revival of fiscal policy in Brunner's analysis, culminating in this paper, does not proceed along Keynesian lines – a direct influence on the output market via the expenditure and tax multipliers. To be sure, a *pure fiscal* effect on the output market is recognised by Brunner, but most of the *total* effect of fiscal policies is attributed to their *financial* effect, i.e. the feedbacks from asset market adjustments to changing financial stocks. The analysis thus focuses on the role of the budget deficit, and therefore of expenditure and taxes, in 'manufacturing' the stocks of base money and government securities.[2]

For reasons made clear by the author, the levels and accelerations of inflation recently experienced by industrial countries cannot be explained by deficits financed with issues of securities. The attention should be addressed to deficits financed with base money, generating the expansion of money and credit. 'Inflation still emerges in this manner as an essentially monetary phenomenon.'

One might then be inclined to think that monetary policy, after all, is ultimately responsible for inflation. But in the author's view it is extremely improbable that an inflationary growth in base money may occur independently of fiscal policies, simply driven by pure open market operations. 'Any relevant explanation must fully recognise the role of *fiscal* policy in the determination of *monetary* growth.'[3]

In addition to these *short-* and *intermediate*-run effects on the output and asset markets, the budget process has *long*-run effects on the level of 'normal' output, via the tax rates and the absorption of labour and output by the government sector. Increases in real government expenditures on goods and labour services and also increases in taxes tend to lower the stock of real capital, the available labour supply, and therefore 'normal' output. This reinforces the inflationary drift built into the economy by a pattern of expanding budgets.

An interesting implication can be discerned in this analysis. Increases in the size of the government budget imply long-run inflationary trends even if the budget itself is balanced. Such familiar features as a growing government debt and a large monetisation of the debt are sufficient conditions for fiscally generated inflations. But even if a more virtuous state of permanently balanced budgets prevails in the long run, the

[2] The 'New Cambridge' approach – readable accounts are 'The Cambridge debate', *The Economist* (27 Apr 1974) and 'The "new Cambridge" ', *The Economist*, (22 Mar 1975) – also stresses the financial effect of government deficits. In contrast with Brunner's framework, however, it apparently does not emphasise the role of alternative ways in which the deficit is financed, essentially holds the 'mark-up' theory of prices, and considers an open economy. For an extension of the Brunner framework to open economies, see K. Brunner, *The Money Supply Process in Open Economies with Interdependent Security Markets: The Case of Imperfect Substitutability*, mimeographed (Apr 1974), and K. Brunner and A. H. Meltzer, *Monetary and Fiscal Policy in Open, Interdependent Economies with Fixed Exchange Rates*, forthcoming.

[3] Italics added.

economy cannot escape inflationary trends as long as the size of the budget increases over time.[4]

The reader will have no difficulty in working out Brunner's long-run prescription about the optimal size of the government sector, a prescription that is familiar among monetarists of all orientations. It is perhaps more interesting to examine his recommendations about the behaviour of the government sector as long as it exists.

Given the importance of fiscal influences on Brunner's economy, he might be expected to recommend some sort of fiscal activism, in contrast with the monetarist position. But my impression is that the intercourse between Friedman and money – a notorious blend of love and hatred – revives here between Brunner and the budget. After having shown how much money matters, Friedman suggests that the reins of monetary policy be taken away from the monetary authorities' discretion and committed to a quasi-automatic rule. Brunner shows how much the budget matters but suggests that the reins of fiscal policy be taken away from the government's discretion and again turned to quasi-automatic rules.

Two differences, however, should be brought into light in this connection.

Friedman's distrust in the authorities' ability effectively to use a powerful instrument like money largely originates from the recognition of objective difficulties connected with its use, such as unpredictable lags. In Brunner's framework – possibly because of its as yet higher level of abstraction – one does not find similar indisputable obstacles to the correct implementation of a discretionary fiscal policy. Even more than Friedman, therefore, Brunner emphasises the *unwillingness* of policy-makers to use correctly the instruments they have available. The incentive structure confronting policy-makers and legislators, he argues, is such that long-run inflationary trends with intermittent accelerations are the most probable outcome of discretionary fiscal policies.

The second difference concerns the specification of the automatic rules which should replace discretionary decisions if a non-inflationary environment is to be created. In Brunner's more elaborate (and theoretically more satisfactory) framework, these take the form of a set of structural arrangements guiding fiscal operations. In particular, (*a*) tax revenues should be at least proportional to the price level, (*b*) expenditure policy programmes should be formulated in nominal terms, (*c*) the government's wage policy should be independent of, or substantially lagged with respect to, wage developments in the private sector, and

[4] In spite of obvious differences (long v. short run, 'normal' v. actual output, operation through the factor markets v. operation through the output market), it is perhaps worth noting the resemblance between this result of Brunner's and a full employment application of the balanced budget theorem developed long ago by T. Haavelmo in the Keynesian tradition.

(*d*) the rate of monetary growth should be confined within a specified control band (this would implicitly constrain the creation of base money and the budget deficit).

Friedman's rule is but one component of Brunner's set of rules. The preceding three may be interpreted in part as a net addition to the automatic control system, in part as an operational specification of necessary conditions for the monetary growth rule to be implemented effectively in a context in which base money is not really an exogenous instrument.

I hope the remarks above have been of some use in placing Brunner's important contribution to this Conference within the framework of current macroeconomic literature.

Two comments may be appropriate at this point.

A conjecture about an inherently *stable* and shock absorbing private sector and a *destabilising* government sector underlies Brunner's analysis, as well as traditional monetarism. I still consider this conjecture a postulate, but an interesting effort is discernible in this paper to translate the postulate into a set of testable propositions.

As far as the government is concerned, the incentive structure confronting policy-makers is partly specified and there is some description of the transmission mechanism of policy-generated uncertainties on to such economic variables as the anticipated net yield on capital. In this and other respects,[5] fiscal monetarism incorporates some of the factors identified by 'institutionalist' theories. Incidentally, application of this procedure makes the institutionalist and the monetarist approaches somewhat less antagonistic in my view than they are in Brunner's.[6]

With respect to the stability of the private sector, the author emphasises the role of the wage adjustment equation,[7] which determines a process producing and disseminating information over the economic system. This aspect is not explicitly incorporated into the present paper but the author plans to develop it at another occasion. Similar developments may contribute significantly to generating testable hypotheses about the crucial issue of the inherent stability of the private sector.

Turning now to my second comment, I have some doubts about the consistency between Brunner's analysis of the incentive structure confronting policy-makers and his recommendation that discretionary fiscal policy be traded-off against a system of automatically operating fiscal arrangements. If really fiscal policy is destabilising because policy-makers and legislators do not refrain from a *day by day* use of their discretionary powers which produces inflation for the economy and political rewards for themselves, how can they be expected to give up those powers *once and for all*? 'Institutionalist' critics might argue that

[5] Particularly the hints at a rationalisation of 'wage push' in terms of union hierarchy behaviour (section II.2.e). [6] Section I. [7] Equation (5).

Brunner's prescriptions, as well as the more modest traditional monetarist prescription, are not in fact any more feasible than are changes in the system by which prices and wages are determined, advocated by proponents of incomes policy.

I will now turn to a few remarks of a rather more technical nature on the analytic framework developed by Brunner.

AGGREGATION IN THE OUTPUT AND CREDIT MARKETS

The author's emphasis on relative prices is well grounded – and well known. The prices considered in this model are the output price, the price of existing real capital, the wage rate and the interest rate.

The occurrence of one aggregate price level associated with an aggregate output variable does not imply or presuppose – the author warns – that the analysis is confined to a single commodity world. It is simply the analytic counterpart of his assertion that variations in relative prices among components of output are not significant with respect to aggregative processes like the inflation problem, or at least are of second or third order of importance compared to variations in the price of capital relative to the output price, or to relative variations in interest rates.

One may share this judgement and yet be convinced that inflationary trends – over the adjustment process if not in the steady state – can better be explained if some disaggregation is performed in the market for goods and services. This disaggregation need not concern *final* output, if the model is not to be burdened with relatively unimportant details. It should rather distinguish between an aggregate final output variable, with one price level associated to it, and one or more intermediate goods variables with their corresponding price levels.

This is of course a shortcoming of all models concentrating on the market for final products, whatever their degree of disaggregation within this market.

A similar point can be made for the credit market. In the model there is no disaggregation within the banks' absorption of earning assets and within the public's asset supply. As in previous works by Brunner and Meltzer, therefore, no distinction is made between the bank *loan* market and the market for *securities*.

In the context of this paper, such a procedure seems to me less appropriate than elsewhere, given the importance of the government budget and of inflationary conditions. It would be interesting, and perhaps vital for a realistic monetary analysis, to trace the absorption of government securities in the banks' portfolio and their substitution effects with respect to bank financing to the private sector, through loans or investments in corporate bonds. Twists in the interest rate structure as between the banks' lending rates and the bond market rates, ceilings on loan expansion, compulsory bank investments in bonds are among the features frequently encountered in economies characterised by relatively large government budgets and inflationary trends. Unless a reader is thoroughly convinced of the 'aggregative irrelevance of these allocative aspects', he would wish the Brunner model threw some light on them, since it is specified to explain precisely the environment in which their occurrence is likely.[8]

GOVERNMENT, WAGES AND INCOME DISTRIBUTION

The formulation of human wealth and of the anticipated net yield on real capital[9] is said to be conditioned by 'an underlying postulate bearing on the regularity of income distribution between ownership of real capital and labour'. The precise nature and the implications of this postulate are not made clear. In particular, it would be interesting to know whether the postulate is consistent with some feedback pattern from inflation to the distribution of real income.

In addition, the relationship among the wage rate in the private sector, the wage rate in the government sector, and the government budget requires a few comments.

Brunner allows for an influence of private wages on government wages and indeed considers alternative arrangements concerning the responsiveness of the latter to the former. There is also a feedback from government wages to private wages, but it is an *indirect* one, via the effects of the government wage bill on the budget and of the budget on the economy.

In my view, three additional *direct* influences of the government sector on wage developments in the private sector deserve consideration:

(*a*) *Tax rates* obviously influence labour supply and they should not be omitted in the wage adjustment equation.

(*b*) If the government sector is large enough, and under certain conditions concerning union policies, wage rates prevailing in the *government* sector are likely to exert an autonomous influence on wage negotiations in the private sector.

(*c*) The volume and quality of *public services* provided by the government sector determine the living standard associated to a given real wage and thus influence the determination of wages in the private sector. In economies with a large government sector this influence is probably very important.

The issue of public services leads us to discuss the role of government

[8] On this subject, see K. Brunner, 'A Diagrammatic Exposition of the Money Supply Process', *Schweitzerische Zeitschrift für Volkswirtschaft und Statistik* (Dec 1973), and K. Brunner, *The Money Supply Process in Open Economies with Interdependent Security Markets: The Case of Imperfect Substitutability*, mimeographed (Apr 1974). [9] Equations (1c) and (1d) respectively.

in Brunner's philosophy and the nature of the government sector's participation in his output market.

GOVERNMENT AND OUTPUT

The government in this framework absorbs output, labour services and credit (including non-interest bearing credit in the form of base money) to produce essentially economic instability and inflation. It produces no goods or services, as shown by the fact that there is no government component on the supply side of the equilibrium condition for the output market:[10] to avoid confusion, the author clearly states that y denotes the *private* sector's output.

The possibility of the government sector producing any goods or services is confined to footnote 6: 'The government sector could be considered as a production process absorbing output g from the private sector and labour services lg as inputs. But what is the output and how does it feed back to the behaviour of the private sector? The government produces goods competing with or complementing consumables offered by the private sector, or modifying the anticipated yield on real capital. This array of problems requires an approach using a variety of analytical developments emerging in recent years.'

But there is no consideration at all of the government's output throughout the text. Besides preventing an explanation of important aspects of wage determination, as mentioned above, this procedure has several implications:

(*a*) It becomes no surprise that an expansion in the budget, even a balanced one, *reduces* 'normal' output: if only private output qualifies as output, any absorption of resources by the government is most likely to reduce output.

(*b*) It also becomes obvious that the formulation of expenditure programmes in nominal terms, as recommended by Brunner, has no drawbacks: inflation would simply cut the real volume of inputs of a productive process which yields *no* output anyway.

(*c*) Disregard for the *manner* in which the government uses the output and labour resources it absorbs may lend theoretical legitimacy to a relaxation of economic and legal controls over its activity. This is an attitude that most of us, certainly including Brunner, would reject.

(*d*) In this framework it is irrelevant, for instance, whether a given budget deficit is entirely generated by government dissaving through a *current* account deficit, or is entirely determined by *capital* account expenditures. This is so not only in the short run but also in the long-run interpretation of the framework.

(*e*) It is also irrelevant whether the government makes a more or a less *productive* use of resources in any given activity. More precisely, in this

[10] Equation (1a).

framework it is logically impossible to define any concept of productivity in connection with government uses of resources, and hence any reference to 'productivity considerations'[11] in this context is, strictly speaking, inconsistent with the framework itself.

I realise that neglecting government output altogether is a tempting reaction to the increasing impalpability of many services provided by our governments and to the misleading distortions they generate in national accounting figures. But a more balanced attitude suggests that careful consideration be given to what the government produces and to its influence on the private sector through its productive activity. This consideration is required even in an analysis dealing exclusively with aggregative aspects. The analytical developments alluded to by Brunner in his footnote 6 can certainly be useful in this respect.

Some relevant problems raised by Brunner could then be treated in a more acceptable way and their crucial importance would be reinforced. One example is provided by the 'skill and knowledge capital'[12] and its stimulating effect on the 'normal' output level. Which particular kinds of taxes, subsidy and benefit policies tend to lower the incentives to acquire that capital? Is it not possible that some kind of services produced by the government (education and research activities, for example) increase the *supply* of that capital?

Traditional monetarism ignores the fiscal role of government. Keynesian economics and Brunner's 'fiscal monetarism' emphasise it. Keynesian economists concentrate on the effects of the budget on the demand side of the output market. Brunner recognises these effects and stresses the financial effects of the budget through the asset markets. Both approaches neglect the influence of the budget through the *supply* side of the output market.

Issues such as the inflation problem cannot be adequately explored, in my view, unless a framework is developed to take account of *what* the government does, in terms of production of goods and services, and *how productively* it does it.[13] How much it spends and taxes and how it finances its deficit are important information, but are only a part of the picture.

Professor Brunner's model is an important contribution to the literature, because of its theoretical foundations and the relevance of the questions to which it addresses itself. It probably has sufficient elasticity[14] to allow incorporation of the government production process.

[11] Section IV.1. [12] Section II.2.(e).

[13] For a treatment along these lines, see H. I. Grossman and R. E. Lucas, 'The Macroeconomic Effects of Productive Public Expenditures', *The Manchester School of Economic and Social Studies* (June 1974). [14] Not only for the liberal use of ε's.

3 Some Economic Implications of the Indexing of Financial Assets with Special Reference to Mortgages

Franco Modigliani

I THE BASIC ROLE OF INDEXATION OF FINANCIAL ASSETS IN THE PRESENCE OF PRICE LEVEL UNCERTAINTY

As long as loan contracts are expressed in conventional nominal terms, a high and variable rate of inflation – or more precisely a significant degree of uncertainty about the future of the price level – can play havoc with financial markets and interfere seriously with the efficient allocation of the flow of saving and the stock of capital. Indeed it may be argued that this is one of the most damaging unfavourable implications of unpredictable inflation rates, potentially as serious as the capricious redistribution of income and wealth which, in the popular view, is the hallmark of a disorderly inflationary process. It has been suggested by many economists for quite some time now that these unfavourable effects on resource allocation as well as the redistributive effects can be eliminated or at least greatly alleviated by the device of 'indexing' financial contracts, especially long-term contracts. Indexation consists in denominating the principal and the interest in 'real terms', i.e. in terms of 'a suitable commodity basket'. In practice, this means that the nominal value of the principal is revalued periodically on the basis of an index of the changing nominal value of the stated basket, and that the agreed interest is to be applied to the revalued principal.

The reason for the unfavourable effect of inflation on financial markets and efficient allocation of resources and for the view that it can be remedied by indexation can be compactly stated as follows.

When the price level is stable (more generally, perfectly predictable) there exists in society one man-created intangible asset whose outcome is sure, namely that arising from loans to borrowers who are essentially default-proof. The existence of such an asset plays a fundamental role in the process of efficient allocation of capital because it permits separating the function of accumulating and holding wealth from that of managing physical assets and bearing the risk typically associated with such assets. Even though for society as a whole, capital or wealth must finally consist of physical assets (except for net claims on the government and the rest of the world) any individual can shed the risk associated with physical capital by holding at least some of his wealth in the form of claims fixed in terms of money as long as other members of society are prepared to assume more risk than they have wealth by issuing money fixed claims against themselves and using the proceeds to acquire physical assets or financial claims to such assets (equities). The sure contract can, in turn, form the basis for more complex 'intermediation' in which a financial intermediary is the initial borrower and, in turn, lends directly, or through further intermediaries, to the final borrower. This type of contract together with efficient and competitive financial markets permits physical capital to be allocated so as to produce the highest return adjusted for risk as assessed by all wealth holders through the market. The analysis of this process is the essential contribution of modern asset market theory.

When the future price level is uncertain, however, there is no asset which offers a sure outcome. If the uncertainty about future price levels becomes large enough the return from loan contract can become more risky than that from certain physical assets; hence holders of wealth may be induced to invest their wealth in such assets, even though from the point of view of society their real return may be small or even negative (e.g. gold), and this course of action will displace investment in potentially higher-yielding assets. This is the so-called flight into commodities (*corsa ai beni rifugio*) which may also contribute to kindling the inflationary process if the 'flight' is directed towards commodities with inelastic supply.[1]

This outcome may also be encouraged by the fact that monetary authorities quite frequently endeavour to stabilise interest rates, which prevents the nominal interest rate from changing enough to offset the expected changes in the rate of inflation. The result is that, when inflation is growing, even the *expected* real return from lending is reduced and may become negative, compounding the effect of greater uncertainty or dispersion around the expected outcome.

Even when this does not happen, and interest rates are allowed to rise to reflect increases in the expected rate of inflation, misallocation may be fostered by the fact that uncertainty about the price level may also

[1] If the supply is completely inelastic, as would be the case, e.g. with land, so that net investment can only be zero, the final result might well be an increase in consumption spurred by the rise in the (real) market value of private wealth, and a corresponding decline in investment.

tend to increase the risk of the outcome for the borrower, especially for long term contracts (when the nominal 20-year rate has reached, say 25 per cent because the expected rate of inflation over the next twenty years is 20 per cent, a 20-year loan may be quite risky for the borrower as well as the lender). Thus at least the volume of long-term loans may diminish because of the greater uncertainty about the average long-term rate of inflation, reducing the possibility of hedging against future movements of rates (even real rates).

Indexation prevents all this by reintroducing a contract with a 'reasonably' sure real outcome – regardless of the length of the contract and the actual future course of inflation – thus revitalising financial markets and re-establishing the possibility of intermediation and efficient allocation of capital. In addition, of course, indexation has desirable distributive effects in that it eliminates the capricious redistribution of income and wealth resulting from unforeseen inflation (or deflation).

It is sometimes argued that these redistributive effects may have some positive consequences in that inflation typically 'robs' the lender in favour of the borrowers, who on the average have a greater propensity to save and are more willing to bear risk. These effects would seem desirable in a society where both capital and willingness to assume risk are scarce. But the argument about the different propensity to save is, in my view, very doubtful – at least in the long run – on the basis of my own work and that of others on the life-cycle model of saving (cf. the results of a recent analysis of the Italian experience by Modigliani and Tarantelli).

Furthermore, the view that inflation systematically robs the borrower is valid only to the extent that nominal rates are prevented from reflecting the market's best estimate of the future rate of inflation. In this case, however, the inflation will also tend to produce, to a serious extent, the distortion in allocation referred to above. If, on the other hand, nominal rates do reflect an unbiased estimate of the future rate of inflation, lessening the misallocation problem, then the actual outcome is as likely to be a redistribution in favour of the lender as in favour of the borrower.

It has also been suggested that inflation may tend to reduce the overall level of saving and capital formation by reducing the expected real return on financial assets (when nominal rates are kept artificially low) and by causing the return on all assets to become uncertain. Unfortunately the validity of these propositions is hard to assess. As is well known, a fall in the rate of interest may either increase or decrease the rate of saving depending on whether the substitution or the income effect predominates, and at least some evidence suggests that income effect may be the dominant one (cf. Modigliani and Tarantelli and the references cited therein). Similarly recent work on the theory of saving under uncertainty (e.g. Dreze and Modigliani) leads to the conclusion that, under plausible assumptions about attitude toward risk (decreasing absolute risk aversion), an increase in uncertainty results in an *increase* rather than a *decrease* in saving, though in the case of uncertainty about rates of return either outcome is consistent with rational behaviour and plausible assumptions about tastes.

In summary, in the presence of substantial uncertainty about the future rate of inflation, indexation of financial assets would seem likely on balance to do considerably more good than bad, though one cannot rule out *a priori* some minor unfavourable effect. Many economists nowadays point to the Brazilian experiment with indexation as providing empirical evidence in support of the above conclusions, at least in extreme circumstances.

II THE SPECIAL CASE FOR THE INDEXATION OF MORTGAGES

More recently some economists have pointed out that a case may be made for the indexation of mortgage contracts that is even stronger than the general case made above. (See for example Poole, Baffi.) It can be argued that inflation may distort the allocation of resources between housing and other physical assets and variable rates of inflation may contribute to the instability of construction activity – even when inflation is largely predictable and adequately reflected in nominal rates; and that these problems could be relieved by the indexation of mortgages. As a result of these considerations research is presently getting under way at MIT to investigate in depth the theoretical as well as the practical issues involved in indexation of mortgages, and to compare indexation with alternative approaches to the stabilisation of construction by way of improved financial instruments. What follows is largely based on the preliminary and still tentative analysis developed in preparation for that project.

The propositions stated above about the unfavourable effect of high and variable rates of inflation on residential construction rest on two main considerations: (1) in most of the developed countries, the prevailing vehicle for financing residential housing, notably owner-occupied dwellings or small rental units, is the traditional level-payment mortgage; (2) the financing through this instrument is provided by specialised institutions such as savings banks or, in some countries, mortgage banks (frequently also connected with savings-type institutions). Under these conditions a high rate of inflation will tend to curtail the demand for housing, while variable rates of inflation are likely to produce instability in construction both through the demand for housing and through the availability of mortgage funds, for reasons detailed below.

II.1 DEMAND EFFECTS OF THE RATE OF INFLATION

The demand effect occurs because the high nominal rates of interest which result from the addition to the 'real' rate of interest of a premium roughly equal to the expected rate of inflation has the effect of increasing the level of the annual payment relative to the rate of earnings in the early year of the mortgage contract. This point is illustrated in column (1) of Exhibit I which shows the level annual payment required on a $30,000, 30-year mortgage. Assuming a 3 per cent real rate of interest, it is seen that with zero inflation (case No. 1) the first year (as well as all subsequent) payment amounts to $1,517; with a 2 per cent rate of inflation, and hence a 5 per cent nominal rate (case No. 2), it is nearly 25 per cent higher or $1,931; for a 6 per cent rate of inflation the payment is almost twice as high, $2,895. The reason for the positive association between rate of inflation and initial payment is that, in the presence of inflation, the constant nominal payment will imply an annual payment, which in 'real' or purchasing power terms, decreases in time at the rate of inflation. Thus with a 6 per cent rate of inflation, by the year 5, the real payment is $\$2{,}895/(1{\cdot}06)^4 = 2{,}294$; by the year 12 it is 1,525, or about the same as with no inflation and, thereafter, it becomes lower, being reduced in the terminal year to a mere 524. Of course the real present value of this declining stream of real repayments is always $30,000 no matter what the rate of inflation; it is precisely in this sense that the higher nominal rate corresponding to higher rates of inflation compensates for the gradual erosion of the purchasing power of the nominal stream. But precisely because the present value of the real stream must be the same and the stream is declining in time, it must start at a higher level. The higher the rate of inflation the greater the tilting in the rate of real repayment and hence the higher the initial payments. This point is illustrated graphically in Figure 1, which compares the behaviour of the real payment at successive dates over the life of the contract. (In this figure, the assumed real rate is 4 per cent and the mortgage is for $20,000.)

But why is the real rather than the nominal rate of repayment the important magnitude? The simple answer is that under generalised inflationary conditions the income of the typical home buyer may be expected to rise in the long run at a rate at least equal to that of the price index. In the limiting case where the growth of nominial income precisely equals the rate of inflation, the behaviour of the real rate of repayment in Figure 1 is proportional to the behaviour of the ratio of the nominal payment to nominal income. Columns (3) and (4) of Exhibit 1 provide a numerical illustration. One can see from column (4) that for that illustration, in the absence of inflation carrying the house will absorb some 15 per cent of the person's income throughout the life of the contract. But with a 2 per cent inflation the annual payment for the very same house will require 19·3 per cent of his income at the beginning of the contract, and will continue to absorb more than 15 per cent for some twelve years, though in the terminal year, it will take only 10·8 per cent. With a 6 per cent inflation it will absorb at the outset nearly 30 per cent of his income, declining to 5 per cent in the terminal year.[2]

It is obvious from this example that with conventional mortgage financing a rapid rate of inflation even if fully and correctly anticipated may be expected to reduce the demand for owner-occupied housing space by raising the ratio of annual payment to income in the early years of the contract. Exhibit 2, reproduced from Tucker (1973) shows that even the relatively modest increase in the mortgage rate that occurred in the US between 1963 and 1973, as a result of the relatively modest rise in the rate of inflation, has been sufficient to cause the initial payment, computed in column D (from an index of prices of new houses, the average mortgage rate and the prevailing length of contract), to rise appreciably faster than average wage income, shown in column E.

The nature of the unfavourable effect on the demand for housing of a higher nominal rate due to inflation is quite similar to that of shortening the length of the contract. This point is brought out graphically in Figure 2 which shows that a faster rate of inflation, much as a shorter maturity, forces the borrower to repay his real debt – or equivalently to accumulate equity in his house – at a faster rate. Of course the ratio of annual payment to income eventually declines as inflation erodes the purchasing power of the payment. But this only means that inflation causes the burden of owning a house to be very unevenly distributed over time. The extent of this unevenness is even greater than implied by column (4), when it is recognised that a major group of potential home buyers is represented by young households (cf. Baffi). This group can look forward to an increase in income even in the absence of inflation, both because of the general effect of productivity growth, which tends to raise all incomes, and because typically, even in the absence of productivity growth, income tends to rise with age, at least for a while (though the specific shape of the life cycle of income will be influenced

[2] On the assumption of a steady rate of inflation, $\dot{p}$, fully incorporated in the nominal rate $R = r + \dot{p}$, where r is the 'real' rate, the effect of inflation on the annual payment (which is also the initial real payment) relative to what it would be without inflation, is given by

$$(a) \qquad \frac{r + \dot{p}}{1 - (1 + r + \dot{p})^{-T}} \quad \frac{1 - (1 + r)^{-T}}{r}$$

T being the length of the contract. If the borrower's income is growing at the rate $\dot{p}$ then the ratio of nominal payment to nominal income in the nth year of the contract is proportional to

$$(b) \qquad \frac{(r + \dot{p})}{[1 - (1 + r + \dot{p})^{-T}]\,(1 + \dot{p})^{s}}$$

To find the number of years over which the ratio of annual payment to income is above the level prevailing with no inflation, one can equate (a) to $(1 + \dot{p})^{s}$ and solve for s.

by individual factors such as education, social institutions, etc.). Column (7) exhibits the share of income absorbed by the payment under the conservative assumption that income rises but 2 per cent per year. It is seen that even in the absence of inflation a conventional mortgage already implies a rather uneven burden over life. But if the rate of inflation reaches 6 per cent the unevenness becomes rather dramatic.

It should be apparent, in fact, that if the rate of inflation becomes very high the conventional mortgage contract becomes so onerous for the potential buyer as to become practically unusable, except possibly for those who already have the means to pay in cash a substantial portion of the price. To be sure, this problem could be remedied, in perfect markets, by recourse to second mortgages or similar devices. But such facilities are seldom readily available, and are unlikely to develop in an inflationary climate. On the contrary if, as frequently happens in such periods, the rate of interest on deposit is kept artificially low, and falls short of the rate of increase in the price of houses, there may be little hope for lower income groups, having a very limited menu of assets available beyond some type of savings deposit, ever to accumulate a sufficiently high equity to use as down-payment. One of the serious consequences of this situation is that, in many countries, pressure has developed to provide relief for the home buyers through various types of government subsidies – e.g. direct contributions to the interest.

In addition to the above effect there may be unfavourable dynamic effects on construction from a *rise* in the rate of inflation if, as frequently happens, the seller of a house cannot transfer his mortgage to the buyer but instead must repay his loan. This tends to 'lock' the owner in the house he initially owns when a rise in the rate of inflation raises the mortgage rate on new contracts, and by selling his house he loses the benefit of the lower rate on the present mortgage.

II.2 SUPPLY EFFECTS

In addition to these demand effects, rapid changes in the rate of inflation have tended to have a destabilising effect on residential construction by destabilising the supply of mortgage funds – though the precise nature of this mechanism depends on the nature of the institutions providing funds to the mortgage market.

In the US and other countries, the bulk of these funds has come from specialised thrift institutions that secure funds through deposits – essentially a short-term liability – and then invest them in long-term mortgage assets. When a spurt of inflation raises money market rates these institutions find it hard to offer competitive deposit rates, because their earnings do not promptly adjust upward; in addition as the market value of their assets declines they may even approach technical insolvency. In order to limit the losses that these institutions would face if left free to raise competitively their deposit rates, as well as to hold down the overall level of long-term rates in order to minimise the negative effect of rising rates on these institutions and on potential home buyers, monetary authorities have imposed ceilings on the deposit rate that can be offered by the thrift institutions and by their close competitors, such as on time deposits at commercial banks. But ceilings have contributed to induce the public to switch their savings from traditional deposits to other types of assets (disintermediation). Thus even if the ceilings may have helped to protect the solvency of the intermediaries they have tended to dry up their inflow of funds and, hence, their ability to supply funds to the mortgage market, curtailing construction activity through supply of fund effects.

A similar mechanism has been at work even when, as in the case of Italy, mortgage funds come in part from the floating of mortgage bonds by specialised mortgage banks. This has come about because the mortgage banks have endeavoured to stabilise the price of their bonds in the face of rising long-term market rates on competing instruments, by limiting net new issues, even to the point of making negative new issues, using the repayment flows to buy back outstanding bonds. To pursue this course they have been led to ration funds at the artificially low rate they endeavoured to maintain (though the cost to the borrower has been allowed to reflect to some extent market rates through variations in the spread between the market price of mortgage bonds and the amount paid to the borrower).

II.3 THE ROLE OF INDEXATION IN ELIMINATING DEMAND AND SUPPLY EFFECTS

The institution of indexed mortgages (IM) could help considerably in eliminating both the demand and the supply effects. On the demand side, since the rate on an IM is a real rate, it should be largely independent of the rate of inflation, making the initial payment equally independent of inflation. It is true, of course, that if the anticipated inflation occurs the level of payment will rise precisely at the same rate as the price level as illustrated in column (2) of Exhibit 1. In fact in the presence of productivity – or real income-growth – the ratio of annual payment to income will still tend to decline in time as shown in column (8). However, this declining pattern is independent of the rate of inflation. Furthermore, it could be eliminated – or modified to any desirable extent – by combining indexation with another reform of the mortgage contract, namely non-level repayments. We need not be concerned here with this reform which is quite separate from indexation, but it should be pointed out that indexation can be readily combined with any appropriate contractual repayment schedule stated again in real terms, thus giving rise to a non-level repayment schedule in real terms. We may finally note that indexation should also greatly reduce, if not eliminate, the lock-in effect, since all available evidence suggests that the major source of variation in nominal rates is due to changing rates of inflation, and related changes in *expected* rates of inflation.

On the supply side, where mortgage funds come from mortgage bonds, indexed mortgages would be matched by the issue of indexed mortgage bonds. This instrument, one should expect, would be very attractive to investors, especially small investors, under conditions of high and uncertain rates of inflation as it would provide them with a hedge against inflation whether predicted or not. Hence it might, on the average, raise the flow of funds available for mortgages, especially if mortgages were the only, or main, type of indexed long-term instruments. More important, however, the indexed mortgage rate needed to equate the supply of mortgage funds with the stabilised demand for mortgage funds might be expected to be fairly stable, even in the face of wide movements in nominal rates on other instruments, in so far as these reflect changes in inflationary expectations unrelated to the real rate; there would, therefore, be little need for the mortgage banks to endeavour to stabilise the market price of indexed mortgage bonds by restricting issues and rationing funds.

Where the mortgage funds come from depository institutions, these again would now be in a position to offer indexed deposits, whose principal would be adjusted periodically to the price level, since any change in their liability due to such revaluation would be matched by similar changes in the value of their assets; and again the indexed deposit rate needed to maintain a stable inflow of deposits should remain reasonably stable despite inflation-induced variations in the nominal rates on competing financial assets. Alternatively the depository institutions could continue to offer nominal deposits but the rate they could offer on such deposits could be based on the contract (real rate on their indexed mortgages plus the rate of change of the price index: that is, the revaluation of principal could be treated as income currently available to remunerate depositors, on the ground that the mortgage could then be carried on their books at nominal value. Being able to pay such a nominal rate they might be expected to remain competive with market rates on competing short-term instruments.

When the rate of inflation is not only high but also subject to a high degree of uncertainty, the indexation of mortgages, as well as possibly of mortgage bonds and other instruments, such as deposits which are used to provide funds for indexed mortgages, would also achieve the desirable result of enabling borrowers and lenders to hedge against the risk of uncertain price fluctuations. This would be true even if indexation were limited to mortgages and mortgage market related instruments.

II.4 VARIABLE RATE MORTGAGES AS AN ALTERNATIVE TO INDEXATION

It is worthwhile noting briefly that the unfavourable effect of high (and variable) rates of inflation on the financial health of depository intermediaries and on the supply of funds might be also eliminated or reduced through another device which is also receiving considerable attention and has already been tried out to some extent (e.g. in the UK, in Canada, and to a very limited degree in the US), namely through so-called variable rate mortgages (VRM). In this version the interest rate charged to the borrower is not fixed in the contract but is allowed to float up and down being tied to some market rate, generally a short-term one. This approach clearly enables the intermediary to offer deposit rates competitive with other short-term market instruments and also disposes of the need for rate ceilings and other related disruptive devices. Furthermore, in so far as short-term rates reflect fairly accurately the actual rate of inflation over the life of the short-term instrument, VRM could also provide a reasonably good hedge against uncertainty of the price level.

However, in our view, this approach is distinctly inferior to indexed mortgages in three important respects: (1) the welfare of the borrower, (2) its effects on the level and stability of the *demand* as distinguished from the *supply* side of the market, and (3) the ability of the monetary authority to pursue an appropriate monetary policy.

The basis for propositions (1) and (2) can be most conveniently clarified by reference to Exhibit 3 which compares the annual payment required of the borrower under three alternative arrangements: conventional level mortgage (CLM) – block 1; variable rate mortgage – block 2; and indexed mortgage – block 3. The rate currently applied on the VRM is a nominal rate; hence it will be higher, the higher the rate of inflation, and so will the initial annual payment, just as in the case of CLM. Accordingly in the presence of high inflation VRM, in contrast to IM, has the same unfavourable effect on demand as CLM (see column 1 of Exhibit 3). In addition, if the rate of inflation, and hence the applicable interest rate *changes*, VRM will cause changes in the next annual payment which may be quite great and largely unrelated to the rate of inflation and hence to the changing income of the borrower. This can be seen by inspection of column (1) and (2) in the last row of the VRM block and by comparison with the corresponding figures for the IM block. If the rate of inflation rises from 3 to 5 per cent the scheduled payment under IM rises by 2 per cent above what it would have been if inflation had remained at 3 per cent, an increase commensurate with the likely effect of the higher inflation on the borrower's income. On the other hand, under VRM the scheduled payment rises from \$1,453 to \$1,798 or some 24 per cent; the reason for this much higher percentage change is that the higher inflation, by raising the nominal rate used in computing the constant payment for the rest of the contract, implies a further tilting of the real repayment schedule – a higher front-end load as it were. For similar reasons a decline in inflation produces a large percentage decline in the scheduled payment (cf. columns (3) and (4)).

Thus while the VRM approach protects the intermediary (and presumably insures a smoother supply of funds), it does so at the expense of imposing a good deal of additional real risk on the borrower, especially since short rates, as well as the short-run behaviour of $\dot{p}$, may be quite variable (see for example Kaufman). For the same reason it might do little to mitigate variability on the demand side. In contrast, IM tends to reduce the real risk to the borrower, as well as to reduce variability.

Some of these undesirable features of VRM can be eliminated by an alternative design, that has already been applied in some countries, under which the variable rate is used not to change the rate of annual payment, but rather the length of the contract, while the payment itself remains fixed. However, this alternative creates other difficulties, notably that the length of the contract can grow uncomfortably long, when the floating rate rises substantially above the one used in fixing the initial level of the annual payment; indeed the maturity will approach infinity if the rise in the rate is such that the fixed annual payment approaches the interest bill due on the remaining principal. This difficulty is intimately related to the fact that, in the presence of high rates of inflation, a level payment in nominal terms does not make much sense. Tucker (1973) and (1974), has suggested an interesting modification of the VMR which would combine it with the variable repayment scheme. His proposal relies on two basic ingredients: (1) the annual payment would be scheduled to rise in time at some constant rate which could be based initially on the rate of inflation expected at the time the contract was written: this would permit an initial rate of payment similar in size to that prevailing under IM; (2) the rate used in computing the annual payments would be revised periodically, as under VRM. But the change in rate would change neither the current payment nor the length of maturity but would instead change the rate of growth of the scheduled annual payment. Under some fairly reasonable assumptions this scheme would work in a way rather similar to indexed mortgages. But one can see little reason for preferring this roundabout 'imitation' to straightforward indexation.

Finally the IM retains one desirable feature of the traditional level mortgage under constant prices, that would be lost under any form of VRM, namely that it permits the borrower to hedge against future movements of the 'real rate', since this is fixed by contract. To have available such a hedging option would seem to be rather valuable when entering into a long-run commitment such as the acquisition of a house, considering the sizeable transaction costs associated with changing houses.

The third drawback of VRM listed above is suggested by the consideration that variations in the nominal rate affect very significantly the rate of payment of all mortgage borrowers. This feature is likely to generate a lot of pressure toward avoiding or delaying changes in nominal rates which might be desirable from a stabilisation point of view. Under IM, on the other hand, the payment rises only because of inflation and hence the pressures will be toward avoiding it, whereas changes in nominal rates as such would be of no consequence.

III THE EFFECT OF INDEXATION OF MORTGAGES ON OTHER FINANCIAL MARKETS

The considerations developed in section II suggest that considerable advantages might be anticipated from making available to borrowers an indexed mortgage instrument – possibly with non-level real repayment schedule – and to lenders indexed mortgage bonds, and/or deposits, or at least deposit rates reflecting more nearly the rate of inflation. However these conclusions were based, as it were, on a partial equilibrium analysis of the residential and mortgage markets, more or less in isolation. Before we can confidently advocate that legislation be adopted to make such an instrument available one has to give some consideration to at least two other major issues: (1) the effect of indexation on other financial markets and, (2) implications it may have on the effectiveness of traditional stabilisation policies and/or the stability of the economy as a whole. Both topics are being included in the pilot phase of the MIT project, and the best that I can do at this time is to report some preliminary thoughts on the issues and on the methodology by which the issues might be attacked.

The questions to be examined under heading (1) range all the way from whether there would, in fact, be a sufficient market for indexed mortgages and supporting instruments to warrant the costs of establishing such markets, to the issue of whether the introduction of such instruments would play havoc with the markets for conventional nominal instruments. The latter concern has been often put forward as an argument against allowing the introduction of any indexed instrument.

These issues can be partly attacked by examining the experiences of the few countries that have made use of such instruments in the postwar period. But it needs to be attacked also through the tools of economic analysis applied to financial markets, especially since the experience so far has been quite limited and for various reasons not too conclusive.

III.1 COUNTRY EXPERIENCES

A summary of experiences with indexation is provided in a recent OECD publication (1973).

The main countries which have had significant experience with these devices are Finland, Israel, and some Latin American countries, notably Brazil. In every case, indexation was applied more generally to instruments to finance housing. The most favourable experience seems that of Brazil, to which reference was made earlier. The one raising most questions is that of Finland. Exhibit 4, reproduced from the OECD publication, shows that the proportion of bond issues taking the indexed form rose rapidly to some 80 per cent from 1952 to 1956 and, thereafter, fluctuated between one-quarter and four-fifths, responding apparently positively, but with some lag to the rate of inflation in the recent past. However, the marginal rate was fairly uniformly above the average rate so that the share of the stock of bonds outstanding having indexed form rose fairly uniformly to 3/4 in 1967. In the case of deposits the trend is similar but at a lower level, reaching one-third by 1967. Unfortunately, in that year indexation was abolished, though apparently for reasons having little to do with market acceptance of the instrument as such. It appears that, following the devaluation of 1967, aimed at bringing under control the large trade deficit, it was felt necessary to abolish the indexation of wages. To secure labour consent to this step, indexation was abolished also on mortgages and other instruments. In Israel some forms of indexation (namely on foreign exchange) were abolished under circumstances somewhat reminiscent of those of Finland. This experience, which *prima facie* is not encouraging, will bear closer scrutiny. One lesson that it seems to suggest is that, at least in a small open economy subject to significant changes in terms of trade, the index used for indexation of financial instruments as well as of other contracts like wages should perhaps not be that of the basket of goods bought like a 'cost of living' index but that of the basket of goods produced, or domestic value added like the GNP deflator; in other words, it should aim to protect against redistribution of domestic income arising from wage or mark-up push, but not protect against changes in purchasing power due to changes in terms of trade. Had indexing been of this variety, it might have survived the devaluation.

III.2 SOME INFERENCES FROM ECONOMIC ANALYSIS

Several attempts have been made recently to examine the implications of the presence of indexed financial assets on the working of financial and other markets, as testified, for example, by the bibliographical references in recent studies – for example, one by the OECD cited earlier, and the essays by Scholtes. The most recent of these endeavours is represented by the just completed and still unpublished paper of Fischer which is especially valuable because of its rigour and promise for further development, and on which I will lean heavily in this section.

Fischer relies for his analysis primarily on the powerful approach developed by Merton for the study of individual saving and portfolio decisions under uncertainty and their implications for asset-market equilibrium. In this approach economic agents are assumed to make instantaneous and continuous decisions about their rate of consumption and the allocation of their wealth between the menu of assets available to them so as to maximise the expected utility of consumption over life. It is further assumed that investors' expectations about the return on assets as well as the behaviour of the price level, are identical and can be described by a continuous-time stochastic process, known as Ito process; the instantaneous stochastic distribution is essentially normal, though the resulting distribution of returns over any finite length of time is log normal. Fischer analyses a succession of models of increasing complexity, but for our present purpose it will be sufficient to concentrate on the results of his simplest model in which there is a single consumption good, and three assets: (1) a bond indexed on the consumption good with contractual non-stochastic real return r_1; (2) equity, with (instantaneous) expected return r_2, and (instantaneous) variance σ_2^2; (3) nominal bonds with contractual nominal return R_3. The price of the consumption good is also stochastic; the expected rate of inflation is π and its variance, which is also the variance of the rate of return on the nominal bond is σ_3^2. (Note that because the real rate of return on the nominal bond depends on the reciprocal of the price level, its expected real rate of return turns out to be $r_3 = R_3 - \pi + \sigma_1^2$.)

Assuming at first a deterministic labour income, Fischer derives the instantaneous demand equations for the three assets. Letting w_i denote the proportion of net wealth invested in asset i, and ρ the correlation coefficient between the real rate of return on equity and the rate of inflation, he finds

$$(1) \quad w_1 = 1 - \frac{A}{(1-\rho^2)\sigma_2\sigma_3}\left[\frac{(r_2-r_1)(\sigma_3+\rho\sigma_2)}{\sigma_2} + \frac{(r_3-r_1)(\sigma_2+\rho\sigma_3)}{\sigma_3}\right]$$

$$(2) \quad w_2 = \frac{A}{(1-\rho^2)\sigma_2}\left[\frac{r_2-r_1}{\sigma_2} + \frac{\rho(r_3-r_1)}{\sigma_3}\right]$$

$$(3) \quad w_3 = \frac{A}{(1-\rho^2)\sigma_3}\left[\frac{r_3-r_1}{\sigma_3} + \frac{\rho(r_2-r_1)}{\sigma_2}\right]$$

where A is a positive number measuring the so-called relative risk aversion. ($A = J_w/-WJ_{ww}$ where J_w is the 'derived' marginal utility of wealth, W.)

From these results he draws the conclusion that in order for the investor to choose to hold a positive quantity of indexed bonds, the contractual real rate of return on indexed bonds r_1 may have to exceed the expected real rate of return on nominal bonds (and hence *a fortiori* to exceed the nominal rate R_3 less the expected rate of change of prices). In other words, the indexed bond need not command a premium over the nominal bond; this result he finds striking and surprising since it runs contrary to the intuitive view that, with risk aversion, indexed bonds would be preferred to nominal bonds, other things being equal. A necessary condition for this counterintuitive outcome to occur is the not implausible one that the real rate of return on equity be positively correlated with the rate of inflation. Under these conditions some doubts might arise as to whether indexed bonds could, in fact, exist, or whether instead they might not be dominated by nominal bonds.

My own interpretation of his results, however, is rather different; specifically, they can be shown to imply that, at least, in a closed system without government, in which the *net* supply of both indexed and nominal bonds must be zero (i.e. the value of bonds privately held exactly offsets the liability of the private issuers) and, under the usual assumption of homogeneous expectations, indexed bonds dominate nominal bonds. That is, only indexed bonds would be issues and held, while the gross amount of nominal bonds issued and held would tend to be zero.

To establish this conclusion we merely need to note that the coefficient of the square bracket in (3) is necessarily positive under the assumption of risk aversion. Hence, if the quantity in square brackets were positive, then every transactor would have a positive net demand for nominal bonds; but since the net supply is zero, there would then be a positive excess demand for nominal bonds. By the same token, if the quantity in square brackets were negative, there would be an excess supply of these bonds. Hence the market can only clear if the relation between the rates is such that the quantity in brackets is precisely zero. But this means that at these market-clearing rates no one would either wish to lend or to borrow in the form of nominal bonds. In other words, the existence of the indexed bond would cause nominal bonds to disappear. This is clearly a rather remarkable result which, incidentally, readily generalises to the case where there is not one but many 'equities'.

One may throw some further light on this result by observing that, for the problem on hand, the demand equations derived by Fischer with Merton's approach are analogous to those obtained under the mean-variance approach of Tobin and Markowitz. It is well known that the basic result of their model is that, when there exists a sure asset, and a plurality of risky assets (in our case the equity and the nominal bond), for every wealth holder the optimum portfolio is a linear combination of the sure asset and a portfolio of risky assets; furthermore, the percentage composition of the portfolio of risky assets is the very same for all investors. In our case then, the optimum portfolio is a combination of the riskless indexed bond and of a portfolio containing the equity and the nominal bond in fixed proportions. But since the net supply of the nominal bond is zero, in market equilibrium, i.e. when the returns have been adjusted so as to clear all markets, the proportion of the nominal bond can only be zero.

With the help of Fischer's equations, we can establish just what the market clearing relation must be between r_1 and r_3. Specifically from (3) the necessary and sufficient condition for $w_3 = 0$ can be stated as

$$(4) \quad r_3 - r_1 = -\rho\frac{\sigma_3}{\sigma_1}(r_2 - r_1)$$

This equation is readily recognised as the basic equation of the Capital Asset Price Model (CAPM) of Sharp-Lintner-Mossin, since

$$-\frac{\rho\sigma_3}{\sigma_1}$$

is the regression (or β) coefficient of the return of the nominal bond on the return on equity (which, when the net supply of bonds is zero, is also the return on the market portfolio). Since $r_2 - r_1$ must be positive under risk aversion, we can conclude that

$$r_1 \gtreqless r_3 \quad \text{as } \rho \gtreqless 0$$

This result, of course, conforms to Fischer's conclusion: however, it now appears that a positive correlation between the real returns on equity and the rate of inflation is both necessary and sufficient to make the market-clearing expected real rate on the nominal bonds smaller than the return on the indexed bond.

This result can be given intuitive meaning as follows. A positive value of ρ implies a negative correlation between the return on equity and the return on nominal bonds. But then lenders holding only indexed bonds could reduce portfolio risk by substituting nominal for indexed bonds. Hence, if r_3 equalled r_1, there would be a positive demand for nominal bonds. However, by the same token, people wishing to lever their portfolio would find nominal bonds unattractive, since the negative covariance of the return on equity with the real rate to be paid on nominal bonds implies that borrowing through nominal bonds rather than indexed bonds would increase portfolio risk. Accordingly they will be willing to pay a real rate on indexed bonds sufficiently higher to induce lenders to accept these instead of nominal bonds.

At the same time, Fischer's analysis suggests that if there existed in the market some positive net supply of nominal bonds – say because they were issued by the government or were the result of earlier contracts – the presence of indexed bonds would by no means have a disruptive effect on the market for nominal bonds. On the contrary, at least if ρ were positive, nominal bonds might well command a premium over indexed bonds.[3]

[3] Allowing for a net positive supply of positive nominal bonds, say issued by the government, would mean that w_3 would have to be positive for all private investors.

It should be added that Fischer shows that once we allow for a stochastic labour income, then it will no longer be the case that indexed bonds must drive nominal bonds out of existence, unless for all participants real labour income was uncorrelated with the real rate of inflation. But especially if for some participants interested in borrowing this correlation was negative, making for them the issue of nominal bonds relatively more attractive, then the two kinds of bonds could be expected to coexist. Dropping the assumption of homogeneous expectations would also work in this direction. It is also clear from the above reasoning that the presence of stochastic labour income would, on balance, act in the direction of a positive premium for indexed bonds if the correlation between real labour income and the rate of inflation was prevailingly negative, and of a negative premium in the opposite case.

In summary Fischer's results suggest that if inflation had no real effects on the economy (or to use an expression coined by Tobin, money were not only neutral but also 'superneutral') then the expected real rate of return would tend to be similar on both indexed and nominal bonds. On the other hand the well-known debate on the Phillips curve would lead one to expect a prevailingly positive correlation between (unexpected) inflation on the one hand and real labour income and return on physical assets on the other. Unfortunately, there is at present little empirical evidence to settle the issue, at least with respect to the effect of inflation on the return on equity, though casual observation suggests that, in recent years, the correlation has tended to be negative. The analysis, however, does suggest that in the case of indexed mortgages, considering also the advantages that such an instrument would offer the borrower, one should not be too surprised if the market-clearing real rate for such instruments were to exceed the expected real rate of nominal instruments.

IV EFFECTS OF INDEXATION OF MORTGAGES ON THE STABILITY OF THE ECONOMY

The analysis so far suggests that indexation of mortgages should help to stabilise residential construction without disrupting markets for nominal instruments. This conclusion, however, was based on a 'partial' equilibrium' analysis; to understand the full implications of such a reform one needs to consider also the interaction of construction with other components of aggregate demand and, in particular, effects on the stability of the economy as a whole and on the effectiveness of stabilisation tools, especially monetary ones. There seems little question that reliance on conventional mortgages and the specific institutional arrangements controlling this supply of mortgage funds, has helped to

It appears from (4) that if ρ were zero or negative, $w_3 > 0$ would require a negative premium on nominal bonds; but with ρ sufficiently positive and the net supply of nominal bonds sufficiently small, the premium could still be positive.

make residential construction very sensitive to monetary policy; and to bear the brunt of stabilisation policies through monetary tools. In particular, it would appear that it has made possible the containment of aggregate demand with smaller fluctuations in interest rates than might have been required otherwise. This is true both because the demand presumably responded in part to variations in *nominal* rates; and because the restraint has been obtained in part by quantity rather than by price rationing. One point is worth mentioning in this connection. While the measurement of real rates is extremely difficult in the absence of indexed instruments because of the difficulty of measuring price expectations, in so far as one can rely on past rates of inflation as at best a rough indication of expected rates, at least for the US there is little evidence of large changes in the real rates in the post-war period. This might well reflect the fact that, through residential construction, aggregate demand could be influenced by nominal rates alone.

IV.1 EFFECTS OF INDEXATION OF MORTGAGES IN THE PRESENCE OF EXOGENOUS CHANGES IN AGGREGATE DEMAND

With the indexation of mortgages residential construction, like other components of demand, should tend to respond mainly to real rates, and only through its effect on demand. Thus, if real rates were to remain stable, this reform should indeed tend to stabilise residential construction. But in the presence of exogenous changes in demand some components must adjust, and this means that, unless stabilisation rested on fiscal policy, real rates would have to fluctuate. Thus some instability in construction could not be avoided. Presumably, for given fiscal policy, the fluctuations would be smaller since other components would share more in the role of accommodating the exogenous changes. However, since it seems likely that the elasticity of construction with respect to real rates would be larger than for other components, variations in construction activity might still bear a major burden. The question here is fundamentally an empirical one. Some efforts are presently being made in the course of the MIT research to shed some light by simulation with econometric models – such as the MIT-Penn-SSRC model which has a well-developed housing and mortgage sector – though the model will require modifications to allow more explicitly for the likely effect of indexation on the demand for housing. These simulations should also help to throw light on the interaction between indexation, the conduct of monetary policy, the variability of real and nominal rates, and the overall stability of the economy and thereby help to assess the desirability of indexation.

IV.2 SHOULD CONSTRUCTION BE STABILISED?

For a full assessment, however, it is not sufficient to determine the effect of indexation on stabilising construction. Since this stabilisation must be at the expense of unstabilising other components, one also needs to be concerned with the issue of the social cost of instability of various components. A case might be made that residential construction is a particularly suitable sector to absorb fluctuations, for at least two reasons. First because of the durability of housing short-run variations in construction activity have but a small effect on the stock of houses and hence on the supply of housing services, although the force of this argument is considerably weakened by the geographical immobility of houses. But the very geographical dispersion of housing also means that construction activity is widely dispersed and hence variations in this activity produce equally dispersed variations in the demand for labour. Furthermore the skills of the construction labour force may be fairly readily transferable to other uses, such as non-residential construction. Also, in developing countries, employment in construction seems frequently to constitute the gateway through which labour enters the modern sector. Hence fluctuations in employment in this industry may tend to have smaller social costs than in other segments of the modern sector since the labour force can be more readily attracted and also more readily returned to earlier activities (though the evaluation of this social cost is a complex task). These arguments, as well as others pointing partly in the opposite direction (e.g. the effect on the supply price), need to be assessed carefully to reach a balanced judgement as to the relative costs of instability.

V SUMMARY AND CONCLUSION

The major themes developed in this paper, many of them in a preliminary and tentative form, can be summarised as follows:

(1) Indexation of financial activities can perform a very useful function in the face of substantial uncertainty about the future course of the price level. In addition to the traditional argument centring on the elimination of capricious redistribution of income and wealth, we have stressed its role in maintaining well-functioning capital markets with ample opportunities for financial intermediation, portfolio diversification and resulting efficient allocation of resources.

(2) A special case can be made for the indexation of mortgages, because inflation has major effects on the demand and supply of this instrument even when perfectly predictable. It reduces the demand for mortgages and housing by increasing the ratio of annual payment to income in the early years of the contract. Also because of the special nature of the institutions involved in the provision of mortgage funds, short-run variations in interest rates, even if due entirely to variations in expected inflation, produce sharp variations in the supply of funds. Both difficulties could be eliminated

or alleviated through indexation, possibly supplemented by variable real repayment schedules.

(3) It would seem perfectly possible to limit indexation to this instrument and perhaps to some related ones, in the sense that such a reform should not produce serious disturbances or dislocation in the markets for nominal assets. Indeed our analysis suggests that it would not be at all surprising if indexed mortgages were to command a higher expected real yield than corresponding nominal instruments.

(4) While indexation looms as a useful and powerful device for stabilising residential construction, one risks to exaggerate its effect if one considers the housing market in isolation. Taking into account the economic system as a whole suggests that the very forces which tend to stabilise construction must tend to unstabilise real interest rates and other components of demand, and the greater variation in real rates may be expected to feed back on to the housing market reducing the direct stabilisation effect.

(5) In assessing the desirability of mortgage indexation and the resulting likely stabilisation in construction, one must also assess the social costs of instability in residential construction versus instability in other sectors.

(6) Many of the conclusions summarised above, especially those under (2) to (5) must be regarded, at present, as tentative. Hopefully the research which is presently getting under way at MIT will help to confirm them, reject them or modify them and provide a firmer footing for those that survive.

EXHIBIT 1 Lifetime Comparison of Index-linked and Conventional Mortgages* ($30,000 30-year mortgage)

Year	*Annual payment*		*Payment/salary*					
	Conventional Mortgage	*Index-linked Mortgage*	*0% Real salary growth* Salary	*Payment/Salary* Conv.	Indexed	*2% Real salary growth* Salary	*Payment/Salary* Conv.	Indexed
Case 1	0% Inflation			3% Real interest			3% Interest on conv. mtge	
	(1)	(2)	(3)	(4)	(5)	(6)	(7)	(8)
1	1517	1517	10,000	15·2	15·2	10,000	15·2	15·2
5	1517	1517	10,000	15·2	15·2	10,833	14·0	14·0
10	1517	1517	10,000	15·2	15·2	11,972	12·7	12·7
15	1517	1517	10,000	15·2	15·2	13,323	11·4	11·4
20	1517	1517	10,000	15·2	15·2	14,623	10·4	10·4
25	1517	1517	10,000	15·2	15·2	16,160	9·4	9·4
30	1517	1517	10,000	15·2	15·2	17,786	8·5	8·5
Case 2	2% Inflation			3% Real interest			5% Interest on conv. mtge	
1	1931	1517	10,000	19·3	15·2	10,000	19·3	15·2
5	1931	1643	10,833	17·6	15·2	11,735	16·3	14·0
10	1931	1816	11,972	16·0	15·2	14,333	13·3	12·7
15	1931	2021	13,323	14·4	15·2	17,507	10·9	11·4
20	1931	2218	14,623	13·1	15·2	21,382	8·9	10·4
25	1931	2451	16,160	11·8	15·2	26,117	7·3	9·4
30	1931	2698	17,786	10·8	15·2	31,899	6·0	8·5

Case 3	4% Inflation		3% Real interest			7% Interest on conv. mtge		
1	2393	1517	10,000	23·9	15·2	10,000	23·9	15·2
5	2393	1780	11,735	20·4	15·2	12,712	18·8	14·0
10	2393	2174	14,333	16·7	15·2	17,160	13·9	12·7
15	2393	2656	17,507	13·7	15·2	23,164	10·3	11·4
20	2393	3244	21,382	11·2	15·2	31,268	7·7	10·4
25	2393	3962	26,117	9·2	15·2	42,207	5·7	9·4
30	2393	4839	31,899	7·5	15·2	56,973	4·2	8·5
Case 4	6% Inflation		3% Real interest			9% Interest on conv. mtge		
1	2895	1517	10,000	29·0	15·2	10,000	29·0	15·2
5	2895	1928	12,712	22·8	15·2	13,771	21·0	14·0
10	2895	2603	17,160	16·9	15·2	20,544	14·1	12·7
15	2895	3514	23,184	12·5	15·2	30,648	9·4	11·4
20	2895	4743	31,268	9·3	15·2	45,721	6·3	10·4
25	2895	6403	42,207	6·9	15·2	68,208	4·2	9·4
30	2895	8643	56,973	5·1	15·2	101,754	2·8	8·5

* All calculations assume continuous compounding of interest and inflation as well as payments on a continuous basis.

EXHIBIT 2*

Year	*A* Price index of new 1-family houses sold	*B* Contract rate for mortgages on new houses	*C* Average mortgage term on new houses	*D* Index of monthly payments required for level-payment mortgage of average term on standard house	*E* Index of average wage and salary income of employed civilians
		%	yr.		
1963	90·2	5·84	25·0	98·1	91·2
1964	91·1	5·78	24·7	99·0	95·0
1965	93·2	5·74	25·2	100·0	100·0
1966	96·6	6·14	24·7	108·6	106·5
1967	100·0	6·33	25·2	113·5	111·0
1968	105·1	6·83	25·5	124·4	118·5
1969	113·6	7·66	25·5	144·9	126·0
1970	117·4	8·27	25·1	158·7	131·9
1971	123·2	7·60	26·2	155·0	138·6
1972	131·0	7·45	27·2	160·7	146·7
1973 (est.)	143·0	7·72	26·3	181·6	156·0

Sources:

Column A: U.S. Department of Commerce, 'Price Index of New One-Family Houses Sold', *Current Construction Reports* No. C27–73–2 (Nov 1973).

Columns B and C: Table 'Terms on Conventional First Mortgages', *Federal Reserve Bulletin*, various issues.

Column D: Derived from columns A, B, and C, assuming same percentage down-payment in every year.

Column E: Index of series derived by taking the sum of ('total wages and salaries' plus 'proprietors' income' minus 'military wages and salaries') and dividing by 'total employed' (excluding armed forces), from US Department of Commerce, 1971 *Business Statistics* and various issues of *Survey of Current Business*.

* From Donald Tucker, 1973.

EXHIBIT 3 Computation of Annual Mortgage Payments Illustration

	(1)	(2)	(3)	(4)
Year	1	2	3	4
Real interest rate, *r*	3%	3%	3%	3%
Rate of inflation, *q*	3%	5%	5%	4%
Nominal interest rate, *i*	6%	8%	8%	7%
Years to maturity	30	29	28	27
Conventional mortgage				
Beginning principal	20,000·00	19,747·00	19,478·82	19,194·55
plus interest (6%)	1,200·00	1,184·82	1,168·73	1,151·67
less annual payment	1,453·00	1,453·00	1,453·00	1,453·00
Ending principal	19,747·00	19,478·82	19,194·55	18,893·22
Scheduled payment (next period)*	1,453·00	1,453·00	1,453·00	1,453·00
Variable rate mortgage				
Beginning principal	20,000·00	19,747·00	19,873·76	19,665·28
plus interest (nominal rate)	1,200·00	1,579·76	1,589·90	1,376·57
less annual payment	1,453·00	1,453·00	1,798·38	1,798·38
Ending principal	19,747·00	19,873·76	19,665·28	19,243·47
Scheduled payment (next period)*	1,453·00	1,798·38	1,798·38	1,627·23
Index-linked mortgage				
Beginning principal	20,000·00	20,166·99	20,707·15	21,236·13
plus interest (3%)	600·00	605·01	621·22	637·08
less payment	1,020·40	1,050·90	1,103·48	1,158·64
Ending principal	19,579·60	19,721·10	20,224·88	20,714·57
Ending principal (adjusted for inflation)	20,166·99	20,707·15	21,236·13	21,543·16
Scheduled payment (next period)*	1,050·90	1,103·48	1,158·64	1,205·12

* Annuity required to amortise principal over remaining life of mortgage at applicable rate of interest.

EXHIBIT 4 Index-tied Financial Assets in Finland

		Bonds* so d during year			Bonds* outstanding at end of year			Deposits outstanding in all banking institutions		
			Index-tied			Index-tied			Index-tied	
Year	Cost of living index change %	Total million marks	Million marks	% of total	Total million marks	Million marks	% of total	All term deposits million marks	Deposits million marks	% of total
1952	4·0	45	6	13·3	516	6	0·1			
1953	1·8	279	46	16·5	600	51	8·5			
1954	−0·5	142	96	67·6	675	145	21·5			
1955	−3·0	94	69	73·4	724	204	28·2	3,158	3	0·1
1956	11·4	121	102	84·3	901	284	31·5	3,230	225	7·0
1957	11·4	122	101	82·8	899	348	38·7	3,390	824	24·3
1958	6·5	210	111	52·9	924	412	41·6	3,852	833	21·6
1959	1·6	190	56	29·5	999	422	42·2	4,542	281	6·2
1960	3·3	216	173	80·1	1,077	544	50·5	5,405	151	2·8
1961	1·9	220	112	50·9	1,089	589	54·1	6,270	38	0·6
1962	4·4	486	299	73·6	1,295	807	62·3	6,707	68	1·0
1963	4·8	518	125	24·1	1,611	844	52·4	7,185	281	3·9
1964	10·4	478	224	46·9	1,803	919	51·0	8,158	1,287	15·8
1965	4·9	768	472	61·5	2,073	1,163	56·1	9,199	1,670	18·2
1966	3·9	704	427	60·7	2,221	1,468	66·1	10,437	2,217	21·2
1967	5·3	276	216	78·3	2,022	1,502	74·3	11,538	3,997	34·6

* Excluding Government indemnity bonds.

Source: OECD, 1973.

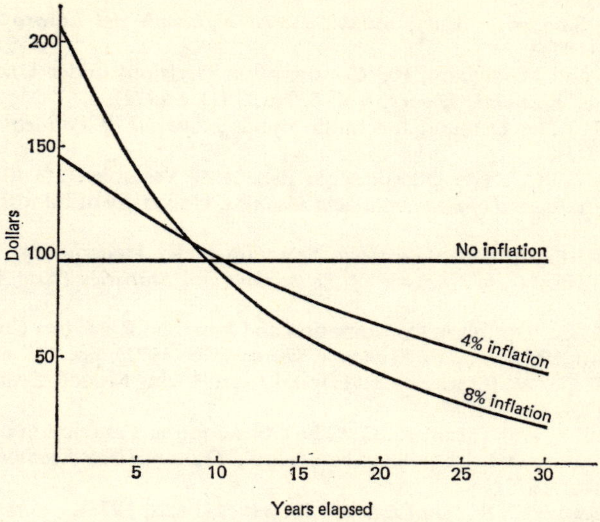

Figure 1. Real Value of Monthly Payments

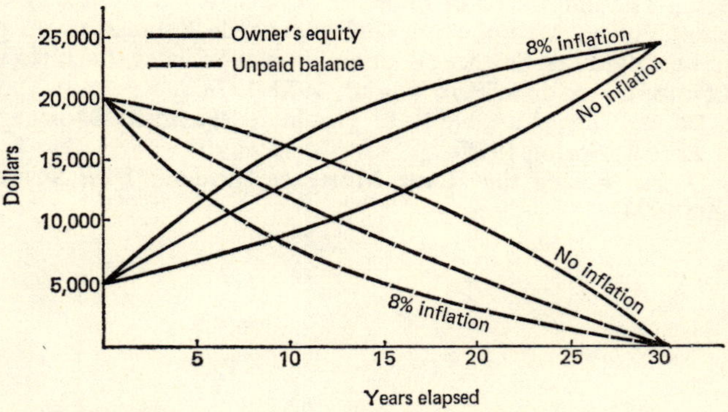

Figure 2. Real Value of Owner's Equity and Unpaid Balance

REFERENCES

Baffi, P., 'Savings in Italy, today', *Banca Nationale del Lavoro Quarterly Review* (1974).

Dreze, J., and Modigliani, F., 'Consumption Decisions under Uncertainty', *Journal of Economic Theory*, Vol. 5, No. 3 (Dec 1972).

Fischer, S., 'The Demand for Index Bonds', *Journal of Political Economy* (June 1975).

Kaufman, G. C., 'The Questionable Benefit of Variable-Rate Mortgages', *Quarterly Journal of Economics and Business*, University of Illinois (Autumn 1973).

Merton, R. C., 'Lifetime Portfolio Selection under Uncertainty: The Continuous-Time Case', *Review of Economics and Statistics* (Aug 1969), pp. 247–57.

Merton, R. C., 'Optimum Consumption and Portfolio Rules in a Continuous-Time Model', *Journal of Economic Theory* (Dec 1971), pp. 373–413.

Merton, R. C., 'An Intertemporal Capital Asset Pricing Model', *Econometrica*, (Sep 1973), pp. 867–87.

Modigliani, F. and Tarantelli, E., 'The Consumption Function in a Developing Economy and the Italian Experience', *The American Economic Review* (December 1975).

OECD, *Indexation of Fixed Interest Securities* (Paris, 1973).

Poole, W., 'Housing Finance under Inflationary Conditions' in *Ways to Moderate Fluctuations in Housing Construction*, Board of Governors, Federal Reserve System (Washington, 1972).

Poole, W., and Negri Opper, B., 'The Variable Rate Mortgage on Single Family Homes' in *Ways to Moderate Fluctuations in Housing Construction*, Board of Governors, Federal Reserve System (Washington, 1972).

Scholtes, C., The Indexation of Financial Assets: An Economic Analysis for Monetary Policy, Memoire presenté en vue de l'obtention du grade de Licencie et Maitre en Sciences Economiques et Sociales, Facultés Universitaires Notre-Dame de la Paix-Namur, 1972–1973.

Tucker, D. P., 'The Variable-Rate Graduated-Payment Mortgage', *Real Estate Review* (Spring 1975).

Tucker, D. P., 'Easing the Home Mortgage Burden', *Wall Street Journal* (12 June 1974).

Discussion of Chapter 3

Siro Lombardini

My comments will be concerned with the major theme of Professor Modigliani's paper, namely the problem of indexation and in particular the indexation of financial assets (I will be concerned with the indexation of wages and salaries only to the extent that this is necessary for the analysis of the indexation of financial assets). I will start by reviewing the reasons why indexation has been proposed. These reasons can be critically evaluated on the basis of the following considerations:

(*a*) the effects that the introduction of indexed assets would have on the financial market (and on the rate of accumulation);
(*b*) the nature of the inflationary process at work in the modern economy.

I will then show why the indexation of financial assets cannot become a permanent characteristic of a capitalist system. This conclusion will be further reinforced by reference to some specific aspects of the Italian financial market.

In the final portion of my comments I will discuss the more limited proposition of the indexation of mortgage bonds which are used to generate finance for housing construction in Italy.

1. THE AIMS OF THE INDEXATION PROPOSALS

The aims of the proposals for indexation can be summarised as follows:

(*a*) to create an asset with a constant purchasing power over time;
(*b*) to avoid the unforeseen and undesirable modifications in the distribution of income caused by variations in the price level;
(*c*) to facilitate the ability of the financial system to carry out its essential role of guaranteeing a more rational distribution of saving among various investments and to reduce the uncertainty faced by consumers in their decisions concerning the distribution of their income between present and future consumption;
(*d*) to favourise the passage from a state of affairs dominated by high rates of inflation and an inflation-oriented economic policy to conditions of relative price stability.

The first three objectives, which are in general related, revive proposals already made by Jevons and by Marshall.[1] The last objective is at the heart of Milton Friedman's analysis of the problem.

2. THE ROLE OF INDEXATION IN THE FIGHT AGAINST INFLATION

The strong inflationary pressures of recent times have regenerated interest in the proposals for indexation. In fact Friedman firmly believes that this instrument is primary to the successful fight against inflation. The following arguments essentially provide the foundation for this belief:

(*a*) A policy formulated to stop inflation will have strong social reactions as side effects. Indexation could make such a policy socially acceptable. In fact, with general indexation these undesirable side effects could be reduced to an acceptable level.

On this point Friedman observes: 'Indexation will temper some of the hardships and distortions that now follow from a drop in the rate of inflation. Employers will not be stuck with excessively high wage increases under existing union contracts, for wage increases will moderate as inflation recedes. Borrowers will not be stuck with excessively high interest costs, for the rates on outstanding loans will moderate as inflation recedes. Indexation will also partly counteract the tendency of business to defer capital investment once total spending begins to decline – there will be less reason to wait in expectation of lower prices and lower interest rates. Business will be able to borrow funds or enter into construction contracts knowing that interest rates and contract prices will be adjusted later in accord with indexes of prices.'

(*b*) The introduction of indexed assets increases saving and could thus limit inflationary tendencies.

(*c*) Savers who wish to protect themselves from inflation do not need to resort to the purchase of real assets, e.g. houses. Thus the demand for real goods will be dampened. This contributes to a reduction of inflationary pressure.

(*d*) The repayment obligations that the Government has undertaken through the issue of indexed assets encourages anti-inflationary government policy.

To judge the validity of these statements it is necessary to visualise the possible effects that the introduction of indexed assets would have on the financial market and to recall some of the peculiarities of the current inflationary process.

[1] W. S. Jevons, *Money and the Mechanism of Exchange* (1875) and A. Marshall, 'Reply to the Royal Commission on the Depression of Trade and Industry' (1866), and 'Remedies for Fluctuations on General Prices'. Both quotations can be found in M. Friedman, *Monetary Correction, A Proposal for Escalation Clauses to Reduce the Cost of Ending Inflation* (Institute of Economic Affairs, 1974).

A large literature concerned with the effects of the introduction of indexed assets now exists. Modigliani has cogently surveyed the results of a particularly sophisticated research which, in its formal development, is undoubtedly of great interest. However, to judge its limits and to indicate the ways that the analysis might be extended it is useful to make some methodological considerations. We will then be better prepared to judge the possibility of achieving the objectives attributed to indexation and to assess their desirability.

3. SOME METHODOLOGICAL CONSIDERATIONS

The analysis of the consequences of the introduction of indexed assets that Franco Modigliani has referred to is derived from the basis of an equilibrium model. It is my belief that equilibrium models are particularly inappropriate to the analysis of monetary phenomena. Money, by its very nature, is a source of disequilibrium, and at the same time the instrument used to remedy pathologic disequilibria.[2] In fact, equilibrium in the goods market corresponds to an objective need which seems obvious: that the use of the various goods should be limited to the quantities available, whether by production or imports, is a necessity that is found in all socioeconomic systems. On the other hand the equilibrium conditions for financial markets are by no means clear since a fundamental characteristic of money is its zero cost of production. Wicksell's attempt to define equilibrium in the money and financial markets as a part of a general equilibrium analysis by means of the notion of the natural rate of interest has been justly criticised, even within the Swedish School (cf. Myrdal[3]).

In a capitalist system, as will be explained more fully below, money cannot be neutral. It is sufficient to consider the influence of monetary phenomena on accumulation to be able to exclude as impossible any definition of an equilibrium rate of interest (as Wicksell's natural rate was meant to be) based on initial conditions (the quantity of resources, consumer preferences and technology) and resulting from market equilibria. The theories of Schumpeter and Keynes support this position by spotlighting the function that money, and only money, can have as a transmission mechanism between expectations and the realisation of technical and organisational innovations. The type of analysis relied upon for the treatment of the effects of the introduction of asset indexation essentially leaves these particular functions of money out of account in as much as it assumes that: (1) it is nearly the sole implied function of the financial market to guarantee an efficient distribution of savings (the level of which would vary with variations in the rate of interest) among the various demands for investment funds forthcoming

[2] E. Lundberg, *Studies in the Theory of Economic Expansion* (New York, 1955).
[3] Gunnar Myrdal, *Monetary Equilibrium* (London, 1939).

at a given point in time; (2) it would be desirable to avoid all income distribution effects that result from the working of financial markets.

The acceptance of these two premises would justify the use of an equilibrium model. They are not however very satisfying premises. The assurance of the optimal distribution of resources is not the only function of the financial market. It also has the function of assuring an accumulation adequate to the needs and potentialities of growth in the economy. It is interesting to note that this function of financial markets has been given – in certain countries – considerable importance for the 'take-off' phases of an industrial system. This function has recently taken on major importance in present-day economies where the tendency towards falling profit rates has obliged firms, to an increasing degree, to rely on the financial market for investment funds, and obliged the banking system to operate in a manner that guarantees an adequate availability of finance for investment through operations that are similar to forms of primitive accumulation. It is useful for our purpose to recall, even if briefly, these diverse functions of financial markets and to recall that they are related to some structural characteristics of the system which explain the range of possible actions and reactions occurring in the market. These characteristics allow us to outline the most probable among the various possible effects that might result from the introduction of asset indexation.

From Marshall to Friedman the major recognised advantage used to justify the introduction of indexation is the creation of a financial asset with constant purchasing power. This reasoning is open to serious criticism. The development of methodological considerations helps us to clarify the problem and open the way to a more realistic analysis of the advantages and disadvantages of asset indexation.

4. THE FUNCTIONS OF THE FINANCIAL MARKET

There is no doubt that the financial market has the function of selecting the most efficient of the diverse investment programmes in order to assure the greatest rate of growth for any given level of accumulation. This function cannot be adequately understood if one remains within the context of a one-period equilibrium model. Better suited to this task is the Schumpeterian theory which relates the process of distribution of resources amongst the various productive activities to the initiatives of innovating entrepreneurs thereby assuring the maximum technical progress. The financial market can develop its functions of selecting investment programmes more efficiently under certain conditions suggested by Schumpeter, e.g. the market should be independent of both entrepreneurs and politicians.[4] A condition which is

[4] J. A. Schumpeter, *Business Cycles*, abridged by R. Fels (New York, 1964) p. 92.

in fact seldom realised. In the past the dependence of banks on entrepreneurs has caused concern, but recently the influence that can be, and is, exercised by politicians on the banking system is of even greater concern.

The other function of the financial market, the support of an adequate level of accumulation, is also of notable importance. It is not without significance that Fisher, one of the most convinced supporters of indexation, was largely responsible for the theory in which optimal saving depends on the informed choice of savers being made compatible with the choice of the entrepreneurs, who invest the savings, through variations in the rate of interest. Changes in the level of accumulation are brought about mainly (but not solely) by operating on the rate of interest through appropriate monetary and financial policy. Let us recall that these variations in the rate of interest – as the neo-Keynesians have demonstrated (Kaldor in particular[5]) – act on the level of saving more through changes in the distribution of income between classes (capitalists and workers) with differing propensities to consume, than through the individual's adjustment of his distribution of present versus future income. Monetary processes, however, can also influence accumulation through disequilibrium adjustments, the effects of which cannot easily be visualised through equilibrium-comparative dynamic analysis. Variations in the price of assets may impose losses on some groups who are thus constrained to increase their propensity to save for the reasons set out in Modigliani's analysis of savings behaviour.[6]

The second important function of the financial market is systematically underestimated by methods of analysis that employ the models of equilibrium theory. To the extent that variations in the level of accumulation are seen to be desirable it is not possible to maintain the second assumption – given in the preceding section – implied in the method of analysis that has been suggested as appropriate to the discussion of the introduction of indexed assets.

5. IS AN ASSET WITH CONSTANT PURCHASING POWER POSSIBLE?

It is argued that the existence of indexed assets would allow savers to maintain the purchasing power of their savings constant in an economy where price stability is impossible. But even this proposition is not as straightforward as it might seem at first sight. The sufficient condition for a monetary measure whose value remains constant over time would be that the system grows at a constant rate (semi-stationary equilibrium). Under such conditions any good could serve as money (the

[5] N. Kaldor, 'Alternative Theories of Distribution', *Review of Economic Studies*, XXIII (1956) pp. 83–100.

[6] F. Modigliani and R. Brumberg, 'Utility Analysis and the Consumption Function', in *Post-Keynesian Economics*, ed. K. Kurihara (London, 1955).

Walrasian *numéraire*). Let us now suppose that with the existence of a suitable system of indexation (supposing for the sake of argument that it could exist) the same result could be achieved in a system that did not grow at a constant rate. Let us also suppose that the problems of a proper index number scheme and the appropriate period of adjustment have been resolved. Changes in the general price level will thus have no effect on real quantities. Therefore, the postulate of homogeneity holds.

Let us recall that this postulate implies:

(*a*) that any general price level is compatible with the process of growth implied by the real structure of the system (indeed, in a semi-stationary equilibrium only relative prices are uniquely determined);
(*b*) changes in the quantity of money can have no effect in the elimination of any potential disequilibrium in the financial market.

Money would thus cease to be an instrument capable of setting the system in equilibrium if it were to stray from its equilibrium growth path. This, of course, is the normal situation for a system which does not grow at a constant rate and in which it is consequently highly improbable that all expectations could be realised. The mechanisms of stabilisation would be sharply reduced and would perhaps not operate at all. Fortunately this possibility is not realistic and in fact when one takes a concrete system into consideration, in which the relative as well as the absolute level of prices changes, it is not possible to find a good or an asset whose value can be made constant. In the first place because it is impossible to find a unique solution to the problem of the price index, for it depends on the sign of the change and on the representative individual whose real income can be measured by means of the basket chosen (is there any?). And even if one could overcome the complications of the required aggregation process it is unthinkable that the indexation of bonds could produce the constant purchasing power asset that is necessary to reduce the risks involved in the investment of monetary savings. Indeed it would only be possible if two conditions were met: (1) the real rate of interest, which should correspond to the rate on indexed assets, is constant; (2) the money rate of interest – the rate on non-indexed bonds – is just equal to the real rate plus the anticipated rate of change in prices for the stipulated period.

In fact it is only with reference to a semi-stationary system – both in relative values and average expectations as assumed by Kahn[7] – that one could rigorously satisfy these conditions. It is therefore more accurate to state that indexed bonds will diminish only some risks of changes in the value of capital.

[7] R. F. Kahn, 'Exercises in the Analysis of Growth', in *Selected Essays on Employment and Growth* (Cambridge, 1972).

6. THE PHASES TO BE FOLLOWED IN AN ANALYSIS OF THE EFFECTS OF THE INTRODUCTION OF INDEXED BONDS

After these necessary methodological clarifications we can indicate the general lines to be developed in the analysis of the effects that the appearance of indexed assets could have on the financial market. Having done this we will investigate some of the results derived from Fischer's analysis and utilised by Modigliani. This rigorous analysis of comparative dynamics is carried out in an equilibrium model based on rather restrictive assumptions (the assumptions of uniform expectations and symmetry in the market behaviour of suppliers and demanders of funds are particularly heroic). Our analysis will be developed in three steps.

(1) In the first part it is assumed that past history has no effect on the present, i.e. that a kind of retroactive adjustment in past time is possible (recontracting).

(2) In the second, the effects which depend on past history are examined. It is necessary in this context to distinguish two cases:

(*a*) the first which holds when the past and present variations in prices are within a sufficiently limited range to allow the rates of interest to reflect the expectations of future changes without substantial distortion;

(*b*) the second – closer to present conditions – which holds when there are large jumps in the rate of price increase in excess of the maximum level that is considered plausible given the experience of the recent past.

(3) In the third phase the analysis is enlarged to take into account the repercussions that the disappointment of expectations might have on the system.

7. THE REACTION OF THE FINANCIAL MARKET TO THE INTRODUCTION OF INDEXED BONDS ON THE ASSUMPTION THAT PAST HISTORY HAS NO EFFECT

What relations are established between indexed and non-indexed bonds and what is the effect of the introduction of indexed bonds on the rate of interest? Assuming uniformity of expectations and the nominal rate of interest in excess of the real rate by the expected rate of change in prices, the preference for indexed bonds is based solely on risk-aversion in the sense specified by Friedman and Savage.[8] Things become more complicated when savers and investors act to maximise utility and

[8] M. Friedman and L. J. Savage, 'The Utility Analysis of Choices Involving Risk', *Journal of Political Economy*, LVI (Aug 1948).

profit over time and there is a defined relation between the changes in prices which take place in succeeding periods. If corporate shares are now introduced, in addition to indexed and non-indexed bonds, and their rate of return is assumed to be positively correlated to the rate of inflation then, as the analysis of Fischer and Modigliani shows, it is possible that the real rate of interest on indexed bonds will exceed that obtained on non-indexed bonds. Thus the existence of indexed bonds, through variations in the real rate of interest, can affect the volume of investment with potentially important feedbacks.

As Modigliani points out, Fischer's analysis takes as a starting point the postulates that allow the proof of an important result in the analysis of portfolio selection developed by Markowitz and Tobin: the optimal portfolio is a combination of a non-risky asset (in this case, indexed bonds) and a combination (similar for all investors) of the various risky assets (in this case non-indexed bonds and shares). Non-indexed bonds enter this combination with a non-zero weight only when the correlation between the rate of return on shares and the rate of inflation is negative – which seems to correspond to recent experience – and when the real income of labour is negatively correlated with the rate of inflation. Only under conditions where inflation has no effect on the economy will the expected real rate of interest for indexed and non-indexed assets be equal.

Fischer's model then gives a large range of possibilities despite the highly simplifying assumptions that are necessary for the validity of the results.

It can be demonstrated that the aggregation of risky assets in a single composite asset of constant composition (which brings to mind certain properties of a golden-age growth process and which is the principal result of the Markowitz-Tobin analysis) is much less certain if systematic differences in the expectations of different agents exist, and if the assumptions of perfect flexibility and independence on past changes of current decisions (to take account, for example, of money illusion) are dropped.

If we want to take more realistic assumptions as our starting point for the analysis of the effects of the introduction of indexed assets, we have to give up sophisticated analyses such as Fischer's and return to more simplified and essentially static one-period equilibrium models in which one assumes that individuals choose among the different types of assets on the assumption that the present conditions can be extrapolated into the future. We could thus examine the consequences of abandoning the assumption – in truth too heroic – that expectations are homogeneous. Given the supply of indexed bonds, and supposing an adjustable supply of non-indexed bonds, the difference in their rates of return reflects the inflationary expectations of the marginal buyer.

The relation established between the two rates of interest is more complicated if indexed bonds are introduced into a market in which savers have, in the past, invested their savings only in bonds and shares. We shall come back to this complication below. Here we will be concerned only with what determines the supply of indexed bonds. They could be supplied either by firms or by the government. The government could have an interest in issuing indexed bonds if it expects the rate of increase in prices to be smaller than that expected by savers, provided that the government is capable and willing to make the required financial calculations. This argument has been reversed by Friedman. The indexation of bonds having been established, the government will be led to act to reduce the rate of inflation. In fact, such a reversal is unacceptable because the government is not able, in the current economic and social system, to control the inflationary process. We shall have to return to this fundamental proposition.

Let us now consider the supply of indexed bonds by firms. For simplicity we assume that the volume of investment has been decided and that the choice of the method of finance is the only problem. Let us also suppose, to start with, that inflationary expectations are uniform (an assumption which is, as already stated, heroic). Thus a preference for indexed bonds would be justified only if firms are highly risk averse, and especially if the probability distribution of the rates of inflation (of which the expected rate is the mean or the mode) is skewed rightwards. On the other hand if firms like to gamble, non-indexed bonds are preferred.

We now pass to the more realistic case of differing expectations. Firms that expect a rate of inflation higher than that reflected in the difference between the rates of interest on non-indexed bonds and indexed bonds, see an advantage in issuing non-indexed bonds. Only firms with weaker expectations of inflation would find an advantage in raising funds by the issue of indexed bonds. It would seem reasonable to assume, in general, that firms (at least dynamic ones) are risk-takers. It also seems realistic to assume that the expectations of entrepreneurs are normally more inflation-oriented than the expectations of savers, or at least the greatest proportion of them. In these conditions if firms only supply indexed bonds their rate of return will tend to be depressed, especially if the risk aversion of savers is strong; while the return on other bonds will probably be increased.

In fact, under the assumption of diverse expectations, it is difficult to give a precise quantitative meaning to this proposition in as much as one faces different probability distributions of the expected rates of price changes, for we know that the aggregation of different expected values is a doubtful operation even on the ground of pure logic.

If we now introduce the government, which could be favourably disposed to the issue of indexed bonds for reasons we will outline in a moment, then private savings tend to move on a larger scale to the government. The adjustment of the prices of the various assets brings about an increase in the rates the firms use to decide their investment plans. The consequence would be a reallocation of resources from the private to the public sector, a reallocation that would be desirable only in special cases.

8. THE EFFECTS OF INDEXED BONDS ON THE LEVEL AND STRUCTURE OF SAVING AND INVESTMENT

When inflationary expectations are diverse and uncertain it is difficult to distinguish money interest from real interest, as will be more fully explained below. Some people however insist that it is possible, none the less, to affirm that the indexation of assets has positive effects on the level of savings. They argue that the introduction of indexed assets reduces the risk of variation in the purchasing powers of accumulated savings (but does not, in fact, eliminate these variations as was pointed out above) and thus produces a larger volume of saving. This assumes that indexation, by reducing the undesired risks, is equivalent *ceteris paribus* to an increase in the interest offered to savers (the net rate of interest is in fact considered equivalent to the gross rate of interest less a percentage that reflects risk). But even admitting this possibility it is not possible to affirm absolutely that saving will increase for it is not absolutely certain that an increase in the rate of interest would bring about an increase in saving. If in fact savers save in order to attain a given amount of purchasing power in the future, it is possible that the existence of indexed assets, by eliminating risk as explained above, could produce the opposite effect and reduce saving.

It is said that the presence of indexed assets together with other assets acts to improve the efficiency of the distribution of savings to the extent that it impedes firms with higher expectations of price increases from being led to excessive increases in investment, while on the contrary the rate of interest appears to be excessively high to firms with more moderate expectations of inflation. In a static analysis this proposition seems reasonable. The contribution of indexation to a more efficient utilisation of savings seems more doubtful when the growth process is taken into consideration. A Schumpeterian view of the problem would involve the hypothesis that the more inflationary-minded firms are also the most innovative, while stagnating firms are more easily led to believe that prices will remain sufficiently stable. If this is true, the introduction of indexed assets – if obligatory for the firms or if adopted by them because of the difficulty of issuing non-indexed assets – can have a negative influence on the rate of productivity growth in as much as the effects of indexation penalise the most dynamic firms.

9. THE INFLUENCE OF PAST HISTORY AND ITS INFLUENCE ON EXPECTATIONS AND ADJUSTMENT

We continue the analysis of the effects that the introduction of indexed assets can have by considering the repercussions that depend on past history. Here it is necessary to distinguish the two separate cases indicated in section 6. A preliminary consideration of the behaviour of the agents in the financial market under conditions of uncertainty is also required.

9.1 SOME REMARKS ON THE 'MODUS OPERANDI' OF THE FINANCIAL MARKET

No agent in the financial market takes his decisions on the basis of complete information on all possible alternative combinations of events, each conceived distinctly and assigned a given probability. Each combination of alternative events taken separately is never complete, and this has a residual uncertainty attached to it.[9] As a result of this residual uncertainty an agent may undertake actions that would not normally be justified. An individual might thus hold liquid funds even at a negative rate of return. Residual uncertainty will also differ for different agents and can thus, in part, explain differences in their financial market behaviour. Agents then differ not only by their different utility functions but also by their different expectations. This is an essential characteristic of the financial market that is linked to other essential features of the capitalist system. The difference between rentiers, speculators and active capitalists is in fact of particular importance in understanding the formation of the diversity of expectations. The expectations of rentiers are characterised, in general, by a large degree of inertia and are thus subject to sharp, but discontinuous change. When the inflationary process achieves a certain continuity and intensity, the rentiers react sharply and then, by the same inertia which had maintained their previous faith, e.g. in fixed income assets, they tend to extrapolate the tendency towards acceleration currently under way into a time frame much longer than objective conditions might justify. The speculator must thus manoeuvre between two lines of action. The first is to exploit the inertia of the rentiers (thereby accentuating and prolonging a tendency towards a rise or a fall in prices), the second, to anticipate a change in the tendency.

Active entrepreneurs (firms) are generally characterised, as Knight has sharply observed,[10] by a greater willingness to optimism and this – above all in the present system – leads them, in general, to look on the process of inflation with favour for the following reasons.

[9] S. Lombardini, 'L'Incertezza nella Teoria Economica' in *Studi in memoria di G. Borgatta*, 2 vols (Bologna, 1953) p. 39; J. E. Meade, *The Theory of Indicative Planning* (Manchester, 1970) pp. 39–42, 70.

[10] F. H. Knight, *Risk, Uncertainty and Profit*, Ch. IX (Boston, New York, 1921).

(1) Because it favours, at least within certain limits, the growth, or at least helps to limit the reduction, of demand.

(2) Because it eases the problem of finance. To the extent inflation is unanticipated (or in general to the extent that the actual rate of inflation exceeds the expected rate which is reflected in the money rate of interest) it favours the existing firms to a greater or lesser extent in relation to the greater or lesser proportion that their investment is financed by borrowing in the bond market. Innovating firms can however find the justification, and the possibility, to enter the market, above all if they foresee that the rate of inflation will continue in the future at a rate higher than predicted by the market.

(3) Because it eases – within certain limits – relations with the unions. This may seem paradoxical but it is not. Even if the stabilisation of the value of money succeeds it is probable that union pressure will remain strong and in any case continue to try to bring about changes in the distribution of income in favour of the workers. In many situations these distributive changes can be made compatible with the rate of growth necessary for the attainment of the objectives of development only if the insufficient contribution from profits to accumulation is compensated by a larger contribution from tax receipts (and by using stimuli – foreseen or facilitated by efficient planning – capable of substituting for the weakened stimulus of profit). But just because the possibility of ultimately increasing the fiscal yield to the required degree is, even in countries like the USA, rather limited, the only remedy for the excessive increases in wages that harm the necessary accumulation lies in the inflationary process. It is precisely in the expectation of a resumption of inflationary pressures that entrepreneurs are led to an easier acceptance of union demands which, on the contrary, are in general more confident about the possibilities of the adoption of anti-inflationary policies.

(4) Because it reduces the real value of debt.

The substantially favourable attitude of entrepreneurs towards inflation is then not without influence on the dynamic of their expectations. The exploitation that the entrepreneurs can inflict in this way on the rentiers can be explained by the substantial divergence in the expectations of the two groups.

9.2 SOME EFFECTS OF PAST HISTORY AND CHANGES IN EXPECTATIONS

We are now ready to examine some effects of the introduction of indexed bonds. Under normal conditions the introduction of indexation can constitute an alarm bell which influences expectations. Savers, realising the greater danger of inflation, are led to substitute indexed bonds for normal bonds. The money rate of interest on these assets then undergoes a drastic increase reflecting the new expectations of a more intense inflationary process. In general, however, indexation is proposed when inflation is already proceeding at a sustained rate. We then see savers deserting the financial markets, searching safety in investment abroad or in real goods. The effective monetary rate on bonds then does not reflect the real rate adjusted by inflationary expectations, since the market for bonds is in effect paralysed. This is what has happened in Italy where the new issues of bonds, though supplied in limited volume, are now mainly absorbed by the banking system which is certainly not interested in a rise in effective rates, for this could reduce the value of the bonds held in bank portfolios. The effective rate on bonds, which is relatively low, then has to compete with the high rates that the banks, to procure liquidity in a period of overall credit restriction, have to offer on deposits to attract the flow of private savings. At the same time the central bank requires the banks to employ a percentage of these deposits (or of the increment in them) in the purchase of bonds. This process enormously increases the long-term risks associated with the liquidity structure of bank assets. These risks, however, are common to all the banks, and for this reason the banks believe they can ultimately transfer them, if necessary, to the central bank or public institutions.

What would happen if indexation were adopted in these conditions? There are two possible cases. In the first, indexation is undertaken within the framework of a policy that, given the power that the state can exercise on the unions in certain political conditions, is widely believed to be capable of the control and drastic moderation of the rate of inflation. This is the case represented by the experience of Brazil. In these conditions indexation can have the success that Friedman expects, at least for a period of time until it is necessary to abandon it, either because of the necessity of an increased exploitation of rentiers, or because of the impossibility of keeping the rise in wages within the desired limits (two situations that can be seen to be interconnected), or finally as a result of developments in the international situation. In the second case – where there is no overall and credible policy for the control of inflation – the introduction of indexation could have diametrically opposite effects. Indexation then offers to savers the possibility of safeguarding their accumulated savings. This possibility could lead many savers to sell their holdings of bonds. The price of bonds would thus fall sharply and inevitably result in a sharp rise in the rate of interest which might exceed the rate of interest established for indexed bonds by an amount substantially greater than that justified by the rate of inflation that was previously expected by the marginal investor and *a fortiori* by the average expected rate of inflation. The introduction of indexed bonds can have another affect on the attitudes of savers and other agents. It could create a larger number of people with no particular interest in the control of inflation. The social pressure for economic and social developments which bring strong inflationary pressures – already strong for reasons to be given below – could be reinforced with particularly serious consequences for international relations. Indexation that is carried out in only a few countries can make the maintenance of equilibrium in the international markets even more difficult.

10. NOMINAL INTEREST AND REAL INTEREST

The coexistence of indexed and non-indexed bonds brings up the difficult problem of the relation that should be established between the money rate of interest (interest paid on non-indexed bonds) and the real rate received by the owners of indexed bonds. It seems, at first sight, that the problem does not exist for it could be argued that it should be left to the market to establish the difference between the two rates in relation to marginal inflationary expectations. In fact, the determination of the two rates depends not only on the available savings and the number and size of investment projects seeking finance, but also on the supply of indexed bonds that the government decides to make available as well as on the stance of monetary policy.[11] The government has, essentially, two types of decisions to make: the first concerns the excess of public expenditures over tax receipts, the second, the form of the finance for the public sector deficit. The first type of decision can be taken in relation to overall economic criteria, at least to the extent that public expenditure policy is part of a stabilisation policy. Most often, however, the decisions on the level of public expenditure are primarily influenced by political factors. It could be maintained that the second type of decision, concerning the method of financing the deficit, is strictly related to economic criteria. But even this may not be true when it is recognised that the decisions of the government can be influenced in a substantial degree by the behaviour of the central bank. If the central bank, through a policy of credit restriction, creates difficulty for the government in financing the deficit, this could be overcome by the issue of indexed bonds, which the firms may not be willing to issue. The government could thus absorb a greater amount of private saving than would otherwise have been possible. The issue of indexed bonds could then confirm, in the eyes of the savers, the government's willingness to continue a policy of public expenditure expansion. Since this expansionary fiscal policy is associated with the restrictive credit policy of the central bank, the prospective of future events becomes somewhat uncertain. Depending on whether the central bank's monetary policy or the government fiscal policy appears more credible, inflationary expectations will be dampened or reinforced with concomitant effects on the distribution of savings between indexed and non-indexed bonds. It might be thought that the government is expressing its valuation of the

[11] These three variables are related to each other. The effects of an issue of indexed government bonds can be analysed only by a cybernetic model.

expected inflation through the issue of indexed bonds. And in fact this valuation should be reflected in the level of the effective rate they offer on indexed bonds relative to the effective rate that is being obtained on savings placed in non-indexed bonds. At the same time, at least in those countries with a system of national planning, the government is required to make known its expectations concerning the rate of inflation within its official estimates of the predicted values of the various macroeconomic variables. Thus the consistence of the economic plan shown by the balancing of the estimated national accounts provides a unique indication of the inflationary expectations that have government approval. This official evaluation can differ quite substantially from the evaluations that may be generated by the conditions in which indexed bonds are issued. The net result is an increase in uncertainty for those who have to operate in the financial market. In this respect we should mention the difficulty faced by the government in formulating the official forecasts of the rate of inflation. Realistic evaluations that might be more pessimistic than those generally held by the public can themselves modify current expectations. This is one reason why official forecasts of the rate of inflation almost always turn out to be underestimations *ex post*. In these conditions of uncertainty and differing risk preferences it is rather difficult to attribute the difference between the rates on indexed and non-indexed bonds to the inflationary expectations of the marginal investor.

11. INDEXATION OF WAGES

We now take the indexation of wages into account. This can have the effects suggested by Friedman if the rate of growth of productivity is particularly high and is substantially higher than the rate of increase of the general price level. In such conditions there is, in fact, room for union action which, looking for further increases in wages, succeeds in gaining a redistribution, in favour of the workers, of the increment in value added resulting from the higher productivity. Such a redistribution may also be in the interest of firms – as will be explained more fully below – if it is necessary to support an adequate growth in the demand for final goods. If, however, the rate of increase in wages as a result of indexation (corresponding to the rate of inflation) is higher than the rate of productivity growth there can be an intensification of the inflationary process, in as much as unions cannot give up their autonomous efforts to obtain higher wages. The firms may find it in their interest to accede to the union claims if they are able to pass on the higher cost of labour, at least in part, in higher prices, thus deceiving the workers' expectations.

Even if the rate of productivity growth is greater, but only just greater, than the rate of price rises there can still be an intensification of inflationary pressures when sufficiently strong unions are determined to gain wage rises in excess of those automatically conceded by the operation of indexation.

In addition, the large differences in the rates of productivity growth in different sectors may cause further inflationary pressures under a policy of wage indexation. Increases in wages more easily conceded in sectors of high productivity growth can easily spread to lower productivity sectors where profit margins can only be maintained by further price rises which, through the mechanism of indexation, will produce additional increases in wages.

12. THE NEW INFLATION

The inadequacy of the indexation proposals as an instrument in the fight to control inflation seems even more evident when one considers the particular nature of the inflationary process at work in the modern economy. The causes of this process have been generally located in external factors (the special role played by the dollar in the international monetary system which gives monetary policy in the USA a large degree of freedom and allows the USA to maintain a deficit on the balance of payments; the petroleum crisis) or in the behaviour of the unions. In fact, a more profound analysis should take into consideration certain interactions between economic phenomena and other phenomena usually classed as socio-political, emphasising that neither monetary and fiscal policy nor the strategy of the unions are the result of errors or malicious intentions, but may instead be explained in objective terms by reference to the current process of growth. There are, in fact, two types of explanation linked to each other. The first is associated with the different influences of wages in the growth process (in consumer capitalism it is no longer possible to maintain that the rate of growth is higher when wages are lower) and the different mechanisms at work which bring about an expansion of public expenditure. In the second type of explanation come considerations of the reasons why certain mechanisms (homeostatic) which in the past have kept the movement of wages at a level compatible with the growth of the system, no longer seem to operate with sufficient efficiency. The possibility for growth in a consumer-oriented capitalistic system depends not only on the possibility of accumulation, but also on the purchasing power allocated to the consumption of new durable goods which the commercial and promotional activities of firms render desirable. The necessity of accumulation puts a limit on the increase in wages, the necessity of sales requires that the purchasing power of workers increases at certain rates.

An increase in public expenditure may be necessary to reconcile these two requirements. The resulting inflationary process can reconcile the accumulation requirement, which must be undertaken by the system as a whole, with the required expansion of labour income, which is demanded by the unions and recognised especially by those firms most involved in the production of consumer durables. The process of inflation thus transfers that part of the cost of accumulation that cannot be financed by declining profits[12] on to other social classes (to some strata of the middle-class and agricultural workers).

The expansion of public expenditure then responds mainly to the requirement – discernible at the macroeconomic level – of making the growth of real consumption and investment consistent with the attainment of a full-employment level of output. Such a necessity can be considered Keynesian even if in certain situations this macroeconomic compatibility requires variations in the distribution of income rather than changes in the level of employment (the redistribution of income produced by inflation may in fact be necessary to make the rate of increase of final demand consistent with the rate of accumulation). The observed growth of public expenditure is not explained however, solely by reference to this Keynesian requirement. The expansion of government activity has in many cases been necessary to the creation of some of the underpinnings of the growth of consumer capitalism (motorway construction) and to maintain, through an adequate growth of public demand for certain goods, the rate of growth of certain sectors (engineering industry for example) at a sufficient level to preserve the existing structure of power in the market (economic power). The workers are also interested in the increase in public expenditure for structural as well as anti-cyclical reasons, e.g. to increase the level of social consumption. The principle of deficit spending, justified when the expansion of public expenditure is considered within a stabilisation framework, cannot be invoked to resolve the problem of financing expenditure programmes that for structural reasons are in continuous expansion, not only in absolute terms but also relative to GNP. This brings up the problem of the increasing proportion of income that has to be taken by taxation and is thus removed from the realm of private decision-making. This problem has been solved relatively easily in countries where, for a combination of reasons (among them the lesser virulence of certain socio-economic characteristics associated with the maintenance of consumer capitalism), it has been possible to bring about a more equitable distribution of income (e.g. the Scandinavian countries). In other countries it has not been possible to increase sufficiently the tax yields. The only recourse left to the government for the resolution of this structural problem has been deficit spending. Then the government found itself in a position to take advantage in inflation and encourage, with activities that Friedman justly considers morally reprehensible, the divergence of expectations that, as we have seen above, is an essential

[12] A. Glyn and B. Sutcliffe, *British Capitalism, Workers and the Profit Squeeze* (London: Penguin Books, 1972).

characteristic of the financial market. We cannot, however, now complain about this result after having asked the government to support the level of economic activity and to increase the development of the social services. You can't have your cake and eat it too! Two reactions follow from these developments. We must consider them to understand both the process of inflation and the role of the indexation proposal. The first, which has taken on especially dramatic proportions in some countries (such as Italy) is the means by which purchasing power has increased without any relation to the growth of productivity. When the governmental bodies created to undertake new duties of economic policy have attained dimensions that produce a socially noticeable relation between the growth of their own activity and the ever more numerous interests of certain social classes (in general the middle classes), the way is opened to growth of purchasing power that is independent of the rate of growth of productivity.

The only obstacles that such a process may encounter are the internal and external homeostatic mechanisms that we have mentioned. To the extent that these mechanisms are ineffective for reasons to be explained below, the rate of expansion of public expenditure tends to take on a pathological character and reinforces the inflationary process. This helps to explain the particularly high rates of inflation that in fact existed even before the petroleum crisis, as well as the interest in the indexation proposals. Indeed a kind of indexation of wages is already being exercised in many countries. This is the result of a reaction to defend the share of income that goes to profit recipients and to productive labour in counter measure to policies that aim to increase the distributive share that goes to the middle classes, who are the prisoners of objectively contradictory behaviour. On one hand they are partially interested in the increase in wages (many parasitic emoluments take the form of wages), while on the other hand, being recipients of income that is fixed in money terms, they are damaged by the strong-arm measures, used by the unions and the firms to raise wages and prices, which aim to transfer the consequences of inflation to rentiers, and which they oppose. Now overall indexation would offer valid protection to rentiers. This can only be done, however (it is quite another thing if this is desirable), if conditions suitable for the stabilisation of income shares can be created – as has been the case in certain phases of development and in certain countries (e.g. Brazil and Finland).

13. THE CRISIS OF THE HOMEOSTATIC MECHANISMS

Let us now turn to another cause of inflation, more precisely to consider the reasons for the breakdown of certain mechanisms (homeostatic) which normally come into action to impede the reinforcement of tendencies toward the pathological growth of some income (wages in particular). To clarify the nature of these mechanisms it is useful to refer to the assertion that equilibrium in the financial market is both feasible and desirable.

As we have already observed such an equilibrium does not correspond to any objective necessity as it does in the case of the goods market. In actual fact the theory of financial market equilibrium is a mystified version of the theory of homeostatic mechanisms, mechanisms that tend to reinforce certain structural characteristics of the system and only allow for limited variations in the distribution of incomes. Macroeconomic equilibrium is thus enforced to adjust accumulation to the growth requirement: it cannot be – contrary to what neo-classical theory asserts – a by-product of the equilibria in the goods markets.

There are two basic homeostatic mechanisms.

(1) A domestic mechanism that depends on a relation being established between the level of unemployment and the evolution of wages (this provides the basis of Phillips's explanation of the evolution of prices while for Marx such a relation is linked to the competitive mechanism which conditions the process of innovation and the effects of innovation).

(2) An international mechanism that comes into action when an excess of domestic demand provokes a balance of payments deficit and acts through the international monetary mechanism, or more generally international economic relations, to impose a correction of the deficit through domestic deflationary policies.

If the government decides not to use the first type of mechanism by adopting a deflationary policy when wages increase excessively, the consequence will be an intensification of inflation which will provoke a weakening of the currency in the exchange markets and at the same time an increasing deficit on the balance of payments. At this point the international homeostatic mechanism leads the government to rethink its policy and recognise the necessity of equilibrating the movement of wages. This two-sided homeostatic mechanism is currently in crisis. The different reasons that led to the crisis of the international mechanism cannot be fully outlined here. It is enough to point out that the relation between a devaluation of the currency and the balance of payments deficit is increasingly complex. In some cases – as has been seen in recent years in England and more recently in Italy – it may be in many employers' interests to accede to unions' requests for higher wages for devaluation allows domestic prices to rise without hurting international competitiveness or the ability to sell exports. On the other hand, in some situations, despite the balance of payments deficit, the value of the currency is defended. The financing of the deficit becomes in large measure a problem of international politics. In addition, international speculation, which can be carried on virtually without limit due to the existence of the Eurodollar market, can impose devaluations and revaluations of the currency to a larger degree than the condition of the balance of payments itself would justify.

But more interesting for present purposes are the factors responsible for the crisis of the domestic homeostatic mechanism:

(1) the differential effects that an increase in wages, through the increase in workers' purchasing power, implies for different firms (those producing consumer durables being more disposed to granting wage rises);

(2) the increase, relative as well as absolute, of white collar employment which is difficult to reduce when there is a reduction in productive activity and who, in many countries like Italy, enjoy the guarantee of employment;

(3) the possibility which is available to workers to respond to a slowing of productive activity by a temporary reduction of consumption;

(4) the increasing recognition by firms of the negative effects of the slowing of economic activity;

(5) the possibility of transferring cost increases due to wage rises directly on to prices;

(6) the strengthening of trade union power.

Empirical research based on the Phillips curve supports the view that systematic changes have occurred in the economic system. These changes place in doubt the relation between the rate of change of wages and the level of unemployment, once thought to be universally valid. In fact, during the recession of 1970–71 in the USA, the substantial rise in unemployment did not prevent a continuous rise in wages. In Italy the unions succeeded in obtaining a considerable rise in wages (more than 70 per cent while prises rose only about 22 per cent) in a period (from 1969 to 1972) when the economy was in recession or in stagnation. In fact this experience indicates that the workers, when faced with the prospect of recession, do not reduce their union action but rather reduce demand much more than would be justified by the contraction of real incomes. This also points up why some form of indexation or guaranteed wage would now be more easily acceptable politically.

14. THE DOUBTFUL EFFECTS OF INDEXATION ON THE INFLATIONARY PROCESS

The discussion in the preceding paragraphs suggests several important reasons why it appears doubtful that the indexation of assets and wages could stop inflation. In fact, indexation could not succeed, except in the special case where the government has the political power to control the social classes who desire to increase their share of the national income and to stabilise the distributive structure. Indeed, Friedman only recommends the use of indexation to eliminate undesirable side effects that would result from the successful fight against inflation carried out by the government. Friedman's position, however, is based on the belief that the origin of inflation rests in errors of monetary policy. After what has been said above about the particular characteristics of the inflationary tendencies at work in modern economies, we are not ready to accept Friedman's point of view, nor to consider the problem of controlling public expenditure merely as one of political ethics. Indexation, especially if it is in fact almost exclusively limited to government bonds, could indeed encourage interested parties to press for a policy of expansion of public expenditure. The cost in terms of growing inflation pressure of such action would, in fact, be passed on to future generations. However, there are some who believe that inflation can be reduced by some structural effects brought about by indexation, more precisely,

(*a*) by an increase in personal saving,
(*b*) by a reduction in the demand for real goods as stores of value.

The first effect, as we have already pointed out, is rather doubtful. The same can be said of the second. If indexation should encourage inflationary expectations which, as we have explained above is not at all improbable, the demand for real stores of value need not undergo a strong reduction for the process of inflation is, in general, associated with a rising relative value of such goods, e.g. houses.

On the other hand, there are some indirect effects of the introduction of indexation that could favour inflationary processes. If indexation improves, even relatively, the incomes of rentiers, it could lead to a more active demand for consumption goods. As we shall soon point out, indexation has, in general, negative effects on accumulation. These two effects taken together would result in a worsening of inflationary pressures.

If, then, indexation should have the success that Friedman hopes for and, thanks also to the appropriate use of instruments of economic policy, the government should succeed in effectively slowing inflation to an extent greater than expected, this would in fact result in advantages for those who had purchased non-indexed bonds. The feedback effects could produce serious disequilibrium in the financial market.

Even admitting that indexation can constitute a valid policy instrument for the control of inflation, it does not appear desirable from the point of view of its effects on the process of growth that we have called attention to in the initial sections.

Particularly disconcerting are the effects on the rate of accumulation which, in countries like Italy, has to be maintained at a high level if the structural transformations necessary to allow the economy to attain a level of productivity sufficient to maintain its competitiveness and to move to a new model of development (with an expansion of social consumption) are to be realised.

We recall that indexation can act negatively on the rate of development of productive investment if it represses the activity of risk-taking entrepreneurs. It can also bring about an increase in the flow of saving to the government with negative effects on industrial investment, effects which it may be impossible to neutralise even with the most permissive monetary policy. To the extent that indexation succeeds in protecting savers and the income of rentiers, the phenomenon of forced saving is eliminated. But, in certain conditions it is the existence of this forced saving that allows the maintenance of the high levels of accumulation necessary to guarantee an adequate rate of growth in the presence of a decline in profits.

15. SOME SPECIAL REQUIREMENTS IN ITALY

The depressed state of the Italian bond market is certainly one of the most disturbing features of the present situation. Equally disturbing are conditions in the banking system which, in a certain sense, are linked to those in the bond market. This is not only because of the danger to bank liquidity, the elimination of which would require a greater than planned creation of money, but also from the growing instability of the propensity to consume. Those who have invested their savings in bonds can, it is true, increase their consumption by disinvesting. Such actions however involve economic and above all psychological costs which make them difficult except in exceptional circumstances. On the other hand those who have deposited their savings in banks due to the high rates of interest offered on deposits can utilise these deposits to increase their consumption above the limits of their current income with extreme facility.

It is possible to introduce measures with more certain results and lower risks than indexation to re-establish normal conditions in the bond market. The principal measures are: fiscal measures, limits on bank deposit rates, a variety of assets that offers the saver the possibility of a portfolio structure suitable to his expectations of the variations in rates of inflation and the real rate of interest (if it is meaningful to speak of such a rate).

16. SOME CONSIDERATIONS ON THE OPPORTUNITY OF INDEXING MORTGAGE BONDS

To evaluate the social benefits that a system of indexed mortgage bonds could produce in Italy it is necessary to consider some of the peculiarities of the operation of that market in Italy.

The highly irrational existing system of frozen rents has reduced the private savings available for the construction of non-luxury primary-residence rental housing. The investment of saving in this sector no longer seems profitable. In fact, private construction activity is, in growing measure, in luxury housing and second or third residences. The fact that public construction has dropped to an almost non-existent level has meant a large deficiency of non-luxury lodgings. Many have been led to resolve their lodging requirements by house purchase, stimulated undoubtedly by increasing inflationary expectations. The indexation of mortgage bonds in a period of strong inflation has the undoubted advantage of greatly reducing the real value of the initial repayment instalments. On the other hand this reduces the incentives that result from the expectations of large reductions in the real value of future repayments that the repayment schedules of traditional mortgage loans involve. One might then maintain that indexation would increase the flow of funds to the building sector. In fact as we have observed, the issue of indexed bonds or indexed deposits can be advisable in certain circumstances; but provided these assets are made available only to particular categories of savers, in limited amounts and with some restrictions placed on their disposition. It would also be advisable to use the largest part of the savings thus acquired to develop public housing. There appears to be no necessity to resort to indexed assets to finance private construction as long as a certain money illusion assures the investment of available liquidity in non-indexed bonds (the present situation is highly anomalous and constitutes an exceptional case, being the consequence of the traumatic impact that the prolonged stabilisation of the price of mortgage bonds and then the sharp fall which was thereby made inevitable, has had on the market). One could say that in this way a redistribution of income – ethically reprehensible – could be brought about from rentiers to workers who contract loans for house building. This is certainly an undesirable result that is, however, in a certain sense, inevitable in the actual irrational system which through the freezing of rents places the cost of housing on the community as a whole.

It is hardly necessary to recall, again, that the process of growth in capitalist systems is always accompanied by redistribution effects that could be considered ethically undesirable. But in as much as these are inevitable aspects of the process that aims at socially valid objectives they must be accepted as inevitable. The solution of the housing problem in Italy then requires a series of interventions which are preliminary with respect to the problem of the optimal financing methods.

A first set of interventions can be outlined only after it is decided whether or not one wants to replace the free market for lodging with he distribution of housing services by the government, which would mply that the latter take full charge of housing construction and mainenance.

There are, however, many serious difficulties that must be overcome efore transforming housing into a fully social service. These concern in he first place the social and administrative difficulties associated with he allocation of the available stock of houses, which will always be maller than the stock demanded by households at a zero (or nearly ero) price. There are other difficulties that concern the possibility of the ollection of the means necessary for the construction of lodging by the public sector. There are already serious difficulties in the tax increases necessary to assure the normal financing of the increased activities undertaken by the State.

If it is necessary to reject the idea of complete socialisation of housing, it is equally unthinkable to leave the solution of the problem to the free market. Housing should become at least partially socialised.

This could be brought about in various ways:

(*a*) a rationalisation and partial subsidisation of industries producing standardised building materials;
(*b*) reduction of land rent and of the cost of construction of the infrastructure that could be rationally erected and constructed in line with appropriate urban building norms;
(*c*) intervention to assure, at least for non-luxury houses, that prices and rents are justified by objective technical costs;
(*d*) the concession of subsidies to families whose income does not permit payment of normal rent.

Many think that housing construction should be carried out in part by public entities (*Istituti di Case Popolari*) that rent to the poor at political prices and in part by the free market. This position, if public housing is to achieve adequate levels and the allocation problems can be solved, would mean that subsidies for poor families were no longer necessary. This, sadly, is not a prospective for Italy in the near future.

It is thus urgent for us to resolve the structural problems. To this end it is necessary to put an end to the policy of ignoring the problem and to decide either to leave the problem to the free market or to favour a partially socialised service. In the latter case (the only realistic one), it is necessary to establish the time-scale for the adjustment of rents and the methods to be used to carry out partial socialisation. This is possible if the other measures mentioned above are put into action for they are necessary if the cost of housing is to be reduced to a tolerable level, for at least a large part of the population. In the meantime and while the greatest support is given to public housing, an adequate fund should be established for the payment of interest subsidies on the mortgage loans taken out by unhoused workers to build or buy a house. The fund could be financed by a tax on capital gains on houses. Such a mechanism can be rapidly introduced with immediate effects. This appears to be the best way to put the housing sector back in motion and to combat the persistent tendency to recession.

Interest subsidies can vary over time in relation both to the conditions of the financial market and the prospects that it offers savers, and to the cyclical pattern of the housing sector. The government could thus gain an effective instrument for economic stabilisation.

This is a temporary measure for the period until all the conditions for the creation of a semi-socialised housing service – in the sense given above – can be achieved (this will require at least ten years in Italy).

Such a programme avoids the disturbance of the financial market that indexed mortgage bonds would create. Their introduction cannot be considered as a valid alternative to a stable solution to the problem.

These considerations are naturally relevant to the situation in Italy. With reference to those other countries which do not show the pathological characteristics cited above, the use of indexed mortgages for building finance may well be advisable for the reasons clearly illustrated by Modigliani.

4 The 'New Inflation' and Flexible Exchange Rates

Robert A. Mundell

In the past ten years the scourge of inflation has swept across Western and Southern Worlds and become a global epidemic. Consumer prices have risen by more than half measured in even the most stable currencies. In the past five years many commodity prices have tripled and some have quadrupled. And in the past two years alone, from 1972 to 1974, there has been an acceleration of the price indexes in all the major countries so that one speaks today of 'two-digit' inflation as if it were a 'new' phenomenon. But nothing and everything is new under the sun. There is a uniqueness to all events, and yet at the same time there is a common structure of causation in things that suggest repetition:

> All nature is but art unknown to thee
> All chance, direction thou canst not see
> All discord, harmony not understood

Science looks for (and sometimes finds) the harmony in discord and the direction in chance, the general in the unique and the repetition in the new. Thus inflation is a fall in the value of money, and there is nothing new in that, in this century or any other. But inflation ebbs and flows and when it increases, as it has recently, the science of economics should be able to say why it has increased. The cause of the change may be new or old.

Is the 1974 acceleration of the world price level 'new'? Less than two years ago an OECD report contended that the cause of inflation in each of the countries it studies is different, a proliferation of causation that struck many economists at the time as absurd, and which, in the hindsight of the past two years, must strike even the layman as preposterous. It is a bit like saying that the sun has a different reason for 'rising' every morning. (It is, of course, true that I get out of bed each morning for a different reason.)

But look at the different reasons for 'inflateration' – *acceleration* of the price level – over the past decade. We can find fresh causes or concomitants every year. In 1965 it was the monetary aftermath of the 1964 tax cut in the US. In 1966 it was the escalation of the Vietnam war. In 1967 it was cost inflation in the wake of the 1966 credit 'crunch'. In 1968 it was the consequence of the UK devaluation of the preceding November and the US balance of payments deterioration, or else the two-tier gold system. In 1969 it was again the US balance of payments deficit and expansion in the Eurodollar market. In 1970 it was the collapse of interest rates, easy money and the introduction of the SDR. In 1971 it was the new green avalanche that showered Europe with new liquidity and the collapse of the Bretton Woods system. In 1972 it was the devaluation of the dollar, a rise in oil prices, and an incipient wave of hoarding of raw materials. In 1973 it was the collapse of the Smithsonian system, the abortive formation of the snake, and the drift on to flexible exchange rates, not to mention the world-wide materials boom and the hoarding of inflation hedges. This year it is the big increase in the prices of gold and oil.

Is this year's inflation new? Yes, of course. Is this year's inflation New? No, certainly not. Both answers contradict one another. Both are nevertheless correct. We can find what Alfred Marshall called the 'unity in substance' underlying the 'many varieties of form'.

What is not new is the cause of inflation. There are, of course two schools of thought regarding causation in inflation. The 'monetarist' school believes inflation has a *monetary* cause. The 'structuralist' school believes inflation has a *real* cause. But monetary causes have real consequences, and real causes have monetary implications. Indeed, both are and have to be connected. A glass of water that is half empty is also half full. The connection is Walras's law: the excess supply of money is identically equal to the excess demand for goods (including claims to future goods). The monetarists assert that the cause of inflation is the excess supply of money, while Keynesians fiscalists or structuralists like to say it is due to the excess demand for goods. Both are half right (and half wrong).

There is, however, an issue of substance. Consider economic policy and ask whether an inflationary process is correctible, or automatically self-correcting, and whether the source of the disturbance is a change in monetary supply factors or a change in the real environment. Droughts, famines and plagues have, historically, caused rapid price increases, as have changes in the quantity of money. Now the famine and plagues of the fourteenth century caused steep price increases, but should we choose our language to say that the inflation was caused by an excess demand for goods arising from a decrease in goods supplied and a breakdown of production; or should we say that it was caused by an excess supply of money induced by a shortfall in the population willing to hold the existing monetary stock? Or again, in the sixteenth century, should we attribute the great inflation to the influx of precious metals from America, or should we instead recognise that the price levels rose about six times while the stock of gold and silver only doubled, so that the gap in the bullionist explanation has to be filled by an explanation based on currency debasements which also allow for economic growth?

Analogous problems confront us in our specification of causes of the current inflation. Unless we try to sort them out we will make policy mistakes. More correctly, since we are bound to make policy mistakes in the current confusion of thought, we will compound error if policy advice is not supported by rational and tested theory. But I hope that one conclusion can command fairly general concensus among economists. That is that monetary policy is a crucial determinant of prices, and that an acceleration of money is inflationary and a deceleration of money is anti-inflationary. This is true in the sense that the supply of money cannot be divorced from any theory of *money* prices. Prices are ratios with both numerators and denominators, and money is always in one or the other. In *that* sense every economist worth the name is always a monetarist. The glass may be half empty but it *is* half full. The importance of recognising this truism is that we can do something about the supply of money, but what can one do with a drought?

The fact is that there has been a wholesale explosion of liquidity in the world as a whole in the last few years. The world money supply has doubled in the past five years by any calculation that is comprehensive. This means that inflation has had a monetary cause. Period. It does not mean that money is the sole cause of the increase in particular prices which make up the aggregate price index. But when confronted with major upheavals, amounting to a monetary revolution, when the production mechanism for the world money industry has gone through such a profound change, we have to be monetarists. In that sense we are all monetarists now.

Surely this observation, however, does not prevent us from asking why the quantity of money has increased at this particular time? What caused the surge of liquidity that promoted the inflation and was in turn induced by it? We must, of course, recognise that while money expansions cause prices to increase (or fall by less), increases in prices cause the demand for money to increase and may in turn stimulate money production. What are the inducements to money production, first by the banks, and second by the central banks, and third, by the monetary authorities?

In this paper I want to argue that, while nothing is new under the sun and the cause of the current inflation is an excess supply of money (and an excess demand for goods), the current inflation is *new* in one very important sense. Its newness needs to be underlined. The new feature of it is that the production mechanism of money has been changed. This change goes beyond institutions to the heart of our political system.

What is the change in the money supply function? Put bluntly, it is that the money supply increases when the money demand increases. And the money demand increases when the price level rises and makes liquidity (real money balances) scarce. Money becomes both cause and consequence of inflation.

It is necessary to realise that this is a sharp departure from current monetarist theory, or from the monetary systems of the past, to which so many of us tend to look with nostalgia. It is flatly opposite to the gold standard. Under the gold standard a rise in prices raised the costs of gold production and reduced the supply of gold, squeezing liquidity and forcing deflation (or disinflation). It is also different from the gold exchange standard either of the 1920s vintage or the Bretton Woods system. Under the gold exchange standard a rise in prices (not induced by higher gold supplies) increased the liabilities of the reserve centre, lowered its ratio of gold to liabilities, and prompted defensive contraction of the supply of money, a process that was also reinforced by gold drains to the public and a reduction in gold production. Under the gold standard and the gold exchange standard inflation brought about its own cure, a reversal of the original inflation. Monetary mistakes in the sense of monetary excesses were punished. Crime and punishment were joined.

This is not the case under the present system, as I shall seek to demonstrate below. The new mechanism is that price increases raise liquidity needs, which tighten money markets, raise interest rates, and induce commercial banks to reduce their liquidity ratio, increase their borrowing from the central bank, and prompt open market purchases of the central banks of the Anglo-Saxon countries, and foreign exchange purchases of the central banks of the Continental countries. Concurrently the Eurodollar market expands to meet the needs of customers engaged in financing the higher value of international trade, drawing, as it needs, upon the reserves Eurobanks hold in New York or London. Even the price of gold, in so far as it is still used as a monetary reserve or treasure, reinforces the mechanism by which the value of international reserves rises with inflation. Inflation is thus self-ratifying. If inflation is a crime then crime and reward are joined.

The cause of the current inflation, then, is the breakdown in monetary discipline, which has made the international money supply more elastic than it has ever been in modern or ancient history. It bodes ill for the future stability of prices. It suggests that we need to rethink our institutions and mechanisms, and in particular, our international monetary system. For we have moved with lightning speed from the Bretton Woods collapse, through the Smithsonian system and its collapse, to the flexible exchange regime now in force. There are some who see this as a progression and who want to index contracts which will ratify or redistribute the misery of the 'progression'. But a regime of flexible exchange rates is the most unstable of all systems because it leaves monetary policy the hostage of politicians, only too humanly focused upon the short-run and cosmetic view of the economy on election day. The national discipline of fixed exchange rates and the global discipline of convertibility are abandoned to the gales of inflation.

In the following analysis it seems best to proceed informally, taking account of historical phenomena as well as the idiosyncrasies of current attitudes and theory, and noting the underdeveloped state of monetary systems analysis. I shall give, unfortunately, scant attention to our future needs on the grounds that a correct diagnosis is necessary before we can sensibly proceed with future reconstruction.

THE BREAKDOWN OF DISCIPLINE

We have to ask why the acceleration of money took place and how it spread internationally. The acceleration of home-based money during the Vietnam war seems to place the origin of inflation in the US. But this view grows increasingly unacceptable as time passes. It is too one-sided; it does not sufficiently recognise the importance of the growth of the Eurodollar market and the contribution of European countries to the explosion of liquidity. In the later 1960s a breakdown in monetary discipline occurred and with it a degeneration of the monetary order. In 1967 Britain devalued the pound instead of enforcing measures of internal monetary and fiscal restraint. Britain's bad example set a tone for subsequent adjustments in other countries. The US balance of payments jumped up. In March 1968 the gold pool countries gave up their sales to the private gold market and set the private market price of gold free, establishing the 'two-tier' system'. These changes disclosed the lack of collective will to establish a monetary order and fostered the beginnings of an inflationary psychology throughout the commercial world. However, we still need to explain why and how the US could accelerate the money supply without running into financial difficulties in its balance of payments accounts. Events occurred both in and out of the US that enabled excess dollars to be created and encouraged them to be accepted.

Between 1965 and 1968 two events occurred in the US. They did not receive much publicity at the time, but were (and are) of great long-run importance. First in 1965 the US abandoned the gold reserve required behind Federal Reserve liabilities to member banks; later, in 1968, she abolished the requirement of gold 'backing' the issue of US notes. These two events laid the foundations for the subsequent inflation, in the sense that they freed the US monetary authorities from the discipline of a relation between gold reserves and reserve (or 'high-powered' money) created by the Federal Reserve. It was the end of what Schumpeter called the 'Golden Brake', the organic link between the currency world and the commodity world. The significance of this change is enhanced (rather than diminished, as many economists argue) by the fact that the US was the last country to free its internal money supply from gold.

Between 1969 and 1971 there was an explosion in the liquidity of the Eurodollar market. The total size of the Eurodollar market in 1963 was only \$15 billion, but in 1974 it was over \$200 billion. With this more than ten-fold explosion, the Eurodollar moved from being less than one-twentieth of the world's money supply to perhaps one-fifth. This privately-created new component of the world's money stock is not subject to international control and has been the fastest growing element by far in the recent growth of the world money supply.

Meanwhile, in 1970, the IMF was adding to the fund of reserve media with a new world currency facsimile the SDR. In the three years from 1970 to 1973 SDRs increased in relation to global liquidity; it represented a 25 per cent increase in high-powered gold liquidity. More important, it demonstrated the existence of an enabling mechanism that led to a change of expectations, as the commercial markets recognised that the world liquidity base could now be adjusted by simple agreement of IMF governors. There was no longer an effective constraint on the inflationist proclivities of modern central bankers.

Up to 1971, it should be recognised, the US dollar liabilities to European central banks had continued to mount at an alarming rate. The European central banks, however, did not demand gold conversion, principally because they were afraid of the implications of a change in US gold policy, a breakdown of the Bretton Woods system, US pressures in other directions (especially within NATO) and possibly also because the international commercial banks were making huge profits in the Eurodollar markets with the inflationary system as it was working. However, a new wave of inflation swept over Europe in the spring and summer of 1971.

The policy-engineered recession of 1970–71 in the United States had resulted in a collapse of US interest rates and a vast capital outflow to Europe that wound up as cash in the vaults of central banks. These dollars were, astonishingly, fed back into the Eurodollar market by European central banks, bolstering redundant reserves and then re-lent, as the money multiplier process worked itself out on the Eurodollar market and the multiplier itself increased.

These new European-created dollars brought pressures on the exchange markets and showed up again and again in European central banks, increasing the velocity of deposits and the world money multiplier. The ebb and flow of money between London and the Continent inflated the volume of commercial and official liquidity and the international money supply. The process was, it is true, curbed for a time in the spring of 1971 after the mark crisis, ending the artificial dollar glut.

But now a real dollar crisis developed in August, as the US money machine in that fateful summer blasted new dollars into domestic banks and foreign reserves, accelerating the US and Eurodollar money supply in an effort to combat the domestic recession and prepare the groundwork for a prosperous election year employment level in November 1972. Imprudently, in August 1971, the Joint Economic Committee publicly recommended the devaluation of the dollar, an indiscretion that the European press could not be expected to realise had no legislative teeth. This brought about a $3 billion request for gold conversion from the UK. The US, threatened with the loss of most of their remaining gold stock, which would quickly follow, 'suspended' (or perhaps forever abandoned) convertibility. With this action the link of the world monetary system to a metallic base – a link maintained by at least one country for more than twenty centuries – was ended.

It would be comforting to consider the 15 August abandonment of the gold exchange standard as a deeply conceived philosophical decision on the part of the world's financial authorities, in view of the long years of advance notice of its probability. Yet that would foster a dangerous illusion. It is much closer to the truth to regard it as the outcome of the inability of the world's monetary authorities to identify and co-operate with a common interest in a carefully planned international monetary order. More specifically it arose out of disenchantment with US leadership in monetary matters and a surge of confidence in Western Europe.

The spring and summer of 1971 also saw the emergence of a new attitude of independence and monetary nationalism in the US and abroad. Convertibility was regarded as an albatross around the neck of US policy-makers. Not much weight was placed on the long-run costs of a breakdown of convertibility in 1971 because there were few who appreciated its importance. US Treasury representatives even said that convertibility was not important since dollars had not been converted to gold for ten years! But of course the *de jure* inconvertibility of the dollar had a deeper significance. It ripped away the façade of the global liquidity control mechanism of the Bretton Woods system, and ended confidence in a system that had worked, however imperfectly, better than any other since the days of the international gold standard.

HISTORICAL FLASHBACK

The long-run importance of convertibility in the monetary system has been overlooked in the preoccupation with short-run policy objectives of modern democracy. This is not the place to discuss the relation between political systems and monetary standards except to remark that the anti-inflation bias of gold-convertible monetary systems is best validated by governments with long time horizons.

The Bretton Woods system, as Sir Roy Harrod aptly put it, was an 'episode in the history of the dollar'. So was the Smithsonian system. For over half a century, the dollar had been acquiring international monetary properties *pari passu* with the rise of the US to its preeminent industrial position, assuming the role that the pound was relinquishing with the recession of power of the British Empire.

In the first half of the nineteenth century, the international monetary system had used both gold and silver interchangeably, with France and a rapidly growing America fixing the bi-metallic ratio. Both France and the US dropped silver after 1870. In the 1870s most countries demonetised silver and joined Britain on the gold standard. Gold currencies were the principle media of settlement until 1914 and the pound sterling the principal unit of account due to the financial importance of the London capital market and the political strength of the British Empire. During this period countries that stayed on a silver standard experienced inflation. Gold countries – which represented the mainstream of the world economy – experienced a mild deflation until 1895, because of rapid economic growth and gold scarcity. After 1885, with the immense gold discoveries, principally in South Africa, gold production increased enabling Austria, Hungary, Russia and India to move to gold without deflating the world economy (except for the Baring Crisis in 1891). Subsequently, coupled with the great banking expansion, the increased gold base led to a monetary acceleration that caused an upward trend in world prices even before the credit inflations of the First World War.

When war broke out in 1914, capital naturally moved to London, still thought to be the most secure haven, as old habits die hard. But as the idea dawned in the public and capital markets that the World War would be a long one, and that even the British Empire might not be invincible, money sought a more secure haven in New York far away from the threat of blocking of gold balances and fears (probably exaggerated) of a submarine menace. The UK link with gold was broken in 1915 while the US, which had already before the war become the largest economy and was for most of the war a non-belligerent, maintained gold convertibility. In 1917 there was a centralisation of gold in the US, but the US nevertheless emerged from the war as an industrial supereconomy with enormous gold reserves. Growth of the US in the 1920s exacerbated the gold scarcity as the US sucked gold from abroad, and world-wide economic growth coupled with greater economic uncertainty increased world liquidity needs. A higher gold price or a gold substitute was needed to supplement liquidity if deflation was to be avoided. The solution that emerged, after the 1923 Genoa Conference, was the gold exchange standard in which countries used gold convertible currencies (mainly pounds) as reserves. This system broke down when Britain decided, in 1931, that the costs of maintaining convertibility of the pound became greater than the benefits – a British decision that was to be repeated in the US four decades later. But the effects were different because the gold exchange standard of 1925–31 was different from the Bretton Woods system.

Prior to the British abandonment of gold, the 1929 Wall Street Crash had greatly increased uncertainly, dried up international lending and led to bank failures in Central Europe. When Britain dropped gold it seemed to everybody that the gold exchange standard had collapsed. But this was an illusion. Major countries, including the US and France, remained on gold. The gold bloc at that time was more important than the sterling bloc and the British Empire. The gold base of the system, however, was still too narrow to maintain the world price level. Gold hunger created an excess demand for gold and deflationary monetary policies. Britain had opted out from the deflationary standard, and the US was soon to follow. In 1933 three major currency areas emerged – the dollar area, the sterling area, and the gold bloc (now centred around France). A floating bloc system emerged for a short period. Unfortunately, the US now embarked on a policy disastrous in its international ramifications. It began to buy gold and silver. It raised the price of gold from \$20·67 to \$35·00 per ounce. This action now distorted exchange rates. It created a franc overvalued with respect to the dollar. The undermining of the franc and other allied currencies weakened France at a precarious time in its relations with a Germany bent on rearmament. The US silver-buying policy also appreciated the Chinese currency which was based on silver and probably played a part in strengthening the hand of Mao Tse-Tung forces by throwing China into depression. The tragedy of this episode is that the US policy was not conducted in an environment in which global implications were sufficiently taken into account (any more indeed, than the British and French were sufficiently aware of the influence of the 1931 liquidity crisis on Japanese actions on the other side of the globe in Manchuria). Gulliver had grown up, physically, but was still underdeveloped in social maturity.

From 1934 to 1971 the US gold parity of \$1 = 1/35 ounce of gold = 0·888671 gramme of gold was maintained. The 1944 gold dollar was adopted as the unit of account of the International Monetary Fund, and dollars became the dominant world currency. The whole world was a vast dollar area. Dollars were accepted world wide *as if* they were as good as gold. The official gold parity of the dollar gave the system a legal basis for settling accounts and with the opening of the London gold market in 1954, an economic basis. Even though in later years the dollar was not, in practice, convertible even for foreign central banks the legal framework remained. But a major difference between the British dropping of gold in 1931 and the US change in 1971 was that in 1931 Britain was not the only country tied to gold.

THE PROBLEM TWINS

We can see the importance of the distinction in the deflationary aftermath of the 1931 episode and the inflationary aftermath in 1971. There are two fundamental problems for the monetary management of the world economy that need to be distinguished. The first problem was the 'exchange rate problem' – the method by which currencies were to be linked to one another. The other was the 'liquidity control problem' – the relation of the global money supply to international reserves. I shall refer to the exchange rate problem as problem A and to the liquidity control problem as problem B. Under the gold standard problem A was solved by the gold content of currencies, and problem B by a stable gold relation between gold reserves and national money supplies. Under the gold exchange standard, problem A was solved asymmetrically, by the major countries pegging their currencies to the dollar, the supply of which was kept scarce, by the gold convertibility solution of problem B. The world supply of liquidity was thus, in principle at least, kept under restraint.

Both problems have to be solved in a well-functioning monetary order. Unfortunately, in the wake of picking up the pieces after 15 August 1971, the world monetary authorities failed to solve or even sensibly try to solve problem B. The Smithsonian system introduced in December 1971 effectively tackled only problem A. It set new exchange rates of the major currencies *vis-à-vis* the dollar which, despite its short-term weakness in the summer of 1971, retained its position as the leading key currency and the pivot around which exchange rates were set. But there was no solution to problem B. There was no mechanism of restraint inhibiting the growth of world liquidity. The dollar convertibility link to gold that had been cut in August remained unmended and no other country or group of countries took it up. The Smithsonian system thus set the world on a multiple-currency standard with no international constraint on the world money supply through convertibility of the major currencies into gold or even SDRs.

The particular feature of the period after the Second World War (until 1971) had been that only one currency (the dollar) was pegged to gold and all other currencies were pegged to the dollar. The major function of the gold link of the system – the gold convertibility of the dollar – was to provide a brake against excessive monetary expansion of the key currency. Whereas the threat of dollar shortage disciplined the other countries, the threat of gold shortage disciplined (in theory) the US.

It was because of the unique role of the dollar that the crisis of 1971 was a 'system crisis' and not just a dollar crisis on the same footing as a pound, franc or lire crisis. Even if convertibility of the dollar into gold had not been exercised in fact the psychology of the system was nevertheless dependent on that relationship. The system was asymmetrical with respect to the dollar, but what made the asymmetry palatable from a legal standpoint was the unique responsibility of the convertibility pledge. The other countries had a 'right' to insist that the US control its balance of payments, and to warn that neglect of its balance was not 'benign' but malignant. A discipline was thus exerted over excess monetary expansion by the need for dollar convertibility on the one hand to solve problem A and gold convertibility on the other to solve problem B. Whereas the Smithsonian system restored a kind of dollar convertibility and thus solved problem A, it proved to be unacceptable without gold convertibility or an alternative solution to problem B. Whereas all countries had a balance of payments constraint under the Bretton Woods system, the Smithsonian system demoted the dollar and created a vacuum with respect to the global liquidity mechanism. With a flexible gold price generally rising with inflation, reserves, subjectively valued, rose with inflation. US monetary policy was kept easy and Eurodollars supplied rose rapidly. The consequent materials boom, which was both cause and effect of the increased reserves, led to the most rapid upsurge in prices since the Second World War.

THE OIL INFLATION

It became apparent, as world inflation developed, that the oil countries have to be paid a high enough price for their oil to induce them to part with it rather than leave it in the ground for their own use. The OPEC was able to exploit a monopoly position which revolutionises balance of payments history. The current imbalances – at annual rates in terms of billions of dollars – could endure for several years. The reserves of the OPEC will be tens or even hundreds of billions of dollars by 1980 if real transfers are not made to pay the petroleum exporting countries with goods rather than gold or claims. But the demand for capital goods imports and weaponry of the oil-rich countries will effect a substantial part of the transfer in real terms.

The oil payment crisis presents great transfer difficulties. Venezuela, Nigeria and Iran, Indonesia and Algeria have substantial populations and development needs and can absorb enough goods to end their surpluses. The absorptive capacity for efficient spending in Saudi Arabia, Libya and the Gulf States is severely limited. Reinvestment of the liquid holdings by the oil bloc in both the industrial countries and the LDCs is limited by political problems. The surplus reserves could be channelled through the IMF and IBRD to longer-term finance of development projects. This sort of dollar transfer link to long-term finance was needed even before the oil crisis to deal with the problem of the 'overhang' of US liquid assets of the EEC countries.

The oil price increase is inflationary under the present elastic system of international reserve provision. With a constant world money supply (as under the gold standard) such a price increase as the oil price increase would have been deflationary and could not have been maintained. But the oil deficits will probably be financed by an increase in global liquidity under the current anchorless system and for that reason it is inflationary in its consequences for the world price level; at the same time it can, through its effects on costs and its implicit tax on the rest of the world economy, create unemployment.

THE RESERVE EXPLOSION

The oil problem underlines the precarious stability of the present system. Excessive price increases are usually reversed in a well-functioning system because they make liquidity scarce. But we have moved into a dangerous system in which higher prices create the demand for more liquidity, which is in turn supplied by the system, thus ratifying the higher price. We have indeed seen a phenomenal increase in world reserves – a doubling since 1970 or, if we value gold at more realistic prices, a tripling.

What is even more interesting is the composition of international reserves. In 1970 total foreign exchange reserves amounted to $45 billion – a three-fold increase. Gold reserves were upvalued in this period from $37 billion to $43 billion. However, the liquidity value of these gold reserves is at least three times this figure. The recent German-Italian agreement valued gold at a 'market-related price' of $120 an ounce.

The regime of flexible exchange rates provides no control over international monetary reserves. With the advent of flexible exchange rates the great dollar overhang disappeared as countries became aware that the uncertainties of a world of flexible exchange rates require more not less international liquidity. In order to increase dollar reserves countries can simply buy them in the foreign exchange supermarket. Under floating rates depreciation of a currency may be a discipline. But now all countries inflate. The expansion of money supplies in all countries makes inflation possible without depreciation. And politicians in each country can blame inflation on the world economy where it is nobody's responsibility.

There does exist a control over the quantum of gold reserves but no control over the value. When the price of gold increases, due to changes in supply or demand factors, the currency value of gold hoards in central bank vaults as well as in private hands increases. Money itself becomes indexed. If the currency value of gold reserves increases with the world price level, the Golden Brake is released and regulation of the inflation rate ceases.

CONVERTIBILITY DISCIPLINE

The United States, the dominant reserve currency country, should not simultaneously maintain an elastic supply of dollars in the face of a rising demand for dollar reserves, and in addition allow a flexible price of gold. When both occur there is no control over the global quantity of reserve money, and hence no check on global liquidity. Inflation becomes a self-sustaining process; the opposite danger of deflation is also possible when there is no mechanism guaranteeing stability of reserves.

The world money glut was not only caused by the above factors. These factors are merely symptomatic of a breakdown of discipline in the entire economic system. For the United States, convertibility discipline meant the acceptance of gold reserve losses when US monetary expansion was excessive. For the rest of the world, convertibility discipline meant that US dollars or gold had to be given up when national monetary expansion was excessive. The Italian inflation of 1962–63 illustrates the importance of the discipline habit. The Italians did not in 1963–64 resort to devaluation as a means of solving their inflationary problems. They absorbed the economic punishment of recession and unemployment resulting from tight monetary policy. It was costly in the short run but essential in the long run. It built up a legacy of confidence later. In 1968–69 many international newspapers predicted that Italy would have to devalue as a result of the inflation of the previous year. But the Bank of Italy again held the lire rate and confidence was quickly restored because of the legacy of their past success. Britain in 1957 and 1961 and 1964 also illustrates the economic advantages of the discipline habit in a world of fixed exchange rates and gold convertibility.

The chain was, however, broken in 1967. The UK broke the tradition of accepting the discipline when she devalued in 1967. The gold pool nations abandoned the discipline of the private gold market when the free market price was set loose. The US followed when she refused to accept reserve losses in 1970 when urged to do so by the IMF managing director. The will to accept monetary restraint in defence of a stable price level was now at an end.

What followed was, as we know, the appeasement of inflationary pressures by a breakdown of all control over international reserve expansion. The Smithsonian system adopted fixed rates but no global discipline of convertibility. By opting out of the Snake, Britain and Italy accepted more inflation than even the other members of the Snake. The Snake countries developed a miniature Smithsonian system but without an external or commodity convertibility discipline. Despite the much cherished anti-inflationary stance of the Bundesbank, the German consumer price index in May 1974 stood at 127 while the US index stood at 126, as compared to a 1970 base year of 100. The Snake area has not been successful in stopping inflation despite the appreciation of its currencies relative to the dollar. Flexible exchange rates have not lived up to the promises attributed to them even for the least inflation-prone countries.

In the long run the viability of a separate currency bloc and a separate identity as a unit of account depends on it having a very large capital market. A small currency bloc cannot be a rival or visible alternative to the dollar as an international currency and the movement towards a distinct European monetary identity that is not inflationary depends on the ability of the group to centralise on a dominant currency in a very large monetary bloc encompassing all the major European countries and a fixed commitment to a monetary rule. The capital markets of the Snake countries are even collectively too small compared to the US market to go it alone in the long run. The international financial world is still dominated by the dollar.

A very large currency area provides protection against inflation based on its size alone. Monetary disturbances are more easily absorbed in large currency areas. The United States provides the outstanding example in this century as the British Empire did in the last century. If an important union tries to negotiate a very large wage increase and is successful in doing so in a particular area, employers will shift to an area where wages are not so high. Industries are mobile – if the incentives are high enough. If we have a large trading and currency area national trade unions cannot 'gouge' without suffering immediate unemployment, and in the event of a strike, the loss of the strike funds. But with floating rates, an increase in unemployment will force the central bank to expand the money supply, which will culminate in more inflation. The union gains will thus be temporary and to the extent that the aggregate union share is increased, the starvation of capital needs will lower both economic growth and future wage increases.

The analogy to the increase in oil prices should be apparent. The oil price increase could not have been sustained under the gold exchange standard. The quadrupling of oil would under the gold standard have led to an immediate deflation of all non-oil prices and a vast excess supply of oil, forcing cutbacks of production in producing countries and straining their own income and liquidity positions. It is no accident that the price of gasoline in the United States is less than half or even a third of that in Europe. Even apart from government control there is no way in which Texan oil producers could have achieved a quadrupling of domestic oil prices. Had they attempted to do so an incipient depression would have forced oil prices back down, as oil reserves would have tumbled. With a control of the quantity of money even as weak as it is in the United States, the demand for oil is elastic and the kind of gouging that is possible at the international level is ruled out.

This situation contrasts with that in the international economy where the system of flexible exchange rates without convertibility has broken down the monetary unity of the world economy. The building up of exchange reserves is creating a 'strike-fund' for the oil exporting countries that will enable them to outlast the oil reserves of the importing countries. This shifts the balance of bargaining power to OPEC, and each day brings the western importing countries further from the *status quo ante bellum*.

The flexible exchange system has proved too elastic to provide that ingredient of discipline and fast adjustment needed to prevent arbitrarily high prices of specific commodities. The best system is a fixed exchange system governed by the rules of asset convertibility of the currencies that make it up. Through this system *relative* prices everywhere become equalised (except for transport costs, tariffs and information interuptions). There is a harmony in the world order of fixed exchange rates that is not obvious, but is nevertheless visible. The lire and the pound are at the levels not much different from their positions seven years ago *vis-à-vis* the US dollar. This is despite all the turmoil of the last few years. The big change which has occurred is in the relative position of the mark and the yen. Germany and Japan are special cases and have been for two decades. Their exchange rates were in disequilibrium fifteen years ago due to the aftermath of wartime reconstruction. The change in their rates reflects the dynamic energies of these economies catching up from two decades of wartime interruption. Their monetary needs go far beyond what the central banks are willing to provide by domestic credit alone. Because of the wiping out of their internal debts after the war they need to buy foreign exchange every year to keep their money supplies growing. They pay a seigniorage cost by using this method, but their reserve build-up has created appreciation expectations for their currencies.

Under fixed exchange rates the money supply is endogenous since there is in general only one level at which international equilibrium can be achieved. The adjustment mechanism works as it does between regions of a common currency area. This system is neutral with respect to long-run unemployment. With the correct monetary and fiscal policy mix the costs of curbing inflation can be minimised while income policies or more generally supply management has a chance to work itself out in the long run. The credit policy of the central bank can be directed to long-run growth needs while the reserves fluctuate and preserve the equilibrium quantity of money. Meanwhile fiscal policy can achieve the needed short-run level of effective demand while wage or incomes policies adapt to preserve the long-run equilibrium level of employment.

In the long run, at the national level, the decline in the terms of trade of oil importing countries due to the increased price of oil means a reduction in real income which will have to be absorbed by the importing economies. The rise in the price of oil is a real phenomenon and no new resources or escape from pain are achieved by letting the exchange rate float downward. Devaluation does not create any new resources; it is primarily a tax on money creditors and a subsidy to debtors (including the government). The sole effect of devaluation is an increase in the rate of inflation and a redistribution of wealth. The February crisis in Britain also illustrated another feature of it: a reinforcing ratchet effect. The dollar value of the pound declined to $2.20 while the forward pound price fell toward $2.00. Britain by this depreciation, did not gain new resources; it raised the price of raw materials, food, created upward wage pressures and further increases in the cost of living which were not reversed when the position of the pound improved. The temporary exchange rate change thus lifted prices permanently higher. Depreciation brings increased prices which lead to further wage increases which in turn lead to further price increases and monetary expansion. Appreciation, on the other hand, appears to be asymmetric because of different timing effects. It does not seem to lead to corresponding price and wage reductions. Destabilising outward capital flows that are later reversed can themselves lead to permanently higher price levels, as the devaluation – even if temporary – raises prices, lowers real wages and forces money wages upwards, where they remain. An economy that experiences an evenly fluctuating exchange rate would thus set in motion forces that lead to secular wage and price trends higher than would otherwise be the case.

It is questionable whether appreciation combined with restrictive monetary policy can be an effective defence against inflation because of the differential timing of price reductions and money wage changes. But in theory it should be. Where the theory does seem to fit the practice is the case where there is a threat to depreciate a currency against an already inflating international monetary standard. The case of Italy is suggestive.

If Italy devalues during the current crisis no new resources will be created for the Italian people. It would merely be another episode of evasion of monetary or political discipline and foreshadow the breakdown of the lire as a stable unit of account. The commitment to a fixed exchange rate, especially in a country more inflationary than the mainstream of the world economy, is the best defence against excessive monetary expansion and inflation.

GLOBAL DISCIPLINE AND THE FLAGSHIP'S COMPASS

What holds for Italy and the UK is true for the world in general. Monetary discipline is a *sine qua non* of monetary stability and monetary stability is essential to the survival of non-totalitarian political systems. There have been two major exceptions. The first was the British float after 1931, which allowed the sterling area to deflate at a slower rate than the rest of the world; it could be justified as a defensive reaction against world deflation. The second exception was the German float upward in 1969 and the early 1970s which can be justified as a means to help gain a lower inflation rate than the rest of the world. Britain in 1931, by exporting deflation by exchange depreciation, and Germany in 1970, by exporting inflation by exchange appreciation, may be examples where single powerful nations can gain at the expense of the rest of the world when a strong case can be made that the rest of the world is off compass. But we should not condone that as a system. All countries cannot depreciate or appreciate together except in a world of convertibility where universal changes alter the real value of liquid reserves.

A stable monetary system for the world as a whole depends on general acceptance of a single monetary rule to which all countries commit their policies. That rule could be a gold standard, a regulated (or dominated) gold exchange standard, as under Bretton Woods, a Smithsonian system with convertibility, or an SDR standard in which global reserves are managed. Exceptions to it will mean some exchange flexibility but general principles cannot be made out of exceptions.

I do not believe that inflation will be controlled until we restore fixed exchange rates and convertibility. We need a pivot for exchange rates or a dominant currency to serve as flagship. And the course of the flagship must be set right. If we do not restrain inflation we risk 'inflateration', two-digit interest rates, a breakdown in long term capital markets, a shortening of time horizons and a breakdown of Western society as we now know it. There will be some who will argue that society is not worth preserving. But economists cannot be ostriches that put their heads in the sand to shut from their vision all the non-economic consequences of shifting from one rate of inflation to another.

New leadership needs to be established that is committed to an informed and responsible internationalism. The integration of the world economy that has developed in the third quarter of the twentieth century has generated, and been caused by an increased interdependence of national economies. That interdependence has been beneficial. It should not be allowed to disintegrate. There is no need to get bogged down in the technical difficulties of resolving the problem of finding a viable substitute for the Bretton Woods system. In the immediate future we cannot avoid the optimum currency areas solution. But we must not lose the vision of an integrated world economy centred on a stable and usable world money into which the major currencies are convertible. The pure gold standard has had its day; so perhaps has the pound and perhaps also the dollar and the mark. But we cannot afford to dispense with gold and dominant currencies overnight.

We could move towards an international currency based on a revised SDR. But in the transition process we have to start from the living assets of the market-place. The SDR is not yet a usable world money. Rome was not built in a day and neither will our new international monetary system be. The transitional currencies will have to include the dollar, the Eurodollar and the European currencies. We shall have to experiment by linking the dollar area and the European currencies as well as the yen and other currencies by arrangements that emerge from experience as manageable. As more countries link their currencies directly to the SDR or indirectly through the dollar or the mark, we shall reduce gradually the instabilities associated with exchange gyrations and evolve an SDR exchange standard with a mechanism for global control of all international liquidities including central bank reserves, swaps and the Eurodollar. The first step is to agree on the world currency because that is the centrepiece of capitalism (and for that matter socialism). After the flagship is identified and its compass is set right, the rest of the fleet will fall into line.

If, on the other hand, we do not move steadily towards the goal of a monetary unity we risk repeating the disasters of the 1930s and a breakdown in the traditional form of Western European and North American civilisation. The choice is ours.

Discussion of Chapter 4

Luigi Spaventa

I would like to apologise for what may be an incomplete and certainly insufficient commentary on Professor Mundell's paper for, like other participants, I have heard it for the first time here today. As a consequence I have not had the benefit of advance reflection on the written text. I shall thus be improvising, or thinking aloud, with the risk (or better, the probability) of being inexact.

I think we should welcome favourably Professor Mundell's attempt to open our discussion to international problems. In our discussion so far, in fact, we were perhaps too preoccupied with the internal causes of inflation, which differ among individual countries, without giving sufficient attention to causes operating on a world-wide scale.

Today, even individual countries which seemed to show the most success in the control of inflation, for example the case of Brazil which has often been discussed, seem to be facing serious inflationary problems once more.

In the first four months of this year inflation in Brazil has again reached an annual rate of 35 per cent – despite the balanced budget, despite the control of wages and salaries, and despite the whole series of instruments that have been used.

Thus I would maintain that there may be much truth in what Professor Mundell has said about the importance of international influence on inflation in the present situation.

Having said this, however, I feel that I must withhold my complete agreement on a number of other points that have been proposed. It appears to me that there are two principal themes in the paper: I am in greater agreement on one than on the other. The first theme of the paper concerns the following problem: Is there an excess of international means of payment? Professor Mundell believes so, if I am not mistaken, and attributes the primary responsibility for the current inflation to this excess of international means of payment. The second argument that Professor Mundell treats concerns the adjustment problem and how adjustment should be carried out.

I will start with the first question – whether there is an excess of international means of payment. This question can, I think, be divided in turn into two points which should be held separate: (1) First of all, is it true that an excess of means of payment has generated inflation in recent years? (2) Can it be deduced from this that *today* there is an excess of means of payment on a world scale? (I should make it precise that, when I speak of means of payment I am referring essentially to international reserve instruments and not to international liquidity in general.)

As far as the first point is concerned, I doubt that it is possible to establish precisely the cause and effect relation described by Professor Mundell. It is certainly true that there has been a complete absence of discipline on the international level; as it is certainly true that there has been an uncontrolled production of means of payment. However, one should also observe that this uncontrolled production occurred before the declaration of inconvertibility of the dollar into gold, and that there have been very powerful real causes which acted upon countries internally as well as on the international level. The recognition of these facts makes it difficult to establish a one-way relation between the quantity of international money and inflation. It remains to be said, naturally, that the presence of these means of payment was a necessary condition for the development of the inflationary phenomenon; this is obvious, but also of little significance, since it does not imply that condition to be sufficient for the phenomenon.

It seems to me that the second point is of greater importance: can one show that there is, today, an excess of means of payment? Professor Mundell's position seems to me to be related to that (shown in international organisations by representatives of the Federal Republic of Germany and often by representatives of the United States) put forward to justify opposition to the creation of new Special Drawing Rights, to the mobilisation of gold reserves, and to the establishment of a link between monetary reform and aid to underdeveloped countries. I point out that this is not a purely theoretical problem, but it touches difficult questions that are, above all for us in Italy today, of the greatest practical importance.

On these problems I have to disagree with Professor Mundell's position for several reasons. In the first place I would like to remark that the distribution of reserve instruments may be much more important to these problems than the absolute amount of such instruments. In a situation, like the present, in which the largest proportion of existing reserve instruments are concentrated in a country with a balance of payments surplus, the quantity of international means of payment can be inadequate, while it would not be if the distribution were different. In other words, to adopt a monetarist terminology, an equal amount of means of payment can have a different velocity of circulation according to its distribution amongst countries. Today this distribution is extremely unbalanced and this makes the actual situation as if it were a situation of scarcity, this quite independently of the absolute amount of existing means of payment. In the second place I should like to remark that the opinion, according to which every increase in international means of payment has inflationary effects is valid if, and only if, one can demonstrate that the creation of new means of payment brings about an increase in the world level of demand.

Now I do not believe that this is true in the present situation and above all after the increase in the price of petroleum and of other primary commodities. One could say, though somewhat imprecisely, that because of the feeble propensity to import and spend of the petroleum producing countries, the propensity to save has risen for the world taken as a whole. One could also say, again in very general terms (and I ask my colleagues to forgive me for the theoretical imprecisions of these statements) that liquidity preference has risen (or the preference to hold reserves has risen for the world as a whole). Thus the volume of world demand has diminished for these reasons as well as from the influence of restrictive demand policies followed by various countries. On the other hand, while the value of world trade is higher, as a result of the increase in petroleum prices, the velocity of circulation of the existing means of payment has at the same time diminished. This then is an argument that justifies the creation of new international means of payment; and their distribution amongst countries not according to market principles, but according to some internationally agreed criteria.

This brings me to the consideration of the adjustment problem. I am in complete agreement with Professor Mundell concerning the inefficiency of a float, and naturally of a downward float, for countries with a deficit on their balance of payments: this primarily for the UK whose deficit is expected to reach 10 billion dollars at the end of the year, and for Italy with a predicted deficit of 8–9 billion dollars. I would like to add to this that one of the principles apparently accepted by all parties discussing the reform of the international monetary system was that a country in structural surplus causes as much damage to the international monetary system as that caused by countries in deficit. One could say that a country that 'lives beyond its means' is no more guilty, from the point of view of international monetary order, than a country that 'lives below its means'.

Now, if one accepts this principle one should also accept its corollary which also used to constitute one of the keys to the reform of the international monetary system: the burden of adjustment should be borne not only by deficit countries but also by those in surplus. The USA succeeded in imposing these principles after the declaration of inconvertibility in 1971 as a result of their imposing economic position: the USA accepted the loss of the virginity of the dollar – if I may use that expression – but obtained at the same time the revaluation of the currencies of the surplus countries, thereby shifting a part of the burden on to them.

Today, the surplus countries should be able to contribute to the reduction of international disequilibrium in two ways: above all in terms of their domestic policy, and secondarily through variations in exchange rates. One might naturally object that the Deutsche Mark has already been revalued several times without effect. Here I think I can agree with Professor Mundell when he says that we cannot compare the effects of a number of small revaluations, which continually engender destabilising expectations, with the effects of a large, once-and-for-all revaluation equal to the sum of several small revaluations. But even more than a revaluation, a change in domestic policies by surplus countries would be helpful. We are living in an absurd situation today. The Federal Republic of Germany, whose reserves exceed 30 billion dollars and which at the end of this year will have a current account surplus of the order of 7 billion dollars despite the rise in petroleum prices, is carrying out a restrictive domestic policy. The same thing is happening in the USA where the non-oil surplus is such as to completely offset the considerable oil deficit. The oil deficit for the industrialised countries (40–45 billion dollars in 1974 for the OECD countries) falls most heavily on only a small number of them, which are asked to support the entire adjustment burden. But, if the deficit countries are to carry the adjustment burden alone, without any change in the internal policies of the surplus countries, it will necessarily require a larger contraction of the level of world demand and activity, implying an ever-worsening recession being transmitted from one country to another.

The damage will fall on the entire international economy, the surplus countries included. In addition, the surplus countries, accumulating liquid assets and therefore claims on the future resources of other countries, are making an irrational choice even from their own purely domestic point of view, to the extent that they refuse, in this manner, to ameliorate the standard of living of their own citizens or to increase their own national wealth: to improve the standard of living, via an expansion of demand larger than the growth of output or, in the case of a revaluation, via a reduction in the prices of imported commodities; to increase national wealth as a result of direct investment abroad.

I repeat that countries with deficits larger than their oil deficit, Italy in the first place, should undergo all the necessary sacrifices to re-establish a stronger equilibrium. I do maintain, however, that it is our duty as economists to recognise that the grave problems of the international economy have been faced in the worst possible manner; in a manner that one would hope to have been overcome after the experience of the 1930s.

Part Two

5 Address

Emilio Colombo

In modern times inflation strikes economic systems with increasing frequency and for ever-longer periods. It is an illness to which no country is immune. It is not rare that the violence of inflation provokes damaging effects, not only on the strictly economic level, not only on the social level. It also extends to the political life of a country. In countries where the strength of the democratic system is thereby weakened, inflation can affect the system of liberty which is the very foundation of democratic political systems.

From the authoritative scholars participating in this conference we expect some enlightenment for the formulation of government policy against inflation in this and other countries.

Italy is now experiencing a high rate of inflation and, as a result, serious monetary problems.

I do not think it would be outside the objectives of this conference if I were to make some observations on our current experience here in Italy and on the guidelines that have been laid down by our government to overcome the present difficulties.

Reflection on the causes of our current problems is not only useful in highlighting oft-forgotten truths, but also in finding guidelines for future government policy and for all the economic and social forces whose actions are not secondary in the process of initiating and developing inflation, and whose actions will play a major part in the realisation of policies suitable to combat inflation.

In Italy 1973 was a year of considerable expansion in both employment and production. The national product in real terms grew at a rate above the long-run trend. Employment increased by more than 100,000 and most of the increase was in the area of dependent labour.

The real growth of the economy was also evident in the expansion of investment, particularly in plant and equipment.

This positive evolution was however accompanied by growing pressure on the price system as well as a growing disequilibrium in the foreign accounts. Both external and internal causes for inflation existed at the same time. The final result was a large increase in prices and a current account deficit in the region of 2,500 billion lire.

In order to maintain an adequate level of reserves it was necessary to contract for compensatory foreign loans of more than 5 billion US dollars.

The situation has not improved in the first part of this year. Indeed the already difficult prospects have been further depressed by the forecasts of an even higher trade deficit due to the new price of petroleum. In spite of this, in January a deficit on the current account of the balance of payments for 1974 of around 5,000 billion lire could be foreseen (of which 3,000 billion would be due to the increased cost of oil) as well as a rise in consumer prices of between 10 and 15 per cent.

This situation in itself could not be allowed to continue, also because of the increasing difficulty in obtaining foreign loans. This was true not only for Italy but for all countries that had suffered the impact of the new price of petroleum on their balance of payments positions. Neither was it easy to adjust the balance of payments through a large increase in exports, in an international scenario dominated by the general determination to combat inflation.

These observations implied the necessity of an adjustment process aiming at reducing the non-oil current account deficit, partly in 1974 and partly in 1975, by means of a quantitative limitation on total domestic credit expansion and measures of fiscal restriction of the order of 500 billion lire. A combination of monetary and fiscal measures were considered necessary to re-equilibrate capital movements.

These objectives were the subject of the government's letter of intent to the International Monetary Fund (IMF).

The public debate which took place before the government was authorised to sign the letter to the IMF, and the discussions which followed to determine the ways and means of increasing tax yields, took a good deal of time, too much time. It would have been much better to get straight to work.

It would have been still better to use the time which was spent even before that in discussing the state of the economy, more so in that the discussions were not always inspired by a realistic assessment of the problems involved.

In the absence of any other timely decision, the government found itself compelled to react only through monetary measures, the only true barrier that we could put up in a situation that risked escape from our control.

The situation did in fact worsen in the first months of 1974. From January to May the current account deficit of the balance of payments has been of 3,400 billion lire, implying a projected annual deficit of 7,000 billion lire taking account of seasonal factors.

At the same time we have had to realise that the rate of inflation in Italy was the highest amongst industrial countries. The rise in the consumer price index in the twelve months to April 1974 was 16·3 per cent in Italy, compared with a maximum rise of 15·2 per cent in United

Kingdom and Denmark and a minimum of 7·2 per cent in Germany.

Through the mechanism of cost-of-living escalator the process of rising prices found and would continue to find, in the absence of economic policy decisions, new impetus.

It is true that the expansion of production remains satisfactory, and that as much can be said for the level of employment, but both are seriously menaced by the high rate of inflation. Equally true is the fact that it would have been impossible to find international financial assistance sufficient to compensate a current account deficit of 7,000 billion lire. Neither was it possible to overlook the fact that at a rate of price increase of the magnitude of 20 per cent per annum our exports could not long remain competitive on international markets.

It has thus become necessary to take more incisive stabilising measures than those required at the beginning of the year, when they would have been less harsh.

Controls on the expansion of total domestic credit had already been adopted. In addition, an obligatory import deposit scheme covering 40 per cent of the value of imported goods was adopted with the effect of a further reduction in the liquidity available to the economy.

The fiscal drain of 500 billion lire, thought at the beginning of the year to be sufficient, in present conditions must be raised to 3,000 billion lire, especially if some flexibility is to be allowed in monetary policy to support production and investment.

The parties of the parliamentary majority coalition, and thus the government, intend to move on the lines outlined above and to adopt promptly the measures required to make them operative.

It can be understood that the determination of a strategy of economic intervention acceptable to all the parties of the majority requires a difficult and intense political debate. The decisions to be adopted, in fact, impinge on normal habits of life and an apparent welfare that could, however, be painfully interrupted if the present economic difficulties are not cured.

To this end, in the twelve-month period from July 1974 to June 1975, additional net fiscal revenues of 3,000 billion lire, will be levied by means of increases in taxes, social security contributions and public service fares, if Parliament approves the package proposed by the government.

The reduction in domestic demand caused by this drain of 3,000 billion lire should reduce the rate of inflation and the current account deficit of the balance of payments.

Our objective is to eliminate our non-oil deficit before the end of 1975 and at the same time to contain the inflation rate in Italy within the average rate prevailing abroad.

The determination of the measures capable of reducing the excess monetary demand is based on four fundamental criteria. In the first place we have determined an increase in fiscal receipts, as outlined above, in such a way as to generate a decrease in imports through a reduction of domestic demand. In fact some of these measures act very selectively on goods with high import content. In the second place, those particular measures have been chosen that are apt to reduce demand promptly. Thirdly, recognising the imperative of obtaining the reduction of demand within short and predictable lags, a required combination of increases in direct and indirect taxes and in public service fares has been adopted. Finally, both in direct and indirect taxes as well as in fares, the differential effects on the incomes of various social groups have been taken into consideration.

Some of the fiscal measures can undoubtedly have an upward effect on some prices, but the measures as a whole are intended to produce a considerable reduction in private consumption over the next twelve months and cannot fail to slow the rise in prices and defend the monetary equilibrium and the purchasing power of wages.

This short-term action, directed to resist the ills that weigh upon us, is related to the recognition that the final realignment of our external account will come through the expansion of production which can in future be devoted to a higher volume of exports; and through a substantial modification of capital flows. Here I refer not only to the investments that can come to Italy from abroad, but also to the ending of the non-authorised outflows of Italian savings and to the return of Italian capital that has been exported in the past.

This government has introduced new and modern regulations, including fiscal measures, to encourage the investment of savings in corporate shares.

As indicated above, one of the objectives of the adoption of fiscal measures to restrict the aggregate domestic demand was to give credit policy a more flexible role in supporting production and investment. This then poses the problem of the manner and the time period in which credit policy should be operated to achieve this result.

Given the decisions concerning the reduction of the excess monetary demand, it has been possible to plan a more flexible credit policy than would have been possible if no other measures had been taken to oppose the rise in internal prices and the balance of payments disequilibrium.

It has now been agreed that a credit expansion sufficient to finance new investment of around 22,000 billion lire will again be permitted to take place between March 1974 and March 1975. The domestic credit expansion should however not exceed 22,400 billion lire. The Interministerial Credit Committee will periodically monitor, and in particular in September, the path of credit expansion to keep the volume of credit within the desired limits in relation to the inflation and balance of payments developments.

It has also been decided that 500 billion lire of bonds will be issued immediately to furnish medium-term credit to small businesses, exporting firms, and to firms located in the *Mezzogiorno*. In addition, as soon as the bill already under examination by Parliament has been approved, a further issue of 1,000 billion lire will take place, the receipts to be put at the disposition of the *Cassa per il Mezzogiorno*.

Finally, in order to give continuity to investment finance, it has been decided that the banks will be required to increase their bond portfolios during the second quarter of 1974 in such a way that their investments in bonds during 1973 and 1974 are no less than 12 per cent of their own deposit liabilities at the end of 1972.

In 1973 the amount of private consumption was about 52,000 billion lire.

It seems to me that the policy to reduce demand by the proportion cited above was an important action to have been agreed by the governing parties.

We think that the adoption of the required measures should be promptly carried out, not only with the aim of correcting our disequilibrium in the shortest time compatible with this burdensome task, but also to encourage international cooperation in our efforts. This will help prevent the effects of our disequilibrium from spreading to other countries and re-establish international confidence in the Italian economy. Italy can then once again become a stabilising element in Europe and in the larger international organisations.

But when such a reduction of demand is decided, also with the aim of replacing unproductive uses of resources with productive uses, it is necessary that Parliament, the government, the unions and the employers all act responsibly and in concert to avoid a subsequent, contradictory increase in demand and thus to safeguard the measures already established to protect the lower paid.

In this respect the public sector requires particular attention. The rise in current expenditures has been 3,066 billion lire in 1973 and 3,411 billion lire in 1974.

Continual increases of this order of magnitude would not only frustrate the initiatives that are taking place today, but would make impossible the programmes for financing further productive activity. The support of productive activity, and in particular of small and medium enterprises makes no sense if it comes *a posteriori*. It only makes sense if their financial needs are taken into account before deciding particular types of behaviour which would inevitably result in restricting the sources of funds available to them.

In regard to local governments, particularly at the city and provincial level, the difficulty in which they find themselves must be recognised. It is impossible not to realise, however, as the present experience shows clearly, that no local government can increase its expenditures, particularly current expenditures, and plan its own financial requirements without reference to the real resources which the country has available and relying upon savings capacity as if this were indefinitely high.

Looking to the past in order better to foresee the future, it must be remembered that the problems of today are also linked to the operation of past policy concerning the distribution of income among the factors of production and the geographical imbalance of investment.

Both of these factors, along with the inordinate behaviour of the public sector, have frequently influenced the continuity of our growth process and made it more difficult to overcome the traditional disequilibrium of the Italian economy.

Today the country asks what benefits will result from these sacrifices. Despite its importance the answer is not only, and cannot simply be, to stop inflation and defend the purchasing power of wages and salaries. Neither can it be, though no less important, to re-establish our balance of payments equilibrium and to avoid a ruinous recession which could result in the bankruptcy of the country.

More important than these essential aims are those of defending the highest possible level of employment, of producing a pattern of development more responsive to our social needs, of promoting our agricultural production, of restructing certain sectors of industry to make them more responsive to the evolution of international markets, of finally overcoming our traditional tendencies to disequilibrium, especially those which produce the differences that divide the South from the North.

For all these reasons the things at stake today are critical and require a sense of national unity as well as the determination to attain the objectives that have been specified.

6 Address

Guido Carli

I am afraid I cannot present a scholarly contribution suitable for a conference like this. In accepting Professors Gasparini and Stammati's invitation I hope to demonstrate my friendship for them. Nevertheless, I repeat, I am unable to present a thought-out contribution worthy of the quality of the audience. Indeed I anticipate that I will disappoint you.

Everyone talks a bit about inflation, even governors and presidents of central banks. They talk about it when they meet in Basle. Each brings the contribution of his own experience. Some join in the debate to reinforce their own points of view, invoking the authority of this or that academic economist. Others, when they want to convince their colleagues of the justness of the measures undertaken, point out that in their own country they have encountered the total disapproval of all the academics. I myself belong to the group which from time to time takes refuge behind one or another academic. Most often I rely on the authority of English language academic economists, not because Italian economists are less distinguished, but because the works of the former are more widely circulated than those of the latter.

A while ago, during a break in discussions between ministers and governors at the European Economic Community, the ministers formed into a separate group, as did the governors. This always seems to happen in such circumstances. When the two groups were later brought together again I was told that one of the ministers had asked a colleague 'These governors talk and talk, but what about?' My response to his question was, 'They talk about inflation.' The minister looked at me, incredulous. Perhaps he could not believe that a group of sensible men could talk about the same problem for so many years with so little success in finding a viable solution.

During the evening discussions of the governors of central banks it once happened that one of them, when his turn arrived, and having listened to his colleagues' meandering expositions, simply said: 'My country is against inflation', and sat down. That affirmation seemed to me very concise, but perhaps for all its conciseness it was not without significance. That governor wanted to affirm that in his country, out of all the possible policy objectives, priority was given to the fight against inflation. Stability took precedence over all other objectives. In fact it became evident that the attainment of other objectives was to a large extent influenced by the attainment of stability.

The discussions carried on during the past decade can be divided into two periods according to the issues which were of major concern. The first period encompasses 1965–69, the second 1970–74. In commenting on these discussions I do not intend to give away any trade secrets, but rather to give some of my personal impressions.

In the first period the focal point of interest was the inflation in the USA, its spread to the rest of the world and the instruments suitable to stopping that spread. It was believed generally that if an international monetary system suitable to contain the inflationary impulses of the US could be found, the problem of inflation would be solved.

Those were the times when all discussions centred on the reform of the international monetary system, and concerned the opposition between those who believed that the reform should be based on gold and those who preferred reform based on an abstract monetary unit which is now called the Special Drawing Right (SDR). But the two positions held the common belief that it was necessary to build an international monetary system in which all countries, irrespective of their economic size, were bound to observe the constraints imposed by keeping their balance of payments in equilibrium. It was then believed that the quantity of money should be adjusted in relation to the surplus or deficit on the balance of payments. And it was thought that when such procedures were followed equilibrium in the balance of payments would be re-established along with a more rational co-ordination of the development of different countries.

During 1968–71 there were two important measures which contributed to the movement of the international system in a direction quite opposite to that which was thought to be desirable on the basis of the ideals of the reformers. In March 1968 came the decision to suspend intervention in the free gold market. This intervention had been carried out over the years by a pool of central banks to ensure the correspondence between the 'free market' and the official gold price. That year, some central banks, the Banca d'Italia among them, argued that if, due to the refusal to accept a higher gold price, continued intervention on the free market was necessary to impose the official price on the free market, central banks should not be forced to exhaust their own reserves in such a defence. This was the position of the Banca d'Italia. The gold reserves of the Banca d'Italia used for such intervention operations were replenished by means of repurchase agreements with the US Federal Reserve System. Thus one comes to the breaking of the link between the two circuits, the official and the free market. In 1971 the dollar was declared inconvertible by breaking the link between dollar and gold. At the end of that year there was a realignment of parities preserving the principle of fixed rates. Here was an adventure into the unknown: a regime of fixed rates without convertibility.

Experience was quick to show that the maintenance of such a system in the face of non-uniform cyclical patterns among countries was very difficult. The system was to be subject to violent shocks and the defence against capital movements within the system was to be sought in exchange-rate flexibility.

Let me summarise. Initially it was believed that inflation was exported from the USA to the rest of the world. Thus it was necessary to erect a defensive system against the inflation exported from that big country. This defence was first sought in the reform of the international monetary system. Such a reformed system, whether based on gold or on a surrogate, would have constrained all to accept the link between the balance of payments and domestic monetary creation. While the discussions proceeded, two events took place, the division of the gold market into a free and official tier, and the ending of convertibility between the dollar and gold. At the same time what we call, perhaps inappropriately, the Eurodollar market was expanding rapidly. Large quantities of dollars flowed to this market and brought about a multiplicative process that increased international liquidity by considerable proportions. Many people spoke of the opportunity of placing this multiplicative process under control. At the same time there was a not inconsiderable number of experts who denied that the multiplicative process was taking place or even that the market existed. Later, however, some of these opinions came around to the point of view that it would have been better if the market had been immediately placed under international control. The system of defence was shifting, as I have already pointed out, from the search for a defence of itself through the reform of the international monetary system, to the introduction of flexible exchange rates.

In September 1969, after a period of experimentation, the Deutsche Mark was revalued. In 1971 there was a new experimental float limited to the Deutsche Mark. During April 1972 the currencies of the EEC were united on the basis of an accord which linked them in respect to reciprocal movements within a margin of 2·25 per cent around their respective parities. An extension of the system of flotation continued during 1973. One group of currencies maintained a link among themselves, a link given the name 'joint float'. By means of the 'joint float' it was believed that a protective wall could be erected around an area of relative stability, protecting it from the instability raging in the rest of the world. Measures were introduced to slow – or which were believed to slow – the process of inflation, based on limits placed upon the rate of growth of the money supply. These limits are specified to the extent that they concern the growth of money and quasi-money. Once again the quantitative conception reappears. If it is possible to contain the growth of the quantity of money (M_1 or M_2, however defined), it is possible to control the inflationary process. But experience quickly showed that the inflationary process could not be brought under control simply through the control of monetary expansion. In some cases experience demonstrated that it was not possible to contain the expansion within the desired limits, in other cases that even when this intermediate objective was achieved, the battle against inflation remained still to be won.

What was happening in the rest of the world and within each country in the meantime? A vast process of redistribution of income was taking place, both between nations and within them. Up to 1967–68, in the economies of industrialised countries the relation between the prices of manufactured products and the prices of primary commodities remained constant, except for the period of the Korean war. The curves representing the movement of prices of manufactured products and prices of primary products intertwine one with the other with a tendency for the prices of manufactured products to rise more than the prices of primary products, or for the second to fall more quickly than the prices of the first; overall the relation of manufactured to primary products prices moved in favour of the first.

In numerous countries wages and salaries were contained within the limits of productivity and in some cases the labour cost per unit of output remained constant or showed direct signs of diminution. But from 1968–69 onwards the conditions change fundamentally. There is a vast process of redistribution. The prices of primary materials rise. The quadrupling of the price of petroleum represents the culmination of this process. The relation between price of primary products and manufactured products changes fundamentally, the terms of trade change. Industrial countries are faced with the problem of adapting the structure of their own economies to the new terms of trade. In individual countries there is a redistribution of income to the advantage of employed labour, the increase in wages surpassing the rise in productivity and unit costs of production thus tending to rise. What are the financial and monetary consequences of this process? I do not intend to give an exhaustive account. I only want to direct your attention to some of the problems that have concerned and are concerning most immediately those responsible for financial and monetary policy; to some of the problems that are the subject of the conversations which take place in that invisible club regularly held by the governors of central banks in Basle.

I would like to limit my considerations to the financial and monetary aspects of the most discussed problem of present times, the rise in petroleum prices and its consequences for the monetary and financial system. A consequence of the rise in the price of petroleum is a large accumulation of income in a small group of countries. Some of them are unable to spend this income in the medium term, while others are able to spend on investment programmes. In both cases, however, the greatest accumulation of incomes is taking place in countries that in the short run are unable to spend them. This produces inflationary and deflationary effects at the same time. A new problem is thus posed for those looking towards a reform of the world monetary system, i.e. to adapt the system to the requirement of supporting large surpluses and deficits on the balance of payments in the medium term and to undertake their financing in a form that is anti-inflationary. Surpluses and deficits imply that some countries accumulate financial claims on other countries. The problem then is the form that these assets should take to minimise the effect that their creation might have on the price system.

When the rise in the price of petroleum was announced, and above all when it had shown effects on the surplus and deficit positions of the exporting and importing countries respectively, it was thought that the financing of the surplus and deficit would take place via the Eurodollar market. The exporting countries, it was thought, would desposit, as they now deposit, part or all of their proceeds in this market. The banks operating in this market lend to the banks of the importing countries, who in their turn, reconstitute their own financial assets. The Eurodollar market in fact accomplishes the function of duplicating the gross reserves of the international monetary system, for the exporting countries consider short-term bank credits in the Eurodollar market as part of their own reserves, while the central banks who have taken loans from the market consider them as reconstituting their own reserves.

Could such a process continue indefinitely? What would be the consequences? Only recently has the new system been fully functioning. Nearly a billion dollars per week is flowing to the exporting countries in payment for 'equity oil' and 4–5 billion dollars a quarter for 'participation oil'. Where are they going to employ this revenue? It seems that a growing portion is being placed with US banks, and is concentrated in the largest banks. This presents problems. To the extent that the larger banks are reluctant to accept all these deposits, they go to smaller banks. To the extent that smaller banks show reluctance, or the potential depositors prefer to put their funds elsewhere, these funds are pushed into the security markets. In these conditions, how is it possible to obtain the required closure of the circuit without which the system could not continue? Would it not be necessary to insert a lender of last resort into the system? And who is the lender of last resort? Suppose that all the dollar proceeds of the exporting countries were concentrated in the US and that they were all in US government bonds. In this case only the Federal Reserve could be the lender of last resort. But one aspect should attract the attention of both exporting and importing countries. This concerns the instability of a system in which an increasing volume of financial assets is capable of free movement from one market to another, from one bank to another within the same market, from the banks to the open market and back again, and from one currency to another. Such instability disturbs the development of international trade. It contradicts the very interests of the exporting, as well as the importing countries. Hence the continued search for better co-ordination of the system.

Rational solutions such as those proposed by the managing director of the International Monetary Fund satisfy the requirements sought for with the medium-term financing of large deficits by an international institution. This would limit the mobility of funds from one point to another in the system, thereby limiting the violent shifts which damage the continuity of the expansion of the exchanges. But there is a further aspect of the problem that should be underlined. Accepting the statistic according to which the accumulation of surpluses on the part of the exporting countries during 1974 would be of the order of 60 billion dollars, the greatest part concentrated *vis-à-vis* a few large industrial countries, and supposing that each of these countries intends to carry out policies designed to re-establish its own balance of payments equilibrium in the short run, the consequence would be that in some countries there would be the double effect of the disequilibrium of the balance of payments between importers and exporters of petroleum, plus payments disequilibrium provoked by the policy of restraint carried out by other countries to equilibrate their own payments position. In fact, if all the industrial countries, autonomously, without co-ordination of their actions, exercised policy to re-establish short-period equilibrium of their own balance of payments, the system would necessarily move towards a diminution of productive activity, which would eventually degenerate into conditions of recession. This again confirms how much the search for a solution to our current problem should be based on an intensification of international co-operation.

I would like to summarise what I have said concerning the problem of the petroleum deficits and their financing.

Deficits and surpluses signify, in the absence of co-ordinated action, the creation of financial assets. If these assets take the form of deposits, either in the Eurodollar market or in the USA or both, the instability or the dangers of instability to which the international monetary system is exposed, increases. The possibility that these funds may suddenly be converted into real goods, stimulating demand and thus accelerating the rise in prices, also grows. The possibility that these funds may be shifted from one market to another, from one asset to another, from one bank to another also grows and with it the possibility of a liquidity crisis in this or that bank, increasing the size of fluctuations of the exchange rates. In addition, the non-co-ordinated search for balance of payments equilibrium by all the industrial countries could expose the system to the dangers of a slow-down in economic activity which could take on the proportions of a recession. Thus the necessity of international policy co-ordination.

I earlier referred to the great process of redistribution of wealth taking place among countries, and among social groups within countries. This second type of redistribution has repercussions not unlike the first. The relative changes in income among social groups produce as a consequence a reduction in the profits of manufacturing firms, an increase in household incomes, and for a given investment, a greater dependence of firms on household savings. To enlarge financial intermediation in this way increases the volume of financial wealth and, apart from the form that it assumes as bonds, deposits or currency, it increases the danger that, in certain circumstances. the financial wealth may be converted into an expansion of demand adding to a rise in prices. This phenomenon is shown to a large extent in those industrial countries in which the volume of financial intermediation relative to national income has risen more than in other countries. In these countries it is more difficult to succeed in the control of the inflationary process because such a policy of control must not only try to keep within given limits the expansion of means of payment, but must also attempt to protect the existing financial wealth in order to prevent it from being transformed in one form or another, into an expansion of aggregate demand. Besides this, the redistribution of income takes place through the higher demand for social services provided by public entities – national and local governments, public corporations, and social security bodies – without a corresponding increase in taxes, i.e. without a transfer of income equivalent to the cost of the additional services demanded.

The deficit of the public sector, at national and local levels, is thereby enlarged. The increase in this deficit imposes further restriction on monetary policy which is thus increasingly constrained by the pressure exercised by the transfer of revenue to sections of the population with a higher than average propensity to consume.

To sum up, we have been witnessing a greater dependence by firms on external finance, brought about by the transfer of savings from the household sector. The creation of greater financial wealth increases the possibility that this wealth may on occasions be converted into a higher level of demand. The financing of the public sector deficit can be carried out either by selling securities in the market, in competition with those used to finance the private sector; or by creating new money, which adds to the multiplicative process of financial assets and is a major danger to price stability. This is further supported by inflationary pressures coming from abroad, for the reasons already indicated. Thus there is increasing instability of the system on the international level as on the domestic level as financial wealth grows in relation to the deficits through which it is created. In sum, we are faced with a system that, on both the international and internal level, is more susceptible to the dangers of inflationary pressures than in the past.

I do not intend to suggest what the remedies might be, nor am I able to do so. I will only point out that there can be no possible policies to control inflation if they are continually stymied by the size of the public sector deficit and continually faced with the problem of choosing methods of finance from either securities floated in the market in competition with private issues or by the printing of new money. The experience of some countries shows how closely the deficit on the balance of payments is related to the money-financed deficit of the public sector. In some countries those who lament the effects of credit restriction too often forget that such effects, rather than being provoked by the deliberate policy of the monetary authorities, are frequently a mechanical consequence that results from the fact that in an open economy the quantity of liquidity which is internally created flows to the exterior in the form of balance of payments deficits.

In conclusion, the public sector deficit, its finance by means of money creation, the deficit on the balance of payments through which the money creation is destroyed, reflect the co-existence of inflation, deflation and a balance of payments deficit. This is why I share the view of those economists – including some who have given papers at this conference – who maintain that the solution to the problem should be sought through appropriate fiscal policies placing some restrictions on the behaviour of the public sector. I am well aware of how easy it is to make such propositions and how difficult it is to obey the imperatives that they imply. Credit policies in an open system are also largely influenced by the existing proportions between the public's financial wealth, aggregate demand and the balance of payments, independently of the possibility that the larger the financial wealth of the public, the greater will be movements from market to market for reasons of profitability or other considerations.

Thus the problem lies in large part beyond the scope of action of the monetary authorities. It concerns the co-ordinated behaviour among nations, and internally, among social groups. It is hard to succeed in resolving the problem of inflation if better co-ordination cannot be established, a co-ordination which would result in the consistency between the demands for real resources and the supply of them.

I might mention that in a conference similar to this one, organised by the American Economic Association and chaired by Professor Galbraith, the speakers set out conclusions not much different from those I have indicated. In that conference, Professors Okun, Gurley and Friedman responded to the question 'Have fiscal and monetary policies failed?' Professor Okun responded that the answer was a function of the objectives which fiscal and monetary policies were set to achieve. He believed that some objectives, in the light of experience, had been satisfied, some not. Professor Gurley responded differently to the question by pointing out that, since Western economies were founded on the profit motives of private enterprise, the response to the question depends on the effect of fiscal and monetary policies on the level of firms' profits. Professor Friedman confirmed his personal faith in monetary policy, maintaining that a policy of appropriate growth in the quantity of money would allow inflation control. But he himself admitted in the end that this remedy would encounter problems when demand exceeded the limits of supply. He concluded his response in the following way: 'I believe that we economists in recent years have done vast harm to society at large and to our profession in particular by claiming more than we can deliver. We have thereby encouraged politicians to make extravagant promises, inculcate unrealistic expectations in the public at large and promote discontent with reasonably satisfactory results because they fall short of . . .' I am not so sure that the governors of central banks should not also be included under the reproach that Professor Friedman made of economists. Perhaps for reasons of *esprit de corps* it seems to me that the reproach is not merited.

Part Three

7 Report on the European Economic Community

*Ugo Mosca**

I SCOPE AND PURPOSE OF THIS PAPER

Inflation is by no means a new phenomenon, either in Europe or elsewhere. The Roman emperors' victualling decrees are a reminder that even in those times the cost of living was creating public alarm.

In more recent times, politicians, economists and sociologists have carried out innumerable studies of the causes and effects of inflation and the remedies therefor; today, however, more and more frequent references can be heard to a 'new type of inflation'. It may well be asked whether this qualification 'new' is really nothing more than a pretext to justify our perplexity when faced with the perennial phenomenon of monetary erosion.

This short paper makes no pretence of putting forward new insights for the theoretical debate on inflation at present in progress; the author's object is merely to highlight those aspects of the evolution of prices within the European Community from 1958 to today which seem the most striking and, on that basis, to make certain empirical observations.

To this end, the following points will be briefly discussed:

progress and characteristics of inflation within the European Economic Community;
reactions of member countries' economies to inflationary pressures;
lessons to be drawn from the most recent Community experience.

II PROGRESS AND CHARACTERISTICS OF INFLATION WITHIN THE EEC

The first comment that should be made is that, until the end of the 1960s, the rate of inflation in the nine Community countries was held – although with cyclical oscillations – down to a maximum of 4·7 per cent. From the beginning of the 1970s onwards an exceedingly rapid acceleration occurred, which developed by the end of 1973 into the inflationary explosion we see taking place today.

* The opinions expressed by the author, who wishes to thank all those who helped him with their advice, are entirely personal and do not necessarily represent the views of the Commission of the European Communities.

According to estimates by the EEC Commission's departments, the increase in the implicit price index for private consumption in 1974 will range between 12 and 20 per cent for seven member countries, whilst the other two, showing relatively better results, will range between 7·5 and 9 per cent.

TABLE 1 Trends of consumer price indices

Percentage increase

	D	*F*	*I*	*NL*	*B*	*L*	*EEC-6*	*UK*	*DK*	*IRL*	*EEC-9*
1963–68	2·5	3·3	3·4	4·4	3·4	3·6	3·2	3·7	5·7	4·6	3·5
1969–72	6·9	5·5	6·4	7·6	5·4	5·9	6·3	7·8	7·1	10·2	6·7
1973	7·1	7·2	11·0	9·0	7·0	6·1	8·0	8·6	9·3	11·5	8·0
1974*	7·5	13·8	20·0	10·5	12·0	9·0	12·5	15·7	16·2	17·0	13·2

* Estimated figures.

This inflationary phase differs from previous such phases in its persistence, intensity and widespread dissemination, both within and without the Community. A greater danger exists than in previous phases, therefore, that irreparable economic distortions and disastrous political and social tensions will result.

As regards the Community in particular, the differing capacities of national economies to react to the accelerating rise in prices has virtually brought all progress towards economic and monetary union to a halt. It is to be feared that if the present state of things persists, the Community may even be compelled to take a pace backwards.

How do we come to find ourselves in this position?

As stated above, this paper will confine itself to certain empirical observations. No attempt will be made, therefore, to analyse the deeper causes of inflation in the 1970s, which would be quite an ambitious undertaking.

More modestly, comments will instead be made on certain factors which have undoubtedly helped to give the inflationary phenomenon its present scope and might therefore provide some useful indications for possible future action.

With this in mind, and without claiming to be exhaustive, the following points will be examined:

the trends of raw materials prices;
the trend of liquidity;
exchange-rate policy;
trends in income distribution.

TRENDS IN RAW MATERIALS PRICES

The rise in raw materials prices, which has been substantial in recent years, is often cited – together with other elements – to demonstrate that the phenomenon we are at present witnessing in the Community is primarily a matter of cost inflation.

It is a fact that oil prices rose by more than a factor of three at the end of 1973 and that prices of other basic materials have also increased sharply. Taking the 1967–70 average as 100, it will be noted that for member countries overall the prices of minerals and metals were up in 1973 by an average of 45 per cent, agricultural produce by an average of 80 per cent and textile fibres by 100 per cent.

According to econometric calculations carried out by the Commission's departments, these recent developments correspond to a direct effect on the implicit price index of GNP of the order of 3–4 per cent (about 2–3 per cent for oil products and about 1 per cent for other basic materials).

It should be pointed out, however, not only that the general rise in consumer prices greatly exceeds this effect, but also that inflation had already begun to accelerate whilst the prices of raw materials – especially oil – were still relatively stable.

Whilst, therefore, it may be asserted that these price increases made a significant contribution to the acceleration of inflation in 1973 and at the beginning of 1974, it would be difficult to maintain that they are the root cause of the inflationary cycle we are experiencing at present. It may be asked whether they are not merely – at least in part – a consequence of the 'boom' in demand in the industrialised countries.

At the beginning of 1973, all the industrialised countries were simultaneously in a phase of buoyant economic activity. This was one of the first occasions on which such a generalised trend has occurred. The fact that trends in Europe and in the United States were in phase – a consequence at once of the growing interdependence of the respective economies and the increasingly rapid dissemination, both at a European and a worldwide level, of cyclical changes in activity – therefore amplified reciprocal stimuli to the development of inflation. The extremely sharp rise in prices of raw materials imports should be seen in this particular light. This rise corresponds, broadly speaking, to an attempt by raw materials producers to reverse the deteriorating trend in their terms of trade in evidence throughout the post-war period. The abruptness of this reversal accentuated inflationary pressures; however, it was only made possible by the inflationary climate already existing.

THE TREND OF LIQUIDITY

From the end of the war until 1969, international liquidity grew by an average of 2–2½ per cent per annum. From 1970 to 1973 the rate of increase jumped to 20 per cent and even 30 per cent. As a result, the volume of international liquidity rose from about 90 thousand million Special Drawing Rights in 1970 to approximately 180 thousand million in 1973.

The result of this phenomenon, especially whilst the fixed exchange-rate system was observed, was to oblige European countries (principally Germany and the Netherlands but, in certain periods, also France and other countries) to absorb growing quantities of dollars, resulting in a corresponding increase in the money supply.

An external element in the expansion of the money supply thus supplemented the internal elements, complicating the task of the monetary authorities.

In general, however, member countries cannot attribute the responsibility for the increase in their domestic liquidity primarily to international monetary disorder. In fact, in the first place, inflows of foreign exchange – particularly where movements of speculative funds are concerned – do not necessarily result in a corresponding increase in domestic liquidity. There is no lack of instruments for controlling capital movements or neutralising their effects. The effectiveness of such instruments, whilst of course conditioned by the violence of the monetary movements concerned, is nevertheless not to be brushed aside.

In the second place, in some member countries – and Italy must be numbered among them – the expansion of domestic liquidity has been determined essentially by internal factors, above all the uninterrupted rise in the deficit of the public sector.

However, quite apart from the factors causing domestic liquidity to expand, a glance at Table 2 (trend of the money supply) and Table 1 (trend of the consumer price index) will suffice to show the degree of parallelism in the trends of these two economic aggregates.

Similarly, a glance at Tables 2 and 3 will show the degree of parallelism between the trend of public sector deficits and that of the money supply.

THE FOREIGN EXCHANGE SYSTEM

The disruption of the international monetary system and the collapse of the system introduced by the Bretton Woods agreement resulted, *inter alia*, in the generalised adoption of floating exchange rates. This is a matter of recent history, which there is no need to repeat here.

In the present situation, whose principal features are inflation, the violent impact of the rise in oil prices on the balance of payments positions of the industrialised countries and the consequent disorganisation of international capital markets, the floating exchange-rate system seems likely to persist.

The Group of Twenty in fact legalised this system at its last meeting on 12 and 13 June. At the same time, the Group shelved the question of the reform of the international monetary system, despite the fact that this was the main objective of its terms of reference.

Within the Community, only five member countries (Germany, Belgium, Denmark, the Netherlands, Luxembourg) have maintained a system of joint floating among themselves. The other four have abandoned the 'Community snake'; the UK and Ireland in June 1972, Italy in February 1973 and France in January 1974. The fact that those countries which have remained faithful to the Community exchange system, besides conducting a high percentage of their trade with each other, also have very similar economic structures and cyclical trends (Table 4) is not without significance.

This confirms that, not only at a world level, but also at the more limited Community level, greater exchange-rate stability cannot be re-established in the absence of any real convergence of economic policies.

This being said, we may go on to ask whether floating exchange rates are really a panacea and – particularly – whether the acceleration of inflation may not be attributable to them, at least in part.

Floating exchange rates permit surplus countries with strong currencies to limit inflows of hot money. The purely monetary machinery by which inflation is transmitted then plays a lesser part than in a fixed exchange-rate system, even though central banks continue to intervene on the market to guide or limit exchange-rate adjustments.

At the same time, the appreciation of strong currencies improves the terms of trade of the surplus countries, with the result that inflation is exported to the deficit countries.

Conversely, in deficit countries with weak currencies fluctuations tend to increase the inflation rate cumulatively, either through a deterioration in the terms of trade, or by creating the illusion that there is no further need to take external equilibrium into account. This illusion, that independence in the conduct of national economic policies has been re-acquired, is a complete fallacy in an open economic system and in practice results in giving renewed impetus to inflation.

In conclusion, the belief that the floating exchange-rate system is, by no means, a negligible cause of the accelerating inflation observed in recent years is gaining ground more and more.

The validity of the reasons – I would say of *force majeure* – at present preventing the reorganisation of the international monetary system on more stable bases should not lead us to forget this aspect of the problem, whose importance seems all the greater as the struggle against inflation becomes more urgent and more imperative.

TRENDS IN INCOME DISTRIBUTION

The forms taken by the struggle for income redistribution and the means employed to this end have considerable importance for the trend of prices in all member countries of the Community.

This question is much more political than economic and should therefore be approached with caution. We shall thus confine ourselves here to certain observations – certainly not exhaustive – concerning two problems: the trend of wages in the various sectors of production, and the respective shares of wages and profits.

In all Community member countries, although to a greater extent in some than in others, wage-rate levels as a whole tend to align themselves on those showing the most rapid increases, i.e. those granted by sectors in which productivity is highest. The result is that low productivity sectors are obliged to increase their prices, thus becoming factors in the general upward movement of prices.

This phenomenon is aggravated by the fact that the geographical and sectoral mobility of Community workers is still relatively limited, whilst the mobility of enterprises themselves or of capital is wholly insufficient.

As regards the respective shares of wages and profits, it must be noted that the social strains experienced at the end of the sixties in many Community countries contributed to a sharp acceleration in the upward movement of wages in money terms and unit costs of production.

Nevertheless, the rise in prices had the effect of appreciably limiting the decline in the share of profits in the national income.

Although the situation is not identical as between member countries, the implication is that, in general, the various social groups have as far as possible maintained their relative positions, but at the cost of sacrificing monetary stability.

There is, of course, no question of uttering a value judgement on the behaviour of the respective social groups; the object is merely to draw attention to an observed fact, i.e. the consequent stimulus given to inflation, not so much by the income distribution struggle itself, but by the conditions – more or less – under which it took place.

In this respect it is significant that those member countries in which social conflicts have been the most acute (Italy and the United Kingdom) are precisely those in which prices have risen the most rapidly, whilst the reverse is true in countries in which more has been done to ensure participation by workers' representatives in economic policy decision-making (Germany and Belgium) and the management of enterprises (Germany again).

III REACTIONS OF MEMBER COUNTRIES' ECONOMIES TO INFLATIONARY PRESSURES

In connection with the acceleration of generalised inflation, two phenomena may be noted regarding the contrast between inflation rates in the various member countries.

In relative terms, the disparities between rates of price rises have narrowed appreciably: from 1960 to 1969, the lowest rates corresponded to about one-third of the highest, whilst from 1970 onwards the lowest corresponded to about two-thirds of the highest.

Conversely, in absolute terms, disparities between inflation rates in the various member countries have widened considerably, rising from a minimum of two to three points to a maximum of four to five.

The first point to be observed (decline in relative disparities) suggests that at high inflation rates the 'pull' exercised by high inflation-rate countries on countries traditionally more stable is stronger than in periods of more moderate inflation.

The freedom for any Community country to select its appropriate degree of stability is thus seriously eroded if its partners are experiencing a price explosion.

The second point (widening of absolute disparities) is a more dramatic illustration of the problems of competitiveness and external equilibrium faced by countries with the highest inflation rates, making the needs for adjustment the more imperative.

This situation involves a risk that member countries in difficulties may be compelled to adopt external measures running counter to interests of the Community (such as the reintroduction of restrictions on intra-Community trade) or, alternatively, internal measures liable to have a drastic effect on production and employment (and therefore detrimental not only to the country concerned, but to the Community overall).

There is a danger, therefore, that inflation may become a disintegrating factor within the Community, affecting the behaviour of member states and pushing them towards unilateral action. If ever this comes about, the opportunities for a demonstration of Community solidarity are likely to be jeopardised exactly when they would be most needed.

IV LESSONS TO BE DRAWN FROM THE MOST RECENT COMMUNITY EXPERIENCE

As I come to the concluding part of these brief remarks on the Community experience in recent years, I do not propose to define a complete programme to combat inflation.

The structures and economic situations in the member states are so diverse that it would be necessary to study the situation in depth in every single country and draw up specific guidelines for each of them. Such a task, apart from being too ambitious, would be outside the limited scope of this short paper. I will confine myself to a few general comments.

First, it is obvious that an anti-inflation policy becomes all the more painful the longer inflation continues and accelerates, because it always makes it more difficult to achieve the other objectives of economic policy: full employment, development and social progress.

In the present circumstances, with an inflation rate which is over 10 per cent nearly everywhere in the Community and which, in some countries, is even likely to reach and pass the 20 per cent mark, it is therefore essential to act as quickly as possible and energetically.

Such action is all the more urgent and necessary in countries with both a high rate of inflation and a very precarious balance of payments situation because, as we have seen, such a situation is likely not only to perpetuate internal and external imbalance through a cumulative process of currency depreciations, but also to impair the cohesion of the Community, perhaps immediately.

Throughout all the Community countries, the simultaneous rising rate of inflation and expansion of the monetary supply confirm that effective control of liquidity is an essential condition for the achievement of a non-inflationary development policy.

Whatever the causes of inflation, its development, particularly at the present rate, in fact presupposes that a 'permissive' policy is being applied to the evolution of money supply. This brings us to the question of the correct dosage of credit policy and budgetary policy.

Better control of liquidity is certainly within the powers of the monetary authorities, but the real problem is to predict the possible consequences, for productivity and employment, of applying the monetary brake. Not even the most recent economic and monetary theory throws much light on this subject, but in the present circumstances in some countries of the Community, it is all too necessary to give priority to efforts to control runaway prices and restore the equilibria of the balance of payments.

If the present imbalance continues it is likely to lead the deficit countries into insolvency, which would have far worse consequences for economic development in general, and for the standard of living of workers in particular. Consequently, it would be better to accept sacrifices now to avoid worse to come.

When speaking of sacrifices, one should be quite aware that behind the apparently abstract macroeconomic calculations are millions of human beings with all their personal and family problems.

It is now certain that the dimensions of the inflationary phenomenon will call for containment of overall demand (a step all the more necessary in industrial countries, where the terms of trade are deteriorating *vis-à-vis* the countries producing raw materials). Furthermore, in carrying out such an operation constant attention must be paid to social justice.

In this context, budgetary policy has a special role to play, both to ease the task of the monetary authorities and to ensure, through adjustment in taxation and the determination of public expenditure, that the twofold objective of equity and social progress is safeguarded.

At the present time a particular responsibility also devolves on the two sides of industry, without whose co-operation it would be impossible to carry out an effective stabilisation policy which does not preclude the possibility of the economy picking up in more stable conditions.

In some Community countries there are procedures and institutions of co-ordination which make it possible for various social groups and categories and the authorities responsible for economic policy to initiate a broad dialogue on the orientation of the major economic choices. Using these procedures and institutions it would be possible to define which sacrifices each socio-occupational group should accept in order to overcome the inflationary crisis and lay the ground for a better future.

With regard to the Community as a whole, collaboration should also be improved between the member countries. Since their economies are so closely interwoven no single country can fight alone against inflation nor be indifferent to the fate of its partners.

A start towards aligning the rates of inflation in member countries, or at least reducing the divergencies to tolerable levels, would seem to be a necessary condition to prevent a general return to protectionism and to open the road to economic and monetary union.

Obviously such harmonisation cannot be carried out to the detriment of the fight against inflation. Should the actual rate of price increases continue, not only will the cohesion of the Community itself be endangered but so will the social and political body of each member state.

The major effort to restore economic equilibrium must now be made and first by those countries which, like Italy, have a very high rate of inflation and a very heavy external deficit.

It is therefore also in the interests of surplus countries, such as Germany, that the efforts of adjustment made by deficit countries should be sufficiently gradual and balanced. An abrupt deflation would be against everyone's interest.

Surplus member countries, even if they so wished, could not indefinitely finance the deficit countries. They are, however, certainly prepared to contribute according to their means to the economic recovery of those that are at present in difficulties, provided the latter bear their share of the efforts and sacrifices necessary.

Far-reaching collaboration, which should not be limited to the financial sphere is, therefore not merely to be hoped for but could become a reality between the different countries. In particular, surplus countries should manage their own economies in such a way as to make room for resources freed in the deficit countries as a result of the brake on domestic demand.

With this prospect in view the problem of sharing the burden of adjustment between member countries cannot be avoided. For such a division to be in the interests of the Community it will be necessary to arbitrate between the different national interests, which are frequently self-seeking. It is on this very point that the authorities of the Community, Commission and Council have so far not always lived up to the expectations of the European public.

The problem is much more political than economic because, in substance, it means transferring real responsibility and decision-making powers to the Community.

The difficulties at present besetting the Community are both a danger and an opportunity: the danger is that of a turning aside of the European integration process; the opportunity – which has to be grasped – is the possibility of taking a resolute step forward towards the political union of Europe.

TABLE 2 Trends in the Stock of Money and Quasi-money (M_2) in the EEC Member Countries Since 1969

Percentage increase

Annual average

Countries	1969	1970	1971	1972	1973
FRG	10·0	10·5	14·3	16·9	14·0
France	6·3	15·2	18·2	18·6	15·1
Italy	11·4	13·6	17·1	18·2	23·3
Netherlands	10·2	11·0	9·0	11·9	21·9
Belgium	7·7	8·2	13·1	16·1	14·4
United Kingdom	3·0	9·4	13·5	27·6	28·9
Ireland	12·6	—	—	10·2	22·6
Denmark*	10·5	3·1	8·6	14·8	12·6

* End of year increase

TABLE 3 Trends in General Government Net Lending by EEC Countries since 1965

Countries	Unit	1965	1966	1967	1968	1969	1970	1971	1972	1973	1974	1975 (prov.)
Germany (FR)	mrd DM	−1·80	−0·53	−6·35	−4·59	7·00	3·29	1·53	−1·19	13·97	−11.7	−70·0
France (*a*)	mrd fr.	1·82	1·61	−1·57	−5·40	5·42	7·39	5·38	5·73	6·24	6·3	−16·4
Italy	mrd lire	−1158	−1312	−733	−1179	−1410	−1447	−2945	−4517	−6396	−3760	−5700
Netherlands	mill gld	−557	−636	−1051	−764	−511	−920	−640	110	2400	3280	−5500
Belgium (*b*)	mrd fr.	−11·8	−7·2	−10·6	−25·8	−18·5	−13·5	−29·5	−49·6	−46·0	−54·6	−68·0
Luxembourg (*a*)	mill fr.	−557	−636	−1051	−983	280	1638	1410	1480	1592	2500	−3100
United Kingdom	mill £	−753	−121	−599	−434	−417	1295	740	−1279	−2523	−3617	−7480
Ireland	mill £	−40·5	−27·1	−35·1	−40·2	−58·7	−67·6	−72·6	−96·5	−124·1	−269	−543
Denmark	mill Kr.	1269	1770	297	1033	1496	2429	3651	5412	7348	n.a.	n.a.

Source: OECD National Accounts.

(*a*) Because of a change in definitions the figures from 1970 for France, and from 1968 for Luxembourg are not consistent with those for earlier years.

(*b*) Excludes net receipts of capital transfers.

TABLE 4 Exports. Percentage market shares in 1972

	(A) 5—EC	(B) 4—EC2	(C) non-EEC	D	UEBL	N	DK	F	I	UK	IRL	(D) rest of world	A+B+C+D
5—EEC Community snake[1]	30·7	26·5	4·8	12·3	7·4	9·4	1·6	13·4	6·9	6·0	0·3	38·0	100
4—EEC Separate float[2]	28·8	17·2	3·3	16·0	6·6	4·8	1·4	5·7	5·3	4·5	1·8	50·7	100
2—Non-EEC joint float[3]	26·4	23·9	11·2	11·2	2·8	3·7	8·7	4·5	3·0	15·9	0·5	38·5	100
FRG	20·5	26·5	4·6	·	8·3	10·2	2·0	13·0	8·4	4·7	0·3	48·4	100
Belgo-Luxembourg Economic Union	44·6	29·4	2·5	25·0	·	18·7	1·0	20·3	4·6	4·4	0·2	23·5	100
Netherlands	49·7	23·9	2·8	34·4	13·8	·	1·5	10·6	5·5	7·5	0·3	23·6	100
Denmark	16·1	26·5	22·9	12·3	1·3	2·5	·	2·8	3·7	19·6	0·5	34·5	100
France	38·8	17·2	2·0	21·2	11·4	5·5	0·8	·	11·5	5·5	0·2	42·0	100
Italy	31·7	18·6	1·6	22·9	3·7	4·4	0·7	14·2	·	4·3	0·2	48·1	100
United Kingdom	17·2	13·0	6·1	6·1	4·0	4·6	2·5	5·2	2·9	·	4·8	63·7	100
Ireland	10·3	66·7	1·0	4·6	2·9	2·7	0·2	4·0	1·6	61·2	·	22·0	100

[1] 5 countries in joint EEC float.
[2] France, Italy, United Kingdom, Ireland.
[3] Sweden, Norway.

8 Report on the United States (1)

*James L. Pierce**

The inflation problem in the United States is in many ways similar to that of most industrial countries. Inflation rates accelerated in the late 1960s primarily because of excess demand pressures. This process was followed by a large number of inflationary shocks in the 1970s, which were superimposed on the already high inflation rates. The new shocks included rapidly rising prices for food, raw materials, and more recently oil. The consequence has been inflation rates that are so high that there is little prospect of returning to pre-1960 price behaviour for a long time to come. Even if there are no new shocks or if some shocks reverse themselves in the near future – which seems unlikely – a strong inflationary process has been set in motion that will be extremely difficult to slow down. Wages and prices in the US will continue to respond to the large price increases in 1973 and 1974, and it will take the inflationary process a substantial amount of time to work itself out.

This prospect has led many observers to wonder whether the costs of trying to eliminate inflation totally is really worth the effort. Why not aim at a constant inflation rate, encourage indexing and let the economy adjust? Quite aside from the possible implications for economic stabilisation policies that might occur from indexing, there would be a great social cost during any transition period to a steady inflation rate. It is essential, therefore, to attempt at least to reduce inflation rates in the US. It is relevant, however, to wonder whether it is desirable to aim for inflation rates as low as those experienced in the US in the 1950s.

I want to focus my discussion on the very recent experience in the US because Mr Burger has provided a paper to the conference on the experience of the mid- and late-sixties. Perhaps a couple of remarks on the 1960s, however, would provide a useful background at this point. First of all, the 1960s were characterised by excess demand in the US

* Associate Director, Division of Research and Statistics, Board of Governors of the Federal Reserve System, USA. The views expressed in this paper are my own and do not necessarily reflect those of the Federal Reserve Board or its staff. I wish to thank MaryAnn Graves for her help and advice in converting the original taped version of this talk into a form suitable for publication.

economy and I think that the sources of the excesses are well understood. Monetary and fiscal policy proved to be overly expansive during the period, in part, to avoid – or better postpone – paying for a very unpopular war.

Because prices respond slowly to excess demand, it did appear during much of this period that the country could have both more guns and more butter. Unfortunately by the end of the 1960s and the beginning of the 1970s the fallacy of this guns *and* butter proposition were obvious. As the price rise accelerated, real demand was reduced for those who could not manage to keep up. Real income did get redistributed but not as a result of increased taxes and/or interest rates, but as a result of rising prices.

Let us turn to the recent record which is depicted in Table 1. It shows that in 1970, inflation in the United States was running somewhat above a 5 per cent annual rate as measured by the broader price indexes. This is high by historic US standards. Beginning in 1971, but more so in 1972, some – but not all – prices accelerated. Table 1 shows that the GNP deflator, which is probably the best global indicator of prices in

TABLE 1 Selected Wage and Price Indicators for the United States (annual rates of change of seasonally adjusted data)

	Prices					*Wages*
	GNP implicit price deflator	*Consumer price index*	*Wholesale price index*	*Farm products and processed foods*	*Imports*	*Average hourly earnings private non-farm economy*
1970						
1st half	5·5	5·9	1·9	−2·0	5·3	5·9
2nd half	5·2	5·1	2·7	−0·4	6·6	7·3
1971						
1st half	4·8	3·8	4·4	6·8	4·2	7·6
2nd half	2·2	2·9	3·7	5·5	5·1	5·6
1972						
1st half	3·7	2·9	4·1	4·5	10·3	6·9
2nd half	3·7	3·9	9·1	25·1	7·0	6·2
1973						
QI	5·5	8·4	19·5	46·8	10·9	5·0
QII	7·3	7·5	20·9	44·8	34·9	6·7
QIII	8·3	10·2	13·2	33·5	18·5	7·9
QIV	8·6	9·2	8·7	−8·7	34·3	7·1
1974						
QI	12·3	14·2	24·5	10·8	66·1	6·0
QII	9·4	10·9	12·2	−29·3	50·8	10·4

the US, did not indicate much inflation until 1973. The explanation is that price controls were introduced in August 1971 and were relatively effective even in 1972. However, the behaviour of the wholesale price index beginning in the second half of 1972 signalled the weakening and eventual demise of price controls. Also, neither imports nor food products were included in the price controls, a fact that is clearly evident from looking at the table. The rise in food and import prices greatly exacerbated the inflation last year and this. By the first quarter of 1974 price controls had been lifted in the US, and prices accelerated further.

The final column of Table 1 shows an index of wage earnings. During the entire period shown, which includes the first quarter of 1974, wages were remarkably stable in the United States, even though the inflation rate was high and accelerating (note that consumer prices started accelerating before the GNP deflator itself, in large part because of the import prices). Thus workers in the private non-farm sector suffered a decline in real wages. Wage controls went along with the price controls in the US and apparently were more successful than price controls.[1] The relatively low rate of wage increase during this period indicates that wages have really not responded yet to what has been happening in the rest of the economy. This implies that we can expect a rather sizeable acceleration in the rate of wage increase now and in the future. The behaviour of wages in the second quarter of 1974 confirms this suspicion.

Unemployment in the United States has been rising, and real output has not grown much for a year, in fact, it declined in the first two quarters of 1974. The relatively high unemployment rate in the economy will tend to offset in part the effects of employed workers trying to recoup their lost real wages.

Wages will also react to additional surges of prices as firms attempt to re-establish more normal profit margins now that price controls have been lifted.[2] Despite the relatively weak aggregate demand in the economy, there are still capacity problems and bottlenecks in certain important industries such as steel, aluminium and petrochemicals. These supply problems are no doubt due in large part to a combination of distortions stemming from price controls and from the oil embargo.

[1] Two recent studies suggest, however, that the rate of price increase was sufficiently small in the controls period to account for the behaviour of wages. Wages respond to price increases with a lag so that the run up of consumer prices in 1973 and 1974 will be felt on wages in 1974 and 1975. See Robert J. Gordon, 'The Response of Wages and Prices to the First Two Years of Controls', *Brookings Papers on Economic Activity*, 1973:3, pp. 765–79. James L. Pierce and Jared J. Enzler, 'The Effects of External Inflationary Shocks', *Brookings Papers on Economic Activity*, I:1974, pp. 13–61.

[2] Both the Gordon and the Pierce–Enzler studies indicate that profit margins were depressed during the price control period.

Until they are eliminated, however, they will be an additional source of price increase in the US economy.

What are the consequences of this situation for monetary policy? My first response is that monetary policy cannot do very much about inflation in the short run. A given maintained rate of money growth implies a given maintained rate of growth of prices, at least up to an approximation, only in the *long run*. All of the empirical research that I have seen of the US experience, including the 'monetarist' model of the St Louis Federal Reserve Bank indicates that the lag from money to prices is quite long. In the current environment, pursuit of a money growth path that is consistent with price stability would have disastrous implications for the economy in the short run because most of the initial effect of this policy would be felt on real output and employment. Some of the rise in prices must be accommodated with more money growth. How much depends upon the unemployment that can be tolerated. To avoid unacceptable unemployment rates, money growth can only be reduced relatively slowly to the 'appropriate' long-run growth rate.

The inflation rate over the next year or so in the US is largely predetermined; there is little monetary policy can do about it. My best guess right now is that if oil prices do not rise any more – leaving aside the wishful but unlikely prospect that they may fall – and if food prices do not rise significantly, then the inflation rate will go back fairly quickly to some place within a 7 to 8 per cent range. The problem lies in trying to get below this range which involves the painful dilemma of trading off unemployment against inflation. To reduce inflation quickly, unemployment would need to rise to unacceptable levels. To avoid massive unemployment, the process of unwinding the inflation will require a long time.

I would like to make a couple of points to distinguish between the effects of external inflationary shocks on the one hand (effects that come from the increases in food and oil prices) and the effects of the more classical demand-induced inflation on the other.[3] In one sense, external shocks are more difficult to deal with because there is no way to anticipate them. While policy cannot prevent them, it must react to these shocks. The effects of the external inflation surges are particularly dangerous when the economy is already running quite high inflation rates, as was the case for the US in the early 1970s.

In another sense, and I think an important sense, the effects of external shocks are easier to control than those that come from internal excess demand sources. The oil price increase, and to a lesser extent the effect of devaluation, have acted to raise prices without raising domestic incomes and wealth. Since domestic real income and wealth are reduced by these external price increases, there is a natural built-in stabilisation

[3] For a more detailed discussion see Pierce and Enzler, op. cit. pp. 13–61.

effect that acts to dampen domestic demand, provided that the income and wealth reductions are not offset by policy action. The devaluation presented a more complicated case because it tended to raise the income of farmers, as well as the prices of non-traded goods, and thus generated incomes. To some extent, then, the devaluation had some excess demand effects within the short run.[4]

The final comment that I want to make about external shocks is that it is quite possible that wages do not react in the same way to this kind of price increase as to that which stems from purely internal sources. The reason is that even though consumption goods prices rise, the value of the marginal product of labour does not rise concomitantly. Thus, it is more difficult for labour to get wage increases because there is no increase in the demand for labour on the part of business firms. Furthermore, labour unions cannot point to high profits of business firms as a rationale for demanding wage increases, thus removing another impetus for increased wages. One possible explanation for why wages were so well behaved during the price control period is that even though the real wage went down, there was no increase in the demand for labour because profit margins did not increase. The income went elsewhere.

The effects of the external inflationary shocks might be expected to wear out more quickly than for internal shocks, such as a rise in defence expenditures, because of the reduction in real incomes and real wealth, and also because of the possibility that wages will not react as strongly, at least in the short run, to these external price increases. Eventually, of course, wages will react, but in a different way than if the shocks were domestically induced.

On the other hand, some recent empirical evidence produced in the United States indicates faster speeds of adjustment of wages to prices and also a larger total response of wages to prices than has been observed in the past. Recent evidence seems to indicate that the Phillips curve is probably vertical in the long run (i.e. there is no trade-off between inflation and employment in the long run), and that the response of wages to prices is relatively rapid.[5] There is also evidence from observed wage increases and nominal long-term interest rates that inflationary expectations have not fully developed in the US economy; expectations have not adjusted to the kind of inflation rates that seem in prospect over the next four or five years. To the extent that these expectations have not been fully formed, it is easier for monetary policy to work against inflation now than it will be in the future.

Let me turn for a moment to what is called an 'accommodating

[4] The devaluation may also not be considered an external shock like the oil price increase because the exchange rate was adjusted, in part, as a result of earlier inflation in the US.

[5] See Pierce and Enzler, op. cit.

monetary policy'. This is a very slippery notion, although it is readily bandied about in the US press and in some academic circles, and it is particularly slippery when it is applied to external shocks. Consider what would happen if monetary policy were to tolerate no accommodation. Assume that the monetary authority insisted upon some constant rate of growth of the money stock and assume that there is a sudden upward surge in oil prices. If monetary policy in no way responds to the price increase – that is, does not change its constant rate of money expansion – then there would be a drastic reduction in the real balances available in the economy. Mr Burger in his paper is correct when he states that no central bank can determine real balances in a country; all it can do is determine nominal balances. While this is true in the long run, in the short run it can affect real balances. This is because of the long response lag between money and prices. If any central bank had worked to maintain a constant money growth path in a situation where inflation rates have increased as they have – let us say between the third quarter of 1973 and the first quarter of 1974 – the results would have been a disaster.

I want to hasten to add that it would also be disastrous for a central bank to attempt to keep real balances at their previous value. If the initial price surge is accommodated and if money growth is increased in step with every round of price increase, the inflation rate would increase without limit. An attractive – but not unique – definition of policy accommodation is one in which the *level* of the money stock is increased in step with the initial rise in the price level (such as that precipitated by the rise in oil prices), but the *rate of growth* is left unchanged. This policy would remove the initial downward shock to real money balances and real output but it still would put downward pressure on the rate of inflation.

I think the proper way to determine whether monetary policy is tight or easy, i.e. the degree to which it is 'accommodating' inflation, is to look at the growth of the money stock relative to the growth in nominal GNP, which is just another way of talking about real balances. Determine whether the central bank is providing more or less money balances than it did for transactions purposes in the economy in the past. The answer to that question with regard to the experience of the last three quarters in the US has been 'no'. While money growth has been rapid by historical standards, it has been much less rapid than the growth of nominal GNP. As a result, there has been an excess of money demand over supply; nominal interest rates have risen and real balances have fallen. While real balances should not and cannot be a target of monetary policy, the behaviour of real balances and interest rates can be a useful *indicator* of what policy is doing.

I should now like to turn to a question that has been asked by those who have read other country papers: is the current inflation different?

I think in the sense that there have been an unseemly number of external shocks, at least by US standards, the answer has to be yes. I think in the sense of the response of the economy to these shocks as well as to excess demand, the answer is no. There are several bits of information that can be offered as support for this assertion. First, our econometric models are tracking economic behaviour as well now as they have in the past, which suggests that our economic structure has not changed. The price equations have been performing well after adjustment is made for a catch-up following the decontrol of prices. Price controls, of course, were not built into our structural models.

Second, the current inflation appears to be different simply because the inflation rate is so high by historical standards. At first blush, it may appear that recent economic behaviour may be 'new' and different but in fact it could be that price movements have been sufficiently large that what was probably always there is just now becoming evident. Consider, for example, the observation that it is real interest rates that influence spending. Until relatively recently, real interest rates could not be distinguished from nominal interest rates because of the relatively low and constant inflation. This is not the case now and it has become important to distinguish between nominal and real interest rates. Similarly, real wealth seems to be the important variable in the economy rather than nominal wealth. Real wages are relevant, not nominal. Some observers may think that the underlying structure has changed, but I think it is only the nature of the problem that has changed. Price movements are much more important now than in the past. The economy is responding in very much the way that one would expect. The only real surprise has been the degree of inertia in the wage-price process. Recent experience indicates that most econometric models have estimated lags that were too short with respect to prices and wages. Economists who predict prices by non-econometric techniques have also understated the length of the lags. Historical data for the US simply were not rich enough to allow accurate estimates of the dynamics of wage-price adjustments.

There are signs that the economy is beginning to learn to live with inflation. Quite apart from any governmental actions, escalators are beginning to be used increasingly in wage contracts. Also there are more frequent negotiations of wage contracts than in the past, which is another means of handling the indexing problem. Pensions, including government pensions, are being indexed. In financial markets, a floating rate on long-term loans has been introduced, which is again a sort of 'behind the scenes' method of indexing securities in order to protect long-term investors against wrong guesses about future inflation rates. In the past, there has been little reason for having indexing. Now there is, and there has been quite a surge in its use, although in some cases, it is incomplete. For example, in some wage contracts, the formula does not allow wages to go up by the full percentage rise in the consumer price index, thus indicating an unwillingness to go to full indexing.

In conclusion the US economy, like many economies, is very badly out of equilibrium: both unemployment and inflation rates are high and rising. There are no effective short-run solutions. However, with time and patience the economy can be returned to some semblance of price and output stability.

9 Report on the United States (2)

*Albert E. Burger**

Let me begin by setting forth a position on the features of the 'new inflation'. First, the current widespread inflation across industrial countries is a 'new' inflation only in the sense that it is a phenomenon of the last ten years. The current inflation has *not* been largely determined by the supply behaviour of non-industrial countries. The basic cause of the current inflation is the same as the cause of all previous inflations – too much money chasing too few goods.

The most disturbing aspect of the current inflation is not that there has been a movement from one rate of price increase to a new maintained higher level of price increase, but that there has been a periodic upward movement in the *rate* of inflation. There is no reason that this process has to continue. Policymakers have the power to prevent a permanently accelerating rate of price increase. It is true that more attention is being devoted to 'how to live with inflation' rather than 'how to fight inflation', but this is a very dangerous approach. A little inflation leads to a little more inflation which leads to a little more inflation until inflation has become a major disruptive force in the economic as well as the social fabric of a country.

IS INFLATION LARGELY DETERMINED BY SUPPLY FACTORS?

An exogenous decrease in the supply of one good will tend to (1) raise the price of that good; (2) raise the demand for and price of substitute goods; (3) lower the demand for complementary goods and hence put downward pressures on the prices of these goods. The way a market economy adjusts to a change in supply conditions is through changes in *relative* prices and reallocation of resources from one type of production to another. Assuming no government controls on prices, resources will be bid away from those industries producing complementary goods and will move into industries producing substitute goods. Initially, the average price level will rise, assuming prices of complementary goods are not immediately flexible downward, and unemployment will

* The views expressed in this article are the responsibility of the author and do not necessarily reflect the views of the Federal Reserve System.

temporarily rise since resources do not immediately move fully from producing complementary goods to producing substitute goods.

For a decrease in the supply of one good to cause a permanent increase in inflation, holding growth of total expenditures constant, would appear to require that the item was so vital to production that no substitute existed or could be developed. In that case, reducing the supply of that good means that the potential growth of real output is reduced. This seems a highly unlikely case, except in the short run. Man seems capable of finding a substitute good for almost any item. However, even if this were the case, the increase in inflation is not ultimately due to the reduction in supply, but results from the fact that growth of total expenditures is not reduced along with the reduced growth of real output. If the growth of total expenditures is maintained, but the growth of real output is reduced, then prices will rise more rapidly. The monetary authorities cannot affect the supply situation, but they can follow policies that reduce the growth of total expenditures.

Inflation began to develop in the United States long before any so-called supply-induced effects developed. For example, over the 1963–69 period real output rose at an average annual rate of 4·7 per cent, compared to an average rate of about 3 per cent over the previous ten years. However, from 1963 to 1969 the rate of inflation increased to a 3 per cent annual rate, about double the rate of the previous ten years.[1]

We must look somewhere other than at supply factors for the underlying cause of inflation. The basic underlying cause of the inflation currently being experienced in the United States is simply that the trend growth of money has been accelerating over the last ten years, approaching 7 per cent rate on average over the last three years. This has resulted in a growth of demand for goods and services that is much greater than the long-term average growth of real output.

INTENT OF MONETARY POLICY

The current intent of monetary policy in the United States is to reduce inflation and avoid causing a substantial medium-term rise in unemployment. In fact this is the same 'intent' that has characterised monetary policy since the middle 1960s. No member of the Federal Open Market Committee desired to have the rate of inflation, as measured by the consumer price index, rise from an average annual rate of about 1·5 per cent over the period 1952–64 to an average annual rate of about 4 per cent from 1964 through 1972, or to see price increases accelerate to an average annual rate of over 6 per cent during 1973, as shown in Figure 1.

The basic force underlying the accelerating inflation in the United States has been the accelerating average annual growth of the money stock. As shown in Figure 2, the growth of the money stock accelerated

[1] Unless otherwise noted, all growth rates are computed on an average-of-year basis.

Figure 1. Prices

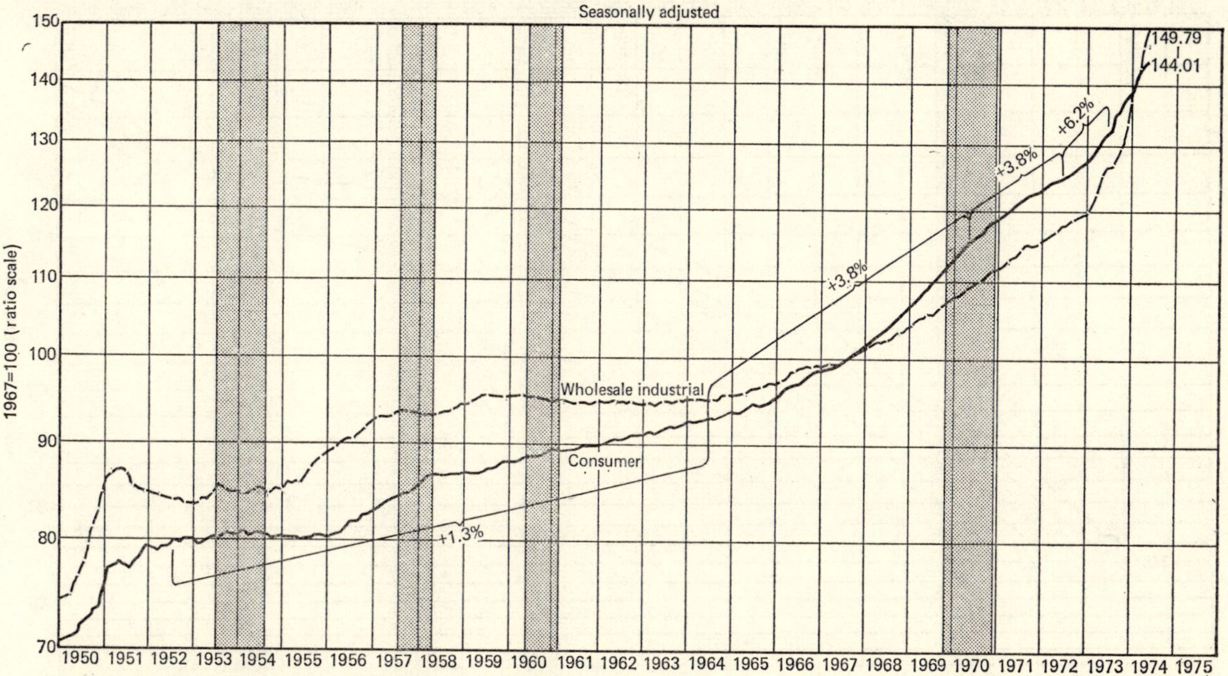

Shaded areas represent periods of business recessions as defined by National Bureau of Economic Research
Percentages are annual rates of change for periods indicated
Latest data plotted: April

Figure 2. Money stock

Monthly averages of daily figures
seasonally adjusted

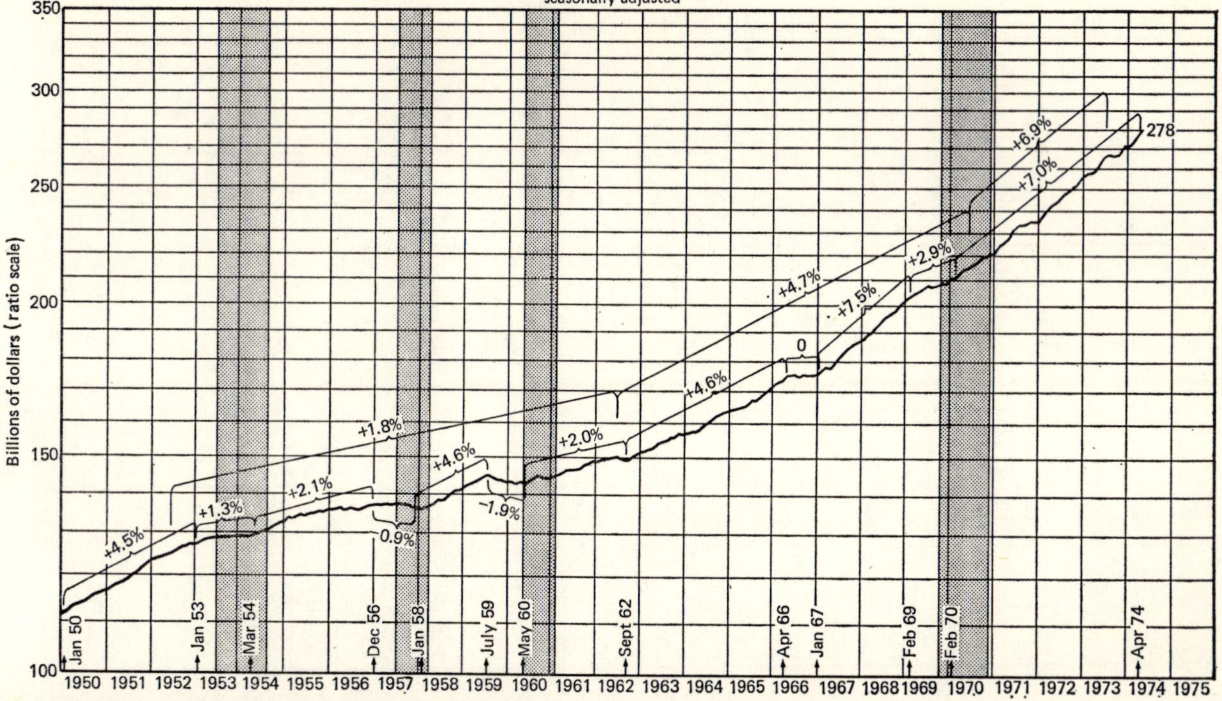

Shaded areas represent periods of business recessions as defined by National Bureau of Economic Research
Percentages are annual rates of change for periods indicated

from about a 2 per cent average annual rate over the period 1952–62 to about a 5 per cent annual rate over the period from 1962 through 1970. Over the period 1962–70 the growth of the money stock followed a pattern of sharp accelerations followed by periods of sharp reductions in the growth rate, for example in 1966 and from early 1969 to early 1970. Since 1970 the growth of money has reaccelerated to about a 7 per cent annual rate. At the same time, real output has grown at an average rate of about 4 per cent since 1962, somewhat faster than its average annual rate of about 3 per cent recorded over the previous ten years. With progressive accelerations in the rate of growth of money leading to markedly faster growth of total expenditure, and with real output growing at only a slightly more rapid rate, prices rose at accelerated rates.

Again, I do not believe that any member of the Federal Open Market Committee desired the progressive upward movements in the growth of money. From 1964 to 1973 the Federal Open Market Committee (FOMC) met 141 times and voted for a policy of restraint at 70 per cent of these meetings. Only in 1967 and 1970 did the FOMC adopt a policy of ease at virtually every meeting.

Given that the intent of policy has not changed, why has there been a progressive rise in the average growth of the money stock and, hence, a progressive rise in inflation? Three related factors appear to account for this situation. First, in the United States since the mid-1960s, there has been a sharp rise in the growth of Government spending. Since 1965, Federal Government expenditures have risen at an average annual rate of 10 per cent, compared to about a 6 per cent rate over the previous ten years. In 1966 and 1967 the major rise was due to defence spending which rose 20 per cent per year. However, since 1967 the growth of defence spending has been much slower, and actually declined from 1969 through 1973. The rise in Federal Government expenditures since 1965 has primarily reflected the public's growing demands that the government sector do more in the way of social welfare programmes. Since 1965 Federal non-defence expenditures have risen at a 12·6 per cent annual rate, compared to a 9·5 rate over the previous ten years.

Essentially, the public has demanded that the Government sector provide a larger flow of goods and services. However, while Government spending was rising, taxes were not raised enough to finance the increased expenditures. This brings us to the second factor. As a result of a rising spread between tax revenues and Government expenditures, the growth of the outstanding stock of Government securities accelerated as the Government was forced to borrow to finance its expenditures. Over the period of fiscal year 1966 through fiscal 1973 Federal Government expenditures exceeded tax receipts by almost $98 billion. The net result of deficit financing was upward pressures on market interest rates.

This brings us to the third factor. The Federal Reserve System traditionally has been concerned with the stability of interest rates and with the 'viability' of financial markets. Consequently, the Federal Reserve has tended to resist demand-determined movements in interest rates and has always stood ready to offer substantial aid to the financial markets in times of stress. The substantial rise in Government financing requirements was bound to put upward pressures on market interest rates and put stress on financial markets. Essentially, the Government was attempting to acquire more funds than before through the credit markets and, assuming no change in the growth of total credit, other demanders of credit would have had to be rationed out of the market.

Among the other demanders of credit was the housing industry. As market yields on Government debt rose, funds were drawn out of savings and loan associations, the supply of funds to finance housing fell, and mortgage interest rates rose. Questions arose about the solvency of the major financers of mortgage credit. These results, along with pressures on the financing of state and local governments, developed quite early in the inflationary process and in 1966 culminated in what has come to be called 'The Credit Crunch of 1966'.

The Federal Reserve came under considerable criticism for permitting the development of the 'crunch' in 1966. However, although certain Federal Reserve policies probably added to the strain on financial markets at that time, the situation in 1966 reflected the attempt of financial markets to adjust to the added financing pressures from the Federal Government. The 1966 Federal Reserve policy of resisting a substantial expansion in money and credit was an attempt to force the adjustment through financial markets. If the Government was going to get a larger share of real output, then some other sector had to receive a smaller share.

The Federal Reserve tried to halt the upward march of inflation again in 1969. From February 1969 to February 1970 monetary policy actions slowed the growth of the money stock to about a 3 per cent rate. This led to the slowdown in economic activity in 1970 and from about mid-1970 there was evidence of a slowing in inflation. By the end of 1970, the market yield on Treasury bills had fallen below 5 per cent, compared to about 8 per cent at the end of 1969. In the first quarter of 1971, yields on long-term corporate bonds had eased to about 7·25 per cent, compared to about 8 per cent in late 1969.

However, after early 1970, Federal Reserve actions resulted in a reacceleration in the growth of the money stock. From 1970 through 1973 Federal Reserve credit grew at an average annual rate of 9·5 per cent and the monetary base grew at a 7·7 per cent rate. On balance, since early 1970 money has grown at about a 7 per cent rate. Although inflation continued at a slower rate through late 1972, how much of this was due to the lagged effect of the previous slowing of money on prices extending into late 1972 is open to question. In August 1971 a fairly comprehensive set of price and wage controls was instituted in the United States. The lag in the response of prices to the reacceleration of money probably reflected the effect of these price controls. Sooner or later the upward pressure on prices had to surface, and price controls appear to have only delayed the upward thrust of prices. The main result of the various phases of price controls was the distortion in supply conditions that the United States is still experiencing.

EFFECT OF INFLATION ON CURRENT POLICY

Inflation affects current monetary policy because inflation affects interest rates and financial markets. Also, accelerating inflation, when joined with price controls, tends to raise questions about the predictive performance of econometric models that are used to forecast the response of the economy to policy actions. A further effect has been the suggestion by some observers that 'real' instead of nominal quantities should be used as indicators of the effects of policy actions.

Recently the United States has been experiencing levels of interest rates that are 'high' by historical standards. However, it would be hard to ascribe these high interest rates to 'tight' monetary policy. As shown in Figure 3, over the last three years the monetary base has grown at a 7·7 per cent rate, compared to about a 5 per cent rate from 1962 through 1970 and less than a 2 per cent rate over the 1952–62 period. Bank credit has grown at about a 13 per cent rate since 1970, compared to a 7·6 per cent rate over the previous five years, and about a 6 per cent rate from 1955 to 1965. These growth rates indicate that Federal Reserve actions have resulted in a large enough growth of the monetary base to support a substantially more rapid expansion of bank credit than in previous periods.

The increase in the monetary base predominantly reflected the fact that the Federal Reserve System purchased a large volume of Government securities and the Treasury monetised the proceeds of the May 1972 and October 1973 changes in the official price at which the US gold stock is valued. The monetary base averaged $20 billion higher in 1973 than in 1970, the Federal Reserve's holdings of Government securities averaged $17·8 billion more in 1973 than in 1970, and the Treasury's actions subsequent to the two official revaluations of the US gold stock added $2 billion to the monetary base.

A central bank policy of buying Government debt and providing the monetary base for a rapid expansion of credit has the initial effect of holding interest rates below what they would be in the absence of such a policy. However, the growth of the monetary base determines the growth of the money stock. The close relationship between accelerations and decelerations in the growth of base and money can be seen by comparing Figures 2 and 3. Therefore, a policy of attempting to resist move-

Figure 3. Monetary base*

Monthly averages of daily figures
seasonally adjusted

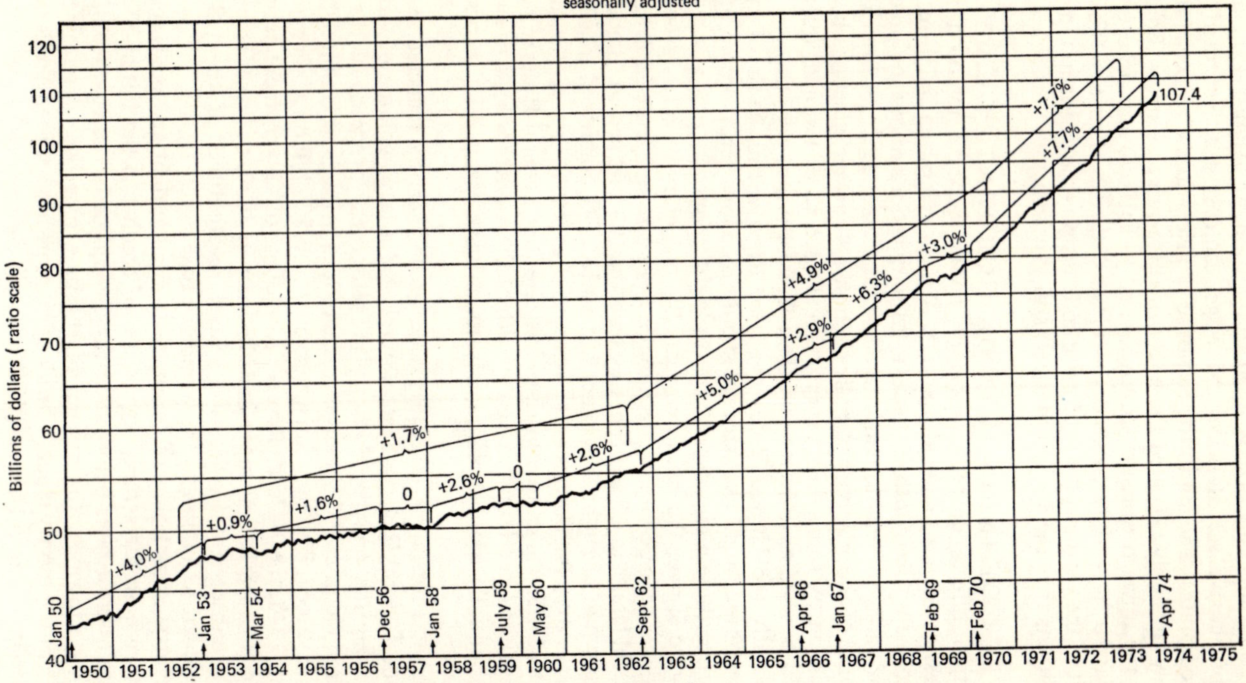

*Uses of the monetary base are member bank reserves and currency held by the public and non-member banks.
Adjustments are made for reserve requirement changes and shifts in deposits among classes of banks
Percentages are annual rates of change for periods indicated

ments in market interest rates also leads to a rapid expansion of the amount of money balances which individuals must absorb into their wealth portfolios. From 1970 to 1973 the money stock grew on the average at a 7 per cent annual rate. This is more than three times as fast as over the 1952–62 period of slowly rising prices. As discussed earlier, the rapid growth of money led to a progressive upward movement in the rate of change of prices and this led to a growth in the demand for credit.

Today's high levels of interest rates largely reflect the accelerating rate of inflation in the United States. When the current rate of inflation is taken into consideration, interest rates are not unusually 'high'. As shown in Figure 4, relative to the rate of inflation, adjusted yields on Corporate AAA bonds are currently lower than any time within the last eight years, with the exception of early 1971. Although long-term

Figure 4. Yields on highest-grade seasoned corporate bonds

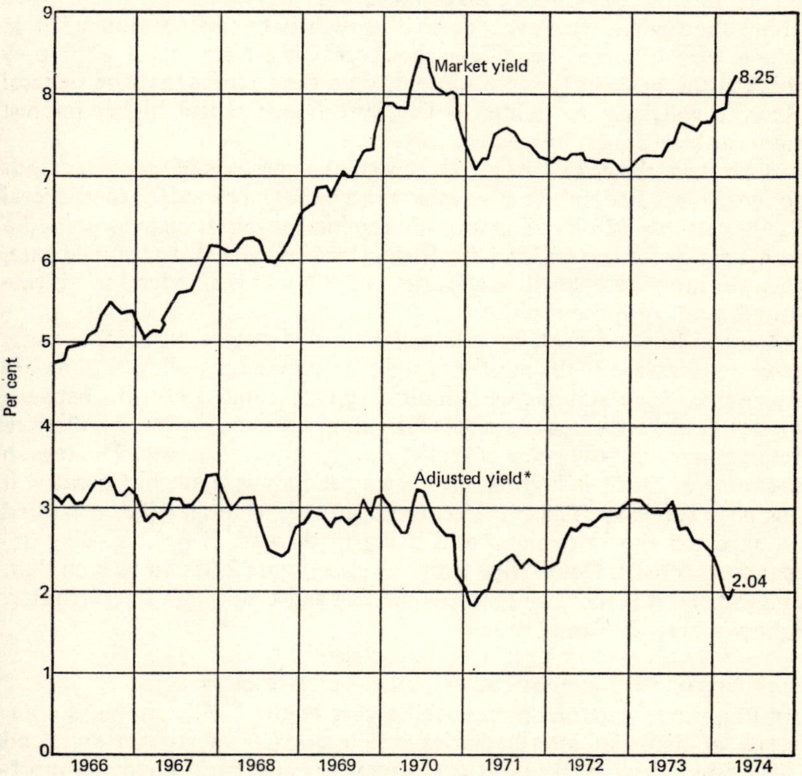

*Market yield less average annual rate of change in consumer prices over three previous years.
Latest data plotted: April

market interest rates have been rising sharply since early 1973, the adjusted yield has been falling since about mid-1973.

In recent months the Federal funds rate, the key interest rate used in short-run operating strategy, has risen sharply. However, there is some question as to whether the Federal funds rate has risen because the Federal Reserve pushed the rate up, or in spite of Federal Reserve actions. In times of rapid increases in the demand for credit, it becomes almost impossible for the Federal Reserve to hold interest rates constant. The more vigorously the Federal Reserve tries to hold interest rates down, the more rapidly the monetary base grows and, consequently, the more rapid the growth in the money stock.

An increased rate of growth of the money stock appears to have two effects on expectations of financial market participants. First, they have learned by experience over the last 8–10 years that a maintained faster growth of money means a higher rate of inflation, and that means higher interest rates. Also, financial market observers have some idea about the Federal Reserve's desired growth path for the money stock. When they observe the money stock growing faster than what they think is the Federal Reserve's intent, then they expect that the Federal Reserve will have to tighten policy, and hence expect higher interest rates, at least in the immediate future.

To restrict the growth of the money stock in periods of rising demands for credit, the Federal Reserve must raise its target range for the Federal funds rate *ahead of* the market-determined level. If increases in the target range for the Federal funds rate *lag* the market-determined rate, then the money stock will accelerate, even though the Federal funds rate moves upward quite rapidly.

Central bankers must be extremely wary of statements that, because interest rates are high, money is tight or monetary policy actions are restrictive. Such statements exhibit a fundamental confusion between money and credit that can be fatal for attempts to slow inflation. Interest rates are the price of *credit*, not the price of *money*. The reason the price of credit is high is not because money is tight, but because it has been too easy. The previous rapid growth of money has generated an expected rise in demand and rising prices and, hence, growing demands for credit. Comparing Figure 5 and Figure 2, it can be seen that, empirically, it is the case that low interest rates, not high interest rates, follow a period of tight money.

EFFECT OF INFLATION ON FINANCIAL MARKETS

An important part of the financial sector of the Unites States is composed of financial intermediaries which borrow short-term and lend long-term. These institutions are primarily engaged in financing mortgage credit demands, and consist of institutions such as savings and loan associations, mutual savings banks, life insurance companies, and

Figure 5. Interest rates

Monthly averages of daily figures

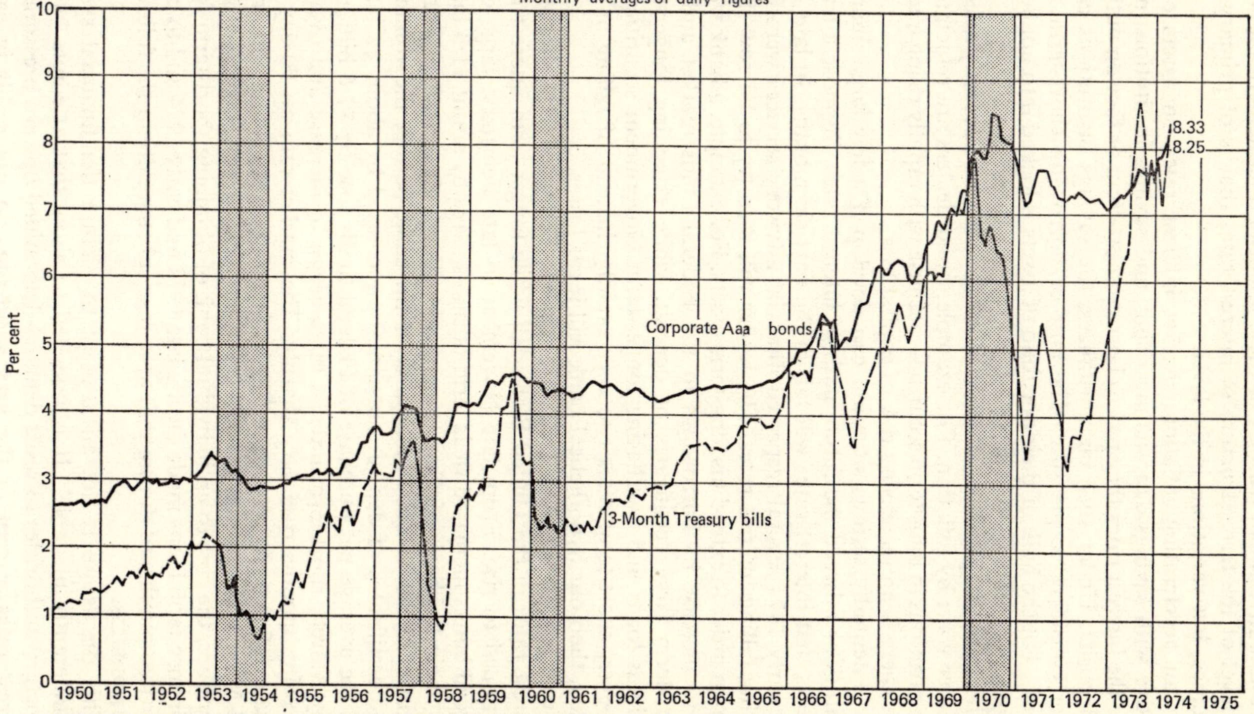

Shaded areas represent periods of business recessions as defined by National Bureau of Economic Research

Latest data plotted: April

real estate investment trusts. For these financial intermediaries it is not the level of the term structure of interest rates that is of primary importance, but variations in the level.

In an accelerating inflation, market interest rates on assets competitive with savings deposits are rising, and savings institutions must raise the interest rates they pay to borrow short-term or face an outflow of deposits. Under such circumstances, the savings institutions come under considerable pressure. The cost of borrowing short-term rises rapidly, but the bulk of their portfolio of assets is locked into nonliquid long-term mortgages that have a fixed interest rate.

The smooth operation of financial markets is also adversely affected in other ways by inflation. For example, bond dealers are reluctant to take positions in long-term securities, because with rapidly rising interest rates there is an increasing risk of capital loss.

A potentially serious situation can develop if a few large financial institutions misread the future path of interest rates. Suppose a lender expects that interest rates will fall in the next six months. In late 1973 and early 1974 several respected financial advisory services were forecasting falling interest rates. The lender will then try to borrow short-term in order to extend his long-term assets. For example, a bank would try to increase its borrowings in the Federal funds market and sell short-term large certificates of deposit, while extending longer-term business loans and purchasing longer-term Government securities. If, however, short-term rates rise very rapidly, instead of falling as predicted, then our hypothetical bank will incur losses.

From early December 1973 through late February 1974 short-term interest rates in the United States fell while longer-term interest rates continued to rise. From late November to late February, large commercial banks increased their term business loans by about \$1·3 billion and their holdings of Government securities with over five years to maturity by about \$600 million. Over the same period, the volume of large certificates of deposit outstanding increased by about \$2 billion and the average net purchase of Federal funds rose by \$2·6 billion. In early March, short-term interest rates began to increase and over the following months rose very sharply. The market rate on 90-day certificates of deposit rose over 300 basis points from late February to mid-May, and the rate on Federal funds rose over 250 basis points. Therefore, the cost to an individual bank of obtaining short-term funds to finance term loans made during late 1973 and early 1974 and to carry securities purchased during that time rose substantially in the following three months.

This discussion is not an attempt to picture the financial system as 'inherently unstable'. It is intended to show that attempts by the monetary authorities to resist demand-determined upward pressures on interest rates, except in the very short-run, do not result in easing financial market pressures. As the monetary authorities expand the monetary base, money expands and ultimately there are greater upward pressures on interest rates as the demand for credit increases. Ultimately, such a policy results in greater, not less, strain in the financial markets, and makes the problems encountered by the central bank when it attempts to slow inflation that much greater. This is especially true because some financial operators still appear to believe that the monetary authorities can hold market interest rates below the level determined by fundamental market factors. The only way to eventually achieve lower interest rates is to slow the growth of money and credit. However, this implies additional temporary upward pressures on interest rates, and further raises the spectre of another 'credit crunch'. These factors further illustrate that, the longer inflation is permitted to develop, the more difficult it is to stop.

EFFECT OF PRICE CONTROLS ON THE PREDICTIVE PERFORMANCE OF ECONOMETRIC MODELS

It is very difficult to judge the effect of inflation on the predictive performance of the Federal Reserve Bank of St Louis model, as well as any other model. During most of the period since August 1971 the US economy has been subject to various types of price controls. These controls probably distorted the behaviour of prices relative to what they would have been without controls. Under these conditions, econometric models are only a guide to the upward pressures that are building on prices.

For example, the St Louis model overestimated the reported rise in prices during the period of price controls, but since the lifting of most price controls, it has underestimated the increases in prices. On balance, the model has fairly accurately projected the long-run behaviour of prices. As shown in Table 1, fitting the model through the second

TABLE 1 Ex Ante Projections of the GNP Price Deflator Using the St Louis Model*

Rates of change from II/71 to:	*Actual* %	*Ex ante* %
III/71	2·6	5·0
IV/71	2·2	5·0
I/72	3·3	5·0
II/72	3·0	4·9
III/72	3·0	4·8
IV/72	3·2	4·8
I/73	3·5	4·7
II/73	4·0	4·6
III/73	4·5	4·6
IV/73	4·9	4·5

* Equation fitted through II/71.

quarter of 1971, the last full quarter before price controls, and projecting through 1973 shows that the model estimated about a 5 per cent growth of the price deflator from II/71 through IV/73. Actual reported prices rose at a much slower rate during the price control period, then accelerated as price controls were lifted.

REAL V. NOMINAL QUANTITIES[2]

The use of real instead of nominal quantities as guides to monetary policy can be extremely dangerous. First, all that policy-makers, as well as other economic agents, observe is nominal interest rates and money balances. They never observe real interest rates or real money balances, and economists cannot agree on how to accurately measure these real quantities. This is not to say that the rate of inflation does not enter into the public's decision to borrow, nor their decision as to the amount of money balances they desire to hold. However, the crucial distinction for central bankers is that, while individuals adjust their money holdings to prices, for the economy as a whole, prices adjust to the amount of money. Second, the ratio of money to some price index is a faulty indicator of tightness or ease of monetary policy because this ratio is determined by the public and is ultimately beyond the control of the monetary authorities. Monetary actions have only a temporary effect on real money balances.

There are five periods from 1955 to 1973 when the ratio of money to commodity prices declined for two quarters or more: 1955–57, 1959–60, 1966, 1969 and 1973. Prior to 1973, each period in which 'real balances' declined for two quarters or more was followed by a significant slowdown in economic activity, ranging from the 1966–67 mini-recession to full-scale recessions in the other periods.

In 1955–57, 1959–60, 1966 and 1969 a large portion of the decline in real balances reflected a sharp drop in the rate of growth of the money stock below its trend. The deceleration in money growth in 1973 was not as abrupt. Instead, the indicated decline in 'real balances' in 1973 reflected, in large part, the reported acceleration of inflation.

Since the adjustment of prices to a change in the trend rate of money growth is estimated to take from four to six years to complete, it is probable that the economy is still adjusting to the accelerated rate of money growth over the last three and one-half years. Supporting evidence for this contention can be found in the movement of interest rates in 1973.

The inflation of last year, instead of threatening to restrict aggregate demand by eroding real money balances below desired levels, reflects instead the efforts of the public to dispose of excess money balances. On

[2] This section draws heavily upon the article by Denis S. Karnosky 'Real Money Balances: A Misleading Indicator of Monetary Actions', Federal Reserve Bank of St Louis, *Review* (Feb 1974) pp. 2–10.

the basis of past experience, if the money stock continued to grow at an average rate close to 6·5 per cent, such as since early 1970, this adjustment would continue at least through 1974.

The arguments which contend that monetary policy is restrictive, on the basis of the recent decline in 'real money balances', imply to some analysts a recommendation to policy makers to increase the rate of money growth above the rate of inflation in order to restore the growth of real balances. Both theoretical analysis and the experience of other countries indicate that there are few more dangerous courses of action that any monetary authority could undertake.

A further increase in the rate of money growth, above its current trend rate of about 6·5 per cent per annum, would only generate pressure for further inflation. It is not possible to avoid the adjustment of real money balances to the level desired by the public by increasing the rate of money growth.

One extreme example of the futility of a policy of trying to make money grow fast enough to prevent desired real balances from falling is given by the German experience in the early 1920s. By late 1923 tax receipts of the German government were covering less than one per cent of its expenditures. To finance its expenditures, the government borrowed from the Reichsbank, which simply turned on the printing presses. The majority of trained economists in Germany refused to believe in a chain of causation running from the growth of the money stock to the growth of prices. Rudolf Havenstein, President of the Reichsbank, tended to believe that the rise in prices created a need for money on the part of businessmen and the government which was the Reichsbank's duty to meet, and which would have almost no harmful effects on the economy. When complaints of 'shortages' of money arose, despite the issue of denominations as large as 100 trillion marks, Havenstein seriously expressed hope that new high-speed currency printing presses soon to be installed would overcome the shortage.[3]

PROPOSALS TO OFFSET INFLATION

Recently, proposals for tying future payments in contracts to some price index (so-called indexing) and explicit payment of interest on demand deposits have been suggested as ways of removing some of the losses associated with unexpected future price movements.

INDEXING

The use of indexing has increased in the US economy as inflation has

[3] The material in this section draws upon Leland B. Yeager, *International Monetary Relations* (New York: Harper & Row, 1966) pp. 269–72 and quotes from the League of Nations Study, *The Course and Control of Inflation.* See also, Frank D. Graham, *Exchange, Prices and Production in Hyper-Inflation: Germany 1920–23* (New York: Russell & Russell, 1930).

accelerated. Recently, the US Congress decided to tie social security payments to the consumer price index, and more wage contracts are being written with cost-of-living escalator clauses, not only for wages, but also for pensions.[4] However, these actions represent only partial indexing. At present, it does not appear that the US is likely to adopt a full economy-wide pattern of indexing. Especially difficult problems would arise when indexing such items as interest rates. For example, attempts to develop variable interest rate mortgages have met with less than enthusiastic support.

Partial indexing probably creates more problems than it solves. Groups whose flow of payments are linked to some price index will be far less willing to support efforts to halt inflation. This is especially true because policies taken to slow inflation also involve some short-run rise in unemployment. It is one thing to explain the reason for tighter fiscal and monetary policy to an individual by pointing out that increased Government spending financed by money creation results in a fall in his real income. It is much more difficult to convince him of the merits of tighter fiscal and monetary policy when his income is tied to a price index.

The actual implementation of generalised indexing presents considerable practical difficulties. What price index will be chosen? Who will decide the way to index prices? What about outstanding contracts? How do you index profits? For example, there has been considerable furore raised over recent attempts to broaden the coverage of the consumer price index. Also, some aspects of indexing would require substantial changes in tax laws, for example, tying the personal exemption to inflation and taking the effect of inflation into account in computing depreciation and capital gains. The effect of many indexing proposals would be to hold the Government's tax revenues constant as inflation increased. In inflation the cost of existing Government operations would rise, and if there was no cut in Government operations, deficit financing would increase. These decisions move us from the field of economic theory into the area of politics and bureaucracy. Having observed the fiasco of wage and price controls, the author is none too confident that the Government can resist the temptation to intervene selectively in the development of an indexing system, and hence is doubtful that a viable system of indexing can be developed.

INTEREST PAYMENTS ON DEMAND DEPOSITS

Generally, the arguments that have been advanced for prohibition of interest payments on demand deposits in the United States are not supported by empirical evidence. Currently, commercial banks pay an

[4] For about 5 million workers, changes in their incomes are tied to changes in the consumer price index. Receipts of an additional 3 million food stamp recipients and 61·4 million social security recipients are also affected by changes in the CPI.

implicit rate of interest on demand deposits: the cost of servicing demand deposits is greater than service charges by banks. This probably leads to some inefficiency in allocation of resources that could be avoided if banks paid a market-determined interest rate on demand deposits and charged depositors the full cost of bank services.

However, as a practical matter, a widespread movement in support of payment of interest on demand deposits does not appear likely in the near future. Changes in legislation would be required to permit commercial banks to make explicit interest payments on demand deposits, and there does not appear to be wide enough support for these changes from any well-organised political group.

CONCLUSIONS

The way to reduce inflationary pressures in the United States economy is to slow the growth of the money stock. On an average-of-year to average-of-year basis, the money stock grew at about a 7 per cent rate from 1970 to 1973. It seems to be a generally accepted proposition in economics that the growth of prices adjusts to the growth of money over an extended period of time. Therefore, if the 7 per cent rate of money growth experienced over the last three years in the United States is maintained, this implies our economy will adjust towards a long-run 6–7 per cent rate of inflation. The recent surge in prices reflects partly an adjustment to the removal of price controls, and partly the continued upward adjustment to the average growth of the money stock.

The only way to halt the upward movement of interest rates is to slow money growth. If our economy is being forced to adjust to a 6–7 per cent annual rate of inflation, then nominal interest rates on long-term bonds will not remain at around 8 per cent but probably will rise to 9–10 per cent.

In the United States the central bank can halt the growth of the money stock. The Federal Reserve, through its open market operations, can control the growth of the monetary base, and hence control the growth of the money stock. The Federal Reserve is on record as having the intent to slow the growth of the money stock. The intent of policy is not to cause a dramatic halt to money growth, because of the short-run effects on employment, but to gradually reduce the trend growth of money.

Whether or not this 'intent' is realised will crucially depend upon (1) the Government's willingness to exercise restraint in its spending, and (2) a willingness on the part of the Federal Reserve to allow market interest rates to rise temporarily to high levels. As discussed earlier, nominal interest rates that seem extremely high by historical standards are not high when the current rate of inflation is taken into account.

It is useful to refer again to the German experience of 1920–23 to see how excessive government spending and central bank creation of money become bound together, and how difficult it is for any central bank to pursue a monetary policy that runs counter to the government's fiscal policy.

> This fundamental cause, in so far as it does not rest on the balance of payments, is . . . the boundless growth of the floating debt and its transformation into the means of payment . . . through the discounting of the Reich Treasury bills and the Reichsbank.
>
> Here too the Reichsbank is alleged to be guilty, because it has not opposed the Reich government and fiscal administration by refusing to continue the discounting of Treasury bills. This reproach is also unjustified and completely misjudges the actual situation. The Reichsbank has done all it could do with any chance of success. For years . . . it has continually called attention to these conditions and demanded a remedy in the most serious and urgent way, but it was not in a position to stop the discounting of Treasury bills as long as the Reich had no other available means to cover its deficit, and as long as all groups in the legislature were not fully convinced that such means absolutely have to be found. For the Reich must live, and real renunciation of discounting in the face of the tasks set by the budget . . . would have led to chaos. The threat of a general refusal to discount Treasury bills would have been nothing but a futile gesture. Only very recently, under pressure of dire necessity, have all groups in the legislature been convinced . . . that fiscal policy absolutely must be based upon adequate sources of income.[5]

Somehow the public must be convinced that once inflation has gained a firm foothold there is no painless way to halt it. Also, the public must realise that goods provided by the government are not free goods. If the government sector absorbs and redistributes a larger segment of real output, then the private sector must be satisfied with a smaller share. Unless these fundamental facts are understood, then the good 'intent' of policy will probably not be realised.

AUTHOR'S NOTE

At the time this paper was completed some slowing of money growth was in evidence. From the second quarter of 1973 to the second quarter of 1974 the money stock grew by 6 per cent, compared to a steady 8 per cent rate of increase over the previous five quarters. From mid-1974 to early 1975 money growth decelerated sharply, averaging only about a 3 per cent rate over these three quarters. The US economy was already in a recession in mid-1974, but aggregate production continued to drop sharply, falling at a 7 per cent annual rate from the third quarter of 1974

[5] Rudolf Havenstein, 'Defending the Policy of the Reichsbank' (Address to the Executive Committee of the Reichsbank, 25 August 1923) in Fritz K. Ringer, *The German Inflation of* 1923 (New York: Oxford University Press, 1969) pp. 93–6.

to the second quarter of 1975. The unemployment rate rose from about 5 per cent in early 1974 to over 9 per cent in early 1975. On the other hand, inflation continued to be a very serious problem, with the general price index rising 12 per cent during 1974. It was not until late 1974 that some slackening in the rate of inflation became apparent.

The sharp deceleration in monetary growth, especially from the second quarter of 1974 to the first quarter of 1975, would have been expected to substantially reduce the rate of growth of real output and lead to a rise in unemployment. However, the actual behaviour of the real economy, especially in the early stages of the recession, was somewhat worse than would have been expected given the behaviour of the money stock. Part of the problems affecting the US economy came from the *supply* side of the market, not from the demand side, as usually had been the case in prior US recessions. A series of circumstances such as the changes in the supply and price of oil, strict enforcement of environmental regulations and occupational and safety standards, and problems in the supply of agricultural products raised the costs of production, and therefore affected real output in the first half of 1974.

In mid-1975 it appears that the US economy has completed a substantial portion of the necessary adjustment to the developments in 1974. The decrease in real output seems to have come to a halt, and the outlook is for a fairly substantial expansion of real output over the next eighteen months. The rate of inflation, after being temporarily raised by supply restrictions is now adjusting back to the rate consistent with the 6 per cent trend growth of money. The deceleration in growth of the money stock has ceased. Money grew at a 9·3 per cent rate in the second quarter of 1975, and Chairman Burns has announced the Federal Reserve considers, at this time, that a 5–7½ per cent growth of money from the second quarter of 1975 to the second quarter of 1976 would be appropriate.

The massive government deficits that the US economy now faces is perhaps the major factor that will influence developments in the financial markets and monetary expansion over the next two years. So far the large deficits have not caused substantial upward movements in interest rates, primarily due to the substantial decline in private demands for credit. However, as the economy recovers and private credit demands grow, substantial upward pressures on interest rates may develop. Over the next two years it will be crucial that the Federal Reserve does not repeat the pattern of resisting upward movements in interest rates that result from surges in the demand for credit. To prevent an acceleration in the rate of growth of money that will increase its trend rate of growth and hence lead to a reacceleration of inflation, the Federal Reserve may have to allow interest rates to rise substantially above their current levels.

Even though the Federal Reserve has announced its intent to permit an expansion of money that is rapid by historical standards, some economists have criticised the Federal Reserve's intent as being too restrictive. However, past experience in the United States, as well as many other countries, shows that a country cannot run a massive government deficit and have the central bank continually accelerate its purchases of government debt to hold interest rates down without suffering severe consequences. The end-result is accelerating inflation and ultimately much higher interest rates. Such programmes, which seem to be working well in their early stages, eventually end in disaster, causing severe social and political, as well as economic strain within the country.

10 Report on Japan

Chiaki Nishiyama

INTRODUCTION

In the last one hundred years of Japan's history there has been no other inflation than that of 1973–74, the cause of which was so purely monetary in its nature. It is a tragic testimony of the importance of monetary policy. Moreover, it seems that the failure of monetary policy has not really been brought about by simple lack of understanding on the part of the monetary authority but greatly promoted by its insistence on the wrong kind of monetary theory.

The core of the wrong theory is the assertion that monetary policy must pay attention to the behaviour of interest rates or changes in the availability of funds, or perhaps to both, and not to changes in the rate of money supply. It has denied any direct (substitution) relationships between money on the one hand and real goods, particularly in the form of capital goods, on the other. The tradition of Keynes-Hicks-Patinkin-Gurely-Shaw-Tobin has led us to lose sight of money itself by guiding us into the world of asset preference theory; just as we lose sight of wood by going into wood. It has been said that the purpose of economic theory is to analyse how to optimise various economic variables. But, money, the *key* variable to our monetary economy, has so far been left out of optimisation analysis. It is no wonder that severe inflation has developed.

Many people seem to like to call the current inflation 'new inflation'. They appear to be inclined to discuss its causes either in terms of some institutional ones such as full employment policy, administered prices, monopolies, oligopolies, labour unions, etc., or in terms of some real causes such as confusions in commodity markets, shortage of resources, etc. It is true that such problems do exist in actual economy; and attempts to solve them are not wrong in themselves. But, however successful we may be in removing those 'exogenous' causes of inflation from our economy, we shall never succeed in really controlling it without knowing the 'endogenous' mechanism for the development of inflation. I believe that the today's inflation is quite old in its nature. In my view it is a 'classical' kind of inflation in the sense that there has been no other inflation which has been caused so typically by monetary factors. Let us stop searching always for something new. It is the task of economic theory to analyse problems as 'endogenously' as possible in the tradition of price theory. The fundamental solutions of economic problems may become possible only on the basis of such analysis.

What is most needed today is the establishment of monetary theory. We must move away from today's financial theory, whose refinements have only led us increasingly to lose sight of money. We must rescue money from oblivion and place it at the top of monetary theory. The close relationships between money on the one hand and other economic variables on the other are quite evident, as will be seen later, in the economy of Japan as well as in other economies. We can perhaps today even claim that such indications are already quite sufficient at least for a while. What is insufficient and, for that matter, too insufficient is monetary theory. I do not believe that I can offer here much to remedy this. But what I will do is to present some simple ideas that seem to be fundamental to the development of monetary theory and end my paper by quoting from Keynes that:

> I am more attached to the comparatively simple fundamental ideas which underlie my theory than to the particular forms in which I have embodied them, and I have no desire that the latter should be crystallised at the present stage of the debate. If the simple basic ideas can become familiar and acceptable, time and experience and the collaboration of a number of minds will discover the best way of expressing them.[1]

JAPANESE INFLATION IN 1973–74

1 THE STRUCTURE OF RELATIVE PRICES AND THEIR LEVEL

Since 1973 Japan has certainly been experiencing severe inflation almost unprecedented in her own history and having hardly any parallel among the advanced countries. The wholesale price index rose at the annual rate of 35 to 36 per cent in the first and second quarters of this year; and the consumer price index at 24 to 25 per cent. The Japanese are naturally unhappy and disgruntled; they tend to blame all sorts of things for this. The business firms appear to them quite unethical and insatiably greedy. In fact the session of the Diet of Japan in the spring of 1974 had an atmosphere of the 'people's court'. The presidents of big corporations were summoned one by one to the session and tried for presumably taking advantage of the situation and raising prices. After wages and salaries were raised on average by 30 per cent this spring, the people are now concerned about cost-push inflation.

In responding to the witch-hunt fever of the people, the economists are busy enumerating various causes for inflation. They usually divide the causes into two categories in a Harrodian fashion; one is demand-

[1] J. M. Keynes, 'The General Theory of Employment', *Quarterly Journal of Economics*, Vol. 51, p. 209.

pull (or demand-side) factors and the other cost-push (or supply-side). They then proceed to subdivide those categories into smaller and yet smaller items. The list becomes quite encyclopaedic. It is as though we are taken by those economists on a guided tour through a fancy department-store, where the varieties of niceties are displayed; though without quite being able to decide which one to buy but simply being dazzled, if not puzzled by the choice. Is it thanks to the Keynesian revolution that economists came to forget to economise on their own theories before anything else? They certainly expanded the number of variables and thus made their theories closer to realities but also, alas, emptier than ever.

It is true that a simple illustration of a goldfish bowl is not sufficient to explain the cause of the current inflation. It is often said that for a given quantity of water (i.e. money) goldfish (i.e. relative prices) swim around and change their relative positions from time to time (some higher and some lower) but always below the surface of the water. However, this time some fish (notably oil-related goods) swam higher than the water surface or, as it were, the water surface bulged because of the surge of those fish. The goldfish that used to swim relatively high did not change their swimming level. Instead other fish came to swim even higher. Income velocity of money clearly increased. Hence some economists assert that it is not money or at least not money alone but something else that has caused the current inflation. Alfred Marshall was early to point this out by saying that 'inflations and contractions of credit and prices will always be caused by wars and rumours of wars, by good and bad harvests, and by the alternate opening out of promising new enterprises, and the collapse of many of the hopes founded on them'.[2] And Sir Roy Harrod made this issue a dividing point for his becoming a Keynesian. But which modern monetarist of positivist persuasion would really assert the absolute constancy of income velocity?

Income velocity does change: it does behave cyclically. The real question is whether non-monetary factors such as wage-push or oil price-rise are capable of forcing it to change against its own cyclical behaviour. Or is it simply that the cyclical behaviour of income velocity is either accelerated or mitigated by those factors? So far as I know, no monetarist claims that money is everything or that monetarism is an all-purpose theory. Money is certainly incapable of eradicating all the disturbances that originate from the real sector. But it is capable of reinforcing those disturbances and amplifying them. As we shall see later, no inflation in the last one hundred years of Japan's history occured without a prior increase in the rate of money supply; and no deflation without a prior decrease. The rate of either inflation or

[2] *Memorials of Alfred Marshall*, ed. A. C. Pigou (New York: Kelly & Millman, Inc., 1956) Chap. VIII, p. 194.

deflation was indeed accelerated or mitigated by changes in the real sector but was never reversed.

The only reason why Japan is suffering from severe inflation today is that the rate of money supply has been increased abnormally by none other than the monetary authority of Japan in spite of our repeated warnings. Up until the summer of 1972, the monetary authority of Japan might be able to offer some excuse; in so far as the volume of dollars that flowed into Japan could be regarded as beyond their control. But even this is quite dubious because dollars flowed into Japan to such an extent precisely because the monetary authority of Japan was so reluctant to adjust the exchange rate of the yen and dragged its feet in spite of our repeated protests. The really terrible fact is, however, that the monetary authority of Japan not only bought up a lot of dollars and failed to neutralise them but also on top of this even increased the supply of the Bank of Japan credit by bringing thus the annual rate of money supply close to 30 per cent in the fourth quarter of 1973. How would it ever be possible to avoid terrible inflation after feeding the economy this amount of money? If awful inflation did not occur consequently, the sun would indeed rise from the west. That is the cold fact that the one hundred years history of Japan tells us. And in this history no other inflation was brought about by so purely a monetary factor and hence by a mistake of the monetary authority than this one.

It is true that the sudden rise in the price of crude oil delayed the occurrence of the turning point in the current inflation in Japan. A turning-point was about ready to appear some time around November 1973, because the rate of money supply had been steadily lowered by the Bank of Japan since January 1973, from the vicinity of 30 per cent (annual rate) down to 16 per cent (annual rate) by the end of the same year. But the rise must also have accelerated the inflation. In other words, it accelerated the cyclical upswing of income velocity still further. But so long as the Bank of Japan steadfastly sticks to the 10 to 13 per cent annual rate which I regard as close to the optimum rate for the Japanese economy, prices in Japan are bound to decline and our inflation will definitely be over by the end of 1975. Indeed, the prices are behaving more or less as predicted since March 1974.

The continued upswing of income velocity of money implies the development of price-rise expectation on the part of the general public. Should such an 'exogenous' factor as the increase of oil prices strike at precisely the moment when otherwise it might well have begun to simmer down, the increase would certainly cause people's price-rise expectation to flare up once again and develop a commodity shortage scare. Hence the general price level will go up. That is what happened in Japan since November 1973 until February 1974. After all, there is no such a thing as general price level or absolute price level as such but only some sort of vector of relative prices. In so far as relative prices go up, so will their vector.

If the central bank were to reduce the rate of money supply to its optimum level (optimum in the sense that the impact of money is more or less totally absorbed into the real sector and not into prices), and keep it there, the vector price would be bound to come down; although the structure of relative prices might well be changed during the process. If the sudden rise of oil price were to have occurred at precisely the moment of the cyclical down-swing of income velocity, it would have been quite possible for the prices of goods as well as the rate of employment to decline, together with the level of general prices. [I suspect that this is more or less what happened in the case of West Germany from the end of 1973 through 1974.]

In so far as it was the 'oil crisis' that was an immediate cause for the acceleration of inflation, it could be said that an 'exogenous' factor was responsible for the current inflation. But inflation as such is caused only by money and can be controlled only by money; although it may be disguised to a certain extent by some other measures. Although money does influence relative prices and, in fact, although the equilibrium of the system of relative prices in monetary economy can be attained only by introducing money into the real sector, monetary policy cannot effectively be used to change at will the structure of relative prices.

2 MONEY, INTEREST RATES, OUTPUT AND PRICES

Our question is why in the face of the enormous inflow of dollars the monetary authority of Japan increased the Bank of Japan credit in the last four months of 1972. It was precisely because of their preoccupation with the behaviour of investment; the preoccupation which was of Keynesian origin and characterised by the asset preference theory bias. It was for the monetary authority of Japan nothing but this investment especially by large-sized industries that was a deciding factor for business cycles. In so far as it did not show any significant increase, the authority apparently did not care at all about how great the rate of money supply already was or how low the interest rates already were.

It is true that in so far as investment is in fact interest elastic, interest rates are the intermediaries between the monetary sector and the real sector. The great contribution of the Keynesian revolution was that it emphasised some essential difference between a monetary economy and a barter-production economy; although, as will be explained later, it really ended up in what I call 'neo-classical' dichotomy. This emphasis was rightly accompanied by the recognition of the function of money more as a store of value than as a medium of exchange as well as of the substitutability between money on the one hand and the wide range of alternative financial assets and the access to credit on the other. But the questions of (1) how elastic investments are to the changes of interest rates and (2) how reliably stable the investment multiplier is, are really empirical questions and not a matter for *a priori* judgements.

The assertion that interest rates are the sole intermediary variables between the monetary sector and the real sector really amounts, on the one hand, to the claim that the income velocity of money is the function of interest rates and, on the other, to the denial of any direct substitutability between money and capital goods. As to the former, the Keynesian assertion of the existence of the liquidity trap implied that income velocity could even be infinitesimal from time to time. If this is really so, monetary policy must indeed be preoccupied with the behaviour of investment via interest rates.

But the interesting fact is that throughout the post-war period of Japan, except for the year 1956, the changes of the income velocity either of M_1 or M_2 really preceded the changes of interest rates. This is only natural because the income velocity has behaved quite procyclically throughout the last ninety years (see Figure 1). Whenever the rate of money supply increased, so did the rate of change in income

Figure 1. The Rates of Changes in Industrial Production – Wholesale Price Index and Income Velocity.

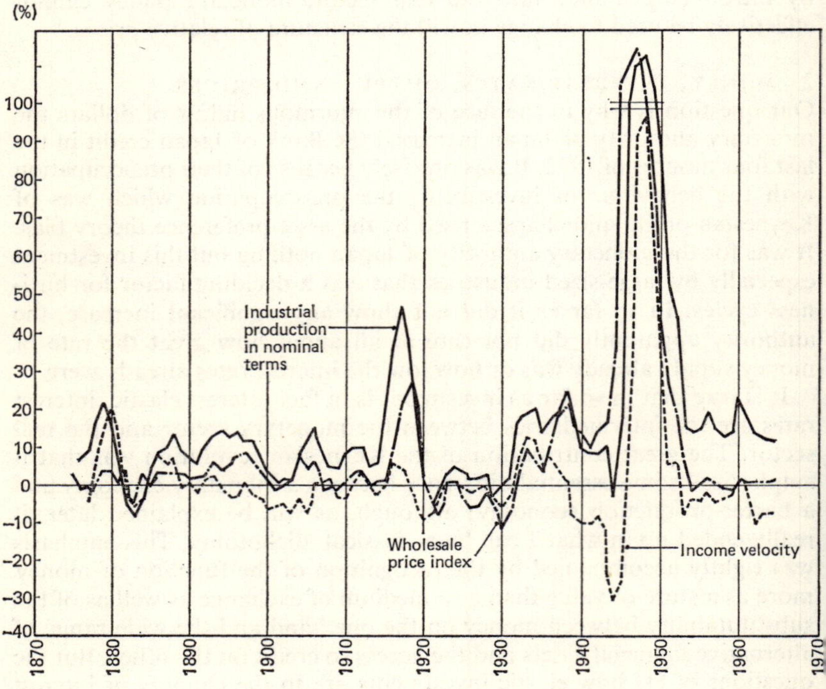

velocity correspondingly; and whenever the former was reduced, so was the latter correspondingly. This pro-cyclical movement of income velocity amplifies the impact of money first on output and later on the vector of relative prices. Such changes of the vector price as will thus occur consequently are bound to influence interest rates as well. Hence the lagged changes of interest rates. It is precisely this behaviour of interest rates that was labelled by Keynes the 'Gibson paradox' and hence came to constitute a wrong starting-point for the Keynesian analysis.

It is true that at least the peaks and troughs of interest rates in the post-war period of Japan either precede, or occur simultaneously with the peaks and troughs of the rate of change in money supply. It thus appears that, as stated precisely by J. M. Keynes, high interest rates appear because of tight money policy and low interest rates because of monetary relaxation. But such correspondence occurs only at the time of turning-point, such as a peak or trough. Otherwise, there exists no meaningful correlation between the behaviour of interest rates on the one hand and that of money supply and, even less, real output on the other.

It is not accidental that we observe some significant correspondence between the behaviour of interest rates and that of money supply at their turning-points. It is because the monetary authority must have enlarged money supply before the rise of interest rates and hence the rise of the vector price prior to the rise of interest rates. Moreover, in Japan, partly because of the law, the changes of discount rates have been used by the monetary authority as the means to express its political determination to shift the direction of monetary policy. Only after such political decisions are made explicit by means of some change of discount rate, will the monetary authority change in any significant way the rate of money supply, the direction of window guidance, etc. It is thus politically as well as phenomenally correct that tight money policy results in high interest rates and cheap money policy in low interest rates. But, economically speaking, its precise opposite is correct.

It may seem, incidentally, that in Figure 2 any significant correlation between money and real output was lost during the period from 1965 through to 1970. But it is only because the relative stability of money supply at a more or less optimum level produced a stability of the vector price. Hence, the impact of money was almost totally absorbed into real output. But, of course, this did not eradicate all the disturbances that originated in the real sector. Instead, it helped those disturbances to show themselves more clearly as they really were.

Now, let us go back to our original question and ask once again why the monetary authority of Japan chose to increase money in 1972 in the face of the already tremendous increase of money supply. It is true that even by the first quarter of 1973 private equipment investment, which

Figure 2. Rates of changes in Industrial Production, Money (M_2) and Prices.

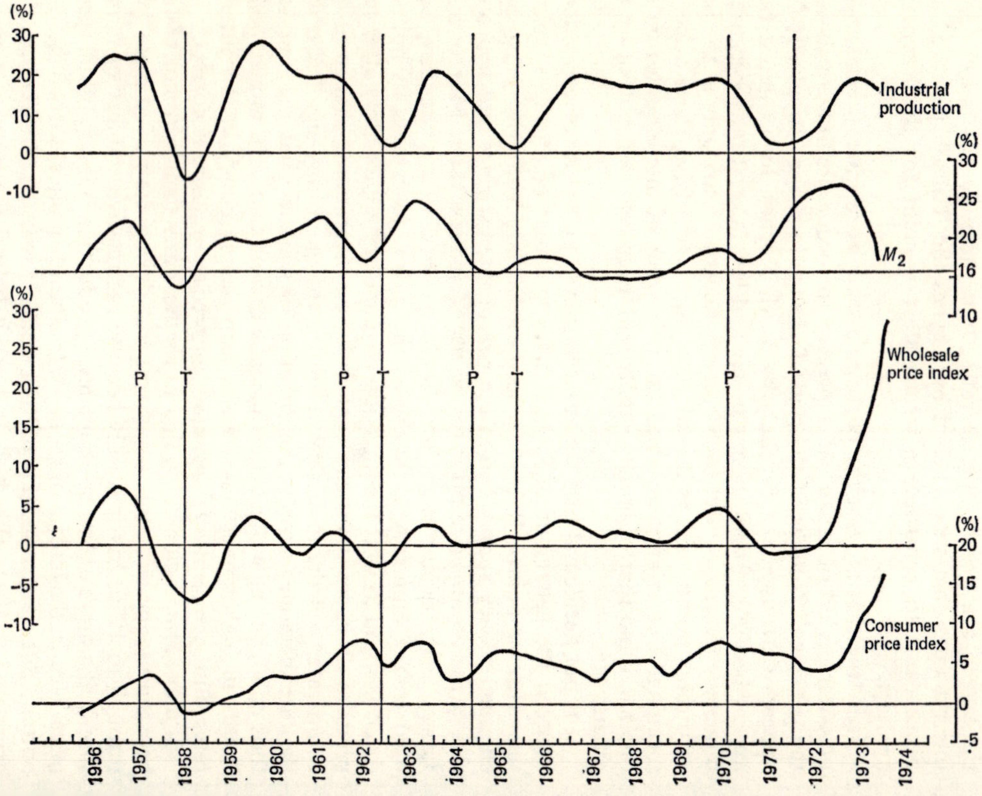

had been growing at the annual rate of 16–18 per cent on average since 1966, did not recover from what the Japanese public called the 'Nixon shock'. The annual rate of its increase declined to the vicinity of 3 per cent. The authority never believed that money as such would ever directly stimulate output or sooner or later was bound to increase investment. We must, of course, sympathise with them to a certain extent; for the Marshallian *K* increased enormously after the 'Nixon shock'. If money is really to be regarded as a substitute for information as will be explained later, the uncertainties created by the sudden announcement of the American 'New Economic Policies' helped to increase the demand for money in Japan. But, as the new exchange rates of the yen became clear, a consumption boom began to take place already in January 1972, the housing investment boom in March and the equipment investment boom of the medium- and small-size industries in June. The rate of private investment as a whole was already back to 11·4 per cent in the second quarter of 1972. Money, the rate of increase of which was enlarged to the 22 per cent annual rate by that time, was bound to activate itself sooner or later and stimulate the economy. But in order to understand this, the financial asset preference theory of the Keynesian orientation does not seem sufficient or even appropriate. We must really ask once again what money fundamentally is.

'MONETARY' EQUILIBRIUM ANALYSIS

1 FINANCIAL ASSET PREFERENCE THEORY AND MONETARY THEORY

I am afraid that financial theory, the gist of which is the optimisation of asset portfolio, has greatly misled monetary policies and seriously obstructed a healthy development of monetary theories. I do not mean that the analytical efforts of the financial asset preference theory are wrong in themselves. It can certainly help to explore the behavioural principles of financial institutions in the private sector, especially when its theories are developed in connection with the profit maximisation behaviour of those institutions. However, this kind of financial theory is neither the essence of the monetary theory that aims most fundamentally at the optimisation of the rate of money supply for a nation's economy nor even its core. Yet it appears as if the asset preference theory has been turned into the dogma that what is important is either interest rates or the availability of funds or perhaps both, but not the rate of supply of money as such. It might thus have only been natural for the thoughts of the monetary authorities to become really those of private bankers and to have lost sight of the proper road to the real development of monetary theories.

There was, of course, a theoretical necessity for financial theory to have become recently asset preference theory. In spite of the marginal revolution, as Professor Hicks precisely put it in 1934, monetary theory was only repeating a tautology in the form of $MV = PT$. Until then, monetary theory was left outside of the marginal revolution. It goes without saying that in the Walrasian tradition of the general equilibrium analysis, there did exist money, the *numéraire* role of which was to be played by one of the goods. But that was just about all that could be said for money. The quite special function of money that it is traded in all markets was simply abstracted from the analysis and never discussed so specifically; except, of course, as a medium of exchange, whatever its meaning was. It was thus rather natural that the 'classical dichotomy', which J. M. Keynes criticised, should occur.

It was recognised that the price of good which is to be used as money was to become higher than otherwise or that the value of money would be proportional to its utility and inversely proportional to its quantity, but nothing more. What was really important for the Walrasian general equilibrium analysis was only a conceptual money in so far as the latter as a unit of account helped in the attainment of a general equilibrium, but money was not really regarded as a tangible good as such. Hence the rise of the 'classical dichotomy' that the equilibrium of the system of relative prices is attained in the real sector and its nominal level or absolute prices only in the monetary sector. Its only consequence was the estrangement of monetary theory from development in the field of price theory.

It was thus only proper for J. M. Keynes to have asserted the necessity of overcoming the 'classical dichotomy' and to have emphasised the substitutability between bonds and money in his liquidity preference theory. It was also natural for Professor Hicks to have stressed the need for marginal revolution in the field of money. With his asset preference theory in response to these assertions Don Patinkin tried to integrate the monetary sector and the real sector together by introducing the rate of marginal substitution analysis. When this theory was first developed, its attention was still limited to 'outside money'. But after Gurley and Shaw emphasised the importance of 'inside money' and hence that of the liquidity position of the economy as a whole, financial theory came to be developed by J. Tobin and his so-called 'New View School' as an asset preference theory, the core of which was the analysis of interest structure.

It was precisely out of this process that a new separation of the monetary sector from the real sector emerged; a separation which I call the 'neo-classical dichotomy'. The new dichotomy is the assertion that what is important is interest structure, fund position or some such and neither the rate of money supply nor the purchasing power of money. Behind this development there are, of course, not only the asset preference theory but also the Keynesian theory of investment multiplier, or the assertion that what counts is investment and not money – the position criticised early on by Professor Modigliani[3] – or, above all, that huge tradition of 'natural interest' theory of Wicksellian origin, etc.

It is theoretically quite correct to assert that interest rate is an intermediary between the monetary and the real sector. And the people involved in the banking business may well find it familiar to their own experience that the liquidity position of the economy as a whole is influenced by the changes of interest structure and in return influences investment and finally the business cycle. But interest rates are neither the only intermediary between money and the real sectors nor even the primary path that combines the two sectors.

It seems that those of the asset preference school confused the matter of financial institutions with the problems of general equilibrium theory. However correct it may be from the institutional point of view that money is issued anew only in exchange for some financial asset and hence changes interest rates in the process, this is not the whole story of importance to general equilibrium theory. This is not to say that interest rates are not important: theoretically interest rates are very important. How important they actually are is the empirical question that has to be decided by how elastic investment or the business cycle is to their changes or in other words by how sensitively income velocity will be changed by their changes.

The mistake of the 'neo-classical dichotomy' is that it regarded interest rates as the sole intermediaries between the monetary and the real sectors and hence came to lose sight of the more primary and direct relationship between money and real goods. It thus reinforced the 'classical dichotomy' by amounting once again to the assertion that while the equilibrium of the system of relative prices or the equilibrium growth path is attained in the real sector, general prices (or absolute prices) alone are determined in the monetary sector. But the truth is that either the equilibrium of the system of relative prices or the equilibrium growth path in a monetary economy can be determined only when money is introduced. Without money there is no such thing as equilibrium relative prices in this economy. And such things as absolute prices do not exist either, but only some vector of relative prices. The proper development of monetary theories as well as the healthy operation of monetary policies can be attained only by the clear realisation of these points.

2 MONEY IS AN INTER-SPATIAL AND INTER-TEMPORAL SUBSTITUTE FOR INFORMATION

There is hardly an assertion that is fresher in spirit and more suggestive in contents than the following words of Professor F. A. Hayek, stated already some thirty-seven years ago. According to him

[3] Franco Modigliani, 'Liquidity Preference and The Theory of Interest and Money', *Readings in Monetary Theory*, ed. F. A. Lutz and L. W. Mints (New York: The Blakiston Co., 1951) pp. 186–239.

> . . . it is only relative to the knowledge . . . that an equilibrium is likely to be reached. . . . While such a position represents in one sense a position of equilibrium, it is clear that it is not an equilibrium in the special sense in which equilibrium is regarded as a sort of optimum position.[4]

And yet the equilibrium analysis of the Walrasian tradition or the so-called perfect competition models have resolved this most important problem either by abstracting the problem of the people's knowledge as that of '*tâtonnement*' or by regarding prices as given. But how can we be sure that the units of economic activities can ascertain equilibrium (relative) prices without paying for them? On the contrary, as Professor Hayek emphasised, if there is genuine competition, the major efforts of the people are directed to find the information of those prices. In order to discover such information and attain equilibrium prices, the people must unavoidably spend their resources, labour and time.

In other words, the information concerning equilibrium (relative) prices are not free goods but economic goods. It is this situation that a nation's economy must face and find it most difficult to solve in its efforts to get out the barter-production economy and prosper. It is precisely in this content that money comes into our picture, for money helps us to solve the specific difficulties in the above. That is precisely why there is such a close relationship between the rate of money supply and the other economic variables. Unless we make this point clear, our equilibrium analysis may well end in being simple tautologies. Once again in the words of Professor Hayek

> Indeed, my main contention will be that the tautologies, of which formal equilibrium analysis in economics essentially consists, can be turned into propositions which tell us anything about causation in the real world only in so far as we are able to fill those formal propositions with definite statements about how knowledge is acquired and communicated. In short, I shall contend that the *empirical element in economic theory* – the only part which is concerned not merely with implications but with causes and effects and which leads therefore to conclusions which, at any rate in principle, can be capable of verification – *consists of propositions about the acquisition of knowledge.*[5]

In responding to the assertion of Professor Hayek, Professor G. Stigler developed a marginal analysis of the information of prices some quarter of a century later.[6] In this analysis, the actual price that the

[4] F. A. Hayek, *Individualism and Economic Order* (Chicago: The University of Chicago Press, 1950) Ch. II, 'Economics and Knowledge', p. 53.

[5] F. A. Hayek, *Individualism and Economic Order* op. cit. p. 33. Italics are mine.

[6] Cf., George Stigler, 'The Economics of Information', *The Journal of Political Economy*, Vol. LXIX, No. 3 (June 1961) pp. 213–25, and 'Information in the Labor Market', *The Journal of Political Economy*, Vol. LXX, No. 5, pt 2 (Oct 1962) pp. 94–105.

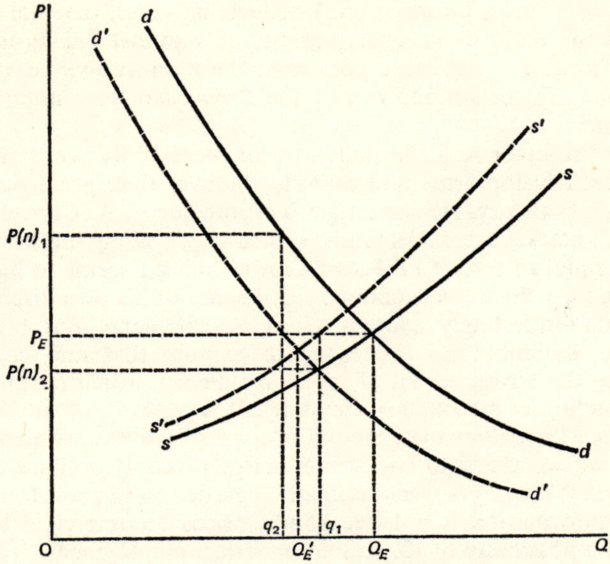

Figure 3. Equilibrium under Information Costs

buyer faces is termed 'asking price' and the actual price that the seller faces is the 'bidding price'. The essential point of the theory of Professor Stigler is that the 'asking prices' are generally higher and the 'bidding prices' are lower than the equilibrium prices in the Walrasian type of general equilibrium analysis and hence the latter require costs for their discoveries. Let us express the asking price by $P(n)_1$ and the bidding price by $P(n)_2$. Then the core of Professor Stigler's assertion, though clearly oversimplified, may be expressed by something like Figure 3.

Since the asking price is at the level of $P(n)_1$ and the bidding price is at $P(n)_2$, the quantity actually demanded at the equilibrium price P_E is q_1 and the quantity actually supplied q_2. This situation is universal at all the levels of the theoretical equilibrium prices in so far as there exist the information costs for all the prices in the demand and the supply functions (actually, as will be explained later, information costs are the function of the scales of economic activities). Then, the demand function *dd* shifts to the actual demand function *d'd'* and the supply function to *s's'*. This means that the actual equilibrium quantity is Q_E' and not Q_E.

If you like, you could call Q_E', Q_E 'deflation gap' in the Keynesian fashion. Professor Stigler himself did not examine the problem implied in this gap which is essentially the gap between a monteary economy and a barter-production economy but paid his attention to the marginal analysis of information costs or of the costs that are necessary for the acquisition of price information. I believe, however, that the potential existence of the gap in Professor Stigler's model led Professor A. Alchian to assert that there does exist the microeconomic and hence endogenous factor for the rise of the Keynesian 'involuntary' unemployment.[7]

It was Professor A. Leijonhufvud who successfully synthesised these theoretical developments and came to discover their great significance for monetary theory. He was taught by Professor R. W. Clower that 'the sum of all market excess demands, valued at prevailing market prices, is at most equal to zero'.[8] Professor Clower himself seems to have failed to realise fully the microeconomic significance of his own discovery and remained, interestingly enough, on a macro plane. But his student Professor Leijonhufvud proceeded to explore that and contributed greatly to the advancement of monetary theory, which means the real understanding of a monetary economy. It was he who made it explicit that in the Marshallian market equilibrium model the adjustment velocity of price was assumed to be infinitely large precisely because the information costs for prices were implicitly regarded to be zero. But in so far as such information is not free goods, prices become rigid and there occurs the possibility of Keynesian imperfect employment.

In this analysis, money is regarded as an indispensable factor for an economy to escape the restraint unique to barter-production economy and leap forward. Money, called 'liquidity', is a particular kind of good, whose price of information cost is zero or close to zero. Therefore, people substitute money for goods they demand; the marginal costs of information of those goods being higher than the marginal returns that can be brought about by investing those costs. But, thanks either to the passage of time or to the (intentional and unintentional) collaboration of the people in the social process, the information costs may well sooner or later approach zero. Then the people will substitute goods for money. That is, putting it in the simplest way, *money is a substitute for information* and by virtue of this function it helps us to attain the 'transitivity of exchange' of Professor Clower to the extent unique only to a monetary economy.

3 'WEALTH EFFECT' OF MONEY

The 'wealth effect' of money is already clear from Figure 3, though it is admittedly an oversimplified diagram. The output that must remain at the level of Q_E' is now enlarged to Q_E thanks to the introduction of

[7] Almen A. Alchian, 'Information Costs, Pricing, and Resource Unemployment', *Microeconomic Foundations of Employment and Inflation Theory*, E. S. Phelps *et al.* (New York: W. W. Norton & Co., Inc., 1970) pp. 27–52.

[8] R. W. Clower, 'The Keynesian Counterrevolution: A Theoretical Appraisal', *The Theory of Interest Rates*, ed. F. H. Hahn and F. P. R. Breckling (London: Macmillan, 1966) p. 122.

money. Conversely, the Walras-Lange type of general equilibrium analysis, which asserted that the equilibrium of the system of relative prices was attained in the real sector, was really a 'real' general equilibrium model that fitted to a low level barter-production economy which was capable of attaining only Q_E' in Figure 3.

However, the discussion on the wealth effect of money has (naturally) not been so simply concluded. Whether money has any wealth effect has been discussed mainly in connection with the assertion that money is really to be analysed in reference to growth theory in so far as it is really to be examined in the field of capital theory. In the course of this discussion, people generally recognised the existence of the wealth effect of 'outside money' or of 'high-powered money'. The best example may be Professor W. T. Newlyn.[9] He asserted that in growth economy capital formation is made partly by the creation of money.

The problem was whether or not 'inside money', which includes interest-bearing time deposits, has any wealth effect. B. P. Pesek and T. R. Saving insisted that not only cash currency but also non-interest bearing demand deposits do create 'net wealth' for the economy as a whole:[10] although, of course, demand deposit sometimes bears interest and sometimes does not. In contrast to this, Professor J. Tobin asserted not only that money does not contribute anything to real income but also even that money really reduces real output per head.[11] This means that Professor Tobin and his 'New View School' must regard Q_E in Figure 3 as attainable without money and hence they must be suffering from the illusion unique to what I called 'real' general equilibrium analysis. Our real question is whether we remain at Q_E' without introducing money into economy or succeed in attaining a higher equilibrium level by creating either 'outside' money or 'inside' money. I cannot see any essential difference for their being substitutes for information except the degree. It is true that the creation of 'inside' money is made only in exchange for the creation of corresponding debts in the private sector. But the fundamental significance of either cash currency or time deposits does not lie there. The real question is, as Professor Hicks emphasised, why people hold money instead of capital goods.

In response to the assertion of Professor Leijonhufvud, Professor Milton Friedman came to build a new equilibrium model, where the constancy of either price or quantity was no longer assumed.[12] This model satisfies Leijonhufvud's condition that information concerning the prices of goods that are other than money must not be regarded as

[9] W. T. Newlyn, *The Theory of Money* (Oxford: Clarendon Press, 1971).

[10] B. P. Pesek and T. R. Saving, *Money, Wealth and Economic Theory* (New York: Macmillan Co., 1969).

[11] James Tobin, 'Money and Economic Growth', *Econometrica*, No. 33 (Oct 1965) pp. 671–84.

[12] Milton Friedman, *A Theoretical Framework for Monetary Analysis*, NBER Occasional Paper 112 (New York: Columbia University Press, 1971).

free goods and yet, I believe, is capable of producing equilibrium solution.

Let P_E and $P(n)$ in Figure 3 be those of the ith good. Then, since

$$P_{Ei} \leqslant P(n)_i,$$

in the Walras-Lange model

$$\sum_{i=1}^{n-1} P_{Ei}S_i - \sum_{i=1}^{n-1} P(n)iD_i \geqslant 0$$

Therefore, general equilibrium can be attained only when

$$\sum_{i=1}^{n-1} P_{Ei}D_i = \sum_{i=1}^{n-1} P(n)_iD_i + M_D = \sum_{i=1}^{n-1} P_{Ei}S_i = X_E$$

Here, X_E signifies the full employment level of output (i.e. Q_E' in Figure 3). The above implies that the equilibrium of a monetary economy, which corresponds to Q_E in Figure 3, can be attained only when money is supplied just in the quantity of M_D and that the equilibrium of the system of relative prices, which is attained without money, limits the output to a very low level (which corresponds to Q_E' in Figure 3). Nevertheless, it is this primitive economy that has been analysed by the traditional equilibrium analysis. It is money that will let us get out of that. It is precisely here that the most fundamental wealth effect of money lies.

K. Brunner and A. H. Meltzer have also come to regard money as a substitute for resource investment in information.[13] But I believe that by so doing they have erred in overemphasising the medium of exchange function of money. It is not only inter-spatial information that money substitutes. It is also inter-temporal information that money more significantly substitutes. In the former function money is ordinarily regarded as a medium of exchange and in the latter as an asset. The Tobinian type of balance-sheet analysis of portfolio is simply incapable of analysing this aspect of the significance of money. But when such a fundamental significance of money is recognised, it may not be difficult for us to realise also that money is important not only in the short run but also in the long run.

A MONETARY ANALYSIS OF THE JAPANESE ECONOMY, 1868–1972

1 THE EPISODE OF ν-SHAPED CURVE

In any meaningful way, money does not directly influence general price level or the so-called absolute prices. I think that absolute price is only a fiction created out of the classical dichotomy. If there is any meaning

[13] K. Brunner and A. H. Meltzer, 'The Uses of Money', *The American Economic Review*, Vol. LXI, No. 5 (Dec 1971).

for it, it is only when absolute price is understood to be some sort of vector of relative prices. If it is so, money can influence the absolute level of prices only by influencing the quantities of goods and services first of all and only then the structure of their relative prices. Even when the rate of money supply is changed, the units of economic activities will try to maintain

$$d \log V_i = d \log X_i - d \log M_i = 0$$
$$(i = i\text{th person}).$$

But their individual efforts of this kind will end up in causing such an aggregate result as

$$d \log V = (d \log P + d \log X_E) - d \log M > 0$$

This is because output is always the function of time, even when below the level of full employment. That is why, as we will see later, money first changes output and later the vector price.

The fundamental significance of money as a good is to be found (as may well be clear by now from its wealth effect) in its being a production factor. It facilitates both production and demand (which is really to be understood to be production function). This assertion does not prevent us from writing out the demand function as follows:

$$\frac{M}{P} = f(I_c; y, w, r_m, r_e, rb; \frac{1}{P}\frac{dp}{dt}; u)$$

Here, I_c signifies the expected information costs concerning prices, y real income, w non-human wealth, r_m, r_e and rb respectively the vectors of the expected rates of returns of money, equities and bonds,

$$\frac{1}{P}\frac{dp}{dt}$$

the vector price or the vector of the expected rate of returns of real assets and u other related utilities. By being a substitute for information, money facilitates the optimisations of not only the production activities of the people but of their consumption activities as well. I do not believe that this fundamental significance of money can be understood in so far as we regard money as a consumption good or a luxury good.

A very universal significance of money as a production factor is most dramatically demonstrated in Figure 4. We observe there a *v*-shaped curve. The gold embargo, its lifting and the final departure from the gold standard clearly disrupted the growth trend of output in one hundred years and came to draw a *v*-shaped curve. In other words, as Professor Friedman emphasised, the great depression was caused by a severe contraction of money and not by its abundant availability (alias

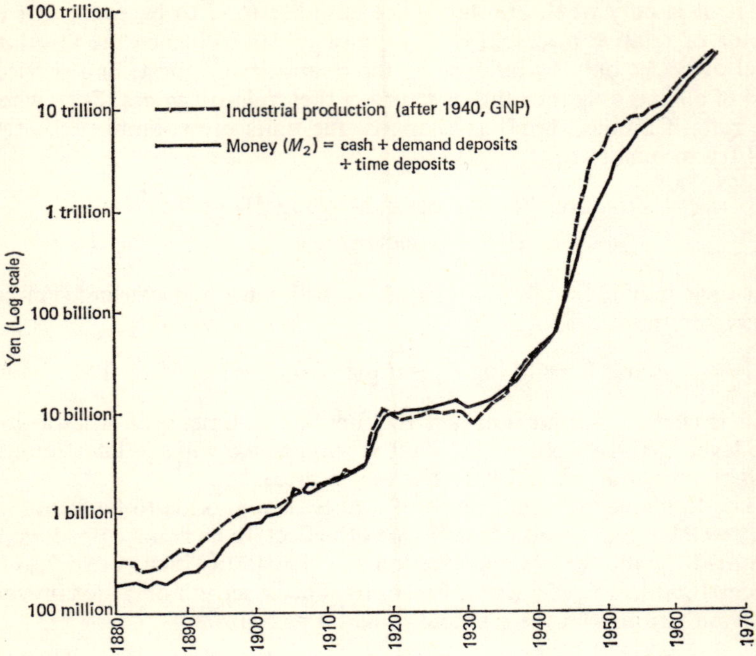

Figure 4. Money and Industrial Production in 100 years of Japan

liquidity trap), as J. M. Keynes and his followers claimed. There is no evidence for the power of money more dramatic than this episode.

2 INCOME VELOCITY OF MONEY

The correlation between money and income is very clear in Figure 5. And, as we have already seen before, the income velocity of money behaves pro-cyclically in the short run and shows a clear trend in the long run. This pro-cyclical movement of money amplifies the impact of monetary policy and tends to create 'overshoot' or 'overkill'.

In fact, however, though income velocity is important for monetary policy, it is not really so theoretically. Theoretically it is simply a mathematical quotient, the product of vector price by real output divided by money. This implies that the pro-cyclical movement of income velocity is only a passive in its nature. What is really important is the rate of change in what I called the 'Friedmanian k', which is a quotient of money divided by some weighted average of real output in several years, a concept that corresponds to Professor Friedman's permanent income. Money per unit of output is still a crude Friedmanian k, which is a proxy for the latter, and which is a simple moving

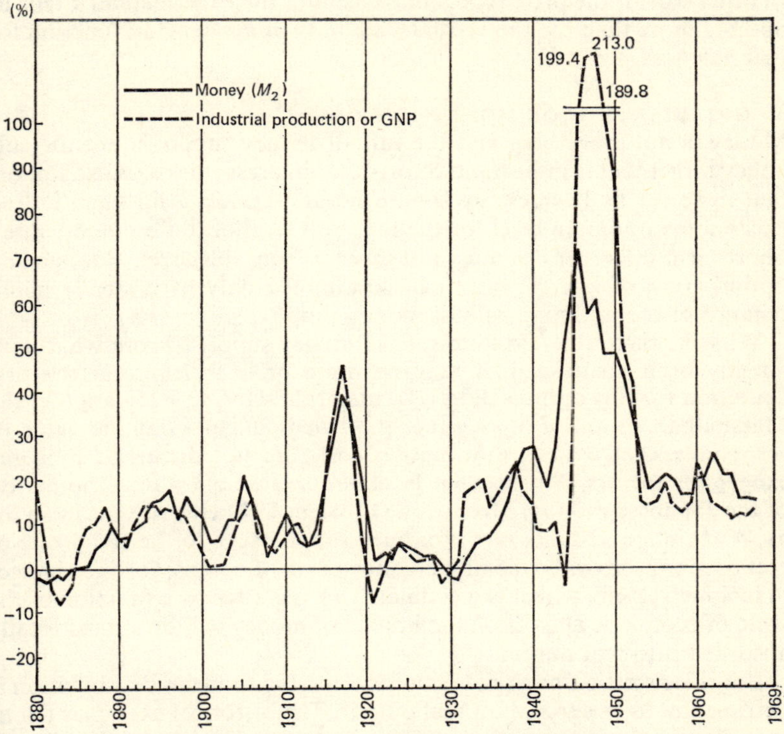

Figure 5. Rates of Change in Production and Money in the last 100 years of Japan

average. Nevertheless, the correlation between this and the rate of change of the vector price is already rather striking. The pro-cyclical movement of income velocity is a mere reflection of this pro-cyclical movement of the Friedmanian *k*.

Let us suppose by simplifying the problem that information cost mentioned before increases at some constant rate as the scale of economic activities grows, i.e. so long as information is not disturbed by some exogenous factors. If under such circumstances the rate of change of the Friedmanian *k* were to grow, it should mean that 'excess' money was supplied. Then, as already explained before, every unit of economic activities will try to maintain its own ratio between his money and his real scale of economic activities. But since

$$\frac{1}{y}\frac{dy}{dt} = f(t)$$

Hence, as mentioned before,

$$d \log V = (d \log P + d \log X) - d \log M > 0$$

In other words, the pro-cyclical movement of the Friedmanian k tells us nothing more than the fundamental stability of the demand function for real balances.

3 OPTIMISATION OF MONEY SUPPLY

Money is not everything and the rate of money supply is not the sole policy target that is important. Short-term interest rates are also important in so far as business cycles are interest-elastic. And there indeed exists some optimum level for the long-run level of those interest rates. Short-term interest rates must not diverge from this level. But such an optimisation of interest rates can be attained only by a steady maintenance of the optimum rate of money supply.

What is, then, the optimum rate of money supply? From what have already been mentioned, it may be more or less clear that the first condition for this optimisation is to maintain $d \log V$, $d \log k_M$ (i.e. the Marshallian k) and $d \log k_F$ (i.e. the Friedmanian k) at the value of zero; unless, of course, information costs are not disturbed by some exogenous factors. But at what level is our next question. The period of the Japanese economy from 1965 through 1970 tells us that in so far as we maintain a stable rate of money supply close to the trend rate of real economic growth (making an allowance, of course, for the changes in income velocity which can ordinarily be regarded as a function of the scale of economic activities), the impact of money will be almost totally absorbed into real output.

But this assertion must not be misinterpreted to mean that inflation is detrimental to the growth of real output. The historical examples tell us that open inflation, however galloping it may be, has hardly slowed down economic growth. The evils of inflation must be found somewhere else. It is wrong because it produces a serious income redistribution effect. But then the standard of value must not be identified with money. Money is a unit of account but is not the standard of value; for, after all, what is usually called the purchasing power of money is a vector price combined with a certain specific set of weights. If our problem about inflation is income redistribution effect or the differentiated lags of price rises among different sectors of economy, some other standard of value must be established. Alfred Marshall, as was pointed out to me by Professor Friedman, was quite early to mention that

> . . . the only effective remedy for them [the fluctuations of general prices] is to be sought in relieving the currency of the duty, which it is not fitted to perform, of acting as a standard of value; and by establishing, in accordance with a plan which has long been familiar to economists, an authoritative standard of purchasing power independent of the currency.[14]

[14] Alfred Marshall, 'Remedies for Fluctuations of General Prices', *Memorials of Alfred Marshall*, ed. A. C. Pigou (New York: Kelley & Millman, Inc., 1956) p. 188.

If we succeed in establishing such a standard and raising all the prices in accordance to it, we may succeed in reducing fairly well the evils of the income redistribution effect. In the meantime, efforts to optimise the rate of money supply will help us to emerge from this problem.

11 Report on Brazil

Américo Oswaldo Campiglia

This essay is an empirical contribution to the study of the effects of inflation on monetary policy, as based on the Brazilian experience throughout the 1964–73 period. Its fundamental purpose is to provide a brief introduction to and analysis of the inflation factors as well as of the steps which have been taken in Brazil with a view to holding down the rate of increase of domestic prices, whilst concurrently propitiating the conditions capable of ensuring the country's socio-economical development. The concurrence of these goals, although apparently conflicting with one another, has undoubtedly posed a challenge to the orthodox articles of faith of the economic theory which had prevailed till then, and according to which *deflation* would have been the sole process capable of containing and neutralising the outburst of inflation.

With the twofold purpose of fending off the social and economical effects of inflationary pressures – even if of a short-run duration – as well as that of triggering a process of expansion of the economy, Brazil has chosen to adopt a pragmatic policy of gradual and controlled 'de-inflation', the performance of which has been evidenced by the decrease in rates of inflation, from 91·9 per cent per annum to 15·7 per cent per annum throughout the period of 1964 to 1973 whilst, as of 1968, the country has succeeded in achieving an average annual growth rate of 10 per cent in its Gross National Product. This policy which is often called 'gradualism', has very likely benefited from the circumstance of having been applied in a 'developing' country possessing very specific features in terms of an abundant availability of both natural and human resources; nevertheless, its success has undeniably had the decisive contribution given by the deep changes which were introduced in the country's monetary and financial structure and which have carved out the paths of recuperation so far achieved.

When analysing the country's economic evolution throughout the last decade, it becomes easy enough to establish that the so-called 'Brazilian miracle' is a mere figure of speech. Actually, what is taking place in Brazil, at present, is a consciously programmed development process, the fundamental support of which relies on social stability, support of private enterprise, logistic infrastructure for fiscal and monetary policies as well as for public works and services – factors contributing to the stepping-up of the pace in the exploration of the country's immense economic potential.

THE BRAZILIAN INFLATION

The determining factors in the case of the Brazilian inflation are fairly notorious for indeed, one way or another, they have been present in the inflationary process of other developing countries – if not in that of some developed countries as well. They may be briefly grouped under four basic variables: (1) public sector deficits and the manner of financing thereof; (2) cost pressures arising from wage adjustments; (3) cost pressures arising from devaluation in rates of exchange; and (4) pressures arising from the private sector of the economy.[1] Such factors correspond to the structuralist concept of inflation, although they may be identified in the behaviour of the monetary mass during the decade of 1960 as well.

The Federal Government's budgetary deficits were the cause of the continuous and growing issues of paper currency and of the increase in level of indebtedness of the public sector – the Federal, the States' and the Cities' Governments included. If, on the one hand, this was propitiated by the loss of money's purchasing power, on the other hand, the tendencies shown by the governments to spend in excess of public revenues is likewise due to the expansion in the demand of public goods and services which had been brought about by the very process of economic development. And in addition to this, due to the state of low degree of trust to which government bonds had fallen (a very common instance during times of inflation), the only way of financing federal budgets was by issuing paper money, up to the middle of the decade of 1960.

With regard to wage adjustments, the reckoning basis taken by worker's claims and by periodically allowed adjustments was the peak of inflation of the preceding year, the notion of an average real salary giving way to a yearly rate of constant inflation, something which, in turn, generated expectations of continued raises in prices over the future. Wage adjustments and budget deficits were, undoubtedly, the two most significant accelerating factors acting on the inflationary spiral.

Devaluations in the rate of exchange played a meaningful part in the process by causing the cost of imports to rise and, consequently, the increase of domestic prices; it should be noted that, throughout the period, exports did not increase at rates compatible with the demand for foreign currencies.

Within the private sector, the behaviour of the economy displayed the classic effects of inflationary and hyper-inflationary systems: price indices continuously on the increase, a steep increase in the velocity-income

[1] Delfim Netto *et al.*, 'Some Aspects of the Brazilian Inflation' São Paulo: Estudos ANPES, 1965).

index of money, a condition of repressed demand for goods and services – particularly for food products, an abnormal growth of means of payment, the withdrawal of medium- and long-term credits, the increase of interest rates, a tendency towards over-indebtedness, and so on.

In all, throughout the years of 1959 to 1964, the Brazilian economy experienced the darkest period of its history, as signalled by a high level of inflation, on the one hand, and by rather meaningless rates of Gross National Product growth as compared with the rates of population growth of the country.

ECONOMIC RECUPERATION: 'DE-INFLATION' AND DEVELOPMENT

By 1964 the rate of inflation in Brazil had reached 91·9 per cent. In 1965 it became possible to clamp down the climbing trend of the process and to keep the year's rate down to 34·5 per cent. The gradual reduction was carried on over the ensuing years and by 1970 the rate was down to 19·2 per cent, decreasing further to 15·7 per cent in 1973. Concurrently Gross National Product rates increased year after year and, by 1973, Gross National Product had reached 60,000 million dollars, whilst exports were recorded at 6,200 millions. This performance enabled the national currency to achieve a measure of stability and Brazil shed the status of a country chronically delinquent in its foreign debt payments, to embark on a schedule of punctuality supported by foreign exchange reserves to the tune of 6,500 million dollars, whilst the *per capita* income reached 500 dollars in 1973, something which Herman Kahn, the futurologist, had predicted for the year 2000!

The measures which were adopted in the country, after 1964, and which made possible both the reversal of the inflationary process and the achievement of high rates of economic growth may be thus summed up:

(*a*) The Reformation of the Banking System (Law 4595 of 1964) which provided for the creation of the Central Bank of Brazil, of the National Monetary Council and of other basic institutions comprising the national finance system.

(*b*) The organic structure of the capital market (Law 4728 of 1965) which entailed the setting-up of a new type of financial institution to specialise in medium-term and long-term credit operations, and which likewise gave out new operational rules applicable to the stock market.

(*c*) The progressive and full suppression of budget deficits pertaining to the Federal, the States and the Municipal governments, together with the economic and financial recuperation of state-owned companies engaged in public services and in operations of transformation.

(*d*) The rebuilding of trust in public bonds, the value of which became indexed on the basis of price levels, through the adoption of the 'monetary correction' system, and which, furthermore, went on to be utilised as an instrument in monetary policies and for the control of means of payment (National Treasury Readjustable Bonds and National Treasury Certificates) through open market operations.

(*e*) The adoption of a new policy for wage adjustments which, by eliminating the excesses and distortions contained in the earlier empirical procedure, contributes to the maintenance of real wage levels compatible with the conjuncture and with productivity scales.

(*f*) The new policy of providing for the distribution of income among the working classes, as adopted through the institution of the Social Integration Programme (PIS), the funding of which is provided by percentages of income tax revenue as the burden of employer companies.

(*g*) The reformation of the social security system, which has created the Employment Time Guarantee Fund (FGTS) by means of nominal bank account deposits earning interest and monetarily corrected, and which may be drawn on by workers in the event of being laid off, as well as for the construction or acquisition of housing and other purposes contemplated under the law.

(*h*) The National Housing System, under which the building or the construction of housing by the working classes has been brought within the reach of the latter's purchasing power through long-term financing.

(*i*) A flexible rate of exchange which is readjusted over short terms, thus enabling the increment in domestic costs to be neutralised and providing the feasibility for exports at world market price-levels.

(*j*) The system for the development of the country's Northeastern and Northern regions through the allocation of funds originating from fiscal incentives assignable to agricultural and industrial projects implemented in those regions by the private enterprise.

(*k*) The national system of long-term oriented credit for the financing of private projects within all sectors of the economy, as granted by the National Economy Development Bank (BNDE), by the Development Banks operated by State Governments, by private investment banks, and by the Central Bank of Brazil.

(*l*) The reformation of the tax system, the new structure of which has rendered possible an equitable distribution of tax revenue among the Federal Government, the States Governments and the Municipal Governments, thus affording all three levels of government the allocation of substantial means for infrastructural investments required to support both regional and national development.

(*m*) Last but not least, the system of indexing (monetary correction), introduced in the country since 1965 and which, on being adopted

> as an instrument for the correction of monetary devaluation, has rendered possible the development of domestic financial relations, thus neutralising the unilateral effects of inflation on savings deposits as well as on commitments callable in terms of duration.

Once domestic and foreign credit had been re-established, the public budget balanced and the national currency strengthened, the Brazilian Government set about executing important programmes with a view to creating infrastructures for transport, communication, electric power generation and distribution, education, basic sanitation, port facilities, expansion of the merchant navy and of other services, all of which have enabled the country's economic growth to increase in pace, a performance which, in turn, has fostered a substantial inflow of foreign investment as witnessed over the last years.

INDEXING BY MEANS OF 'MONETARY CORRECTION'

The gauging of any given magnitude must necessarily assume the existence of a point of reference or of a reckoning basis. The measuring unit is an established and constant magnitude which is used as a standard for the assessment of other magnitudes. And the conventional standard for the measuring of economic goods is money. In terms of international relations, currencies are assessed reciprocally or, again, by comparison with a third currency possessing constant magnitude and stability features.

The instability of a given currency, as constituting an instrument to barters or a gauge to value, when reflecting a progressive loss of its buying power through an inflationary process, generates serious and harmful disturbances in the context of financial relations. Especially in the context of domestic relations, such effects are predominantly felt in the case of deals concluded for a future maturity date, such as is the case of debts assumed, of financial deposits or investments subjected to repayment at nominal monetary values. The principle of indexing, in this case, constitutes a corrective measure whereby the monetary restitution must be worth, on the date of its occurrence, and in terms of currency, the true and actual worth which the same currency had at the time when the deal was concluded. Or, again, original historic values are monetarily corrected at the end of a given duration by means of a factor which corresponds to the devaluation of currency throughout the same duration. This principle can be utilised for various other purposes such as, for instance, the monetary correction of a company's fixed assets, or the reckoning of actual profits through the utilisation of corrective indices applied to working capital, and other assessments.

In the context of income, the great inflationary impact felt in countries where usury laws limit rates of interest (12 per cent per annum, in

Brazil) becomes patent in the generalisation of negative rates of income, when these are lower than the rate of inflation. Monetary correction offsets this distortion since the remuneration of the principal is paid by means of two components: actual interest plus monetary correction, the latter being representative of the currency's devaluation over the period.

In Brazil, indexing at rates worked out and published by the Federal Government has been instituted by law for specific instances, whereas other types of periodical readjustments follow a principle of direct evaluation. A brief description of the most important readjustable items is given below.

NATIONAL TREASURY READJUSTABLE BONDS – ORTN

Federal bonds maturing in 2 or in 5 years and earning from 4 to 7 per cent interest per annum, plus quarterly monetary correction. *Remark* Bonds issued at the nominal value of Cr$10.00 in 1965 now have a corrected value of Cr$86.51.

STATE GOVERNMENTS' READJUSTABLE BONDS

Rotating bonds maturing in one year's time, earning monetary correction and issued at a discount price over that stated for redemption purposes.

NATIONAL TREASURY CERTIFICATES – LTN

Open market operation papers placed by the Central Bank of Brazil with the country's banking institutions and maturing in 180 days. LTNs do not earn interest nor are they monetarily corrected. They are periodically auctioned off in limited volumes and at prices (selling) inferior to nominal, the difference corresponding, approximately, to the summing up of an anticipatedly assessed monetary correction covering the maturity period plus a measure of actual income. LTNs are negotiable and their actual price is quoted in the interbanks market.

TAX DEBTS IN ARREARS

Federal, State and Municipal taxes, when not paid on due date, become subject to monetary correction at ORTN rates throughout the period of delinquency

OLD RENTS AND NEW LEASES

The monetary correction of rents (which had been virtually frozen till then) has been governed by various criteria, all of which were inspired by the need to stimulate the construction of new housing whilst giving due regard to the social implication of the problem. The presently effective indexation allows for deeds to include a clause of yearly correction in proportion to the legal readjustment of minimum wages;

this criterion is likewise allowed in the event of lease renewal, and applies to old leases which were entered into prior to the law instituting the monetary correction thereof.

WAGES

Wages are readjusted yearly through union bargaining conducted under the jurisdiction of Labour Courts. Readjustments become effective for the twelve subsequent months and are constituted by a percentage increase over wages effective throughout the period plus an additional percentage which tends to set the average true salary at levels slightly higher than that of cost of living indices (rate of inflation). It is, therefore, a direct and periodical assessment process, and not one of the 'moving peg' or indexing type.

NATIONAL HOUSING SYSTEM

The unpaid balance representative of liabilities arising out of the purchase of housing, within the National System framework, is periodically corrected by factors specifically applicable to transactions of this nature.

REAL ESTATE ACCEPTANCE PAPERS

These are sold to investors by Real Estate Credit Institutions, earn interest and are monetarily corrected at ORTN rates.

INSURANCE SYSTEM

Life insurance may be purchased under cover of a monetary correction clause applicable both to the annual tariffs and to the eventual indemnity.

TERM BANK DEPOSITS AND CERTIFICATES OF DEPOSIT

These earn interest and are monetarily corrected at preset rates.

SAVINGS ACCOUNTS (SAVINGS BANKS AND HOUSING SYSTEM)

Interests and monetary correction at ORTN rates.

EXPROPRIATION – COURT SUITS – LABOUR INDEMNITIES

After the legally set deadline for settlement, debts become subject to monetary correction at rates given by the Court's ruling in the course of the assessment procedure.

MEDIUM-TERM AND LONG-TERM BANK LOANS

Under the Brazilian bank system rules, medium-term and long-term loans granted by Government and private banks are, in general, subject to the clause of interest payments and monetary correction. In some instances of medium-term financing, the index for monetary correction is conventionally preset to cover the full duration of contract. In the case of long-term financing applicable to lines of credit for development purposes, monetary correction at ORTN rates is applied at the time of maturity of debt.

MONETARY CORRECTION OF COMPANIES' FIXED ASSETS

The yearly revaluation of fixed assets has become mandatory under the law, at periodically issued rates, to cover both the historic value and the accrued depreciation. Amounts thus reported as monetary correction do not constitute taxable income and must be posted to a specific reserve account for subsequent utilisation in capital stock increases.

Table 1 contains a few economic and monetary indicators which illustrate the evolution of the economy throughout the 1960–73 period and include year-by-year ORTN monetary correction rates, since the year of their institution. The analysis of such data can be put to good use when assessing the effects of indexation on the overall behaviour of the country's monetary economy.

The monetary correction of ORTNs is reckoned with on the basis of the wholesale general price index, but certain adaptation occurs when reckoning the basis for some specific corrections such as in the case of rents, real estate mortgage loans and others.

The monetary correction clause is juridicially valid solely when expressly authorised by law. Therefore, it is not a universally applicable institute, one which could be indiscriminately applied to all relations of a financial nature as well as to other instances of reappraisal. This one-sidedness has been invoked in the criticism which certain currents of opinion bring against indexation. Such criticism does indeed concentrate on three basic points:[2]

(*a*) The circumstance of indexation not being, in principle, a generalised procedure for the whole of the economy;
(*b*) the unilateral character of monetary correction in the context of relations between the Government and the private agents;
(*c*) the broad margin of indefinition concerning ultimate nominal values in instances of long-term operations.

Regardless of what arguments may be produced against indexation, the ultimate truth is that its institution has had a positive influence in the process of Brazil's economic development, for it has greatly contributed to introduce a comparative normality in the context of domestic financial and fiscal relations, and has further stimulated the tendency to accumulate savings by offering a shield against the corrosive effects of inflation.

Truly enough, indexation does widen the horizons of inflationary expectations and does foster, to a certain degree, a process of revival of

[2] Chacel, Simonsen and Wald, 'Monetary Correction' (São Paulo: APEC).

pessimistic tendencies; nevertheless, this could be well termed 'corrective inflation' and, anyhow, even while admitting certain shortcomings, there is no denying the positive effects of monetary indexation, in the absence of better solutions.

The timeliness of putting indexation to work as well as its practical variations depends on the social-economic peculiarities of each given country. Furthermore, there is a consensus to the effect that, in Brazil, a developing country, a yearly rate of inflation of up to 10 or 15 per cent ceases to bear any significance, and 'the real loss may be perfectly absorbed by the economy agents' with no need for an indexation system.

If inflation is to be accepted as inevitable, as a process inherent to the liberal systems of economy, the only answer is one of a pacific co-existence with the inevitable; however, this does preclude recourse to corrective mechanisms capable of neutralising or of minimising the factors of disturbance of domestic economy relations, whilst concurrently ensuring the unwavering conditions for the continuity of national development processes.

BIBLIOGRAPHY

Delfim Netto *et al.*, *Some Aspects of the Brazilian Inflation* (São Paulo: Estudos ANPES, 1965).

Simonsen, Mario Henrique, *Inflation: Gradualism and Shock Treatment* (Rio de Janeiro: Apec Editora, 1970).

Chacel, Simonsen, Wald, *Monetary Correction* (Rio de Janeiro: Apec Editora, 1970).

Campiglia, A. O., 'Monetary readjustment within an inflationary system of unstable currency', Italian translation published in *Bancaria*, no. 2 (Rome, 1974).

TABLE 1 Brazil, Economic and Monetary Indicators 1960–73

	General price indexes				*Gross national product*				
Years	*Products for domestic use*	*Aggregate supply*	*Annual inflation rates* %	*Monetary correction rates* %	*Annual growth* %	*Worth* US$ 1,000	*Brazilian exports* US$ 1,000 (*FOB*)	*Exchange rate variation* Cr$/US$† %	*Money supply (at end of the period)* Cr$ *Millions*
1960	7·9	8·0	30·5	—	9·7	12,011,790	1,268,802	3·7	692
1961	11·9	12·3	47·7	—	10·3	12,782,650	1,402,970	21·8	1·042
1962	17·9	17·9	51·3	—	5·3	13,897,684	1,214,185	38·7	1·691
1963	32·6	32·8	81·3	—	1·5	15,904,800	1,406,480	59·4	2·778
1964	63·0	60·5	91·9	—	2·9	13,922,101	1,429,790	100·0	5·128
1965	80·8	79·5	34·5	—	2·7	16,636,963	1,595,479	53·4	9·051
1966	111·0	113·0	38·8	39·2	5·1	24,200,045	1,741,442	17·3	10·482
1967	136·0	137·0	24·3	23·2	4·8	26,330,129	1,653,751	20·0	15·004
1968	171·0	170·0	25·4	25·0	9·3	26,160,241	1,881,344	28·0	21·384
1969	207·0	203·0	20·2	18·5	9·0	30,842,655	2,311,169	19·6	28·348
1970	247·0	241·0	19·2	19·6	9·5	35,710,450	2,738,922	12·7	35·919
1971	297·0	292·0	19·8	22·7	11·3	41,525,519	2,903,856	15·1	47·160
1972	349·0	339·0	15·5	15·3	10·4	48,824,806	3,991,219	12·2	62·982
1973	368·0	381·0	15·7	12·8	11·4*	60,000,000*	6,197,937	3·2	88·870

Sources: Banco Central do Brasil, Cacex/Banco do Brasil, Fundação Getúlio Vargas, Ibge, 'Conjuntura Econômica'.

* = Preliminary data.
† = Cr$ devaluation.

12 Report on the United Kingdom (1)

Paul Bareau

It is my task, and let me say at once a somewhat sombre task, to present a report on the 'new inflation' as it is being seen and operated and endured in the United Kingdom. And if it is sombre, may I add that there is room for mutual commiseration between the United Kingdom and Italy not only because we have similar economic problems in common, but because we have both been finally and I think very unfairly booted out of the World Cup!

What is new about the current phenomen of inflation not only in the United Kingdom but throughout the still free world (note that little word 'still'), is first that it is proceeding hand in hand with a perceptible slowing down in economic activity, or the state of affairs to which the name 'stagflation' has been given; secondly that it is showing a capacity for combined speed, endurance and extent which is unmatched in world monetary history; and thirdly that the power of organised labour has given an entirely new dimension to cost-push inflation.

Let me give you the facts, as they apply to the United Kingdom, then seek the causes, give a passing glance at some of the consequences, look at the corrective measures that have been taken and, finally, peer into the future and try to assess the chances of solving this problem.

The facts need not detain us very long – and I will not bore you with a lot of figures. Inflation, measured by the increase in the cost of living in the United Kingdom has over the past year been proceeding at a gallop of 16 per cent, but the pace has been accelerating and over the past months we are getting very near to 20 per cent. If we look at the figures for a whole year, wage increases have just kept up with a rate of inflation in the cost of living. But in the latest acceleration of the rise in consumer prices, wages, which are of course still held back by the previous Government's wages and incomes policy, are showing a slight decline in real terms. The sharp rise in oil and other commodity prices, together with the tax increases of the recent budget, are beginning to make some impact on real incomes and on domestic consumption. And this is of course an essential condition of diverting more resources to the export market and of going some way at least in solving the immense balance of payments problem that faces us as indeed so many of the countries represented at this conference.

But may I here interpose one important question – the $30 billion question. If all the deficit countries attempted at the same time to correct their deficits by diverting more of their resources to exports, who would absorb the exports? Not the oil exporting countries, since by definition their surplus – a 70 billion dollar unspendable surplus – must for the time being be invested, must in one form or another be recycled.

Let us look at the causes of the so-called 'new inflation'. They are of an international as well as of an essentially domestic nature. Whether of universal or of primarily home manufacture, they do derive from one common philosophic origin – a weakening of discipline which has spread from the area of moral principles to that of economic policy. In our political and economic priorities governments give the highest places to full employment, social security, the sense of social justice, the maximisation of economic growth. Each of these is in most respects highly desirable. But they can and do become suspect if, in the pursuit of them, we sacrifice the honesty, the stability of money.

In the policies of most major countries, stability of prices has now come to occupy a very low place in the list of priorities. The old disciplines that used to obtain under an external standard, such as gold, have vanished. They used to be heeded, in part because they were impersonal; they were virtually automatic responses to the changing lights and guidelines of a set of traffic signals. Perhaps that kind of discipline can no longer be recaptured. Perhaps it is no longer compatible with parliamentary democracy. This mood of permissiveness, leading to instability, has inevitably spread from the realms of domestic to those of external monetary affairs. For example, we accept the inevitability of floating rates of exchange and the best we can do in this context is to ask the Committee of Twenty to concoct a set of rules for official intervention in the exchange market, a 'code for dirty floating'.

At the same time, we continue to intone the now familiar refrain about 'phasing out' gold from the international monetary system. This is to dismiss the sole remaining policeman of monetary policy. As Schumpeter wrote forty years ago, 'The modern mind dislikes gold because it blurts out unpleasant truths.' I might quote in support of this a remark made by Lord O'Brien when he was Governor of the Bank of England. What he said was: 'The enthusiasm for getting rid of gold owes much to the fact that in this inflationary age currencies cannot stand comparison with it.' Fortunately, the proceedings at the recent meeting of the Committee of Twenty and the Group of Ten in Washington and in particular the initiative of the Governor of the Bank of Italy, suggest that the phasing out of gold from the international monetary system will be a very long process indeed.

And to continue my tale of permissiveness, instead of gold we shall install the new form of international paper – Special Drawing Rights, the value of which will be expressed in terms of a basket of currencies while these currencies in turn will be expressed in Special Drawing Rights. Is there not an element of circulatory logic here – and one which could lead to a very vicious circle? If the currencies in the basket continue to be inflated and their value eroded, that surely will react on the integrity and ultimately on the acceptability of the new international unit and anchor.

I have spent some time on this consideration of attitudes to monetary stability, both in the domestic and international context, because they are essential to understanding the problem as it faces us in the United Kingdom. We have been drawn into the vortex of world inflation, a vortex stirred by many forces and in recent years by persistent United States deficits which through the operation of the reserve currency standard have enormously increased world reserve, as well as the liquidity sloshing around in the so-called Euro-currency and particularly in the Eurodollar markets. The oil crisis is adding to this liquidity and to its inflationary implications.

The impact of these external forces on the British economy has of course been enhanced by the depreciation of the floating pound. And for the reasons behind that, we must turn to domestic affairs, to the internal sources of inflation. My presentation of the domestic scene has to be carried back a little way in history but, let me reassure you, not too far. In fact, to the last but one general election, that which in June 1970 brought the Conservative Party into power under the leadership of Mr Heath. That election was fought by the Conservatives on a programme dedicated to the principles of a self-reliant society, relying on market forces, providing greater rewards for efficiency and success; together with penalties for failure and inefficiency. In addition, the Conservatives promised to put the Trade Unions under the discipline of a concisely defined rule of law provided in an Industrial Relations Act. Alas, the programme did not last long. The Industrial Relations Act was passed, but it failed to improve industrial relations. On the contrary, it envenomed them and, worst of all, it led to wholesale successful disregard and open flouting of the rule of law – the first time this had occurred on such a scale since Parliamentary Government and Constitutional Monarchy arrived in Britain more than three hundred years ago.

As for the reliance on market forces, this weakened and then was abandoned after little more than twelve months. By the autumn of 1971 unemployment was creeping up towards the dreaded, psychologically important one million mark. And so came the great retreat. A number of large firms in difficulties, the so-called 'lame ducks', were rescued with government assistance. Credit policy was eased under the provisions of new rules for the control of bank credit. This was set out in new regulations entitled 'Competition and Credit Control'. Substantial reductions in taxation were made in two successive budgets and contributed to deficits, or borrowing requirements which, in the conditions of the gilt-edged government bond market, were in part financed by the banking system and therefore led to an inordinate expansion in the money supply. All this was done in the pursuit of a higher rate of economic growth than had ever been sustained in Britain over any appreciable period. The growth was achieved, for the time, but it was the wrong kind of growth. It did not have its roots in industrial investment or in an adequate expansion of exports. It was based on a consumer boom. And the result inevitably was a return to full employment admittedly but a rapid deterioration in the balance of payments and a steady acceleration in the rise in wages and prices.

The fallacy of this policy, of this obsession with growth, is the belief that sustainable growth can be achieved by the appropriate monetary and fiscal policies. The real sinews of growth are to be found in real things: good management, inventiveness, readiness to invest in new plant, readiness on the part of the workers to operate the new plant; good human relations in industry, absence of restrictive practices, confidence in the political leadership. The danger lies in assuming that manipulation of money supply can be an alternative and a substitute for these basic factors. If these are not present – and they were not present in Britain in the years in question – then the pursuit by monetary means of a rate of growth which, in the circumstances, is unsustainable, will assuredly land us in the kind of inflationary and balance of payments mess in which we find ourselves today.

Our new political masters have not so far improved on the poor performance by their predecessors. The last budget was harshly redistributive, but it still left an overall deficit, a borrowing requirement, which in present circumstances is excessive and inflationary. Food subsidies, rent freezes, attempts to get interest rates down in order to prevent an increase in mortgage rates – all these may be good political manoeuvring, but they are not relevant to the basic problem of inflation. Indeed in that context they are in the long run counter-productive.

The new government has undertaken to repeal the Industrial Relations Act and has substituted for it a voluntary restraint agreement with the Trades Union Congress. But this contract, or 'compact' as it is more modestly called, is with a TUC which wields no real power. The power lies with individual unions; and the demands which have recently been made by coal miners, railway staffs, local government staffs, building workers and many others suggest that the social compact is in fact a man of straw.

It would, however, be wrong to imply from all this and from the evidence so far, that no progress has been made in the anti-inflation campaign. The budget which increased taxes and the higher prices for oil are having some effect on consumer spending. The volume of retail sales is falling. On the monetary policy front, the rules of credit control have been tightened. The commercial banks are now in a so-called 'corset' which will undoubtedly provide a real deterrent to any further expansion in bank credit. All this has had the effect of restricting advances and of checking the commercial banks bidding for money in the interbank market.

The combination of tougher fiscal and credit policies is having its effect on the economy. The property and construction industries are in the doldrums. Their plight has involved a number of smaller banking institutions – the so-called 'fringe banks' – which have had to be rescued, or in one or two cases have been allowed to go to the wall. In other words, there are hints of an incipient recession and, judging by the recent behaviour of commodity prices, these hints could apply to the whole world economy – and not to Britain alone.

We, in Britain can certainly draw some comfort from the fact that at long last the rate of increase in the money supply has begun to fall. The most widely used measurement of the money stock M_3 which increased by over 30 per cent in 1973, was rising at an annual rate of only 10 per cent over the first five months of this year and the progression is still downward. But the interesting, significant and also ominous fact is that these faint harbingers of disinflation and recession have already been followed by demands in certain influential quarters in Britain for an easing of credit restrictions and for an expansionist autumn budget. These demands for re-expansion at a time when the rate of inflation is nearing 20 per cent and when the balance of payments, though improving, is still in massive deficit, make one despair of one's academic colleagues and of the politicians who heed their advice. Keynes, the originator of compensatory budgeting, must be turning in his grave at the manner in which his teachings are being turned upside down.

The world as a whole seems to have committed the ultimate act of surrender in the face of the enemy, in the face of inflation. We are bending our ingenuity to devising means of living with inflation by indexing and monetary correction. I have just come back from Brazil where I studied some aspects of this policy and I was very much impressed by them. But monetary correction merely removes certain of the injustices that flow from inflation. It measures. It does not correct, except in so far as it can encourage savings and investment in indexed bonds. Its success as an adjustment mechanism depends on the correction being accepted by all concerned, including the Trades Unions. It depends, in other words, on the strength, on the authority of the Government and on the means of which the Government disposes to enforce its decisions.

That leads me to my final question; namely whether the 'new inflation' is amenable to the orthodox correctives and control techniques of a free society. If this kind of inflation is to be solved, will it not demand more and more interventionist, dirigiste and ultimately more authoritarian techniques of economic and political control? If I may quote Schumpeter again, was that old Austrian right when he wrote that 'There is an irreconcilable incompatibility between democracy and capitalism'? If there is such incompatibility, it lies in the tendency of parliamentary democracy to beget inflation. But I refuse to end on this note of despondency. I retain enough faith in human intelligence to believe that if the dangers were spelt out, clearly explained, if the grim political and economic alternatives were set out with appropriate conviction and qualities of leadership, the fight for honest money in an expanding economy could yet be won. But it will be a long battle – and what happens in Britain in the months and years and perhaps weeks ahead will play a very significant, instructive and influential part in deciding the outcome of that battle.

13 Report on the United Kingdom (2)

Brian Quinn

I must confess that my first reaction on reading Paul Bareau's paper was, on balance, one of broad disagreement. A second reading revealed more common ground than I first suspected; further reading uncovered additional subtleties – I stopped reading at that point. Otherwise I might have beaten Mr Burger's record for brevity hands down, and our excellent hosts might have considered the wisdom of inviting two speakers from the UK.

I want to make several comments on Mr Bareau's paper, nevertheless. Some amount to no more than a difference of emphasis, while others are perhaps more substantive.

The first comment almost certainly falls into the first category and deals with Mr Bareau's fundamental explanation of inflation, whether internationally or domestically generated; and that, you will remember, is the breakdown or abandonment of discipline in the conduct of economic policy. He calls this 'permissiveness', and at one point appears to regret the loss of the automatic restraint imposed by the Gold Standard. Sir John Hicks has reminded us of the penalties that this system could bring, and indeed it was for precisely this reason that that system was abandoned for one that left governments and central banks with a greater degree of choice in determining what impact the external sector should have on domestic economic activity. I should like to stress that the current mechanism – as well as the one which existed until 1971 – is capable of having the same effect; but that governments have chosen otherwise. Other objectives have occupied a higher priority, as Mr Bareau says. If Mr Bareau will agree to substitute 'discretion' for 'permissiveness' I think we are in closer agreement, although I think our choice of priorities might still differ.

Secondly, I am not sure I would agree that the excessive liquidity, to use Mr Bareau's words, 'sloshing around' – what a beautifully evocative expression – in international currency markets has played a central role in the explanation of inflation in the UK. You would, I think, have to work very hard to observe any relationship between movements in UK foreign currency transactions and domestic monetary expansion; I do not think it exists myself for the UK over the period in question, although Professor Nishiyama has a different story to tell.

This seems a good juncture to move on to another of Mr Bareau's arguments, namely that inflation in the UK is attributable to excessively expansionary domestic fiscal and monetary policies. I want to make two points here:

A. The UK economy had experienced a low growth rate over the period 1968–72 – no more than 1½–2 per cent p.a. on average. By the beginning of 1972 excess capacity, as measured by unemployment, was at a post-war high; these figures do not tell the whole story, but there is little doubt that the economy had developed considerable slack over the period. Indeed the Government at one stage was despairing of ever lifting the economy on to anything even approaching full capacity again. If fiscal and monetary policies were expansionary, it was because that was intended. To show that these policies were excessively expansionary, one would need to produce evidence of overheating, and only in the second half of 1973 was there any evidence of this phenomenon – and I personally have still to be fully convinced. However, prices in the UK began to accelerate in 1969 and, allowing for prices and incomes restraint, have continued to accelerate throughout the period.

B. If part of the monetary expansion was a deliberate reflection of policy, part was also bogus. I will not take up your time with the details, but a good deal of the recorded increase in M_3, the broadly defined money supply, is generally recognised as having reflected (*a*) re-intermediation with the banking system of business lost to other financial institutions during the period of quantitative credit ceilings; (*b*) recycling of advances from and deposits with commercial banks to take advantage of a gap between the rate payable on advances and that received on deposits, notably sterling certificates of deposit.

Reflecting these points, the rate of growth of M_1, the narrowly defined money supply, was less than a quarter of that of M_3 between 1972 Q2 and 1974 Q2; and the expansion of the latter did not accurately reflect the impact of liquidity on spending plans or spending behaviour in the period.

Before our friends from outside the UK think I am suggesting that the authorities were always absolutely content with developments on the monetary front, let me add that during 1973 monetary policy was tightened on three occasions. And as Mr Bareau points out, the expansion of the monetary aggregates has slowed down perceptibly during 1974. Over the three banking months to June, M_3 has grown by less than 1 per cent; M_1 has grown by somewhat more, as one might expect in the circumstances. There is little doubt that the new system of monetary control introduced last December has played an important role in this moderation. But there are signs that the demand for bank credit from the private sector may be slowing down sharply against an outlook of weakening economic activity, a point made in Mr Bareau's paper. With the full impact of oil and other commodity price increases still to make themselves felt on domestic incomes, and the impact of cuts in Government spending now coming through, domestic demand could weaken further this year. Mr Bareau sees any moves to reverse any such development as ill advised. It might indeed be premature to act at present to restimulate output while our balance of payments on current account is still in substantial deficit and inflationary pressures are increasing. But we in the UK also have in mind the costs of operating below full capacity for any appreciable length of time, not least the effects on trade union bargaining attitudes. So there is a careful calculation to be made.

It is here that my own emphasis would probably fall, in interpreting the causes of inflation in the UK. I think it is possible to explain the movement of prices in the UK since 1968 by reference to cost-push factors, both domestic and external in origin. There are signs that the worst may be over from the latter source, although we have been disappointed before. If, however, output should again stagnate at a time when labour costs are rising, and labour is seeking to maintain living standards, the domestic impulse to inflation could again create real difficulties. I feel that much more remains to be explained in the area of income shares before 'institutional' explanations of inflation can be laid aside as irrelevant.

14 Report on Italy

Antonio Fazio

INTRODUCTION: THE REAL FLOWS MODEL

In this paper I propose to illustrate briefly the methods by which monetary policy is carried out in Italy and more specifically the planning and control of financial flows. I shall also try to elucidate some causal relations between such flows and the rate of inflation, but the exposition will be limited to those phenomena which seem to have the greatest empirical significance.

Let us consider the relation of the national accounts:

$$Y = C_{pr} + I_{pr} + G + X - M \tag{1}$$

where C_{pr} and I_{pr} denote private consumption and investment respectively; G denotes the demand for final goods and services by government for consumption and investment; Y, X and M have the usual meanings of national income (= product), total exports and imports. By subtracting T, the total taxes and contributions collected by government, from both sides of (1) and then rearranging terms, we obtain

$$S_{pr} \equiv Y - T - C_{pr} = I_{pr} + (G - T) + X - M \tag{2}$$

This identity makes explicit the relation between the saving of the private sector S_{pr} on one side and private investment, public sector deficit and trade balance on the other. The relations (1) and (2) are always true *ex post*, they would be true *ex ante* at an appropriate level of income.

Since savings for the most part do not take place in the sectors (or better, by the agents) who use them, the financial intermediaries have the task of transferring this purchasing power from the sectors in excess to those in deficit.

In fact, expansive and depressive movements have their origin in the aggregates represented on the right-hand side of equation (2) and the level of saving adapts through variations of the level of the economic activity. In other words, from the financial point of view, credit expansion precedes the formation of the financial assets.

Let us consider the particularly simple case (the essential points of the considerations which follow remain unchanged in more complex or more realistic cases) where there are no capital movements to or from foreign countries and the demand for credit from the firms and from the public sector is exactly equal to the respective deficits (the deficit of the firms is given by the difference between investments and firms' retentions, A_u). The total demand for credit will be equal to

$$(I - A_u) + (G - T) + (X - M).$$

The acquisition of financial assets by the surplus sectors will be

$$(S - A_u).$$

The conditions which guarantee the equilibrium between saving and its uses therefore automatically assure the equality between the demand and supply of credit.

However, the desired composition of financial assets is usually such that it does not correspond to the desired composition of different forms of credit. In practice, the demand for long-term credit tends to prevail on the borrowing side, at least from firms; while for financial assets, the demand is mainly for liquid assets.

Given certain objectives concerning the level of economic activity, employment, prices, investments, and also taking rates of interest into account, the spontaneous evolution of the members on the right-hand side of (2) during a given time period may be consistent with the abovementioned objectives. In this case, monetary policy is limited to the creation of the conditions by which financial intermediation through the credit system and the securities market tends to an equilibrium, both at the overall level and at the level of individual financial assets. In this case, we can speak of 'passive' monetary policy, even if the fundamental task of determining a level and a structure of interest rates consistent with the mentioned values of saving and investment is added to the task of maintaining orderly conditions in financial markets. The latter are particularly important in a country like Italy where financial intermediation turns out to be (after consolidation of the various rounds of intermeditation) about 20–22 per cent of the national income, which is much more than in other Western countries.

In other cases, the levels of investment and of surplus or deficit in the balance of payments and in the government budget, may be unsatisfactory because they do not lead to the desired objectives or because, in the case of the balance of payments, there are international financial constraints limiting the feasibility of its deficit. In this case monetary policy carries out an active role in order to modify the mentioned aggregates and to align them with the desired objectives.

We then have an illustration of the main lines of the type of analysis and interventions necessary to regulate the financial flows when they adapt themselves to the spontaneous evolution of saving, investment, government expenditures and the balance of payments. Such analysis is also a good starting point to illustrate the way monetary policy works when its instruments are used in order to control global demand, and in this way, economic activity, the balance of payments and the rate of inflation.

THE SYSTEM OF FINANCIAL ACCOUNTS

Let us suppose that the objectives, in terms of the principal aggregates of the national accounts, are fixed and that an accepted evolution of prices is assured. The adjustment of the financial flows consistent with the above-mentioned objectives can then be analysed by reference to the following accounts (agents and markets of the financial system):

(1) Treasury, Post Office Savings Fund, and autonomous agencies
(2) Securities market
(3) Banking system
(4) Special credit institutions system
(5) Sources and uses of the monetary base
(6) Financial assets and liabilities
(7) Financing of the other components of public administration and investment

The accounts (1) to (6) form a set of linearly dependent equations so that the definition of five of the equations automatically involves the definition of the sixth (Walras's law). The account (7) isolates the public firms and the public institutions other than the Treasury in such a way that it is possible to define the non-account of the household sector by subtraction.[1]

The appendix shows a set of forecasts for the year 1973 worked out by this means at the beginning of that year. The income expansion forecast was 4·5 per cent at constant prices and 15 per cent at current prices; the forecast of total gross investment at current prices was 16,100 billion lire and the deficit of the sector 'Treasury, Post Office Savings Fund and autonomous agencies' 7,000 billion. A surplus on the current account balance of payments was forecast with equilibrium expected on the overall balance of payments.[2]

It is essential to the completion of our analysis to look at Table 7 and particularly at the last column which describes the formation of the requirements of the firms and housing sector and their financing.

External financing, estimated at 11,400 billion, together with the internal saving of the sector and the transfers from the public sector, exceeded the financial requirements of the forecast investments and

[1] The account system has been developed with G. Caligiuri, F. Cotula, P. Savona, S. Lo Faso, V. Pontolillo and B. Bianchi. An initial formalisation of it can be found in: *Banca d'Italia, Modello M1BI, Settore monetario e finanziario*, by A. Fazio, G. Caligiuri, F. Cotula and P. Savona (Rome, 1970). For a simplified version of the theoretical framework, see A. Fazio, 'Politica monetaria, prezzi e livello dell'attività economica', in *Lezioni sulla politica economica in Italia* (Milan: V. Balloni, 1972).

[2] Banca d'Italia, *Relazione sul 1973.*

implied an increase in the financial assets of the firms of 6,300 billion, a 16 per cent rise over their level at the end of 1972.

The actual evolution of the economy during 1973 presented a distinctly different pattern from the one predicted at the beginning of the year; the increase in income at constant prices was 5·9 per cent, at current prices, 17 per cent. The total gross investments at current prices reached 18,700 billion, the Treasury deficit was 7,500 billion and the current account of the balance of payments was 1,600 billion in deficit with an overall deficit of 2,300 billion.

The total expansion of finance was maintained at a level that satisfied the most important financing requests of the public as well as the private sector, even if through a series of selective measures; the curbing of credit was carried out by favouring long-term credits and containing the supply of bank loans with the consequence of a rise in the respective rates.

From Table 7 we can deduce that the external financing to the firms and housing sector was 15,300 billion. This, taking into account the internal saving and the transfers from the public sector, allowed for the investment of 16,000 billion and an increase in the financial assets of the sector of about 7,000 billion.[3]

The realisation of the indicated financing was associated with the creation of a monetary base of 5,100 billion, of which 1,800 took the form of bank reserves (Table 5). The limitation of free bank reserves, within their total reserves, provoked a rise in interest rates, and especially in short-term rates. This rise in interest rates, even in the face of a strong expansion in the supply of financial assets, liquid assets in particular, was justified, in the borrowers' perspective, by the higher returns to real goods, due to inflation.

FINANCIAL FLOWS AND INFLATION

The variations of the monetary base and of bank reserves in particular, given the existing reserve requirements and the structure of the credit system, allows the control of the expansion of deposits and bank credit (direct loans and investments in securities) to meet demand at the desired level of the interest rates (Table 3). The direct acquisition of securities by the Bank of Italy, in the issue and secondary markets, gives more direct control on the long-term rate of return and thus on the demand for funds and on the supply of these securities. The latter is also directly ruled by the authorisations of issue such that it is possible to provoke variations in interest rates independently of the quantities issued (by taking into account the demand for securities by the private sector and the spontaneous demand by banks).

[3] Banca d'Italia, *Relazione sul 1973*. The actual values have been derived (from the national accounts published in the *Relazione sul 1973*) by G. Caligiuri, M. Caron and G. Morcaldo.

The control of the source components of the monetary base, together with the control of securities issues, influences the division of total credit between short and long term; however when the desired composition of bank portfolios tends to shift from investments to loans, the control of the distribution of credit requires the use of additional instruments of the type used from the second half of 1973.

Given the balance of payments deficit and supposing a desire to leave the banks' position *vis-à-vis* foreign countries unchanged (an increase of their net debt has the same effects on domestic credit as a refinancing by the central bank, but in the latter's assets foreign credits – official reserves – take the place of advances to the banks), credit expansion can be contained by reducing the refinancing given by the central bank to the banks or by diminishing its acquisition of securities.

In the first case, we have a direct action on bank credit and an indirect effect through a smaller creation of monetary base; in the absence of particular portfolio requirements it is likely that the banks reduce their demand for securities and therefore induce an increase in the long-term rates which in the short run will also reduce the demand for securities by the private sector and finally influence the credit expansion in the medium and long term. If there are portfolio requirements which prevent the banks from selling securities, the restriction will tend to concentrate on direct loans with the probability of a larger increase in short-term rates than in other areas.

A decrease in the demand for securities by the central bank has an immediate effect on that market and therefore on the availability of medium- and long-term credit. This method of reducing the total creation of the monetary base also brings about a decrease of bank credit.

So the limitation of the creation of monetary base tends to reduce the credit given by banks and special credit institutions to the firms and housing sector; also direct bond issuing and the issuing of shares on the market are made more expensive by the smaller creation of monetary base. One has therefore a restrictive effect on the volume of investments through the higher cost of credit. But this effect is negligible in the short run, especially in the presence of strong inflation (at least for variations in interest rates similar to those experienced in the past).

A more relevant effect on investment comes from credit availability but in this case the financial assets of the firms act as a buffer which can delay or even cancel the effect of the credit restriction. It should be noted that these assets can be estimated at more than 45,000 billion at the end of 1973, of which more than 30,000 was in liquid form. A large part of such assets consist of foreign credits of various kinds.

A large part of our inability to quantify precisely the effect of the financial variables on investment, and therefore on savings and other macroeconomic aggregates, comes from the insufficient knowledge we have of their distribution, their relation to the rates of interest and, in general, of the way these assets react in different cyclical conditions.

An initial reaction to a credit restriction might be to increase the velocity of circulation of the liquid assets of the firms. A part of the assets held by firms in foreign countries will be repatriated because of the greater necessity of funds inside the country, with a positive influence on the balance of payments and on the rate of exchange. If the latter improves to a sufficient extent, we have a positive effect on the internal rate of inflation, in this case through movements of a purely financial character.

The increase in the velocity of circulation of the firms' liquid balances meets limits due to market imperfections. Beyond these limits the phenomena of a liquidity shortage may begin to appear in particular sectors resulting in a reduction of investment expenditure. The market imperfections come essentially from the fact that some types of expenses, for objective causes, or more often relative to the agent who makes them, depend on particular types of credit for their financing (the entire special credit system and the building sector are examples of the objective aspect; the small and medium firms, an example of the subjective aspect).

The slow-down of the flow of investment influences the level of economic activity, savings of families and firms and, through the smaller tax receipts, public savings (so that the gross savings indicated in the last row of Table 7 will also tend to decrease). Such phenomena reinforce the effects of credit restriction. The decrease of global demand has an influence upon the current balance of payments (we remember the particularly high value of Italy's propensity to import in relation to investment in plant and equipment and in inventories), and in that way once again, favourably influences the rate of exchange and therefore, in a flexible exchange system, diminishes the rate of inflation. We must take into consideration that given a ratio of almost 25 per cent between import volume and national income, every percentage point of variation of the external value of our currency has an impact on domestic prices (or more exactly on costs), of about 0·2–0·3 per cent on average. This initial effect is later amplified through the cost-of-living escalator.

The slow-down of economic activity influences the demand for goods and services produced by the primary and tertiary sectors where prices respond to the level of demand (there seem to be examples of such a reaction in the evolution of these sectors during 1970). Further, in the industrial sector, the transmission of rising costs on to prices, due to cost inflation, will also be slowed.[4]

Finally the slow-down in the level of economic activity has an

[4] Cf. E. Tarantelli, 'Produttività del lavoro, salari e inflazione', Ente per gli Studi Monetari, Bancari e Finanziari Luigi Einaudi, *Quaderno di Ricerche*, 5, pp. 105ff.

influence on employment and in that way on the rate of increase of the wage bill and on prices. This last mechanism operates more slowly and in a more discontinuous manner than the others, but its effects can be most important.

CONCLUSIONS

In Italy monetary policy seems to have the potential to control the rate of inflation in the short run by containing the global level of credit. In fact, the limitation of credit in a system very open to external commercial and financial relations, contributes to support the external value of the currency and consequently to reduce imports costs.

The slackening of that component of private demand which is financed by credit (in the Italian case, essentially investment) is part of the control mechanism on the external accounts (on which monetary policy has on the whole a considerable effectiveness) but it also acts on the level of domestic economic activity and in that way on the rate of inflation.

The available empirical estimates imply high costs in terms of lower investment and employment, for any appreciable impact on prices through this latter mechanism.[5] The anti-inflation effect of credit restrictions appears on the contrary less costly to the extent that it exerts itself on capital movements, but for this purpose the restriction itself must be integrated in an efficient policy of selective credit control.

By concentrating on the relations between credit and expenditure (and therefore essentially on business behaviour) this paper has intentionally neglected another link between monetary and real variables, i.e. between the demand for financial assets and the demand for goods in the sectors where income exceeds expenditures (typically, the household sector).[6] A more complete examination of the possibilities open to monetary policy in controlling global demand, and thus the rate of inflation, should also take these relations into account.

[5] Banca d'Italia, *Modello M1BI, Settore reale e fiscale*, by G. M. Rey, M. Sarcinelli, P. Gnes, P. Miurin, R. Ruberti, E. Tarantelli, C. Tresoldi.

[6] Empirical research in this area shows an appreciable dependence of certain expenses and consumption on the return and other characteristics of financial assets, as well as on the market value of those assets. Cf. F. Cotula, E. Sacerdoti, 'La funzione del consumo e la composizione del risparmio delle famiglie' (forthcoming).

Appendix: *Flows-of-Funds in 1973: Forecast and Actual Values*

TABLE 1 Treasury – Post Office Savings Fund – Autonomous Agencies (Billion lire)

	Forecast 1973	*Actual 1973*
REQUIREMENT (Cash deficit)	7,000	7,507*
FINANCED BY	7,000	7,507
Bonds issued	3,300	4,202
(of which Treasury bills)		(1,550)
Post Office Savings	1,600	1,752
Other operations creating monetary base (Treasury bills for required reserves and borrowing from Banca d'Italia) Other operations	2,100	1,553

* Excluding consolidation of local governments debts.

TABLE 2 Bonds (including Treasury bills) (Billion lire)

	Forecast 1973	*Actual 1973*
ISSUED BY	6,900	11,534
Treasury	3,300	4,202*
(of which Treasury bills)		(1,550)
Other issuers	3,600	7,332
(of which Special Credit Institutions)	(2,400)	(6,438)
PURCHASED BY	6,900	11,534
Banca d'Italia and Ufficio Italiano dei Cambi	1,200	4,007
Banks	3,900	5,598*
Public	1,800	1,929

* Excluding consolidation of local government debts.

TABLE 3 Banks (Net changes in billion lire)

	Forecast 1973	*Actual 1973*
ASSETS	10,700	14,981
Excess reserves	400	112
Loans	5,000	7,641
Bonds	3,200	4,570*
Required reserves	2,100	2,689
(Cash and Treasury Bills)	(1,400)	(1,661)
(Long-term bonds)	(700)	(1,028)
Net foreign position		−31
LIABILITIES	10,700	14,981
Deposits	10,200	13,403
Lending by Banca d'Italia and Ufficio Italiano dei Cambi	100	277
Others liabilities	400	1,301

* Excluding consolidation of local government debts.

TABLE 4 Special Credit Institutions (Net changes in billion lire)

	Forecast 1973	*Actual 1973*
ASSETS	4,100	9,623
Domestic loans*	3,500	5,712
Foreign loans	100	150
Cash and disposable assets	500	3,761
of which: with banks		(1,896)
with Banca d'Italia		(1,865)
LIABILITIES	4,100	9,623
Bonds†	2,400	6,438
Deposits and interest-bearing certificates	550	388
Public funds	400	227
Foreign loans	100	1,888
Other liabilities	650	682

* Excluding financing of agricultural stockpiling system.
† Net receipts of bonds issued.

TABLE 5 Monetary Base (Net changes in billion lire)

	Forecast 1973	*Actual 1973*
SOURCES	4,500	5,077
Foreign sector		− 173
Balance of payments		− 176
Banks' external position and its regulation		3
Treasury	4,900	7,234
Post office deposits	1,600	1,752
Other liquidity creation	2,100	1,475
Bonds purchased by Banca d'Italia	1,200	4,007
Banks		
Financing by Banca d'Italia	100	277
Other sectors	− 500	−2,261
of which: tied deposits in foreign currency with Banca d'Italia		(−1,865)
USES	4,500	5,077
Public and non-bank financial intermediaries	2,700	3,304
Banks' required reserves	1,400	1,661
Banks' excess reserves	400	112

TABLE 6 Financial Assets of Private Sector (Net changes in billion lire)

DOMESTIC FINANCIAL ASSETS	*Forecast 1973*	*Actual 1973*
Cash	1,100	1,593
Post Office deposits	1,600	1,752
Bank deposits	10,200	13,403
Other deposits and interest-bearing certificates	550	388
Bonds	1,800	1,929
Shares and participations	1,150	1,568
Total domestic financial assets	16,400	20,633
Foreign financial assets	650	1,261
TOTAL	17,050	21,894
AGAINST FINANCING OF		
PRIVATE SECTOR		
Financing by Banks and Special Credit Institutions	8,500	13,353
Financing by the Public sector	1,500	1,424
Bonds issues	1,200	894
Share issues (domestic)	1,150	1,568
TOTAL DOMESTIC FINANCING	12,350	17,239
Financing from abroad	150	546
FOREIGN SECTOR (current account balance)	500	−1,405
TREASURY, POST OFFICE SAVINGS FUND, AUTONOMOUS AGENCIES	5,100	5,856
Other items	−1,050	− 483
Discrepancies		141
TOTAL	17,050	21,894

TABLE 7a Annual Investment and Financing Plan (Billion lire)

	Forecast 1973			
	Total	*Treasury, Post Office Savings Fund, Autonomous Agencies*	*Local Governments and Social Security System*	*Firms (including Housing)**
Gross investments	16,100	1,300	800	14,000
Capital transfers	—	1,900	—	− 1,900
Accumulation of financial assets	8,700	1,900†	500	6,300
TOTAL	24,800	5,100	1,300	18,400
FINANCING				
By Banca d'Italia (directly)	2,100	2,100		
By Banks and Special Credit Institutions	8,500		200	8,300
Post Office deposits	1,600	1,600		
Bond issues and Treasury bills	4,500	3,300	50	1,150
(of which Treasury bills)		(300)		
Shares issued	1,150			1,150
By other sectors (State)	1,500		850	650
By foreign countries	150			150
TOTAL EXTERNAL FINANCING	19,500	7,000	1,100	11,400
GROSS SAVING OF THE SECTOR	5,300	− 1,900	200	7,000
TOTAL	24,800	5,100	1,300	18,400

* Including the smaller bodies of the Public Administration.

† Public funds with	Special Credit Institutions	400
	Public firms	650
	Local Governments	850
		1,900

TABLE 7b Annual Investment and Financing Plan (Billion lire)

	Actual 1973			
	Total	*Treasury, Post Office Savings Fund, Autonomous Agencies*	*Local Governments and Social Security System*	*Firms (including Housing)**
Gross investments	18,291	1,151	1,104	16,036
Capital transfers	—	1,666	234	− 1,900
Accumulation of financial assets	9,254	1,651†	735	6,868
TOTAL	27,545	4,468	2,073	21,004
FINANCING				
By Banca d'Italia (directly)	981	981	—	—
By Banks and Special Credit Institutions	13,353	—	1,710	11,643
Post Office deposits	1,752	1,752	—	—
Bonds issues and Treasury bills	5,668	4,774	58	836
(of which Treasury Bills)	(2,162)	(2,162)		
Shares issues	1,708	—	—	1,708
By other sectors	1,424	—	690	734
By foreign countries	407	—	—	407
TOTAL EXTERNAL FINANCING	25,293	7,507	2,458	15,328
GROSS SAVING OF THE SECTOR	2,319	− 2,889	− 884	6,092
Errors and omissions	− 67	− 150	499	− 416
TOTAL	27,545	4,468	2,073	21,004

* Including the smaller bodies of the Public Administration.

† Public funds with special credit institutions, firms, local governments (for the latter, net of consolidations of bank debts by the Post Office Savings Fund).

15 Report on France

Pierre Berger

I INFLATION IN FRANCE

The French economy is characterised by a certain inflationary tendency, the degree of which has been distinctly higher for two or three years now. Under the influence of monetary, economic, sociological or even political factors which have appeared in the Western world as a whole, a movement of acceleration has recently sharpened the internal tendencies towards disequilibrium. It would be rash to speak here of new inflation for, with the exception of periods of abatement, the longest of which lasted from 1928 to 1936, France has been living with inflation for practically sixty years.

A THE CHARACTERISTICS OF PRICE DEVELOPMENT

An analysis of price development shows the particular characteristics of the French economy which have continued to play a certain part in the recent movement of acceleration.

(1) *Permanent tendencies towards inflation*

(*a*) On looking back to developments from 1960 to 1971, France had a mean rate of inflation which was higher than that in the majority of industrial countries.

The annual rate of increase 1960–71

	Average consumer price rise (from GNP deflator)	*GNP (in real terms)*
France	4·2	5·7
UK	5·3	4·8
Italy	4·1	5·2
Belgium	3·1	4·9
USA	2·4	3·9
West Germany	3·0	4·7

(*b*) This relatively strong tendency towards inflation may be explained by a number of different considerations and factors.

The necessity of reconstruction, then the will to expand and the aims of industrialisation which have dominated French economic policy, have led her to give first place amongst her preoccupations to a high level of economic activity. Consequently, the French economy has become extremely strained; its productive capacity is almost constantly at full stretch, and there is practically no unemployment. I think this is the main explanation of the very strong tendency towards inflation.

As a result, investment was favoured by a policy aiming to contain interest rates within narrow limits during the 1950s and the major part of the following decade. But such a policy was not favourable to the voluntary accumulation of savings proportionate in volume to the needs of investment. The creation of money was used to remedy the lack of available capital and the adjustment of savings to investment was achieved in inflationary conditions.

In other words, the division of the national income between consumption and savings was not favourable to a fulfilment of the national ambition for economic growth in a well-balanced way.

The low level of trade between France and foreign countries until the early 1960s delayed structural changes in the system of production which were intended to bring about greater efficiency, with the result that improvement in productivity has been relatively recent in France.

The attitude of private individuals has been to favour a rise in nominal income, which has also contributed towards the continuance of inflationary conditions.

In a general way, the persistence of inflation over a long period conditioned the attitudes of the sectors of the economy which, more or less consciously, are bringing a certain amount of resistance to bear upon factors or policies which stabilise prices.

(2) *The recent tendency towards acceleration*

As in other Western countries a tendency for the rise in prices to accelerate has appeared in France. Yet because of the very fact that the basic price trend was continually on the increase, and also because the system of watching over and controlling prices continued to operate without interruption, the phenomenon of acceleration was less pronounced than in other countries, at least until the beginning of 1974.

Period	*Increase*
From 1966 to 1971	Annual price rise of 5·2 per cent
In 1972	A rise of 6·9 per cent
In 1973	A rise of 8·5 per cent
During the first four months of 1974	Annual rate of increase of 18 per cent

A detailed analysis shows that this phenomenon involves all sectors at both the retail and the wholesale price levels (cf. table below).

Price Developments (by sectors)

	Average 1966–71	*1972*	*1973*
Retail Prices			
Overall index	5·2	6·9	8·5
Foodstuffs	5·0	8·5	10·9
Manufactured goods	3·9	5·4	6·7
Services	8·0	7·4	8·6
Wholesale Prices			
Foodstuffs	4·6	14·1	8·8
Fuel and energy	7·1	0·1	10·8
Industrial products	3·9	8·4	20·9
of which: Raw materials	3·4	9·4	39·1
Semi-finished products	5·0	8·1	14·8

B SPECIFIC FACTORS IN THE RECENT ACCELERATION

Numerous factors – practically all with the same effect – worked together to steepen the price increase, including cost pressure, the behaviour of the various sectors of the economy or international influences.

(1) *The importance of costs in the process of price determination*

(*a*) *The price of oil products and imported raw materials* The trebling of the price of oil products between October 1973 and January 1974 obviously caused pressure on costs in all sectors of the economy. French experts have estimated that this rise alone could well account for a further increase of about 3 per cent in retail prices.

The price of imported raw materials, excluding oil, also underwent big increases (50·7 per cent in 1973).

(*b*) *Wage increases* Since 1968 businesses have had to grant wage rises markedly higher than before. As a result of wage negotiations, particularly in the public sector – which sets an example which the others want to emulate – a number of techniques were applied to ensure increased purchasing power in real terms.

Two other factors were involved in the heavy general upward pressure on wages: the shortage of qualified labour in numerous sectors of the economy; the deliberate policy of low wage improvements which led to an increase in the minimum cost-of-living allowance of 15 per cent in 1972 and 19 per cent in 1973.

The average rates of wage increases in both nominal and real terms were as follows, over the last three years.

	In nominal terms	*In real terms*
1971	+10·7%	+4·7%
1972	+12·2%	+5·3%
1973	+14·5%	+6·0%

(*c*) *Agricultural policy* The principles guiding the agricultural policy applied over the last few years have entailed considerable rises in the price of agricultural products.

Considered overall, the aim of ensuring income parity among farmers and other workers has led to a sufficiently rapid growth in agricultural income.

A similar principle lay behind the fixing of the price of products covered by Community regulations. In addition, shortages arose on certain markets and made the price of certain types of products (beef, for example) rise markedly.

(2) *The behaviour of the various sectors of the economy*
In a climate of more pronounced inflation, the demand for goods and services remained at a high level in nearly all sectors of the economy (with the exception, from the end of 1973 onwards, of the motor-car sector). The demand for equipment by businesses unable to increase production because they were already working at full capacity remained very lively, whilst household demand in consumer goods markets and for services accelerated.

Various factors upheld or favoured the demand pressure: (*a*) In the money and credit fields the tendency for the various sectors of the economy to run into debt was high until the restrictive credit policy was made progressively more restraining at the end of 1972.

A high level of liquidity in the economy facilitated – particularly in 1973 – the reactivation of cash already in hand both in the business and household sectors.

The deceleration of the money supply, namely

18·2% in 1971
18·6% in 1972
15·0% in 1973

was accompanied by the reintroduction of cash in hand into the payments.

(*b*) In the same period inflationary expectations strengthened. This trend was accentuated by the psychological effects of the oil crisis.

On the household front a boom in consumption was observed particularly in January and February 1974, but it was moderated by the check put on the expansion of debt and by the fear of a slowing-down of the economy likely to react upon employment.

As for businesses, in so far as it was possible within the system of price supervision, they tried to safeguard their possibilities of self-financing by rolling over the rise in costs on their sale prices and they even sometimes anticipated increases.

(3) *International factors*
Additional factors related to the expansion of international exchanges and the disorder of the international monetary system reinforced the price trend.

In the first place the devaluation or depreciation of the national currency had the automatic effect of increasing the price of imported products. Furthermore it seems that in a world-wide climate of inflation the adjustment of prices at the time of parity changes nowadays mainly consists of lower prices catching up with the highest world prices.

Secondly, monetary speculation increased the very considerable anticipation of the price rise of certain products on the international market; this was probably the case with German capital goods for example, the price of which greatly increased without preventing a rapid expansion of sales outside Germany. This is to be explained primarily by continued pressure for a revaluation of the Deutschmark and in consequence for an anticipation of a continued rise in the price of German products expressed in currencies other than the Deutschmark.

The recent price rises result in part from factors quite unrelated to the state of the French economy. That is why, while remaining aware of the need to eliminate all the internal disequilibrium, one is led to conclude that the fight against inflation calls for a change in the international situation.

II AIMS AND POLICIES

The aims selected for the monetary policy in accordance with the general economic policy must be specified in operational terms within its own sphere. The choice of means is influenced by financial structures and the behaviour of the various sectors of the economy.

A ASCERTAINMENT OF OBJECTIVES

If defined in general terms, the objectives of monetary policy consist in contributing towards the achievement of a price and balance of payments equilibrium while ensuring economic growth financing. To carry out such a policy, specific objectives are assigned to some monetary aggregates.

(1) *Overall objectives*

(*a*) *Relating to prices* In abstract terms, the public authorities should set themselves an objective of near-stability of prices; but confronted with the causes of inflation, some of them of purely French origin, others well outside the domestic economy, they can only assign at present (at least temporarily) a less ambitious objective aimed at preserving the competitiveness of French products in foreign markets.

Such an objective could be defined by reference to the rates of inflation prevailing in the neighbouring countries in which the tendency is the more moderate (thus the annual rate of price increase in Federal Republic of Germany was about 7 per cent during the beginning of 1974).

The expected results can however only be attained progressively, which was the case in 1973. Equally, the recovery programme set up some days ago by the Government aims at slowing down the rise in prices to 1 per cent monthly at the end of 1974 (12 per cent on a yearly basis) and 0·5 per cent per month from July 1975 onwards (6 per cent per annum).

(*b*) *Relating to the balance of payments developments* In order to avoid a deterioration of the external payments position due to the rise in oil prices which would reach scarcely sustainable proportions, and to contribute to re-establishing the overall balance, the recovery of the trade balance from now on represents one of the main goals of French policy until 1976. Such a recovery is to be based upon the strength of exports.

(*c*) *Relating to the actual economic data* The slowing down of the price rise, even if it contributes to restoring external trade, cannot at the moment be considered the sole objective of the French authorities. Maintaining the level of employment is a necessity as well. Besides, experience has taught us that France is socially a country which does not stand unemployment without serious difficulties.

(2) *Monetary objectives*

Within their traditional concept the French authorities are seeking to control the development of the money supply. Justification of such policy has been enhanced by recent econometric research which has shown the existence of close relationships between the development of the money supply and that of subsequent economic activity both in real and in money terms. However, the monetary objectives are not strictly set in terms of the growth of the money supply; they make allowances for the behaviour of the holders of liquid assets such as are shown in qualitative observations and in the trends of the velocity of money (or of the rotation rates of the sums credited to the quasi-monetary accounts).

(*a*) *Quantitative action* Acting on the development of the money supply is thus based on fixing quantitative goals which make it possible to assess the character of the monetary policy recently carried out.

In 1973 the expansion rate of the money supply was determined as regards both the prospects of economic growth in real terms and price increases seen as inevitable; thus the generally accepted rate of growth of the money supply proved to be smaller than that of the national product in value terms; in those conditions, part of the excess of liquidity built up in 1972 was mopped up. This objective was reached to a certain extent at least.

The liquidity ratio of the economy
defined by M_1/GNP, decreased in 1973 (from 27·5 per cent to 26·5 per cent)
defined by M_2/GNP, levelled off (45 per cent), which does in effect correspond to a decrease.

In fact, in 1973 the GNP deflator was not very representative of the price index of business operations. Moreover, the liquidity ratio of the economy has, in France, a strong propensity to increase in the medium term because of the reluctance of individuals to engage in long-term investments and because of their preference for maintaining their savings in a liquid form.

In 1974 the pressure of monetary policy will continue unabated but is not going to be aggravated. On the one hand, the expected results of such a policy will be more rigorous because the economy has depleted its cash reserves. On the other hand, the problem is to avoid disrupting the impetus of activity through undue credit restrictions at the very moment when the international crisis raises a lot of uncertainties for the future of the world economy.

Such an action implies, among other things, that account should be taken, in the expansion of liquidity, of the price rise which the French authorities think sustainable for the year 1974.

(*b*) *Selective goals* In parallel with this overall objective, specific goals have been set in order: to reserve for businesses the larger part of the credit granted, by discouraging loans to individuals; to direct credit towards export-financing and energy-saving investments; to facilitate company borrowing abroad – public corporations have thus been able to borrow abroad more than 2,000 million units of account since the beginning of the year. Some financial institutions specialising in export credit or in investment loans have also substantially increased their resources with the help of foreign loans.

B THE IMPLEMENTATION OF MONETARY POLICY

During 1973 and 1974, supported by a fiscal policy aimed at freezing a part of the budgetary income surpluses created by worsening inflation, the monetary policy has mainly tried to control the distribution of credit by using to that effect instruments adapted to the structures and behaviour of the French financial system. The traditional method of resorting to interest rates has played an important part but has had to be reinforced by quantitative measures. Finally, selective measures have made it possible to adjust the overall policy.

(1) *Use of interest rates*

When inflation increases, the choice of an interest-rate level which takes into account monetary depreciation tends to moderate the indebtedness of the various sectors of the economy needing finance by encouraging them to make a choice of the best investments and preventing the building up of speculative stocks. Turning to crediting agents, it is possible to limit the disincentive resulting for savers from inflation by maintaining a sufficient return, and this, particularly in the monetary field, is intended to avoid reactivating cash holdings and liquid investments.

(*a*) *The action of the central bank on the money market* Bank liquidity factors (either autonomous factors, or the constraints due to compulsory reserves), create heavy borrowing needs for banks so that the money market equilibrium depends permanently on resources provided by the central bank. This explains why the rates at which the central bank intervenes constitute a point of reference for the banks when fixing their lending conditions.

Independently of the part they play in the field of interest rates, the operations of the Bank of France on the money market – which have lost their automatic character following recent modifications in technical procedures and methods – aimed at altering the banks' behaviour in the supply of credit and at strengthening the links between their credit activity and their liquidity needs.

(*b*) *Overall impact on bank liquidity* The obligation to maintain assets on accounts with the central bank resulting from the reserve system has been appreciably increased in the last two or three years. By adding to the operating charges of banks, the present system has contributed to the rise in the lending conditions of banks.

(*c*) *Borrowing rates* With the exception of sight deposits on which the payment of interest is prohibited, the borrowing conditions – regulated by the monetary authorities – applicable to liquid and semi-liquid investments made with banks and other financial intermediaries have been raised several times. The recent adoption of a 'time-based bonus' applied to the increase in savings deposits aims at checking the return to commercial circuits of a part of the previously existing savings.

As regards large investments or those made for more than a year, the amount of remuneration is freely debated and the interest paid does not vary appreciably from the conditions prevailing on the money market.

(2) *Implementation of quantitative restrictions*

Because of the extent of inflationary expectations, the rise in nominal interest rates remained insufficient to reduce an increasing tendency to indebtedness and to restrain the distribution of credit by banks. This is the reason why the monetary authorities had to resort to a policy of overall quantitative restrictions.

The compulsory reserve system which had already been extended to outstanding credits was complemented in November 1972 by a system of supplementary reserves, the working of which is linked to norms regarding the increase in credits granted.

These norms have been gradually tightened and were fixed at between 12 and 13 per cent (the rate of increase for a period of twelve months) during the first half of 1974.

The rules in force since the last quarter of 1972 aim at getting similar results to those of a statutory limitation of credit (like the so-called *encadrement du crédit*) but without resorting to the imposition of statutory ceilings. This system entails a big increase in marginal costs for the credits which exceed a certain level and has therefore a dissuasive effect.

(3) *Selective measures*

The overall policy calls for corrective measures the aim of which is either to discourage the granting of some credits or, on the other hand, to stimulate the financing of operations considered as being of particular importance.

(*a*) *Restrictive measures* In order to reserve the major part of available credits for businesses, private loans have been gradually restricted.

A ceiling was imposed on personal loans at the level reached at the end of the first half of 1973. Housing credits were subjected to special supervision and measures such as the alteration of eligibility conditions on the mortgage market have made it possible to reserve mortgage loans to meet the need for housing.

(*b*) *Positive measures* Certain types of credits have been encouraged chiefly by means of derogations concerning credits subject to the imposition of reserves.

These measures refer particularly to export credits corresponding to medium- and long-term claims on foreign countries; to housing and agricultural loans with a social purpose; to the financing of energy-saving investments.

The banks were also recommended to avoid letting the main weight of credit restrictions fall on small- and medium-sized firms.

III RESULTS AND PROSPECTS

(1) INFLUENCE ON THE RECENT TRENDS OF ECONOMIC ACTIVITY

Owing to the high level of liquidity reached by the French economy at the end of 1972, the policy applied could not exercise any rapid influence on the economic activity. It was necessary to wait until autumn 1973 to see the first signs of a reversal.

However, independently of their automatic action on prices, the energy crisis and the persistent rapid rise in the price of raw materials have reinforced inflationary expectations, so that the domestic price upsurge has been accelerating since the beginning of 1974.

(2) PROSPECTS

Although political events delayed the introduction of new measures adequate to meet the worsening circumstances, the time seems ripe for the internal pressures to abate. However, without a quick settlement of the international monetary problem and a significant price fall in imported raw materials, inflation will remain relatively strong in France at least during the twelve months ahead.

As previously said, the aims in this field would be to slow down price rises to 1 per cent per month at the end of the current year, then to 0·5 per cent per month from 1975 onwards.

(a) Consequences of inflation

As a result, it is necessary to take measures likely to counterbalance the impact of price inflation on the conditions of economic activity. If certain effects of inflation can be deemed to stimulate the economic activity (with the proviso that certain limits should not be exceeded), it should not be forgotten that from a social point of view inflation is responsible for transfers of wealth which, although not shown in national accounts, are none the less very important with the current rates of inflation, even for the transfers between private creditors and debtors. On the other hand, a depreciation ranging between 8 and 10 per cent in the value of money may amount to a loss reaching 40 per cent of the new gross savings of private persons as far as their financial assets are concerned, or even be equal to the total amount of the taxes levied on individual incomes.

(b) How to alleviate the effects of inflation

Mitigating the impact of price inflation raises the question of whether indexing is desirable or not.

On grounds of equity, the supporters of indexation expect many advantages from this procedure:

Indexing allows fair treatment of savers, especially those in the lower categories who have no access to the more elaborate investments.

It permits a widening of the financial market and a lengthening of maturities. It then becomes possible to reduce the pressures on the creation of money for the sake of investment financing.

It reduces the inflationary expectations of the economic sectors and removes a factor which greatly contributes to the perpetuation of inflation.

However it seems that in modern economies, diversified as they are, indexing presents serious drawbacks which do not lead to its being used extensively.

It is difficult to choose an index accepted by all parties as price rises differ widely between the various sectors of the economy.

It is impossible to find the right amount of indexation needed.

Persistent time lags are unavoidable in the adaptation of the means applied.

It amounts to introducing further constraints in the economic adjustment process with the risk of upsetting altogether the economic machinery.

It is perhaps in the field of interest rates that such action could be taken. However, the introduction of systematic indexing stipulations relating to interest rates, whether coupled or not with capital indexation, would lead to constraints and entail drawbacks similar to those which have been mentioned above. Moreover, it would hardly be compatible with the flexibility required between the different money markets.

However, it is normal that in inflationary times the interest rates should include a premium against monetary erosion on top of the capital interest.

In the short term, the restrictive monetary policies put into action lead to rises in the rates applied to borrowers. This extra cost takes into account a large part of the price inflation and can be cut down whenever the inflationary pressures recede.

On the contrary, the upward adjustment of rates paid on deposits does not always follow the rise in prices. As far as savings invested on sight or very short-term deposits are concerned, the introduction of time-based bonuses on the monetary or quasi-monetary holdings deemed stable (i.e. when minimum amounts are left for a certain time on the books of a financial institution) may be a worthwhile solution.

In long-term contracts, the introduction of fixed rates without any possibility of review has serious drawbacks. If they are too low, they discourage savings and they strongly favour the borrowing process; if they are too high, they reinforce future inflationary developments.

Consequently, one would be tempted to think about adopting floating interest rates in long-term lending and borrowing agreements.

In conclusion, the internal aspects of the problems involved are summed up in the three following comments.

As far as a gap may be seen between the aims in view and the willingness to achieve them, it is necessary to study how savings could be better adjusted to investment. The first solution would be to reduce investment. This is the way chosen by the present government in order to take measures which would be rapidly effective, but the future would be endangered if one did not try to solve the problem in an opposite way, that is by choosing to sustain investment as well as raise the tendency to save.

It is often claimed that the national savings required for the financing of investment can expand only if inflation is combated. It can on the contrary be argued that the tendency to save can only be stimulated by a return to a relative price stability. The growth of voluntary savings can significantly reduce the inflationary pressures for it allows national savings to meet the need for investment without excessive recourse to the channels of monetary creation.

In this respect, experience seems to prove that when savers are offered attractive investment opportunities, which, one must admit, is not frequently the case, but does happen sometimes, the tendency to save gains strength.

16 Report on the Federal Republic of Germany

Kurt Andreas

I

On the evidence of the statistics, inflation problems in the Federal Republic of Germany might appear to be less severe than in the countries we are hearing about at this conference. But in Germany too there is pronounced 'new inflation', in the sense that the term is defined in the questionnaire circulated by the organisers; there too the rates of price increases are much higher than in earlier years, there too the uptrend of prices has constantly accelerated during the last few years, there too the inflation is caused more by 'exogenous' factors than it was.

I.1 PRICES

In the first five months of this year the cost of living index of all households was 7 to 7½ per cent higher than a year before. The steepest increase so far was that recorded in December 1973, at 7·8 per cent, and the 8 per cent mark could easily be reached or passed in the course of this year. This is suggested, among other things, by the faster rise in the producer prices of industrial products, which in April this year were 13 per cent higher than a year before, compared with only 8·5 per cent last December.

If it is therefore assumed that the inflation rate in the present year as a whole will probably approach 8 per cent, the average rate of inflation will have risen continuously for six successive years, from a minimum of 1 to 2 per cent in 1967/68 to about 3·5 per cent in 1970, about 5·5 per cent in 1971/72, just under 7 per cent in 1973 and almost 8 per cent in 1974. In the first half of the sixties and throughout the fifties (with the exception of 1951, the year of the Korea boom) the increase rates had fluctuated only between about 2 and 4 per cent. The 'exogenous' influence more recently exerted on domestic prices by the rise in the prices of imported raw materials, particularly petroleum, is considerable. The raising of oil prices alone seems to have been responsible directly or indirectly for roughly one-fifth of the present increase in the cost of living. The oil-induced inflation of industrial prices must be rated much higher, namely at between one-third and one-half. The index of all import prices is at present over 30 per cent higher than a year ago; the rise in crude oil prices alone comes to over 200 per cent.

I.2 IMPORTED INFLATION

This at the same time touches on the main causes of the recent acceleration in the pace of price rises: the massive price surge from abroad which was caused by the oil crises. This surge came at a time when the efforts of the Federal Government and the Bundesbank to achieve stability were beginning to prove distinctly successful. This promising start was rapidly and lastingly undone, since the rise in oil prices, together with other inflationary trends from abroad, directly affected the price level in Germany through the interlinked world price structure, and since this rise was not at first attentuated by the movement of the D-Mark exchange rate. The external value of the D-Mark, which by the end of July 1973 had risen by over 40 per cent against the US dollar in relation to the central rates of end-1972, declined at a gathering pace from November 1973 onwards. In January the rate of appreciation against the US dollar – again in relation to the central rates of end-1972 – was only about 13 to 14 per cent; in the meantime it has risen again to about 28 per cent.

Thus, during the crude oil supply crisis Germany's lack of primary sources of energy led to a sharp setback in the value of the D-Mark on the exchange market, which intensified the direct price increase coming from abroad. But in January 1974, when the energy crisis began to change from a supply crisis to a price crisis, a new situation arose. Foreign countries' confidence in Germany's exporting power revived, with the result that the D-Mark rose. This new appreciation of the D-Mark moderated the impact of the increase in import prices on domestic costs, and tended to restrict the utilisation of the existing scope for raising export prices. The D-Mark did not depreciate and appreciate to exactly the same extent, however; it is still being valued distinctly lower than in July 1973.

I.3 GENERAL DOMESTIC CAUSES OF INFLATION

In spite of the close price links with inflated international markets, the prime reason for 'new inflation' in the Federal Republic of Germany is to be sought in the domestic sphere. In the last analysis, it resides in the widening gap between, on the one hand, the high income demands to which all social groups have become accustomed in the course of the unparalleled economic growth of the last two and a half decades and, on the other, the possibilities of satisfying these demands in real terms. In all major industrial countries wage increases have far outstripped the growth of productivity in recent years. In Germany productivity in industry went up by as much as 6 per cent in 1973; wages, however, rose in the same period by twice this figure. The larger the discrepancy between real growth and the standard calls for constant or even growing percentage increases in money income, the greater is the likelihood that the distribution struggle between the social groups will be stepped up.

This applies all the more if inflation has already progressed fairly far and compensation for inflation is an additional or even the principal element in the higher wage and salary claims. In such a situation inflation becomes a means of achieving ostensible social satisfaction. Since – ostensibly – nobody suffers, social conflicts can go on being fought out at the expense of the value of money without major social upheavals as long as employment is maintained and savers do not directly realise that financial assets are constantly depreciating. If not before, employment is endangered as soon as the balance of payments moves into disequilibrium because prices have got out of step with those abroad. Then inflationary and recessionary tendencies may combine in an unholy alliance which may produce 'stagflation', with all its disastrous social consequences, or even 'receflation' (as one might call the culmination of such a development, where real growth is negative but the process of destruction of financial assets still continues because the determination of certain groups to obtain compensation in money terms has developed a momentum of its own).

I.4 RESTRICTIVE POLICY AND ITS OUTCOME IN THE FEDERAL REPUBLIC OF GERMANY

In Germany the inflation proceeded in principle in full accordance with this pattern of an inflation of demands, but – particularly in 1973 behind the protective barrier of the float – the Federal Government and the Bundesbank did their utmost to check the dangerous inflationary tendencies as far as possible before the above-described 'automatic intensifiers' could begin to take effect. These efforts were, as noted, not unsuccessful until the oil crisis gave a new international dimension to the struggle for the distribution of the national product and at the same time imparted fresh impetus to the domestic distribution struggle. Anyway, it was probably basically due to the Bundesbank's very stringent restrictive policy, which in 1973 received strong backing from the Government, that the domestic and external surges of inflation did not have adverse repercussions on the balance of payments. On the contrary, trade surpluses rose steeply in 1974, although this admittedly owed something to the favourable structure of German exports on the world market. On the other hand, other consequences of inflation or of the fight against inflation stood out more clearly.

I.5 DISAGGREGATE FEATURES OF INFLATION

The first thing that has to be mentioned in this context is the high level of interest rates, which resulted from the sum of the restrictive measures. The average yield of outstanding fixed interest securities has now reached its highest level since the Second World War, at over $10\frac{1}{2}$ per cent. Since the beginning of 1972 the yield has risen, with only brief interruptions, by more than 3 percentage points. Prices have fallen with corresponding consistency, so that many savers with older security holdings have suffered disappointing losses of nominal wealth. The owners of low-interest bank bonds dating back to the fifties and sixties have been particularly hard hit since such securities were normally issued with very long maturities. The holders have therefore found themselves obliged to provide capital – in some cases until the next century – at a rate of interest which is far too low. Holders of older mortgage bonds are therefore often represented in public as 'special victims' of inflation. It is of topical interest that discussion of the question of compensation for such inflation losses has now started, and that the general public is taking part. A more serious matter for the present state of the bond market is the fact that the disappointing price trend of the last few years has led to nearly all investors being stubbornly opposed to any commitment to a fixed interest rate for a prolonged period. This has been particularly noticeable on the issue market, where maturities of up to four years predominate at present. Sales of a 10 per cent Federal Loan running for seven years, which was recently floated after a break of several months, proved to be very slow. In this situation, with the capital market disrupted by inflation, the debate on the expediency of index-linking interest rates and the capital value of the invested capital naturally thrives.

Outside the monetary sphere, inflation-induced 'dislocations' are mainly to be found in Germany in the construction industry. Activity has also slackened in certain overstaffed or structurally weak sectors, such as the motor industry and the textile and leather industry. After many years of inflation-induced boom in the construction industry, during which it was thought that literally any increase in costs could be passed on, a sharp downturn occurred once the continuation of the inflationary trend could no longer be considered assured and construction demand had been selectively curbed by using instruments of taxation policy, among others. This was the penalty that had to be paid for having largely disregarded actual construction requirements in the urge to possess 'bricks and mortar gold', for there are now more dwellings than households in Germany. The inflow of orders to the construction industry began to decline and there was a wave of failures, particularly of property development companies. In the producing industries, too, the number of bankruptcies and compositions has increased distinctly of late. However, the slowdown in the above-mentioned industries has not so far resulted in appreciable unemployment. In May the number of unemployed was about 460,000, representing a rate of 2·1 per cent.

II

The 'new inflation' has not made any fundamental reorientation of economic and monetary policy in the Federal Republic of Germany seem desirable. However, the restrictive policy of traditional type was tightened to an unprecedented degree when the price surge gained strength in 1973. The essential precondition for more effective employment of monetary policy was created on 19 March 1973 when the D-Mark was released from the obligation to intervene against the dollar and revalued by 3 per cent against the SDR and Germany started the joint float with seven other European countries. Under the protection of this relatively efficient barrier against external influences, which was reinforced by controls on capital movements, it was moreover possible to apply new methods for controlling liquidity. The tighter credit policy was effectively supplemented by the Federal Government's Second Stability Programme of May 1973, which mainly provided for measures of taxation policy to restrain activity. During the oil crisis the Federal Government eased its programme of restraint in major respects, but with the Government's express approval monetary policy remained basically restrictive, if not to the same extent as in 1973.

II.1 NEW APPROACHES IN MONETARY POLICY

In monetary policy new approaches were tried out from the spring of 1973 onwards in as much as stricter and more direct control of the creation of central bank money seemed desirable and, owing to the improved protection against external influences, also possible. The automatic creation of central bank money through foreign exchange inflows and quasi-automatic recourse to Bundesbank credit by banks at the discount and lombard rates were severely restricted or suppressed altogether. By a special open-market policy on the basis of trade bills and by the temporary provision of special lombard credit facilities, additional central bank money was made available for short periods only and at relatively high interest rates, and then as a rule only when it was absolutely indispensable for the fulfilment of the banks' minimum reserve requirements. The banks' so-called free liquid reserves, i.e. the assets they can transfer to the Bundesbank at any time in exchange for liquid funds, were reduced to a level approaching zero in the course of this policy. This noticeably curbed monetary expansion; the money stock increased at a distinctly slower rate than before. M_1 (currency in circulation and sight deposits) did not grow at all between May 1973 and April 1974, after rising by almost 12 per cent in the preceding twelve months. M_2 (M_1 plus time deposits for less than four years) went up by only about 11 per cent in the last twelve months, compared with almost twice as much in the year before.

II.2 CREDIT POLICY BASED ON AN UNDERLYING CONCEPT, BUT NOT TIED TO HARD AND FAST RULES

As regards the instruments employed, the Bundesbank's policy was by no means tied to hard and fast rules or, indeed, guided by rules of any kind. This does not mean that the underlying concept of monetary policy has not, as explained, recently been more strongly oriented towards direct control of the 'monetary base'. The Bundesbank's policy can also in principle be termed 'monetarist' in the sense that its primary aim is to contain the creation of money and that in the process it may be prepared to tolerate pronounced upward swings in interest rates. Of course, it is intent on avoiding 'disorderly market conditions', in which context unduly steep increases in the interest rate on capital, in particular, may be undesirable. In March and April 1974, for example, the Bundesbank tried by interventions of its own to give the capital market a guideline for the yield on public bonds; but it stopped its interventions as soon as the market came to hold the view that they were obscuring the real situation, so that uncertainty increased if anything. Incidentally, the Bundesbank has always welcomed the fact that the rate of interest on capital in Germany has so far regularly been several percentage points above the rate of inflation so that in this sense the saver has always had a real return on his savings. This, however, is not linked with an autonomous 'real interest rate theory' as a monocausal target of credit policy, as is sometimes suspected by the general public.

II.3 NO PLANS TO ENLARGE THE RANGE OF INSTRUMENTS

Events last year showed that a policy mix combining highly restrictive credit policy in the classical mould with supporting fiscal policy can produce quite satisfactory results (even under increased inflationary pressure) if the 'external flank' is sufficiently protected at the same time. Plans to extend the range of credit policy instruments by adding an incremental reserve on assets and conferring the right to impose credit ceilings have been shelved. Similarly, limitation of the autonomy of management and labour in wage negotiations and the introduction of a wage and price freeze have never been seriously contemplated in Germany. Furthermore, the traditional analytical approaches are still being used, based as ever on the nominal value principle.

Nevertheless, a public debate has started in Germany in the course of which a number of commentators have called for the abandonment of nominalism and the increased sanctioning of index clauses, even in capital transactions. But those responsible for monetary policy continue to reject firmly any such relaxation. They fear that if the safeguarding of the purchasing power of financial claims by means of index-linking were sanctioned, it would lead to a general proliferation of escalator clauses. This would speed up inflation, both in theory and on the evidence of foreign experience, especially if – as is the case today – the price rises are largely 'exogenous' in origin.

II.4 BASIC AIMS OF MONETARY POLICY UNCHANGED

Under the Act to Promote the Stability and Growth of the Economy of 8 June 1967 the measures of the Federal and Länder Governments must be taken in such a way as to 'contribute, within the framework of the free market system, at the same time to price stability, to a high level of employment and to external equilibrium, along with steady and adequate economic growth'. According to this statutory mandate, therefore, all four aims are to be pursued with equal vigour. Consequently, policy must depend on which of the aims is in greatest danger at any given time.

At present the aim of price stability is the furthest from being fulfilled. Neither the law nor the general political situation in Germany permits those responsible for monetary policy to tolerate this state of affairs indefinitely. The Government is therefore acting in accordance with its statutory mandate when it supports the central bank in its restrictive credit policy. At present it is not doing so by active fiscal measures, as it did in 1973, but by public recognition and endorsement of the restrictive policy pursued by the Bundesbank. The fact that the Federal Government is currently trying to counteract a threatening decline in employment by means of a special programme to assist areas with particular structural problems is no contradiction. On the contrary, such specific measures against unemployment risks make it easier for the central bank to pursue its restrictive policy, which must necessarily be of a general nature, with determination.

Finally, the fact that a large part of the inflation rate is due to 'exogenous' factors cannot be regarded as a valid reason for a less resolute national fight against inflation. On the contrary, it seems necessary – generally speaking – to curb domestic demand all the more if the countries which supply raw materials want a larger share in the production potential of the industrial countries and the industrial countries cannot refuse this wish owing to the monopoly position of the raw material suppliers. The price increases imposed by these suppliers then assume the character of a 'forced contribution', which ultimately has to be made by transferring real resources. The transfer of an equivalent in goods and services would be hampered and inflationary tendencies would gather pace if the price increases of the supplying countries were offset by compensatory payments on domestic nominal incomes arising from internal money creation.

It is frequently objected that the countries which supply raw materials – at least in their totality – are not in a position to absorb the real equivalent of their additional income from the industrial countries, so that demand in the industrial countries is bound to fall unless the gap is filled by strengthening domestic demand. Such fears are not convincing, at least in the short run. For one thing the present use of the industrial countries' productive capacities by the oil-producing countries is largely additional to the utilisation in the past, so that on the whole this tends to augment demand. For another – and this is the decisive consideration – money incomes in the industrial countries are still growing so quickly that even if this growth were generally moderated step by step there would probably be no gap in demand. Any tightening of the restrictive policy is therefore likely to promote financial equilibrium in the foreseeable future, at least in the deficit countries.

Needless to say, it is not to be expected that the additional demand of the raw material suppliers will be uniformly distributed among the industrial countries, much less that it will conform to these countries' needs to balance their external payments. For those industrial countries which are at a disadvantage, however, this can only be a reason to intensify to the utmost extent their efforts to regain stability. Conversely, for those countries with a strong export trade it cannot be a reason to seek adjustment in inflation. It is obvious that to solve the new balance of payments problems caution and a maximum of solidarity among the industrial countries are essential. For the common good, however, joint steps can at present only be taken towards curbing as effectively as possible the 'new inflation' in the industrial countries.

Concluding Remarks

Innocenzo Gasparini

In concluding this conference, I wish to express our gratitude to the distinguished economists who have presented papers, to the discussants and to all participants in the discussion. I particularly want to thank the Minister of the Treasury, Dr Colombo and the Governor of the Banca d'Italia, Dr Carli, for their stimulating contributions. Also, I am sure I speak for all of us here in expressing our gratitude to Professor Stammati and his collaborators of the Banca Commerciale Italiana for the cordial atmosphere provided for our work.

The object of this conference was to examine the formulation of monetary policies for a country faced with the current inflationary tendencies. In other words there was an implicit question, which can be taken as the starting point of our final considerations and can be formulated as follows. Do the important and distinctive features of the current inflationary tendencies imply a modification of the analytical structures and the efficiency criteria of monetary policies?

To answer this question, it is particularly important to determine whether the current inflation can be regarded as 'new'. In fact, when we consider the group of advanced industrial countries, we find that the inflationary process, although experienced with different intensities, presents different particular characteristics in respect to post-war experience. Given that we are looking at objective characteristics, the first striking factor is the rhythm of the present inflationary process.

On average, the rhythm is higher, even compared with the recent past, in all the countries belonging to the OECD, also in those countries with a higher than average *per capita* income and a more advanced industrial development. In fact, we could say that a 20–25 per cent rate of increase in consumer prices is not as surprising as the fact that the most developed countries have surpassed the threshold of a 10–15 per cent annual price rise. This threshold was once considered as the line of demarcation beyond which only weak countries, in terms of productive structure, of socio-economic system, and of capacity for organising public and private activity, were to be found. For example, the case of Sweden, not to mention Italy, is typical and indeed serious.

The observation of contemporary conditions reveals a second distinctive characteristic. More than thirty years ago, and in other periods more or less recent, there were limited periods in some countries of a very rapid inflationary process. Nevertheless one fact is substantially new. Currently there is an inflationary dynamic in action, not only in a few countries, but in a large group of them, all exhibiting high-productivity economic systems. While the rates of inflation in the various countries differ, they are still highly noticeable in comparison with the recent historical experience.

Among the factors determining the actual inflationary tendencies there is then a component that we can call new, in relation to recent historical experience. As is well known, the prices of raw materials and agricultural products were the first to undergo marked increases because of the speculative demand engendered by the current inflationary process. Some real factors followed afterwards. Considerable increases in imports of wheat, other cereals, meat and alimentary products in general caused subsequent price increases. Then the events linked to the petroleum crisis brought about the rise in the price of petroleum as well as the newly spread conviction that the current reign of scarcity of other raw materials confirmed the tendency given by certain forecasts suggesting that scarcity was not only close at hand but had already arrived. In a certain sense the contemporary situation is similar to a war economy where high prices serve only as a rationing device and give incentives to the rational use of scarce factors because, due to the existence of exceptional conditions, the economic and social system cannot produce a considerable expansion of supply of those factors. In the present case, the analogy must be limited to the short run because we must admit that higher prices will ultimately expand supplies.

The considerations that we have developed thus far suggest a fourth difference. The present inflationary tendencies are distinct from the ones known in the recent past because they are considered as permanent or reasonably persistent phenomena, at least in the short and medium terms. Firms, households, governments, economic agents at all levels feel confronted by forces of strength and gravity that cannot be resisted or overcome in the short run.

Even the least sophisticated observer realises that to cure the significant disequilibrium that such processes involve requires a decisive and well-designed anti-inflationary policy, but that at the same time the raging torrent can only be controlled and brought back to the confines of the river-bed with the passage of a reasonable amount of time.

From these four considerations, we can deduce a fifth, the current preponderance of an attitude that we may sum up as 'how to live with inflation' rather than the more meaningful philosophy and praxis of 'how to fight inflation'. This change is the product and at the same time the expression of a much more serious and preoccupying phenomenon. It reveals the progressive and worrying decline of the Western economies' capacity to pursue the interests of the community in the face of strong sectorial and corporative ends and interests.

To test these assumptions and above all to formulate answers in terms of monetary theory and policy, this conference has followed three basic paths.

The first one was initiated by Professor Hicks's lucid contribution examining the existing linkages between monetary and real factors. Professor Di Nardi provided a penetrating examination of these connections in his stimulating discussion of Professor Hicks's paper.

Professor Hicks's paper can perhaps be summarised in the following way. The post-war period was dominated by an exceptional flow of investment due to innovations. The growth engendered by those investments has practically cancelled, or better, has strongly limited the cyclical fluctuations which existed before the First World War with their well-known historical characteristics. From both the quantitative and qualitative point of view the determining elements in the development of these fluctuations before the First World War, and in particular their turning points, were monetary. A historical factor also emerges clearly from this analysis in the role that the international monetary system, linked directly or indirectly to gold, played in influencing the decisions to restrain the supply of liquidity.

Professor Di Nardi extensively investigates the opposition between monetary and real factors. He concludes that the bottleneck of productive capacity is the main factor determining the turning point in the cyclical path of the economic system. He also re-examines Professor Hicks's conclusion that the likely fall in the flow of major innovations may depress the rhythm of growth of the economic system.

On this point we had several interesting comments. Some feared in particular that increased taxation could have similar effects by reducing profits and thus the incentive to invest. Professor Di Nardi, using a Harrod-Domar analysis, rightly observed that one cannot correctly comprehend the historical reality of the last quarter of the century without taking into account another fact of importance equal to the very rapid rhythm of innovations. This factor is public investment and, in general, the public expenditure necessary to maintain the productive system along the full-employment growth path. Secondly, the forecast of a rapid decline in the flow of innovations may seem a bit premature especially in view of the recent price increases in petroleum and raw materials which should stimulate innovative research. However, the possible negative influence of the future rate of technological progress on the growth rate of the advanced industrial countries' national income remains an open question, although I think there may be only a decline, and a rather small one, of the long-run rate relative to the exceptional levels of the past. If the rate of increase of productivity should slow down, the economic systems would become much more sensitive to inflationary pressures.

A second line followed by the papers and discussions at the

conference concerned the economic logic of inflation and particularly the links that exist between the money supply and the control of the government budget. In the planning of the conference we had consciously interspersed presentations of a theoretical nature and contributions by central bankers from principal world countries. Our aim was to promote experimental verification either of the distinctive features of inflationary processes in different countries or of the various assumptions on the genesis of such processes.

Professor Brunner's paper constitutes an interesting theoretical contribution in at least two directions. First, in the analysis of the links existing in the short- and medium-long term between the control of fiscal and monetary quantities and the equilibrium of the economic system. Secondly, in the particular emphasis that he places on the size of public financing in the model he uses to explain inflationary processes.

While keeping in mind the extreme complexity of real world financial systems, there is no doubt that explanatory schemes of this type can help us to acquire a more correct vision of the supply of financial instruments and of the problems of managing such variables. In other words, the origin of monetary dynamics is explained by a model in which fiscal policy variables have a primary importance while the role of monetary policy is made minor relative to the role necessarily assumed by the budget policy in such conditions. Professor Monti has rightly pointed out in his discussion of Professor Brunner's paper that, in addition to a number of specific questions concerning the logical structure of the model, the fundamental questions of the role of government and of the importance of public finance in determining the welfare of the community remain open. This aspect was also underlined in the stimulating addresses by Minister Colombo and Dr Carli.

Moreover, reports of central banks on the whole favour a rather more complex explanation of the current inflation processes than that of the monetarists. On the other hand, a careful examination of these reports, interesting in themselves for the detail of their monetary investigations, reveals a full awareness of the dangers now posed by inflation as well as an urgency for the adoption of immediate measures on both the national and international level.

Among these measures, the conference stressed the problem of indexation. This proposal, analysed in Professor Modigliani's paper, was perceptively discussed by Professor Lombardini and evoked numerous comments. In this context I would also like to underline the interest of the Brazilian monetary correction system, which runs comprehensively from short-term credits to every other form of medium- and long-term monetary asset and includes wage agreements and balance-sheet valuations of the enterprises. Professor Modigliani expressed himself in favour of an indexing system, particularly in the case of mortgages, in order to ensure an efficient process of capital formation even in conditions of high, sustained rates of inflation. Various reservations were expressed to this proposition, in particular that monetary correction could in itself remove some of the injustices deriving from inflation, but that this would not provide the solution to the fundamental problem posed by such a disequilibrium to a modern society which cannot adapt itself perfectly to inflation. Indeed the costs of inflation, which justify an anti-inflationary strategy in economic and non-economic terms, lie in inaccurate forecasts of price changes which affects all business contracts.

A third component of the problem was the international aspect already mentioned in the discussion of Professor Hicks's contribution. Professor Mundell explained, with a large range of material and analysis in support, the contribution of a widespread system of flexible exchange rates, particularly in the deficit countries, to the diffusion of inflationary trends. Moreover, in his opinion, flexible rates failed just where their contribution was most expected, i.e. in the promotion of the re-equilibrium of the balance of payments. There is no doubt that the breaking up of the international monetary system opened an extremely dangerous vacuum. It was inevitable that a debate on this subject should show a clear difference of opinions. In his discussion, Professor Spaventa neatly emphasised the serious disequilibria resulting from the present distribution of international liquidity, disputing Professor Mundell's position at least on this point.

As I have already said, Western industrial countries are now experiencing an inflationary process with considerable dimensions but with widely different rates. A fixed exchange system seems therefore preferable to the flexible exchange solution from the point of view of the help it can give in restraining inflationary tendencies. But it is paradoxically true that, in the conditions prevailing today, the only possible method for re-equilibrium of the balances of payments would be an increased rate of inflation in surplus countries. A fixed exchange system would be subject to such pressures that they would undermine its existence. It is true that flexible rates of exchange transmit inflationary stimuli but in the reality of the international economic system, composed of numerous countries characterised by prominence in the world economy and trade, the flexibility of exchange has, in a relative sense at least, two favourable effects. First, the constraint posed by the balance of payments upon the decisions of fiscal and monetary policy is more evident; secondly, the international system can function more efficiently under a flexible exchange system when various countries have highly different rates of inflation grouped around a high average rate. While this is true in a relative sense, it is necessary to recognise the long-run danger of ever-increasing instability in the international order which inevitably threatens us, not only from a monetary point of view. A short-term answer to such problems is indeed not easy. A possibility is an organic and long-term system of international aids and the formation of co-ordinated monetary areas, among which flexible exchange rates should persist for some time. But this proposition implies a degree of international organisation that, while desirable, is not yet fully feasible in the present political reality. Reality itself however should encourage the Western countries to move in the desired direction.

The coming months will certainly be very difficult ones in Western countries from the economic and non-economic point of view. But if we are able to overcome the ordeal of inflation, showing that our social and economic systems have the capacity to survive such difficult challenges, we shall have created a strong basis of confidence for future progress. It is necessary to have the wisdom to grasp the occasion to give our countries a common long-term goal.

Index of Names

Alchian, A., 238
Andreas, K., ix

Baffi, P., 93, 116
Bareau, P., ix, 262–4
Berger, P., ix
Brunner, K., ix, 240, 300
Burger, A. E., ix, 197, 202

Caligiuri, G., 268
Campiglia, A., ix
Carli, G., ix, 300
Caron, M., 268
Chancel, 253, 254
Clower, R. W., 238
Colombo, E., x, 300
Cotula, F., 271

Di Nardi, G., x, 299
Dreze, J., 92, 116

Enzler, J. J., 199

Fazio, A., x
Fischer, S., 103–6, 116, 121, 123, 124
Foley, D., 32
Friedman, M., 10, 82, 84, 85, 118, 123, 125, 131, 137, 180, 181, 239, 241, 242, 244

Gasparini, I., x
Glyn, A., 133
Gnes, P., 271
Gordon, R. J., 199
Graham, F. D., 219
Gurley, J. G., 180, 225, 234

Harrod, Sir R., 3, 9, 10, 148, 227
Havenstein, R., 219, 222
Hawtrey, Sir R. G., 5
Hayek, F. H., 235, 236
Hicks, Sir J., x, 225, 234, 239, 262, 299
Hughes, J., 6

Jevons, W. S., 118

Kahn, H., 248
Kahn, R. F., 122
Kaldor, N., 9, 121
Karnosky, D. S., 218
Kaufman, G. C., 100, 116
Keynes, J. M., 7, 9, 22, 119, 225, 226, 231, 234, 242
Knight, F. H., 127

Leijonhufvud, A., 238, 239
Lombardini, S., xi, 127, 300
Lutz, F. A., 235

Markowitz, H., 104, 124
Marshall, A., 118, 143, 227, 244
Marx, K., 135
Matthews, R., 6
Meltzer, A. H., 79, 82, 240
Merton, R. C., 102, 104, 116
Mill, J. S., 5
Mints, L. W., 235
Miurin, P., 271
Modigliani, F., xi, 92, 116, 235, 300
Monti, M., xi, 300
Morcaldo, G., 268
Mosca, U., xi
Mundell, R. A., xi, 301
Myrdal, G., 119

Newlyn, W. T., 239
Nishiyama, C., xii, 263

O'Brien, Lord, 257
Okun, A. M., 180

Patinkin, D., 225, 234
Pesek, B. P., 239
Phillips, A. W., 135
Pierce, J. L., xii, 199
Pigou, A. C., 7, 227, 244
Poole, W., 93, 116

Quinn, B., xii

Rey, G. M., 271
Ringer, F., 222
Robertson, D., 11
Ruberti, R., 271

Sacerdoti, E., 271
Samuelson, P. A., 9
Sarcinelli, M., 271
Savage, L. J., 123
Saying, T. R., 239
Scholtes, C., 102, 116
Schumpeter, J. A., 4, 119, 120, 257, 261
Shaw, G. K., 225, 234
Sidrauski, M., 32
Simonsen, M. H., 253, 254
Spaventa, L., xii, 301
Stammati, G., xiii
Stigler, G., 236–8
Sutcliffe, B., 133

Tarantelli, E., 92, 116, 270, 271
Thornton, H., 6
Tobin, J., 104, 106, 124, 225, 234, 239
Tresoldi, C., 271
Tucker, D. P., 95, 100, 116

Wald, 253, 254
Wicksell, K., 119
Witte, J., 32

Yeager, L. B., 219

Index of Subjects

Balance of payments, 135, 178, 180
  France, 282
  Italy, 168, 169, 267, 268
Belgium
  borrowing requirement, 195
  money stock, 194
Boom, economic, 5, 6, 17, 19, 22
Brazil, 246–55
  banking, 248, 249, 251, 252
  Employment Time Guarantee Fund, 249
  exports, 255
  Gross National Product, 246, 248, 255
  indexation, 102, 249–54
  National Monetary Council, 248
  prices, 255
  wages and salaries, 247, 249, 252
Bretton Woods system, 143, 147–9, 152, 158

Credit control, 18, 19
  France, 285
  Germany, 294
  in 1920s, 7
  Italy, 170, 269, 270, 273
  United Kingdom, 258, 260
  United States, 210, 211, 214, 217
Currencies, 135, 145–59, 250
  Deutsche Mark, 156, 163, 175, 281, 290, 293
  devaluation, 135, 146, 154, 156
  dollar, 8, 19, 146–53, 156, 161, 162
  Eurodollar market, 135, 143, 145–147, 158, 175, 177, 178
  float, 162, 175, 188, 189
  German crisis of 1920s, 219, 222
  gold, 145–54, 158, 161, 174, 175, 257, 262
  lire, 154, 156
  pound, 146, 156
  'snake', 175, 188

Denmark
  borrowing requirement, 195
  exports, 196
  money stock, 194
Devaluation, 135, 146, 154, 156

Economic cycles, 3–23
  'classical' cycle, 4–6, 12, 13, 16–19
Economic models
  accelerator model, 9–12
  Domar model, 21
Eurodollar market, 135, 143, 145–7, 158, 175, 177, 178
European Economic Community, 185–96
  borrowing requirement, 195
  exports, 196
  Group of Twenty, 188
  income distribution, 189, 190
  money stock, 194
  prices, 186, 187
  'snake', 175, 188
  wages and salaries, 189, 190
Exchange rates, 150, 151, 153–8

Finland, indexation, 102, 114
France, 277–88
  agriculture, 280
  balance of payments, 282
  borrowing requirement, 195
  credit control, 285
  exports, 196
  Gross National Product, 277
  interest rates, 283, 287
  money stock, 194
  oil price rise, 279
  prices, 278, 279
  wages and salaries, 279

Germany, 289–96
  banking, 293
  borrowing requirement, 195
  Bundesbank, 290, 291, 293, 294
  credit control, 294
  currency crisis of 1920s, 219, 222
  Deutsche Mark, 156, 163, 175, 281, 290, 293
  exports, 196
  interest rates, 291, 292
  money stock, 194, 293
  prices, 289
  wages and salaries, 290
Gold, 145–54, 158, 161, 174, 175, 257, 262
Gross National Product
  Brazil, 246, 248, 255
  France, 277
  United States, 202

Indexation
  Brazil, 102, 249–54
  Finland, 102, 114
  Israel, 102
  Italy, 138
  mortgages, 93–101, 106–15, 138–41
  United States, 203, 204, 219, 220
  wages and salaries, 131, 132
International Bank for Reconstruction and Development, 152
International Monetary Fund, 152, 168
Ireland
  borrowing requirement, 195
  exports, 196
  money stock, 194
Israel, indexation, 102
Italy, 167–72, 265–76
  balance of payments, 168, 267, 268
  banking, 17, 138, 174, 268, 269, 273
  borrowing requirement, 168, 195
  credit control, 170, 269, 270, 273
  exports, 196
  indexation, 138
  Interministerial Credit Committee, 170
  lire, 154, 156
  Mezzogiorno, 171
  money stock, 194, 274

Japan, 225–33
  Bank of Japan, 228, 229
  industrial production, 230, 232, 242, 243
  interest rates, 229–31
  oil price rise, 229
  prices, 226, 230, 232

Mezzogiorno, 171
Mortgages, 93–101, 106–15, 138–41
  variable rate mortgages, 98–100, 113

Netherlands
  borrowing requirement, 195
  exports, 196
  money stock, 194

Oil price rise, 176, 177, 289
  France, 279
  Japan, 229

Prices
  Brazil, 255
  European Economic Community, 186, 187
  France, 278, 279
  Germany, 289
  Japan, 226, 230, 232
  oil, 176, 177, 289
  raw materials, 186, 187
  United States, 198, 199, 207, 217

Slump, economic, 5–8, 18
Smithsonian system, 148, 151, 152, 158
Special Drawing Rights, 147, 151, 158, 161, 174, 258

United Kingdom, 256–64
  banking, 260
  borrowing requirement, 195
  Conservative policies, 258, 259
  credit control, 258, 260
  exports, 196
  industrial relations, 258, 259
  Labour policies, 259
  money stock, 194, 260, 263
  prices, 146, 156

United States, 197–224
  Council of Economic Advisors, 27
  credit control, 210, 211, 214, 217
  dollar, 8, 19, 146–53, 156, 161, 162
  Federal Open Market Committee, 209
  Federal Reserve, 210, 211, 214, 221, 223, 224
  Gross National Product, 202
  indexation, 203, 204, 219, 220
  interest rates, 213–18
  Joint Economic Committee, 147
  prices, 198, 199, 207, 217
  wages and salaries, 198, 199, 201, 203

Wages and salaries, 176, 177
  Brazil, 247, 249, 252
  European Economic Community, 188, 190
  France, 279
  Germany, 290
  indexation, 131, 132
  United States, 198, 199, 201, 203
Walras's law, 33, 143